Living Together After Ethnic Killing

This volume attempts to critically analyze Chaim Kaufmann's ideas from various methodological perspectives, with the view of further understanding how stable states may arise after violent ethnic conflict and to generate important debate in the area.

After the Cold War the West became optimistic of their ability to intervene effectively in instances of humanitarian disasters and civil war. Unfortunately, in the light of Bosnia, Somalia and Rwanda, questions of the appropriate course of action in situations of large scale violence became hotly contested. A wave of analysis considered the traditional approach of third parties attempting to ensure that the nation was built on the basis of a ruling power-share between the opposing sides of the conflict to be overwhelmingly problematic, and perhaps impossible.

Within this movement Kaufmann wrote a series of articles advocating separation of warring sides in order to provide stability in situations of large scale violence. His theorems provoked extreme responses and polarized opinion, contradicting the established position of promoting power-sharing, democracy and open economies to solve ethnic conflict and had policy implications for the entire international community.

This book was previously published as a special issue of *Security Studies*.

Roy Licklider is professor of political science at Rutgers University. He has been a program officer for the Exxon Education Foundation, a visiting researcher at the New School for Social Research, and a visiting professor at Princeton. His research interests have included nuclear strategy, sources of foreign policy, the impact of economic sanctions (in particular the Arab oil weapon), and how civil wars end.

Mia Bloom is Assistant Professor at the University of Cincinnati's Department of Political Science.

Living Together After Ethnic Killing

Exploring the Chaim Kaufmann Argument

Edited by

Roy Licklider and Mia Bloom

Routledge
Taylor & Francis Group

London and New York

First published 2006 by Routledge
2 Park Square, Milton Park, Abingdon, Oxfordshire OX14 4RN

Simultaneously published in the USA and Canada
by Routledge
711 Third Avenue, New York, NY 10017

First issued in paperback 2014

Routledge is an imprint of the Taylor & Francis Group, an informa business

© 2007 Taylor and Francis Ltd.

Typeset in 11/13pt GaramondMT by techbooks, New Delhi, India

British Library Cataloguing in Publication Data
A catalogue record for this book is available from the British Library

Library of Congress Cataloging in Publication Data
A catalog record for this book has been requested

ISBN 13 978-0-415-41370-1 (hbk)
ISBN 13 978-1-138-01054-3 (pbk)

CONTENTS

WHAT'S ALL THE SHOUTING ABOUT?[1]

MIA BLOOM AND ROY LICKLIDER

N OT long ago it was fashionable to argue that modernization would reduce, if not eliminate, ethnic hatred.[2] Instead, nationalism appears stronger than ever, and ethnic conflict remains a major global issue. The study of ethnic conflict as a distinct field from nationalism itself is only about twenty years old, gaining wide attention mainly in the last ten.[3] It has grown up primarily in response to the decline over the last half century in the number of interstate wars and the simultaneous rise in the number of internal wars, especially ethnic and religious wars.[4]

With the end of the cold war, there was a sudden, if short-lived, upsurge of optimism, especially among liberals, about the ability of the United States and other Western countries to resolve the problems of countries experiencing humanitarian disasters resulting from civil war and other forms of internal strife:

> What is new is that since the end of the Cold War, the U.S. armed forces, and the Army specifically, routinely has been called upon to conduct peace and stability operations aimed at preventing, quelling, or dealing with the consequences of communitarian strife. Moreover, the post–Cold War peace operations are different from earlier peace operations in size, scope, and complexity. Rather than stemming from a purposive grand strategy, U.S. participation in such peace operations stems from its position of leadership

1. We acknowledge with gratitude the financial support of the Center for Global Security and Democracy at Rutgers University, which sponsored and hosted the symposium which triggered this volume. We particularly appreciated the intellectual support and occasional tactful coercion of Edward Rhodes, director, and Richard W. Wilson, acting director, and the cheerful and tireless labor of Jonathan DiCicco and Denise Horn for setting up and running the conference and in preparing some of the papers for publication. Benjamin Frankel has been instrumental over an extended period of time in moving the project toward completion.

2. Larry Diamond and Marc F. Plattner, eds. *Nationalism. Ethnic Conflict and Democracy.* (Baltimore: Johns Hopkins University Press, 1994); Nicholas Stockton, "Afghanistan, War, Aid, and International Order," in Antonio Donini, Norah Niland, and Karin Wermester, *Nation-Building Unraveled? Aid, Peace and Justice in Afghanistan* (Bloomfield, Conn.: Kumarian, 2004), 12–16.

3. Although the technical meanings of the terms "ethnic," "ethnoreligious," "communal," and "national" are not identical, it is becoming an increasingly standard shorthand to refer to the whole field as the study of "ethnic conflict." See Donald Horowitz, *Ethnic Groups In Conflict* (Berkeley and Los Angeles: University of California Press, 1985), 41–54.

4. Horowitz, *Ethnic Groups in Conflict*; Michael E. Brown, ed. *Ethnic Conflict and International Security* (Princeton: Princeton University Press, 1993); and Brown, ed., *Nationalism and Ethnic Conflict.* (Cambridge: MIT Press, 1996/97). David Carment and Patrick James, eds. *War in the Midst of Peace: The International Politics of Ethnic Conflict.* (Pittsburgh: University of Pittsburgh Press, 1997); Peter Wallensteen and Margareta Sollenberg, "Armed Conflict, 1989–98," *Journal of Peace Research* 36, no. 5 (1999): 593–606.

in the world, humanitarian considerations, and a region-specific combination of U.S. incentives and constraints.[5]

This was true, despite a long-standing concern among realists that ending superpower dominance of volatile areas would produce dangerous instability.[6]

Before long many people in governments and NGOs began to argue that the appropriate response to countries with such deep internal divisions was to stop the killing as soon as possible and bring the participants together to negotiate a political settlement which would include power-sharing, democracy, and an economy open to international trade and investment. A representative example of this position came in the form of the 1997 Carnegie Commission Report on *Preventing Deadly Conflict*. The report assessed the strategies appropriate to respond to the increasing lethality of ethnic and civil wars. In it, the commission concluded that early action was the best way to prevent the growing number of noncombatants killed and that a combination of strategies should be pursued simultaneously and in concert—avoiding unilateral action by outside powers.

The Carnegie Commission identified the following key operational strategies as increasing the likelihood of ending violence and conflict: prevent the emergence of conflict, prevent conflict contagion, prevent conflict from resuming, approach conflict resolution in a comprehensive and consistent fashion (clear signals rather than mixed messages), couple political pressures with economic carrots and sticks, and act early and quickly.[7]

All of the Commission's recommendations were excellent, in theory, but the report failed to recognize that there was not always a coalition of countries willing to intervene or act to defend human rights regimes. Also, although the report recognized that NGOs and international organizations may have their own vested interests, and may not be objective arbiters of conflict or provide reliable information about the imminence of violence, it could not offer an alternative measure that would prevent an impending human rights disaster.

Finally, and most significantly for this volume, the report recognized that on some occasions third parties might have to intervene coercively: "The question arises as to when, where, and how individual nations, and global and regional organizations, should be willing to apply forceful measures to curb incipient violence and stop potentially greater destruction of life and property."[8] The report,

---

5. Thomas S. Szayna and Ashley J. Tellis, *Identifying Potential Ethnic Conflict: Application of a Process Model* RAND REPORT MR 1188 (Santa Monica: RAND, 2000), 2.

6. Myron Weiner, The Macedonian Syndrome: An Historical Model of International Relations and Political Development, *World Politics* 23, no. 4 (July 1971): 665–83; Roy Licklider, "Soviet Control of Eastern Europe: Morality versus American National Interest," *Political Science Quarterly* 91, no. 4 (winter, 1976/77): 619–24.

7. Carnegie Commission on *Preventing Deadly Conflict: Final Report* (New York: Carnegie Corporation, December 1997), xviii–xxviii *passim*.

8. *Preventing Deadly Conflict*, xxv.

however, could not provide guidance or criteria indicating which forms of coercion might be effective, especially if these solutions were politically incorrect or ideologically unpopular.

Both the causes of ethnic conflict and appropriate international responses to it remain in dispute.[9] Is it possible or feasible to anticipate specific conflicts, and if so, how can this be done?[10] Under what conditions, if any, should outside powers intervene?[11] How useful is power-sharing among groups within governments as a strategy to prevent ethnic violence? After large-scale ethnic violence, will a single government designed around power-sharing encourage cooperation, or does it make more sense to encourage or even require separation of the groups through partition, at least in some cases?

The experiences of Somalia, Bosnia, and Rwanda, among others, quickly produced a second wave of analyses arguing that nation building based on power-sharing was either extremely difficult or practically impossible.[12] Within this quite

9. Lori Fisler Damrosch, *Enforcing Restraint: Collective Intervention in Internal* Conflicts (New York: Council on Foreign Relations, 1993); Gideon Gottlieb, *Nation Against State: A New Approach to Ethnic Conflicts, the Decline of Sovereignty, and the Dilemmas of Collective Security* (New York: Council on Foreign Relations, 1993); Michael Brown, *The International Dimensions of Internal Conflict* (Cambridge: The MIT Press, 1996); Donald Rothchild, *Managing Ethnic Conflict in Africa: Pressures and Incentives for* Cooperation (Washington, D.C.: Brookings Institution, 1997; David A. Lake and Donald Rothchild, *The International Spread of Ethnic Conflict: Fear, Diffusion, and Escalation* (Princeton: Princeton University Press, 1998); Stuart J. Kaufman, *Modern Hatreds: The Symbolic Politics of Ethnic War* (Ithaca: Cornell University Press, 2002); Chester Crocker, Fen Osler Hampson, and Pamela Aall, *Turbulent Peace: The Challenges of Managing International Conflict* (Washington, D.C.: United States Institute of Peace Press, 2001); International Commission on Intervention and State Sovereignty, *The Responsibility to Protect*, 2 volumes (Ottawa: International Development Research Center, 2001).

10. John L. Davies and Ted Robert Gurr, *Preventive Measures: Building Risk Assessment and Crisis Early Warning Systems* (Lanham, MD: Rowman & Littlefield, 1998); Bruce W. Jentelson, *Opportunities Missed: Opportunities Seized: Preventive Diplomacy and Post-Cold War World* (Lanham MD: Rowman & Littlefield, 2000).

11. Michael O'Hanlon, *Expanding Global Military Capacity for Humanitarian Intervention* (Washington, D.C.: Brookings Institution, 2003); Alan J. Kuperman, *The Limits of Humanitarian Intervention: Genocide in Rwanda* (Washington, D.C.: Brookings Institution, 2001); David Carment and Frank Harvey, *Using Force to Prevent Ethnic Violence: An Evaluation of Theory and Evidence* (Westport, Conn.: Praeger, 2001); Daniel Byman and Taylor Seibold, "Humanitarian Intervention and Communal Civil Wars: Problems and Alternative Approaches," *Security Studies* 13, no. 1 (autumn 2003): 33–78; Kelly Greenhill, "Mission Impossible?: Preventing Deadly Conflict in the African Great Lakes Region," *Security Studies*, 11, no. 1 (autumn 2001): 77–124.

12. Richard K. Betts, "The Delusion of Impartial Intervention," *Foreign* Affairs 73, no. 6 (November/December 1994): 21–33; Fareed Zakaria, "The Core versus the Periphery," *Commentary* 96, no. 6 (December 1993): 25–29;Adam Roberts, "The Road to Hell: A Critique of Humanitarian Intervention," *Harvard International* Review 16, no. 1 (fall 1993): 10–13, 63; Stephen J. Stedman, "The New Interventionists," *Foreign Affairs* 72, no. 1 (winter 1992/1993): 1–16; Daniel Callahan, *Unwinnable Wars: American Power and Ethnic Conflict* (New York: Hill and Wang, 1997); Edward Luttwak, "Give War A Chance," *Foreign Affairs* 78, no. 4 (July/August 1999): 36–44; Michael Mandelbaum, "The Reluctance to Intervene," *Foreign Policy*, no, 95 (summer 1994) 3-18 and "A Perfect Failure: NATO's War against Yugoslavia," *Foreign Affairs* 78, no. 5 (September/October 1999): **2–8.**

substantial literature, three articles by Chaim Kaufmann quickly became the center of attention and controversy for several reasons.[13] What made Kaufmann's argument so provocative was that he suggested the alternative that dare not speak its name—controlled transfer of populations. His argument was straightforward: when ethnic violence involves large-scale killing of civilians, the resulting grievances make it impossible for the survivors to live together in any reasonably open political system. The key mechanism involved, taken from the study of international politics, was the security dilemma[14]—given the high level of distrust and mutual vulnerability of inter-mingled civilian populations, any move by one side, even if defensive, would be interpreted as offensive and responded to accordingly. The only viable solution is thus separation and, in some cases, partition.

Kaufmann's work raised many additional issues and several broad questions for further research:

1. How important is the security dilemma in causing ethnic violence?
2. Is renewed ethnic violence more likely when peoples are intermingled or separated?
3. If separation makes renewed ethnic violence less likely, would autonomy work as well as partition?
4. After large-scale civilian killing, can power sharing agreements between former adversaries result in stable government?
5. What useful role, if any, can third parties play in this process?
6. Are there unanticipated consequences of the separation prescription which make it too costly, compared to realistic alternatives?

All of these issues are discussed in the following papers.

Why were Kaufmann's ideas so incendiary? They proved so provocative for several reasons. (1) Kaufmann stated his argument clearly and framed it in very general terms; it presumably applied to all ethnic conflicts in which the civilian death toll is substantial (although Kaufmann did not stipulate a threshold for such toll). Thus the argument had implications for policy in all parts of the world.

---

13. Chaim Kaufmann, "Possible and Impossible Solutions to Ethnic Civil Wars," *International Security* 20, no. 1 (spring 1996): 136–75; Kaufmann, "When All Else Fails: Ethnic Population Transfers and Partitions in the Twentieth Century," *International Security* 23, no. 2 (fall 1998): 120-56; and "When All Else Fails: Evaluating Population Transfers and Partition as Solutions to Ethnic Conflict" in *Civil Wars, Insecurity, and Intervention*, ed. Barbara F. Walter and Jack Snyder (New York: Columbia University Press, 1999), 221–60.

14. Barry Posen, "The Security Dilemma and Ethnic Conflict," *Survival* 35, no. 1 (spring 1993): 27–47; Barbara Walter and Jack Snyder, *Civil Wars, Insecurity, and Intervention* (New York: Columbia University Press, 1999); William Rose, "The Security Dilemma and Ethnic Conflict: Some New Hypotheses,," *Security Studies* 9, no. 4 (summer 2000): 1–54; Badredine Arfi, "Ethnic Fear: The Social Construction of Insecurity," *Security Studies* 9, no. 3 (spring 2000): 151–92; Daniel Byman, "Forever Enemies? The Manipulation of Ethnic Identities to End Ethnic Wars," *Security Studies* 9, no. 3 (spring 2000): 151–192; and Byman, "Divided They Stand: Lessons About Partition from Iraq and Lebanon," *Security Studies* 7, no. 1 (autumn 1997): 1–29.

(2) The policy prescriptions derived from Kaufmann's argument directly contradicted the position noted above which advocated power sharing, democracy, and open economies as a solution to ethnic conflict; instead, Kaufmann argues for separation or partition. It is true that the prescription was not entirely general; it was supposed to apply only to cases in which substantial civilian killing had occurred, and, fortunately, the number of countries currently engaged in such activities is fairly small. These countries, however, are precisely the countries in which the international community is considering intervening, so that, in fact, Kaufmann was making an argument which called for a complete change in intervention policy.

(3) Population transfers, often involuntary, are hardly novel in conflict situations. Liberals have often approved of the outcome, while deploring the means, as was the case in the expulsion of Germans from Eastern Europe after the Second World War, and even with regard to some of the shifts within the former Yugoslavia. Kaufmann, however, went much further, arguing that international organizations, in order to save lives, should be prepared to separate people, even if these people did not want to move. Many people interpreted Kaufmann's recommendation as ethnic cleansing conducted by outsiders, albeit in order to reduce casualties. The articles appeared in the middle of a debate over intervention in Bosnia-Herzegovina, where ethnic cleansing was being cited as a crime against humanity; no recommendation that outsiders should engage in policies which looked like ethnic cleansing, even if for ostensibly humanitarian purposes, was going to be readily accepted.

(4) At a broader level, Kaufmann's argument undercut the rationale for all multiethnic states (which, of course, means that the argument applies practically to all states). It said that any state composed of people who have previously engaged in a conflict involving substantial civilian casualties is inherently unstable. Moreover, the argument implied that even those multiethnic states which have been involved in such conflicts in the past must live with the knowledge that, if such strife happens in the future, they, too, may be unable to put Humpty Dumpty back together.

(5) For these and other reasons, Kaufmann's arguments were hard for most people involved in international affairs to accept. There did not, however, seem an obvious case or set of cases which would allow us to reject Kaufmann's ideas compellingly. It was true that partition had not always resolved disputes among the peoples involved, but this did not settle the issue since Kaufmann could argue that the level of violence was lowered as a result of partition, and that violence would have been more intense if the groups had been living together; indeed he is now working on a larger study bringing together such cases as India and Ireland. Some research showed that peoples living closely intermingled were actually less likely to resort to ethnic violence than people which lived in separated communities, presumably because closely intermingled people were more vulnerable to

retaliation, but Kaufmann's argument focused on a specific sub-set of cases—those in which there had already been substantial civilian killing, not the entire population of states. The lack of an obvious way to refute the argument seemed to add fuel to the emotional fires it triggered.

Other authors have been more restrained in their view of the rampant diffusion of ethnic conflict. Against the grim view that ethnic conflict is widespread, James Fearon, David Laitin, and Ted Gurr urged us not to exaggerate the occurrence of violence among ethnic groups.[15] Russell Hardin seemed to predict that urbanization would reduce the potential for ethnic conflict since it reduced the ignorance that seemingly constituted a precondition for ethnic violence.[16] Ashutosh Varshney found that ethnic violence in India varied from city to city in ways that suggested practical policy prescriptions to reduce or avoid it.[17]

Kaufmann's position has resonance in several other on-going debates. The common theme in all of them is an increasingly pointed criticism of the notion that outside powers could, rather cheaply, restore peace and create functioning, fairly democratic states in areas of ethnic conflict.

Traditional humanitarianism, for example, focused on giving aid to people in distress and carefully staying neutral on political questions in order to gain access to victims; the International Committee of the Red Cross has been the standard bearer for this approach.[18] As the humanitarian disasters of the 1990s unfolded, however, participants increasingly became concerned that they were "putting band aids on cancer," and that the rules of neutrality prevented them from contending with the causes of the problems, which were clearly political. Indeed, in some situations, classical humanitarianism seemed to be making the situation worse:[19] In the Democratic Republic of the Congo, for example, aid workers helped hundreds of thousands of Hutus fleeing Rwanda into the DRC in the face of the advancing Tutsi-led Rwandan Patriotic Front. Intermingled with these fleeing Hutus, however, were thousands of *genocidaires*—the very people who had led the Hutu government-inspired genocide of the Tutsi. In the process of helping Hutu refugees, the UN was also empowering the Hutu paramilitaries to resume their guerilla war across the border with the new government.

15. James Fearon and David Laitin "Explaining Ethnic Cooperation" *American Political Science Review* 90, no. 4 (December 1996): 717; Ted Robert Gurr, *Peoples vs. States: Minorities at Risk in the New Century* (Washington, D.C.: United States Institute of Peace Press, 2000).
16. Russell Hardin, *One for All: the Logic of Group Conflict* (Princeton: Princeton University Press, 1995).
17. Ashutosh Varshney, *Ethnic Conflict and Civil Life: Hindus and Muslims in India* (New Haven: Yale University Press, 2003).
18. Stockton, "Afghanistan, War, Aid, and International Order," 15.
19. Mia M. Bloom, "Good Intentions and the Road to Hell: the Unintended Consequences of Mixed Messages in the Exacerbation of Ethnic Conflict" (unpub. ms., 2003).

Several influential critics, sometimes called the "new humanitarians,"[20] argued that humanitarian groups had an obligation to enter the political process, either in the local communities or in the intervening countries, as advocates to help change the situations which produced the problems.[21] These issues became more controversial when the United States, after 9/11, declared that humanitarian aid was a critical part of the American political project of regime change in Afghanistan and Iraq, raising concerns that aid workers would now be viewed as parties to the conflict and legitimate targets for opponents.[22]

Kaufmann's proposed policy of separation of peoples by outsiders, perhaps even forced separation, can be seen as the extreme case of such political humanitarianism. It highlights the ethical and normative issues involved in having outsiders not only intervene in internal political issues, but make major political decisions for those on the ground. Is this, as David Rieff says, "recolonization,"[23] and, if so, is it justified by the intention of avoiding future casualties, given the limits of both government intelligence and social science to foretell the future?

At another level, the issue also illuminates a separate discussion—the role of military force in humanitarian activities. Licklider recalls an epiphany in the 1980s when, at a conference of the United States Institute of Peace, humanitarians argued vociferously in favor of using force in Somalia, while military officers argued just as strongly that it was inappropriate. Indeed, Somalia was seen by many at the time as sort of a test case of whether, after the cold war, relatively small military forces could end civil wars and set the stage for peaceful development. The collapse of those hopes in Somalia, and subsequent experiences in the Balkans, led to a much more serious discussion of the numbers and types of military forces required for such expeditions, and whether outside powers really had the political will to pay the costs involved.[24]

20. Mark Duffield, *Global Governance and the New Wars: The Merging of Development and Security* (New York: Zed Books, 2001).

21. Bernard Kouchner, *The Changing Role of Humanitarianism* (New York: Carnegie Council on Ethics and International Affairs, 2004); Mary B. Anderson, *Do No Harm: How Aid Can Support Peace or War* (Boulder: Lynne Rienner, 1999); Alex de Waal, *Humanitarianism Unbound* (London: African Rights, 1995); Peter Uvin, *Aiding Violence: The Development Enterprise in* Rwanda (West Hartford, Conn.: Kumarian, 1998); Samantha Power, *A Problem From Hell: America and the Age of Genocide*, (New York: Basic Books, 2002): Fiona Terry, *Condemned to Repeat? The Paradox of Humanitarian Action* (Ithaca: Cornell University Press, 2002); Stephen John Stedman and Fred Tanner, *Refugee Manipulation: War, Politics, and the Abuse of Human Suffering* (Washington, D.C.: Brookings Institution, 2003): Benjamin A. Valentino, *Mass Killing: Final Solutions and Genocide in the Twentieth Century.* (Ithaca:: Cornell University Press, 2004).

22. See an excellent discussion of these issues in Afghanistan in Donini, Niland, and Wermester, *Nation-Building Unraveled?*.

23. David Rieff, "Foreword," in Donini, Niland, and Wermester, *Nation-Building Unraveled?* xi.

24. Barbara Walter, *Committing to Peace: The Successful Settlement of Civil Wars* (Princeton: Princeton University Press, 2002); Richard K. Betts, "The Delusion of Impartial Intervention," *Foreign Affairs* 73, no. 6 (November/December 1994): 20–33; Richard N. Haass, *Intervention: The Use*

The Kaufmann argument raises another question which much of this literature elides—what is it exactly that military forces should _do_ in such situations? The initial assumption—that interposing forces between conflicting groups would suffice (a sort of heavy United Nations peacekeeping force, which worked in Bosnia)—has been supplanted by a willingness sometimes to fight groups which oppose the preferred settlement, as in Kosovo. (The invasions of Afghanistan and Iraq to bring about regime changes cannot properly be considered humanitarian missions.) Kaufmann, however, implies that there is yet another possible role for the military force outsiders send in to intervene in the conflict: encouraging, or possibly even forcing, civilians to leave their homes, presumably forever.

A major value of the Kaufmann argument is precisely that it forces advocates of particular positions within these different controversies to face an extreme case and explain how they would handle it, given their values and priorities. They must either say that this is indeed a possible, albeit perhaps unlikely, alternative which they would support, or they must explain why they would oppose it. In either case, the intellectual and moral bases of their arguments are likely to be clarified and strengthened.

Interestingly, Kaufmann's argument has remained an isolate in the field: everyone knows about it and cites it, but there has been remarkably little serious research on it.[25] Although academic articles come and go, these issues roused deep emotions for people in the field. During a discussion at a conference a few years ago, Licklider saw a senior political scientist become so angry and agitated that he feared the person would have a heart attack. One of the most respected and temperate people in the field refused an invitation to the conference which produced some of the papers in this volume, saying that he did not want to dignify Kaufmann's ideas by his participation. Thus, when Licklider was asked to suggest a topic for a small research conference at Rutgers in 2000, research related to Chaim Kaufmann's controversial arguments was an obvious choice. The conference was sponsored by the Center for Global Security and Democracy at Rutgers. At the end of the conference it was decided to pursue the possibility of putting some of the papers into a special issue of a journal. Over time several of the papers were

---

of _American Military Force in the Post-Cold War World_ (Washington, D.C.: Brookings Institution, 1999); Michael O'Hanlon, _Saving Lives With Force: Military Criteria for Humanitarian Intervention_ (Washington, D.C.: Brookings Institution, 1997); Alan Kuperman, _The Limits of Humanitarian Intervention: Genocide in Rwanda_ (Washington, D.C.: Brookings Institution, 2001); Robert M. Perito, _Where is the Lone Ranger When We Need Him? America's Search for a Postconflict Stability Force_ (Washington, D.C.: United States Institute of Peace Press, 2004); Greenhill, Mission Impossible?"; Byman and Seibold, "Humanitarian Intervention and Communal Civil Wars."

25. A growing number of young authors are beginning to test some of Kaufman's hypotheses regarding separation against more traditional policy prescriptions of humanitarian action; see, for example, Daniel Byman's _Keeping the Peace: Lasting Solutions to Ethnic Conflict_. (Baltimore: Johns Hopkins University Press, 2002.)

further developed into article form, and, at the suggestion of Benjamin Frankel of *Security Studies*, several more were solicited.

The papers vary widely both in methodology and conclusions. R. William Ayres, in one of the first attempts to test Kaufmann's ideas, starts with his Violent Intrastate Nationalist Conflicts (VINC) dataset of 77 conflicts between 1945 and 1996 and then focuses explaining why some on the 48 which ended during that period resulted in separation and some did not. He finds that higher levels of violence makes separation a more likely ending, as Kaufmann suggests. However, this relationship only holds only when using the Minorities at Risk variable of severity of societal violence, ranging from terrorism through increasing levels of guerilla war to protracted civil war; higher casualty figures (which are more often used by other researchers) do not correlate with separation, either absolute or as a percentage of population. Balanced military capabilities and intergroup perceptions and stereotypes, both of which are significant in Kaufmann's theory, do not seem related to the likelihood of separation endings.

Nicholas Sambanis tests several hypotheses with the Doyle-Sambanis dataset of 125 post-1945 civil wars, which include 21 partitions. He finds that partition is more likely in ethnic/religious civil wars than in others. He also concludes that partition is more likely in wars with high levels of violence, which seem to support the Kaufmann argument but contradict Ayres. However, he also finds that civil wars which have ended by partition are neither less likely to resume nor less likely to have avoided lower levels of postwar violence, two hypotheses which are central to Kaufmann. He also finds no evidence that post-partition governments are any more or less democratic than other postwar governments.

Alexander Downes notes that part of Kaufmann's argument—that autonomy rather than separation may be the appropriate response to ethnic conflict—is in fact now part of the international consensus which calls for federal systems and power-sharing. He suggests, however, that the track record of this strategy is not impressive. He attributed the failures to the fear of each side of their former adversary and the consequent inability to cooperate in a single government, a somewhat different mechanism than Kaufmann's security dilemma. Given this, the only logical conclusion is partition, the part of Kaufmann's argument which most people find most difficult to accept. Downes supports his argument by intensive analyses of Bosnia and Kosovo.

Paul Roe suggests that the security dilemma mechanism is more complex and perhaps less common in intrastate conflict than is sometimes suggested. The standard notion is that both parties want security; the tragedy is that their goals are compatible, but they wind up in conflict nonetheless. Roe distinguishes between three different types of security dilemmas. In a "tight" security dilemma, each side can do what it feels is necessary to achieve security without undermining the perceived security of its opponent. There is no real dilemma, and a concerned outsider should try to eliminate the misperception. In a "regular" security dilemma, one or both sides believe they can have security only by doing things which will, in fact, threaten the perceived security of their opponent. The opponents correctly understand that they have incompatible goals, and it will be difficult to avoid war. The appropriate response is incentives to one side or the other to change its goals. In a "loose" security dilemma situation, one or both sides is not really interested in security at all; the problem is redefined as whether or not war is a rational strategy for one side, and this may depend largely on the particular situation. Under these circumstances, war is very likely, and the prescription would be some sort of military action such as the ones that Kaufmann prescribes. Roe illustrates his argument by looking at the Serb-Croatian conflict in Croatia; he sees it as a regular security dilemma, since, in order to feel secure, Croats needed a "Croatian" republic and Serbs needed a bi-national republic. Presumably the situation could have been resolved by a package of incentives from the outside which would have made both sides feel more secure with more limited goals.

Alan Kuperman notes that two quantitative studies of power-sharing agreements in ethnic conflicts (one of which is Kaufmann's) reach diametrically opposed conclusions. He finds that this is due both to the fact that their cases are almost completely different (only 6 of the 27 and 28 cases in the two articles overlap) and to different definitions of negotiated settlement. He applies each article's definitions to the other cases and suggests that the important difference may not be between ethnic and non-ethnic conflicts, but between ethnic conflicts involving groups which are concentrated and those which are intermingled. In particular, he suggests that groups which are regionally concentrated may find it easier to reach a negotiated settlement of their differences, a conclusion which seems to move in the same direction as Kaufmann's argument, although it is substantially more qualified.

David Laitin uses data from the Minorities at Risk dataset to challenge Kaufmann's argument that renewed civil war is more likely when populations are intermingled than when they are separated. He finds precisely the opposite, that rebellion against the state is much more likely to come when groups are separated, even when we control for other variables. Identifying eleven conflicts among groups which had been intermingled before civil war, he finds that none of these conflicts ended with population concentrations and autonomy or partition, that six conflicts seem to have ended peacefully, that three had another civil war which seems to have ended peacefully, and that only two of the eleven seem to have behaved in the way Kaufmann predicts. He also notes that in several of the cases Kaufmann cites, political autonomy seems to have helped produce peace without population transfers.

David Carment and Dane Rowlands focus on two central issues: can there be peace after civilian killing without partition, and what third party strategies seem to work best in responding to such situations? Looking at wars linked to separatist issues, they find that wars with high number of casualties are less likely to be peacefully settled, and then go beyond the simple statistics briefly to discuss both the cases that seem to support and those which seem to disprove Kaufmann's ideas. They then look at third party intervention in some of the cases. Noting that it is difficult to "code" many of the cases, they conclude that the evidence is inconclusive but that there are cases which seem to cast doubt on Kaufmann's ideas.

James Fearon argues that partition may seem attractive in individual cases but that it would have major effects on other states as well. Granting a state to people who have used violence will encourage violent nationalism in other places. Moreover, since all states are possible targets for such action, the fact that governments are breaking up other states will poison interstate relations. Rather than supporting independence on the basis of violence, it should be based on the behavior of the state toward the minority group to give an incentive to states to treat their minorities well.

In the concluding chapter, Chaim Kaufmann stoutly defends his position and extends the argument to include Iraq. After dealing briefly with each of other chapters, he devotes much of the chapter to a rebuttal of the arguments of David Laitin, taking issue both with definitions of terms and data. He then applies his approach to the current problems in Iraq, in the process developing a clear and original strategy for the United States to follow. This promises to be as controversial as his initial position.

We do not claim that these papers identify all of the major questions raised by Chaim Kaufmann's arguments, much less that they answer all these questions to the satisfaction of all concerned. Indeed, the authors do not agree among themselves. Research, however, is a social activity. We hope that the papers will encourage those who disagree to respond and move the argument from polemics toward the sort of research which, over time, can establish some common empirical ground from which we can move the discussion forward. The issue is too important to be left to emotional responses alone.

R.L and M.B. March 2006

Separation or Inclusion? Testing Hypotheses on the End of Ethnic Conflict

R. William Ayres

Introduction

S INCE the rediscovery of "ethnic conflict" as a key phenomenon in international relations, the question of how such conflicts end has become an urgent one for both scholars and policy makers. We know that some long-running conflicts have been extremely resistant to peaceful settlement—in Palestine and Kashmir, for example. We also know that some "interminable" conflicts *have* made real progress towards peaceful resolution (e.g. Northern Ireland, Palestine, Bosnia), but that the future of these arrangements is unclear and a return to conflict could happen. Finally, the end of the Cold War produced a new and frightening set of conflicts—in the former Yugoslavia, for example—that have reminded us of the existence and tragedy of "ethnic cleansing" and the brutality of nationalist conflict.

All of this has brought the study of ethnic and nationalist conflict to the fore, and has raised a key question in the minds of both scholars and policy makers: How do violent nationalist conflicts end? Can they be peacefully resolved at all, or are the participants "doomed" to cycles of violence and revenge? On this second question, we do have some evidence (Gurr, 1994; Heraclides, 1997; Ayres, 2000)—violent ethnic conflicts can and do resolve, in various ways. The first question—*how*—is now more pressing. What do we know—or what can we discover—about the various ways in which these kinds of conflicts can be ended?

One possible answer to this question is that violent ethnic conflict by its very nature leaves only one possible solution: the permanent separation of warring groups (Kaufman, 1996). Violence, in this argument, makes any solution in which the groups still have access to each other untenable. This logic could have very serious policy consequences, both for the participants in conflict and for those outside who attempt to bring about peaceful resolution. It would suggest, for instance, that a "federalist" solution of one multiethnic Bosnia is bound to fail; it would also lend strength to calls by Israel, for example, for "defensible borders". This paper's initial puzzle, therefore, is to empirically explore the link between levels of violence and "possible and impossible" resolutions, using a different set of cases than are considered by Kaufman's original arguments.[1]

The necessity of separation as a result of violence is not the only logic regarding the resolution of conflict, however. Others have suggested that conflict endings are reliant on the intervention of outside mediators (Walter, 1997; Zartman and Touval, 1996; Crocker, 1996; Regan, 1996), or the depth of hostile perceptions held by the two sides (Ayres, 1997; Stein, 1996; Kelman, 1987; Kaufman, 1996 also includes this as part of his argument), or the balance of military power between them (Posen, 1993). This suggests a multiplicity of possible explanations for the same outcome—types of conflict resolution. This paper will examine these lines of reasoning empirically, by comparing the characteristics of conflicts and types of settlements reached across some 48 violent nationalist conflicts from 1945–1996. The next section will define the dependent variable by laying out what we mean by "resolution", and explore the logic of the alternative explanations suggested above to translate them into testable hypotheses. Data and methods will then be introduced, and results of a series of correlative tests presented. The final section will conclude with a discussion of what these results mean for the different explanations presented here, and how they might guide future research inquiries.

How Do They End? Measures of "Resolution"

IF we are to test these general notions—that violence, or third parties, or perceptions, or military power, condition how conflicts are resolved—we must have some hypotheses that we can test on real-world cases. For this, we need to specify the dependent variable we are explaining: what do we mean by "conflict ending"? There are two ways in which to approach the question of "how conflicts resolve": the results of conflict, and the length of time it takes to reach those results. Addressing what kinds of outcomes end conflicts has been the focus of some previous studies in the arena of civil wars (Mason & Fett, 1996; Licklider, 1995; Wagner, 1993); scholars have looked at whether negotiated or military victories are more likely to last, but these efforts have not looked at the specific terms of the settlement. This

1. The author would like to thank Peter Radcliffe, Donald Sylvan, Andrew Enterline, Volker Franke and Richard Herrmann for their help and advice, and Roy Licklider and David Mason for their suggestions and assistance in locating data. All errors are the sole responsibility of the author. Kaufman explores some of his claims using a set of 27 cases from Ted Gurr's Minorities at Risk data set; this study seeks to use a larger and somewhat different set of cases to explore the same logic.

is the core of Kaufman's (1996) logic—not only that violence matters, but that in particular it determines which terms of settlement will provide viable solutions and which will not. In particular, he argues that high levels of violence necessitate a particular kind of ending—separation into defensible enclaves—in order to be "possible". Therefore, it makes sense to look to the terms of conflict ending—are the parties separated or not?—as an important dependent variable.

It is also useful to ask not only what outcome a resolution produces, but how long it takes to get there. The "conventional wisdom" (at least, as embodied in popular commentary) suggests that violent ethnic conflicts are "intractable"—that high levels of violence, or the depth of historical hatred, make peaceful endings difficult if not impossible. This is also implicit in the logic of Kaufman's argument—unless the "possible" solution of partition is achieved, conflicts will continue for a long time. Similarly, proponents of other explanations also purport to explain conflict length—by reference to how long it takes third parties to get involved, or balances or imbalances in power, or the parties' ability to change perceptions of each other.

Either of these two approaches could be defended as the "outcome" of efforts to resolve conflict; for the purposes of this study we will use both. The next section will explore the logic of each of the four alternative explanations outlined above in light of these different ways of measuring resolution, and bring out testable hypotheses for each.

From Theories to Hypotheses

THESE two approaches to measuring "outcome", combined with the four different explanations offered above (levels of violence; differences in power; strength of stereotyping; third party involvement), yield four different sets of hypotheses—one set of expectations for the effects on various kinds of outcomes for each independent variable. In addition, since violence itself can be considered a dependent as well as independent variable, the following discussion will include explectations about how the other three independent variables might be expected to affect the level of violence—providing a preliminary look at expectations regarding interaction effects among some of these differing explanations.[2] This section thus has four sub-sections, each

---

2. These last hypotheses are offered to guide this as well as future research; because of variable type and data availability problems, multivariate analysis, which might pull out these same relationships, is not available for the tests being done here. See the methods section, below, for a more complete discussion.

laying out, in hypothesis form, the expected effects of that variable on the terms of outcome and length of conflict.

LEVELS OF VIOLENCE

Kaufman's logic argues that sufficiently high levels of violence necessitate the separation of the warring parties "into defensible enclaves". (Kaufman, 1996: 137) The corollary to this is that if a settlement is achieved which does not create such separation, it will not actually end the conflict. Hence, the testable version of this hypothesis is as follows:

- Hypothesis 1: High levels of violence should correlate with separation endings; low levels of violence should have a greater chance of producing an inclusion ending.

  In addition to predicting to type of conflict ending, the level of violence may also affect how long it takes conflicts to end. This is inherent in the logic of "possible and impossible solutions"; if a particular ending is "impossible" or unsuited to a particular conflict, it will presumably not end that conflict. Thus, following Kaufman's original logic that levels of violence are the ultimate fuel to the cycle of conflict, and the conventional wisdom that bloody ethnic conflicts are particularly intractable, we get:
- Hypothesis 2: Greater levels of violence will be correlated with longer conflicts.

BALANCE OF CAPABILITIES

Level of violence is only one possible explanation, of course. Some might suggest that it is not the level of violence per se, but the balance of capabilities between the parties that creates the "possible or impossible" solutions. Since nationalist conflicts are nearly always between an existing state and a nationalist group, we would expect different outcomes depending on which side has the advantage. Where capabilities are relatively balanced, separation might be necessary, because the nationalist group can continue pressing its demands against the state until the state lets them go. However, where capabilities are strongly in favor of the state actor, the state is presumably capable of enforcing its will on the rebelling group, even to the point of forced ethnic inclusion.[3] This leads to the following expectation:

3. One might ask what we should expect if the nationalist group is substantially stronger than its state enemy. In practical terms, this is a moot issue; as we shall see in the measurement section below, in ethnic conflicts between nationalist secessionist groups and states seeking to prevent secession, the real-world range of capabilities runs from relatively balanced to unbalanced in favor of the state. This will be discussed further below in the measurement and conclusions sections.

- Hypothesis 3: When capabilities are balanced between the two sides, separation is the more likely outcome, but when capabilities are unbalanced in favor of the state, inclusion is more likely.

    It might also be suggested that the length of ethnic conflicts—as with the length of most interstate wars—hinges more on the balance of capabilities between the two than on how much damage they cause. This reflects a very conventional Realist notion: conflict with evenly-matched actors will likely last for longer than those where one side has an advantage, presumably because the more powerful side will press its advantage to victory. Thus:

- Hypothesis 4: The balance of capabilities will explain conflict length; more evenly-matched conflicts are expected to last longer, while unbalanced ones should take less time to end.

    We can extend this logic one step further. If the balance of capabilities determines how long a conflict lasts, it may also be the prime determinant of the level of violence, suggesting that the argument that treats level of violence as an independent variable is really focusing on an intervening one. This argument would suggest an additional hypothesis:

- Hypothesis 5: The balance of capabilities will determine the level of violence; greater imbalances will mean lower overall levels of violence (as the more capable side will win quickly and/or decisively), while parties more evenly balanced may experience higher overall levels of violence.

STRENGTH OF STEREOTYPES

There is also the possibility that level of violence (Hypotheses 1 and 2 above) does not exert a direct effect on outcome, but instead influences conflict outcomes indirectly through intermediate causal mechanisms. One such mechanism that political psychologists have recognized as important is the strength of images and stereotypes (Ayres, 1997; Stein, 1996; Kelman, 1987). Kaufman also acknowledges the importance of "harden[ed] ethnic identities" (Kaufman, 1996:137) in arguing for the importance of violence as a determining factor. It is possible, then, that outcome depends not on violence per se, or on capabilities, but on the extremity of perceptions:

- Hypothesis 6: Strength of stereotyping by the conflicting sides of each other will determine outcomes; high levels of stereotyping will correlate with separation endings, while lower levels of stereotyping will have a greater chance to produce inclusion endings.

This same logic suggests that perceptions and stereotyping should be expected to influence the length of conflict. Part of the "intractability" argument sketched above flows through the logic of images and stereotypes; the stronger and more deeply held the two sides' perceptions of each other, the less likely they are to agree to stop fighting and the more difficult the conflict will be to resolve. Thus:

- Hypothesis 7: Stronger stereotypes by conflict participants will correlate with longer conflicts.

Finally, it is possible that the level of violence, rather than being a function of the relative capabilities of the two sides, is determined by their mutual perceptions of each other. If stereotypes matter, we should expect that stronger ones will provide both cause and justification for greater levels of violence against the stereotyped group. This, we should expect:

- Hypothesis 8: Stronger stereotypes will be correlated with higher levels of violence.

THIRD PARTY INVOLVEMENT

Finally, some scholars and policy makers suggest that what third parties do matters in determining conflict outcomes. This has certainly been the logic behind much US (and UN) foreign policy towards areas torn by ethnic secessionist strife—that careful mediation can (in some cases at least) bring warring parties to live peacefully with each other. On the other hand, one would expect that third parties which get involved for the purpose of supporting one side against the other would only exacerbate the existing problems and make separation more likely.[4] This leads to separate expectations for mediators and interveners, which can be expressed as one hypothesis:

- Hypothesis 9: Involvement by mediators will be correlated with inclusion, while involvement by interveners will be correlated with separation.

The logic of third-party intervention (as a mediator or biased ally) also suggests that what third parties do makes a difference in how long conflicts last. Many mediation and peace-making missions are undertaken with the explicit hope of cutting short a conflict that is otherwise expected

---

4. An alternative argument would suggest that, since interveners alter the balance of capabilities between sides, they make inclusion more likely if they line up against the secessionists and in favor of the state. This possibility will be taken into account in the measurement of capabilities, and is thus at least partially accounted for in the testing of Hypothesis 2.

to last into the indefinite future.[5] On the other hand, intervention by third parties to aid one side in the fighting may only prolong the conflict by providing additional sources of arms and support. Therefore:

- Hypothesis 10: Where third parties are involved as mediators, conflicts should be shorter, while third party interveners should be associated with longer conflicts.

The same argument that leads third party mediators to intervene to shorten conflicts also suggests that their involvement may help to lessen the damage caused—to lower the level of violence the conflicting parties inflict on each other. Conversely, parties that are intervening as allies of one side or the other will likely only exacerbate the level of violence by allowing for escalation or more staying power on the battlefield. Thus, we can expect that:

- Hypothesis 11: Involvement by third party mediators will be correlated with lower levels of violence, while third party interveners will be correlated with greater levels of violence.

DATA AND MEASURES

IN order to test these hypotheses, we need some set of cases upon which to test them, measures for each of the named variables, and appropriate methods for examining the hypothesized correlations. This section is divided into two parts: the first will address the question of which cases to use, and the second will introduce measures for the variables named in the hypotheses.

SELECTING CASES

Before we can test hypotheses or measure variables, we need to know what set of cases are appropriate for such measurement and testing. The literature on "ethnic conflict" is fairly vague on this point; there are few if any widely accepted definitions of what constitutes an "ethnic conflict", a "nationalist conflict", or an "ethnic war". Part of this difficulty stems from the behavior of the parties in conflicts themselves, who often have important political interests in how they define their struggles and how those struggles are perceived by the outside world. Part of the fault also lies with us as scholars; although

---

5. Much of the official rhetoric about the Kosovo problem of 1999, and potential attempts to mediate a settlement, made this argument explicitly. See, for example, Steven Erlanger, "US Presses Kosovo Rebels as Violence Claims More Civilians," *New York Times*, January 26, 1999.

there have been some debates over what "nationalism" means (Haas, 1986), few have attempted to create a generalizable definition for the term "ethnic conflict", and some reject the term altogether.[6]

I do not propose a definition to which we should all adhere, but I obviously need a working definition for the purposes of this research. This paper will test the above hypotheses on a group of *Violent, Intrastate Nationalist* conflicts (VINC). These are defined as conflicts *between nations*—groups of people who give their primary identity to the group and who think their group can and should have a sovereign state (Cottam, 1984)—which take place *within states*—entities with governmental institutions which hold sovereignty over a definable territory—and which have a history of *violence*—organized efforts by either side to kill members of the other or destroy values important to them (Ayres, 2000).[7]

In order to study conflict endings and length, we also need definitions of starting and ending points. Conflicts *start* when a group raises a nationalist demand for statehood and either or both parties actively attempt to deal with that conflict (by fighting, or discussing, or some combination of means), at any time between 1945 and 1996; start and ending dates are coded by month and year. Violence must be involved at some point in the conflict, but not necessarily at all times; prior violence both creates a history which indicates that future violence is possible, and carries forward many of the psychological effects of violence to future conflict interactions. Conflicts *end* when both sides are no longer either fighting or talking with each other about what the solution to the conflict should be.[8] Hence, any one conflict dyad or group—say, Kurds in Iraq—could have a number of cases within it, separated by periods during which the parties are essentially doing nothing despite their continued differences.[9] Individual cases within conflict groupings (such as the Kurds

---

6. This last is an argument I heard most forcefully expressed by J. David Singer at the Annual Meeting of the Peace Science Society, International, October 16-18, 1998 in Brunswick, NJ.

7. This definition is similar, but not identical, to Gurr's definition of "ethnonationalist" conflicts (Gurr 1993); Gurr's data set provided the cases for some of Kaufman's own testing. The definition proposed here allows for a more expansive list both in time (up through 1996) and in levels of violence than previous work.

8. This latter criterion excludes talks on *implementation*. Hence, for instance, the 1991 agreement between Morocco and the Saharawis marks the "end" of that conflict, because after its signing, both sides ceased both fighting and arguing over how the conflict should be settled (having agreed on a referendum as the principle of solution).

9. The time period for these behaviors—how long do parties have to refrain from fighting or talking before a conflict episode is "over"?—is set at a 12-month interval. Hence, parties must refrain from either fighting or discussing the conflict for a consecutive 12 month period to be coded as a separation between two individual case episodes; lapses of activity lasting for shorter periods (three-month cease-fires which end, for instance) are considered as part of one episode.

and Iraq) are known as "conflict episodes", to separate each from the broader issue of the "conflict" between any two actors (Ayres, 2000).

Using these definitions, I have put together a list of 77 conflict episodes from 1945 through 1996. Of these, 48 ended prior to the end of 1996; since this study is about how conflicts end, it is this latter group of 48 which will be used to test the above hypotheses.[10]

MEASURING CONCEPTS

There are six important variables that need to be measured to test the hypotheses laid out above. The first two are dependent variables; we need a measure of conflict outcome (separation or inclusion) and a measurement of conflict length. The latter is easily obtained by comparing the starting and ending dates for each conflict episode (see Appendix A); as these are listed by month, conflict length is measured in months.

To measure the former, each conflict episode was coded dichotomously, based on whether its ending produced a situation in which groups were demographically separated or not. The core criterion for this coding was whether, after the conflict ended, members of either side were able to attack members of the other with impunity, or to otherwise engage in easily performed violence.[11] These codings are also presented in Appendix A.

The sets of hypotheses outlined above also require the coding of four independent variables: level of violence; balance of capabilities; strength of stereotyping and perception; and third party involvement. Each requires a somewhat different coding approach, and (across all four) multiple data sources.

Level of violence can be coded two different ways: number of casualties or deaths (adjusted for size of total population), and severity of fighting (from occasional political banditry through various levels of terrorism and guerrilla warfare to full-scale civil war). Both are useful approaches; one assesses the actual amount of damage done, while the other measures the amount of disruption a given population will likely experience based on the behavior

10. A list of conflict episodes, along with starting and ending dates and selected variables, is presented in Appendix A.

11. Note that this criterion does *not* include the inability of one side to assault the other through massive conventional force ... that is, to make war. This would be an almost impossible feat, as war is nearly always possible given sufficient time to build an army. The point here is rather whether violence on a more interpersonal level is possible—whether, absent an ongoing conventional war, members of one group in their normal lives are subject to attack by members of the other. This coding is intended to adhere to Kaufman's understanding of the necessity of partition (see Kaufman, 1996).

of the conflicting sides. This paper adopts both approaches, and uses two separate measures in testing the hypotheses involving levels of violence. Data were gathered on casualty estimates for as many cases as were available (a total of 30 out of 48 cases), from multiple sources (listed in References). These raw estimates are used as one measure of level of violence; they are also divided by total population to get estimates of conflict deaths per 1000 of population.[12] For a behavioral measure of violence, this paper adopts the scale used in Ted Gurr's Minorities At Risk (MAR) data set; it is an eight-point scale, ranging from 0 (no violence reported) to 7 (protracted civil war). The MAR codings were used where these match to the case list here; additional codings were added by the author, based on case data materials, resulting in codings for all 48 cases.

Balance of capabilities is likewise a complex concept, containing a number of possible important factors. Ideally, we want some measure that captures the relative balance of control between the two actors—that is, the ability of one side to force outcomes on the other. Such measurement must, of course, be without reference to the actual outcomes in question; to do otherwise is simply to code tautologically. While there are a large number of potential factors that influence capability to control (terrain, morale, training and equipment), a few factors should give us a rough estimate of this balance. In intrastate nationalist conflicts of the kind to be examined here, we should expect that population, number of men under arms, and strength of outside allies will all play a role in determining the overall balance of capabilities.

The first of these, population size, is coded for each case in thousands of people. For sub-state nationalist groups, this is simply an estimate of the group's population; for state actors, it is an estimate of the state's population *minus the nationalist group*, since the state presumably cannot mobilize a nation against itself.[13] Population is a rough but usable measure of capabilities; it is reasonable to expect that very small nationalist minorities will have less

---

12. In some instances, casualty estimates were only available for a group of cases—for example, the Burmese civil war from 1948 on (within which there are a number of ethnic groups fighting—Mons, Shans, and Karens, among others) In these cases, the total estimate figure was divided proportionally among groups according to their relative troop strength, on the assumption that groups with larger militaries would a) do more damage, and b) be subject to more intense attacks by the opposing government, since they represented a bigger threat. Where further division was needed into multiple cases over time, it was assumed that deaths per month would remain constant over the multiple cases. These calculations were performed for the first 2 Iraqi Kurd cases, and for the Burmese civil war.

13. For states which fight multiple national movements simultaneously, the state's population is calculated *for each dyad* as the total population of the state minus the populations of *all minority nations involved*, for the same reason—that these are populations which, because they are in conflict with the state, cannot be mobilized by it, even against other nations besides themselves.

ability to control outcomes by force than those which make up a much larger proportion of the population of the state in which they reside, although this is not always the case.[14] For both states and non-state groups, the highest estimate of population for the time period of a conflict episode is used. Data for these estimates are taken primarily from the *World Factbook*, published by the CIA; Ted Gurr's Minorities at Risk data; and the US Census Bureau's data on world population.

The second measure, men under arms, is also coded as the highest estimate for each actor for the time period of the conflict episode. For states, this is the total of their armed forces; for nationalist groups, it may be a number of men in an army (for those with organized military arms), or a number of guerrilla fighters, or it may (for particularly disorganized nationalist movements) be none at all. Measuring troops provides a basic measure of military strength and ability to conduct operations on a battlefield—a staple of control efforts. In addition, although counting men is a crude measure for many conventional warfare situations (where measures of the quantity and quality of military hardware may be better predictors of success), it provides the best comparable measure across conflicts which range from conventional warfare through jungle guerrilla tactics to the on-and-off fighting of urban terrorism. Data for states are easily obtained from the *Military Balance*, published by the International Institute for Strategic Studies, and from the Correlates of War Capabilities data set. Data for non-state nationalist groups is also available, in recent years, from the *Military Balance*; coding for earlier conflicts must rely primarily on secondary sources and press reports, particularly Reuters World News Service. Troop estimates for the nationalist group actor were unavailable for 3 out of the 48 cases, restricting this variable (and the composite balance of capabilities variable, below) to an N of 45.

Finally, a measure of strength of allies is included, where allies are those other actors which are actively engaged in helping an actor to fight or otherwise attempt to unilaterally control the conflict outcome. Measuring the strength of allies provides another significant input into the capabilities equation. In many cases, minorities with little military strength and/or population can have their causes greatly assisted by a strong ally willing to lend them assistance. To measure this this, both actors receive a single code, based upon the following rankings:

---

14. Population ratio is not always a very good predictor of ability to control outcomes; blacks in South Africa, despite having a substantial advantage in numbers, were unable to force an end to apartheid for many years. This points to the need for other sources of measurement.

0—No allies
1—Regional Non-State Group
2—Regional State
3—Regional Power/Hegemon
4—Great Power

Each actor receives the code corresponding to its *most powerful* ally; for example, during its war with the Ethiopian government, the Eritrean People's Liberation Front received assistance from the Tigrayans (a Regional Non-State Group), and from Syria and Saudi Arabia (Regional States, but not powerful or close enough to be Regional Hegemons), so it is coded as a 2. Data for coding ally strength for both actors comes mainly from primary news accounts and secondary case histories.

Given these three factors of capability, we need some way to combine them. This is done by creating standardized scores for each measure, so that they can be combined in a manner that makes mathematical sense. Data for troops, population and ally strength for all actors are thrown into three groups, from which means and standard deviations for the population of cases are calculated. In the case of troops and population, the raw data are converted using the natural log (In) function, to control for the extremely skewed nature of the data.[15] Standardized (or z) scores are then calculated for each actor for each of the three components. These z scores are added across all three capabilities components (population, troops and allies), giving a combined score for each actor. These are then subtracted to create a combined balance of capabilities score for each case. Non-state actor scores (usually the lower of the two) are subtracted from state actor scores, creating a scale where higher positive numbers represent a greater capabilities advantage for states; higher negative numbers represent greater advantage for non-state nationalist groups, and numbers near 0 represent cases of near-balance of capabilities. Because of the lack of troop data for a few non-state actors, the total N for this combined score is 45.

Strength of stereotyping—the third independent variable—was measured by coding elite statements for extremity, using the framework of Foreign Policy

15. When grouped together across actors, both the population and troops figures are dominated mathematically by the few cases involving China and the USSR/Russia, which in turn distorts standardized scores created on the raw data alone and eliminates most of the variance at the lower end of both distributions, particularly among non-state nationalist groups. In substantive terms, the process of taking standardized scores on the raw, untransformed data means that nationalist groups with military forces as few as 500 look nearly identical to groups or states with 10,000 troops. Using the logarithmic transformation compresses this distortion and preserves the variance among the vast bulk of cases in the low-to-middle end of both scales.

Images developed by Richard Cottam (1977) and Richard Herrmann (1988; Herrmann and Fischerkeller, 1995). The intent was not to determine *which* particular images (Enemy, Imperialist, Colony) elites were using, but *how extreme* those images were. Elite statements were content-analyzed for image elements, and coded for the extremity of the image being used on a three-point scale:

> 1—Little to No Stereotyping Evident
> 2—Moderate Stereotyping
> 3—Extreme Stereotyping

A "total stereotyping score" for each case is calculated by adding the level of stereotyping of each side, resulting in a scale from 2 to 6. Data for this coding was gathered primarily from Foreign Broadcast Information Service translations and world press sources, particularly the BBC. As with the coding of casualties, data availability limits the measurement of stereotypes to a subset of 23 of the 48 cases.

Finally, we need a measure of third party involvement. It was suggested above that the primary dimension here is *how* third parties involve themselves - as mediators (seeking to broker a peaceful solution between conflicting parties) or as allies and interveners (seeking to advance the interests of one side against the other, or to support one side's position at the other's expense). This leads to a scheme of four nominal categories:

> 0—No Third Party Involvement
> 1—Third Parties Involved as Allies/Interveners
> 2—Third Parties Involved as Mediators
> 3—Third Parties Involved as Both Allies and Mediators

This coding was applied to all 48 conflict episodes; data for these judgments came primarily from news and press coverage (for more recent cases) and secondary history sources.

METHODS AND RESULTS

THIS section is divided into two parts—methods and results. The first briefly lays out the approach and methods used to test the hypotheses on the described data. The second then lays out and briefly discusses, in a series of sections the results of these tests; these sections are grouped by indepedent variable (level of violence, balance of capabilities, strength of stereotyping, third party involvement).

METHODS OF TESTING

These measurements leave us with a variety of different types of variables, requiring different testing strategies. As a first cut at examining the hypotheses above, this paper will limit itself to bivariate testing of each of the hypothesized relationships. This approach is warranted for two reasons: the differing types of independent variables (interval, ordinal, nominal), and the small N of cases for which all of the independent variables are available. Taking the bivariate approach leads to three different testing methods:

- For tests with a dichotomous DV (separation/inclusion) and an interval or ordinal IV, a difference-of-means test is used.[16] This same method is applied (in reverse) to test a nominal IV (third party involvement) and interval DV (length).
- For tests with an interval DV (length) and interval or ordinal IVs, bivariate Pearson and Spearman coefficients (respectively) are used.
- For the one test with a dichotomous DV (separation/inclusion) and nominal IV (third party involvement), a cross-tab is used, with Chi-square used to test the significance of the relationship.

RESULTS: LEVEL OF VIOLENCE

- Hypothesis 1: Levels of Violence and Outcome Type

Since we have three measures of the level of violence (deaths, deaths per 1000 population, and a behavioral scale), there are three separate difference-of-means tests to examine this hypothesis. Results are as follows:

Difference-of-Means Test, Casualties per 1000 vs. Outcome Type

	Mean	Std. Dev.	N
No Separation	4.84	8.59	22
Separation	15.13	32.25	8

Between Groups = 1.9681   Sig. = .1716

Difference-of-Means Test, Total Casualties vs. Outcome Type

	Mean	Std. Dev.	N
No Separation	166841	422962	22
Separation	238663	433514	8

Between Groups F = 0.1671 Sig. = .6859

---

16. Separate checks with difference-of-medians tests will also be used for ordinal IVs; as these provide essentially the same results, the difference-of-means test results are presented for consistency.

Difference-of-Means Test, Level of Violent Behavior vs. Outcome Type

	Mean	Std. Dev.	N
No Separation	5.58	1.52	36
Separation	6.58	0.67	12

Between Groups F = 4.8327 Sig. = .033

These results do seem to support the prediction of Hypothesis 1—that conflicts which end in separation are more likely to have experienced higher levels of violence than conflicts which end in non-separation outcomes. This seems to be true only for the behavioral measure of violence, however;[17] the hypothesis receives weak confirmation (one-tailed significance < .1) using the casualties per 1000 data, and none whatsoever using raw casualties alone. Moreover, if only one case (the Bosnia conflict) is removed from the data set, the borderline significance between casualties per 1000 and outcome disappears (sig. F = .772, and the ordering of group means is reversed). These results suggest that Kaufman's basic premise—that violence matters—is correct, but that what may matter most is not how much damage the two sides do but how they act towards each other. This has potentially significant consequences for how we go about studying these kinds of conflicts, and what sorts of measures we choose to adopt for future research.

- Hypothesis 2: Levels of Violence and Conflict Length

As with Hypothesis 1, we have three different bivariate tests comparing measures of level of violence to conflict length. The results of those tests are as follows:

	Coefficient[18]	Sig.	N
Deaths	−.14*	.433	30
Deaths/1000 Pop.	−.13*	.501	30
Behavioral Violence	.07†	.629	48

The logic outlined above suggests that more violent conflicts ought to be expected to last longer, if violence is connected either with difficulty of settlement or with "intractability". These results, however, show *no* significant

17. A separate difference-of-medians test, dividing the ordinal behavior scale into 2 groups above and below the median, produced similar results, with a Chi-square significance = .065.

18. Coefficients marked with a* are Pearson correlation coefficients; those with † are Spearman correlation coefficients.

relationship between any of the measures of violence and length of conflict—not even between length and total casualties, which we might have expected based on the simple logic that given more time, groups can do more damage to each other. Whatever influence level of violence (behavioral or actual) may have on the outcomes of conflict, it appears to play no role in how long it takes to reach that outcome.

These results are also an indication of the relatively wide range of levels of violence within the phenomenon of violent nationalist conflict. It is clear that some conflicts can go on for a very long time and either cause relatively few casualties (e.g. the Basques in Spain, still ongoing at the end of 1996) or a great many over time (e.g. the Eritreans in Ethiopia). This points to the need to be careful in generalizing across this category of conflict, and may suggest that some important sub-types of conflict exist within this broader category.

RESULTS: BALANCE OF CAPABILITIES

- Hypothesis 3: Balance of Capabilities and Outcome Type
  Since we only have one combined measure for the balance of capabilities, only one difference-of-means test is required. Results of this test are as follows:

Difference-of-Means Test, Balance of Capabilities vs. Outcome Type

	Mean	Std. Dev.	N
No Separation	2.42	1.86	34
Separation	1.48	1.87	11

Between Groups F = 2.1195   Sig. = .1527

Here we see weak support (one-tailed sig. $< .1$), in the expected direction, for the logic of Hypothesis 3. Conflicts that end in separation are characterized by a more even balance of capabilities (numbers closer to 0) than those that end in non-separation situations. There is not an especially strong relationship here, however, suggesting that while capabilities may matter, they are clearly not a decisive factor—that states which have an advantage may still "lose" their separatist populations. This is consonant with observations of individual nationalist conflicts; despite being out manned, outgunned and outnumbered, many nationalist movements have managed to fight on for very long periods of time without being reincorporated into their host states, and some (Chechnya, for example) have even won separation against a numerically superior state.[19]

- Hypothesis 4: Balance of Capabilities and Conflict Length
  This relationship is tested with a single bivariate correlation, with results as follows:

	Coefficient[20]	Sig.	N
Capabilities Balance	.20*	.190	45

The result indicated here shows a relationship opposite the one hypothesized. It suggests (at a very weak level of significance) that conflicts with a greater imbalance of capabilities (in the state's favor) last longer than those more evenly matched. This finding—which should most fairly be treated as a non-finding, indicating support for neither direction—suggests again that traditional measures of capability may not be relevant to the ways in which these kinds of nationalist conflict are conducted. It also suggests that expectations about a particular nationalist group's chances to hold out against a state which are based on such traditional factors are not likely to be accurate; we clearly need a deeper understanding of the factors that enable some conflicts to last longer than others, outside common conceptions of the bases of power.

- Hypothesis 5: Balance of Capabilities and Level of Violence
  This hypothesis is tested by correlating the balance of capabilities score with the three levels of violence measures. Results are as follows:

	Deaths	Deaths/1000	Behavior
Capabilities Balance	−.04*	−.30*	−.13[†]
(N)	(30)	(30)	(45)
Sig.	.851	.106	.408

These data show only weak support for the logic of this hypothesis—that greater imbalances of power should reduce the level of violence, as the more advantaged side can win more quickly. This is not supported at all for the raw casualties data; balance of capabilities apparently has little to do with how many people overall are killed. Likewise, it does

19. Another potential conclusion is that the factors used to measure capability here—men under arms, population, and allies—are not the decisive ones in nationalist struggles. Additional factors, such as a measure of commitment, or ability to mobilize existing resources, may be helpful in clarifying the relationships between power and outcome; these are left for future research.

20. Coefficients marked with a * are Pearson correlation coefficients.

not seem to affect the kind of fighting that happens; an overwhelmingly preponderant state is no less likely to keep nationalist groups from escalating to large-scale guerrilla activity or protracted civil war than one more evenly matched with its opponents. This suggests, for those studying the beginnings and process of these kinds of conflicts, that calculations of capability—at least as measured in traditional fashions—may not play very much of a role (Saideman and Ayres, 2000).

These results *do* support the hypothesis for proportional casualties below the .1 level (one-tailed). This is important because the proportional casualties measure (of the three measures of level of violence) best represents the logic of the hypothesis. There are clearly many factors which can contribute to overall levels of casualties (among them population sizes, weapons available, length of conflict, and so on); likewise, the behavioral level of violence is in large part a result of strategic calculations made by both sides (particularly the nationalist group seeking to secede), which may in turn be swayed by a host of political factors besides raw capabilities. But we should expect that if the capabilities of the two sides affect the amount of violence committed, they might well do so in terms of proportional casualties—how much damage is done given the size of the groups fighting. The hypothesis as stated suggested that when there is a power imbalance (invariably in favor of the host state), damage should be less because the state would use its might to quell the conflict. This result supports this, although the results of these tests and those under Hypothesis 4 rule out two mechanisms by which this could occur: length of conflict (which is not correlated to the balance of capabilities; see above) and intensity of fighting (as measured by the behavioral scale of violence, listed here). This suggests that there is some other means by which states can use a capabilities advantage to limit damage—perhaps by protecting their own populations and troops against armed nationalists. How exactly this works is left for future research.

RESULTS: STRENGTH OF STEREOTYPING

- Hypothesis 6: Strength of Stereotyping and Outcome Type
  This hypothesis represents the logic that the important determinant of how conflicts end is not the "objective reality" of how much damage the parties take or what tools of control they possess, but how they perceive each other. Results of a difference-of-means test between outcome type and strength of stereotyping are as follows:

Difference-of-Means Test, Strength of Stereotyping vs. Outcome Type

	Mean	Std. Dev.	N
No Separation	4.23	1.54	13
Separation	3.40	1.17	10

Between Groups F = 2.0124   Sig. = .1707

While the observed significance level here might suggest very weak support for Hypothesis 3, the direction of the means difference is *opposite* that of the predicted relationship. To the extent that we could attribute borderline significance to this finding (a tentative prospect at best, given the very small N involved), it would suggest that separation outcomes are actually associated with *lower* levels of stereotyping than nonseparation outcomes. However, even this relationship disappears when examined with other methods (a standard cross-tab Chi-square produces a significance above .3, while a two-by-two difference-of-medians table is scarcely distinguishable from chance). The best conclusion that can be drawn is that, for this subset of cases, the strength of stereotyping does not seem to matter much in what kind of outcome a conflict reaches.

- Hypothesis 7: Strength of Stereotyping and Conflict Length

As with the testing of Hypothesis 4 (balance of capabilities and conflict length), this hypothesis is tested with a single correlation, with results as follows:

	Coefficient[21]	Sig.	N
Strength of Stereotyping	.21[†]	.348	23

There is no support here for a significant relationship between the strength of stereotyping and length of conflict. This may seem counterintuitive to those who insist that perception is an important part of conflict resolution; however, we also know that perceptions and stereotypes can change (Ayres, 1997), sometimes rapidly. This in turn suggests the need for further research into the antecedents of such change, and cautions us not to assume that it will take longer to change extreme stereotypes than it does moderate ones.

- Hypothesis 8: Strength of Stereotyping and Level of Violence

---

21. Coefficients marked with a † are Spearman correlation coefficients.

Finally, to test potential effects of the strength of stereotyping on the level of violence, we generate a series of three correlations, one for each of the violence measures:

	Deaths	Deaths/1000	Behavior
Strength of Stereotyping	.40[†]	.19[†]	−.08[†]
(N)	(16)	(16)	(23)
Sig.	.122	.488	.732

These results also show very little impact from the stereotyping variable. Strength of stereotyping has no significant correlation with proportional deaths or intensity of fighting, and has only borderline significance with total casualties (as the coefficient runs in the expected direction, one-tailed sig. $< .1$). This may be a function of the relatively small number of cases for which both stereotyping and casualties data are available, or it may be that it is important to understand the kind and content of stereotypes as well as their intensity (something not measured here).

Another argument is that intergroup perceptions are epiphenomenal—that they are caused by high levels of violence, not the other way around. Kaufman (1996) suggests this logic, as do many popular commentaries on ethnic conflict which use tales of horrific killings to explain to outsiders how deep-seeded hatreds are created. These data do not support this logic either; if violence produces extremity of perception, we should expect proportional deaths to do so at least as strongly as raw death totals (since proportionality helps define the "impact" of violence on a given society). There is clearly a need for more data here, but these initial findings suggest that the various hypothesized links between violence and perception may not work the way we think they do.

Results: Third Party Involvement

- Hypothesis 9: Third Party Involvement and Outcome Type
  In testing this relationship, we cannot use the difference-of-means (or difference-of-medians) approach, since the 4 categories of third party involvement have no ordinality. The best that can be created, therefore, is a cross-tab table, which appears as follows:

---

22. The very low N here is the product of cross-tabulating two variables with missing data in this dataset: stereotyping (N = 23) and deaths (N = 30).

	Type of Outcome		
Third Party Involvement	No Separation	Separation	
None	13	2	
Allies/Interveners	15	2	
Mediators	3	4	
Both	5	4	
Total N	36	12	48 total cases

The relationship between these two is significant (Chi-square significance = .039), and the distribution in the table suggests that there is a fairly clear pattern: where mediators get involved (either with or without intervener involvement), separation outcomes are more likely than when they are not. This is a finding that contradicts the logic set out under Hypothesis 9 above; efforts by mediators seem to make separation, not inclusion, more likely. Also of interest, the contribution of allies (third parties seeking to intervene on one side or the other of a conflict) does not make non-separation outcomes any more likely than if no third party involvement takes place at all. These findings suggest that what third parties do can matter—particularly if they are trying to make peace—but that their mere presence and general intention may not be enough to explain their effectiveness or their impact on conflict outcome.

- Hypothesis 10: Third Party Involvement and Conflict Length

Because the Third Party Involvement measure is nominal, not ordinal, this hypotheses requires a return to the difference-of-means test. Mean length of conflicts were compared across the categories of third party involvement; results are as follows:

Difference-of-Means Test, Third Party Involvement and Conflict Length

	Mean[23]	Std. Dev.	N
None	80.20	77.28	15
Allies/Interveners	149.76	154.00	17
Mediators	42.00	31.13	7
Both	60.33	59.02	9

Between Groups F = 2.5018   Sig. = .0717

These results show that third party involvement does have a significant relationship with length of conflict. Unlike the results for Hypothesis 9, these results confirm the logic of third party intervention suggested

---

23. Length (and therefore mean length) is measured in months.

in the hypothesis section above: mediators tend to be associated with the shortest conflicts, interveners with the longest, and the mixed and no-involvement conditions are somewhere in between. This supports the policy contention that impartial mediation can help bring conflicts to a close sooner than they otherwise would, and also suggests that intervention by outside powers may only lengthen and exacerbate the problem.[24]

- Hypothesis 11: Third Party Involvement and Level of Violence

Because of the nominal nature of the third party involvement measure, to test this hypothesis we must revert to a difference-of-means test procedure. As there are three measures of the level of violence, this produces three sets of results:

Difference-of-Means Test, Third Party Involvement and Deaths

	Mean	Std. Dev.	N
None	80443	119781	7
Allies/Interveners	212033	357710	12
Mediators	7775	14817	4
Both	348743	731413	7

Between Groups F = 0.7343 Sig. = .5410

Difference-of-Means Test, Third Party Involvement and Deaths/1000

	Mean	Std. Dev.	N
None	1.65	3.74	7
Allies/Interveners	5.26	6.35	12
Mediators	0.08	0.08	4
Both	21.79	34.10	7

Between Groups F = 2.2518 Sig. = .1061

Difference-of-Means Test, Third Party Involvement and Behavioral Violence

	Mean[25]	Std. Dev.	N
None	4.93	1.58	15
Allies/Interveners	6.18	1.19	17
Mediators	6.14	0.90	7
Both	6.44	1.33	9

Between Groups F = 3.4869 Sig. = .0235

24. As will be shown below, interveners are also associated with higher levels of violence and greater proportional casualties.

25. Mean of 8-point (0-7) scale of violence. A difference-of-medians test was also performed on these same data, which confirmed a relationship significant below the .05 level with the same ordering of third-party categories.

These data provide fairly strong support for a relationship between third party involvement and level of violence, in the manner predicted by the hypothesis. Involvement by mediators alone is consistently correlated with the lower (if not lowest) levels of violence across all three measures (two of which are significant), while the involvement of interveners is consistently related to higher levels of violence. Curiously, the combination of both mediators and allies correlates with the highest levels of violence; conflicts in this group have the highest means scores across all three measures. This suggests that what third parties do does matter, and provides some support for the notion that mediation by itself can be a way of ameliorating the effects of conflict.

There is an interesting difference among these results: in the behavioral violence intensity data, those conflicts which have no third party involvement at all are on average less violent than those where mediators get involved—a comparison which is reversed in the proportional casualties results. This may be attributable to a problem of endogeneity: what third parties do can be expected to affect the level of violence in a conflict, but it is also possible that third party involvement may be affected by how violent a conflict is. While these results cannot prove directionality one way or another, they are suggestive of a logic worthy of further study, as follows. Third parties may use intensity of fighting (which is knowable at any point in the midst of a conflict) as a cue to involvement. Mediators and interveners alike may be more likely to involve themselves in more intense conflicts—the former because they fear the consequences of fighting gone rampant (including the possibilities of diffusion and contagion to neighboring states), the latter because they may have more cause to fear that whichever side they support is losing. Hence, conflicts with no third party involvement are likely to be the ones with the lowest intensity levels. On the other hand, casualties (total or proportional) are not knowable until the end of a conflict, and thus (as measured here) do not serve a useful cueing function to potential third parties; however, once those third parties get involved, we should expect them to impact the course of the conflict in precisely the ways outlined in the proportional casualties data above—mediation ameliorates conflict, while allied intervention exacerbates it. These results could therefore be construed as supporting relationships in both directions, suggesting that intensity is a cueing mechanism and casualties an outcome. Further exploration of this logic is left for future research.

CONCLUSIONS

THESE results lead to two different sets of conclusions: what they say about the theories and variables examined, and what they suggest for future research. Because of the relatively small N and lack of multivariate testing, we must consider these conclusions provisional at best, though they do shed some light for use in future efforts.

Results for the various tests involving level of violence as an independent variable do not show very much support for the notion that violence, in and of itself, determines what kinds of conflict outcomes you get. The only significant relationship discovered was between behavioral intensity of violence and separation/non-separation outcomes; here, greater levels of fighting are correlated with endings in which the parties are separated. The broader argument that violence is what fundamentally matters, however, does not seem to be well supported.

If level of violence received little support as an independent variable, balance of capabilities received almost none. Knowing the relative sizes, troop strengths, and strengths of allies of the conflicting parties does not help to predict how long a conflict will last, or whether it is likely to end in separation of the two sides or not. There was some evidence that the balance of capabilities has some impact on proportional casualties, but otherwise seems to have no relationship with the outcomes of conflict. This suggests that theories of conflict that emphasize capabilities, as many studies of interstate war do (e.g. Singer and Small 1982), may not be as applicable to this particular class of nationalist, intrastate conflicts.

Approaches that emphasize the importance of intergroup perceptions and stereotypes likewise received little support in these data. Intensity of stereotyping is correlated in these cases neither with outcome type, nor with length of conflict, nor with level of violence. While it may be that perceptions and stereotypes do play a role, it is obviously a more complex one than is captured by the (admittedly simple) measure used here; what effects there are may lie more in the content of perceptions, or their change over time, than in sheer intensity. It must be emphasized that these results are particularly tentative, given the small N (23) involved.

Finally, these results do show that the involvement of third parties plays a significant role in the conduct and outcome of nationalist intrastate conflicts. Involvement by third parties attempting to mediate a resolution makes separation more likely, and is associated with shorter conflicts; mediator-only conditions are also associated with lower levels of casualties. The influence of third parties allied with one of the primary actors, on the other hand, consistently exacerbates conflict, leading to longer, deadlier conflicts. This provides support for both scholars and policy makers who argue that what third parties do matters; that mediation or other attempts to arbitrate a settlement provide beneficial effects; and that biased intervention by outside powers generally only makes things worse.

These results also leave open a number of important questions and suggest further paths of inquiry. The first and obvious next step is to incorporate these variables into a multivariate model which measures the effects of each while controlling for the others. This is made difficult by the variety of types of variables included in this study, particularly the nominal-category third party involvement variable. Based on the results above, there are clearly important potential interactions among IVs; it also appears that there may be some ordinality to the way in which third parties impact conflict outcomes. If this relationship is explored further, it may be possible to construct an ordinal-type third party variable which would allow for inclusion in a multivariate model.[26]

The strength of the third party results also suggests the importance of further study of this relationship on its own merits. If mediators truly are able to ameliorate conflicts and end them with fewer deaths, we would like very much to know why. Another logical next step, therefore, would be to categorize third party mediation strategies and correlate those with various types of outcomes, to examine the impact of what third parties actually do rather than their mere presence. Where the number of cases is too small to use statistical tests (only seven of the cases in this data set involve purely mediator involvement), rigorous comparative case studies may prove useful as well.

Finally, there are a host of timing issues which, because this data set does not include time-series data, are left open to further study. Does it matter *when* third parties become involved? Would perception play a role if we could look at points of change? It is likely that violent behavior and casualties are not spread evenly over the course of many conflicts; do "clusters" of violence matter, and if so, how? To truly understand the process of ethnic conflicts, and how they end, we need time-series data on these and a variety of other dimensions—a very large undertaking, but a necessary one for answering the important questions about ethnic conflict.

---

26. Another possibility would be to break out the different third party intervention categories as dichotomous dummy variables. This approach would overlook any actual ordinality within the concept, but might be a useful next step when more data are available.

REFERENCES

Ayres, R. William. 2000. "A World Flying Apart? Violent Nationalist Conflicts and the End of the Cold War." *Journal of Peace Research*, Vol. 37, No. 1, pp. 105–117.

Ayres, R. William. 1997. "Mediating International Conflicts: Is Image Change Necessary?" *Journal of Peace Research*, Vol. 34, No. 4, November, pp. 431-447.

van Bruinessen, Martin. 1994. "Genocide in Kurdistan?" In George Andreopoulos, ed., *Genocide: Conceptual and Historical Dimensions*. Philadelphia: University of Pennsylvania Press.

Cottam, Richard. 1984. "Nationalism in the Middle East: A Behavioral Approach." In Said Amir Arjomand, ed., *From Nationalism to Revolutionary Islam*. Albany: SUNY Press.

Cottam, Richard, 1977. *Foreign Policy Motivation: A General Theory and a Case Study*. Pittsburgh: University of Pittsburgh Press.

Crocker, Chester. 1996. "The Varieties of Intervention: Conditions for Success." In Chester Crocker & Fen Osler Hampson, eds., *Managing Global Chaos: Sources of and Responses to International Conflict*. Washington, DC: United States Institute of Peace Press.

Gurr, Ted Robert. 1999. "Minorities at Risk" Dataset, www.bsos.umd.edu:80/cidcm/mar/.

Gurr, Ted Robert. 1994. "Peoples Against States: Ethnopolitical Conflict and the Changing World System." *International Studies Quarterly*, Vol. 38, pp. 347-377.

Gurr, Ted Robert. 1993. *Minorities at Risk: A Global View of Ethnopolitical Conflicts*. Washington, DC: United States Institute for Peace Press.

Haas, Ernst. 1986. "What is Nationalism and Why Should We Study It?" *International Organization*, Vol. 40, No. 3, pp. 707-744.

Heraclides, Alexis. 1997. "The Ending of Unending Conflicts: Separatist Wars." *Millennium*, Vol. 26, No. 3, pp. 679-707.

Herrmann, Richard and Michael Fischerkeller, 1995. "Beyond the Enemy Image and Spiral Model: Cognitive-Strategic Research After the Cold War." *International Organization*, Vol. 39, No. 3, pp. 415-450.

Herrmann, Richard, 1988. "The Empirical Challenge of the Cognitive Revolution." *International Studies Quarterly*, Vol. 32, pp. 175-203.

Kaufman, Chaim. 1996. "Possible and Impossible Solutions to Ethnic Civil Wars." *International Security*, Vol. 20, No. 4, pp. 136-175.

Kelman, Herbert. 1987. "The Political Psychology of the Israeli-Palestinian Conflict." *Political Psychology*, Vol. 8, No. 3, pp. 347-364.

Licklider, Roy. 1998. "Civil War Termination 2.1" Dataset, www.rci.rutgers.edu/~licklide.

Licklider, Roy. 1995. "The Consequences of Negotiated Settlements in Civil Wars, 1945-1993." *American Political Science Review*, Vol. 89, No. 3, pp. 681-690.

Mason, T. David and Patrick Fett. 1996. "How Civil Wars End: A Rational Choice Approach." *Journal of Conflict Resolution*, Vol. 40, No. 4, pp. 546-568.

Posen, Barry. 1993. "The Security Dilemma and Ethnic Conflict." *Survival* Vol. 35, pp. 27-47.

Regan, Patrick. 1996. "Conditions of Successful Third-Party Intervention in Intrastate Conflicts." *Journal of Conflict Resolution*, Vol. 40, No. 2, pp. 336-359.

Saideman, Stephen M. and R. William Ayres. 2000. "Determining the Causes of Irredentism: Logit Analyses of Minorities At Risk Data for the 1980s and 1990s," *Journal of Politics*, Vol. 62, No. 4, November 2000, pp. 1126-1144.

Singer, J. David and Melvin Small. 1982. *Resort to Arms: International and Civil Wars, 1816-1980*. London: Sage Publications.

Stein, Janice Gross. 1996. "Image, Identity, and Conflict Resolution." In Chester Crocker & Fen Osler Hampson, eds., *Managing Global Chaos: Sources of and Responses to International Conflict*. Washington, DC: United States Institute of Peace Press.

Wagner, Robert Harrison. 1993. "The Causes of Peace." In Roy Licklider, ed., *Stopping the Killing*. New York: New York University Press.

Walter, Barbara. 1997. "The Critical Barrier to Civil War Settlement." *International Organization*, Vol. 51, No. 3, pp. 335-64.

Wire Service Stories, LEXIS-NEXIS Search; includes Reuters, Agence-France Presse, BBC.

Zartman, I. William & Saadia Touval. 1996. "International Mediation in the Post-Cold War Era." In Chester Crocker & Fen Osler Hampson, eds., *Managing Global Chaos: Sources of and Responses to International Conflict*. Washington, DC: United States Institute of Peace Press.

APPENDIX A

Case Name	Start Date	End Date	Outcome	Deaths	Data Source	Deaths/1000	Intensity	Third Parties
Bosnia	JAN 92	NOV 95	1	250000	Wire	94.162	7	3
Burma—Arakanese	JAN 48	FEB 58	0	600	Licklider	0.0377	6	1
Burma—Kachins I	NOV 49	APR 50	0	700	Licklider	0.0521	7	0
Burma—Kachins II	FEB 61	OCT 93	0	54000	Licklider	1.7988	7	1
Burma—Mons	JAN 48	JUN 95	0	2800	Licklider	0.087	5	1
China—Tibet I	SEP 49	OCT 51	0				6	0
China—Tibet II	FEB 56	APR 61	0	316000	Licklider	0.4899	6	0
China—Tibet III	AUG 66	MAR 70	0				4	0
Croatia—Serbs	AUG 90	NOV 95	0	50000	Gurr	9.992	7	3
Cyprus I	JUN 58	AUG 58				0	4	1
Cyprus II	DEC 63	AUG 74	1	3200	Licklider	5.1282	6	3
Ethiopia—Eritreans	SEP 61	MAY 91	1	350000	Kaufman	11.0431	7	1
Ethiopia—Tigray	JUN 75	MAY 91	0	350000	Kaufman	12.0296	7	1
France—Corsicans	MAY 75	JUN 88	0	0	Wire	0	2	0
India—Kashmir I	AUG 47	JAN 49	0				3	3
India—Kashmir II	MAY 83	MAR 87	0				3	1
India—Mizos	MAR 66	JUN 86	0				6	0
India—Sikhs I	MAR 47	JUN 48	0				6	2
India—Sikhs II	SEP 81	NOV 93	0	40000	Licklider	0.0443	6	1
Iran—Kurds	DEC 45	JUN 47	0				6	1
Iraq—Kurds I	SEP 61	MAR 70	0	95000	Licklider	10.0914	6	0
Iraq—Kurds II	JUN 72	MAR 75	0	31000	Licklider	2.812	7	1
Iraq—Kurds III	SEP 80	AUG 88	0	100000	Bruin.	5.6873	6	1
Iraq—Kurds IV	MAR 91	JAN 92	1				7	2

Conflict	Start	End	Outcome	Deaths	Source		Intensity	Third Parties
Iraq—Kurds V	MAR 95	SEP 96	1	2000	Wire	0.0934	7	3
Israel—Arabs	NOV 47	MAR 49	0				7	3
Mali—Tuareg	MAR 90	JUN 95	0	500	Gurr	0.0518	6	2
Morocco—Saharawis	FEB 76	SEP 91	1	15000	Gurr	0.5616	7	3
Nicaragua—Miskitu	FEB 81	AUG 89	0	1000	Kaufman	0.3026	6	1
Niger—Tuareg	MAR 90	APR 95	0	500	Gurr	0.0549	5	2
Nigeria—Ibos	MAY 67	JAN 70	0	1995000	Licklider	35.4062	7	3
Pakistan—Bengalis I	AUG 47	MAY 54	0				3	0
Pakistan—Bengalis II	MAR 69	DEC 71	1	1250000	Licklider	9.8077	7	1
Russia—Chechnya	OCT 91	AUG 96	1	30000	Wire	0.2025	7	2
Sudan	AUG 55	MAR 72	0	316000	Licklider	19.1992	7	1
Thailand—Malays	FEB 48	FEB 49	0				3	0
Turkey—Kurds	SEP 75	SEP 80	0				4	0
Uganda—Bakonjo I	OCT 62	JUL 82	0	1300	Licklider	0.0821	4	0
Uganda—Bakonjo II	JAN 86	JUN 88	0	100	Wire	0.0052	4	0
USSR—Armenians	AUG 90	DEC 91	1				6	0
USSR—Azeris	DEC 89	DEC 91	1				6	0
USSR—Estonians	MAY 45	MAR 53	0				7	1
USSR—Latvians	MAY 45	FEB 50	0				7	1
USSR—Lithuanians	MAY 45	DEC 52	0	40000	Kaufman	0.2727	7	1
USSR—Ukrainians	MAY 45	MAY 54	0	150000	Kaufman	0.8108	7	0
Yugoslavia—Croats	MAY 90	JAN 94	1				7	2
Yugoslavia—Slovenes	JUN 90	JUL 91	1	100	Wire	0.0079	5	2
Zaire—Katangans	JAN 60	JAN 63	0	126000	Licklider	7.1746	7	3

This list of cases does not include conflicts still ongoing at the end of 1996.

Outcome: 1 = Separation, 0 = No Separation. For Citations of Deaths Data Sources, See References.

Intensity: 2 = Campaigns of Terrorism, 3 = Local Rebellion, 4 = Small-Scale Guerrilla Activity, 5 = Intermediate Guerrilla Activity, 6 = Large-Scale Guerrilla Activity, 7 = Protracted Civil War.

Third Parties: 0 = No Third Parties, 1 = Allies/Interveners Only, 2 = Mediators Only, 3 = Both.

PARTITION AS A SOLUTION TO ETHNIC WAR: AN EMPIRICAL CRITIQUE OF THE THEORETICAL LITERATURE

By Nicholas Sambanis*

INTRODUCTION: THE THEORETICAL CASE FOR PARTITION

IN two influential articles Chaim Kaufmann elaborated a set of hypotheses on the usefulness of partition as a solution to ethnic civil war, building on the arguments of John Mearsheimer and Stephen Van Evera.[1] Before them, a first wave of theorists had considered the benefits and costs of partition. A prominent theorist, Donald Horowitz, suggested that

> if the short run is so problematical, if the constraints on policy innovation are many, if even grand statements need patchwork readjustment, perhaps it is a mistake to seek accommodation among the antagonists. If it is impossible for groups to live together in a heterogeneous state, perhaps it is better for them to live apart in more than one homogeneous state, even if this necessitates population transfers. Separating the antagonists—partition—is an option increasingly recommended for consideration where groups are territorially concentrated.[2]

It is hard to argue with such a statement. Assuming that "the constraints of policy innovation" and "the short run" can be accurately measured ex ante, it would be easy to recommend partition for some countries while trying to patch up others. However, neither the first nor the second wave of theorists was able to produce operational criteria for applying the theory consistently across cases.

*I thank Michael Doyle, Jeff Herbst, Chris Paxson, Russell Leng, George Tsebelis, Philippos Savvides, and three anonymous referees for the very useful comments and suggestions. The opinions and any errors in this paper are the author's and they do not necessarily reflect the views of the World Bank, its executive directors, or the countries they represent.

1. Chaim Kaufmann, "Possible and Impossible Solutions to Ethnic Civil Wars," *International Security* 20 (Spring 1996); idem, "When All Else Fails," *International Security* 23 (Fall 1998); John J. Mearsheimer and Stephen Van Evera, "When Peace Means War," *New Republic* (December 1995).
2. Donald L. Horowitz, *Ethnic Groups in Conflict* (Berkeley: University of California Press, 1985), 588. See also Arend Lijphart, *Democracy in Plural Societies* (New Haven: Yale University Press, 1977), 44-47; Robert A. Dahl, *Polyarchy: Participation and Opposition* (New Haven: Yale University Press, 1971), 121; and Samuel P. Huntington, "Civil Violence and the Process of Development," *Adelphi Paper* no. 83 (London: International Institute for Strategic Studies, 1971), 14. Horowitz also discusses dangers of partition (pp. 588–91).

Despite this lack of operational applicability and clarity, partition theory, with its intuitive appeal, has been shaping scholarly and policy opinion on how to end ethnic civil wars. To help policymakers make informed decisions about the usefulness of partition as a strategy to end civil war, I compiled a new data set of all civil wars in the post–World War II era and used that data set to empirically test the set of hypotheses that constitute partition theory.

I focus on the second wave of partition theorists, who have had the greatest impact on the debate. According to them, ethnic violence implies that civil politics cannot be restored unless "ethnic groups are demographically separated into defensible enclaves ... Solutions that aim at restoring multi-ethnic civil politics and at avoiding population transfers—such as power-sharing, state re-building, or identity reconstruction—cannot work because they do nothing to dampen the security dilemma."[3]

The so-called security dilemma lies at the core of partition theory. The dilemma in its purest form arises when one community faces a distrustful other and one's actions to increase one's own security are perceived as threatening the security of others.[4] Posen argues that this dynamic is intensified when the opponents belong to different ethnic groups.[5] Ethnic civil wars, argue partition theorists, are characterized by strong and fixed identities, by weak ideological and strong religious overtones, by the dissemination of tales of atrocities to strengthen mobilization, and by easy recognition of identities and the existence of only limited scope for individual choice. Therefore, once war starts, the theory goes, all members of the group must be mobilized because other ethnic groups will inevitably recognize them as enemies.[6] This inescapable destiny reinforces the dynamics of war and must lead to partition, since "once ethnic groups are mobilized for war, the war cannot end until the populations are separated into defensible, mostly homogeneous regions ... Ethnic separation ... allows ... cleansing and rescue imperatives [to] disappear; war is no longer mandatory."[7]

However intuitive that reasoning may be, it is nothing more than a series of unsubstantiated assertions. Beyond a handful of self-selected cases, partition theorists have not presented proof that partition is the only viable and credible solution to ethnic civil war. They have not even proven that partition

---

3. Kaufmann (fn.1, 1996), 137, 139.
4. See Robert Jervis, "Cooperation under the Security Dilemma," *World Politics* 30 (January 1978). Such suspicion and fear would be supported by actual or perceived state collapse, which transforms the domestic political environment into a near anarchic environment.
5. Barry Posen, "The Security Dilemma and Ethnic Conflict," *Survival* 35 (Spring 1993).
6. Kaufmann (fn. 1, 1996), 139–47.
7. Ibid., 150.

outperforms other war outcomes in terms of peace-building potential. The theory is indeed plausible under strict assumptions, but are these assumptions realistic?

This paper poses a serious challenge to partition theorists by providing a rigorous test of the theory with a comparison of post–civil war realities in both partitioned and nonpartitioned states. It focuses on countries that have experienced civil war; it does not consider cases of peaceful partition.[8] I begin by summarizing other authors' critiques of partition theory in the next section. I then identify the main determinants of war-related partition and test the three core hypotheses of partition theory: (1) that partitions facilitate postwar democratization; (2) that they prevent war recurrence; and (3) that they significantly reduce residual low-level ethnic violence. My tests lead me to reject the most critical tenets of partition theory. I find that partitions do not help prevent recurrence of ethnic war and that they may not even be necessary to stop low-level ethnic violence. Although it may seem like a clean and easy solution, partition fares no better than other outcomes of ethnic civil war. I turn now to a summary of the debate.

REBUTTALS AND COUNTERREBUTTALS: THE STATE OF THE DEBATE ON PARTITION

THE suggestion that populations must be forcibly separated to prevent them from killing each other has inspired both approval and criticism. The most significant criticism is that partition may be too limiting a solution and that ethnic cooperation may be possible even after civil war, facilitated by both

---

8. Partition theorists also approach the problem in this way: they do not discuss partition as a preventive measure before war occurs but rather analyze it as a strategy to end civil war after it occurs—"when all else fails," as Kaufman (fn. 1, 1998) puts it. Peaceful partitions therefore cannot offer any information on my main research question—war recurrence—since a war is a necessary precondition for war recurrence. My research design is therefore the equivalent of a biostatistician's inquiry into the effects of medical treatment for illness: suffering from that illness is a precondition for inclusion in the study. Studying the relationship between initial war occurrence and partition would be an interesting extension of my study. The research question would have to be reformulated, as would the data set. The dependent variable could no longer be war recurrence or residual violence and one would need a theory of civil war occurrence that included partition as a potentially important determinant of civil war (or civil peace). Such a study would analyze a random sample of countries (or the entire population of countries) and would have to include both countries that experienced war and countries that were at peace. To identify whether partition causes war, one could code a binary variable denoting if the country was partitioned and use it as a regressor in a model of the onset of war. Alternatively, one could estimate two separate regressions on partitioned and nonpartitioned countries and compare the coefficients. In terms of the medical research example above, this study would effectively ask: how does factor x affect one's chances of becoming ill?

ethnic diffusion and third-party security guarantees.[9] Some say that partition is also too severe a solution, as forced population movements cause tremendous human suffering and violate important human rights.[10] The process of partition may also create undemocratic successor states, which would be likely to repress their residual minorities much as their predecessors did.[11] This is important because successor states will rarely be ethnically homogeneous and may incorporate new ethnic antagonisms.[12] Moreover, partition does not resolve underlying ethnic rivalry, so civil wars that end in partition could be transformed into interstate wars between predecessor and successor states.[13] Finally, endorsing some partitions may encourage partition movements elsewhere, leading to new wars.[14]

The debate between partition theorists and their critics is ongoing, although some of the critiques listed above have been settled or are close to being settled in the literature. Below, I summarize three important arguments that other scholars have refuted.

Successful Ethnic Partitions Do Not Encourage Partition Movements Elsewhere

CRITICS have argued that support by the international community for partition in a few countries would encourage partitions elsewhere. Kaufman, however, has successfully rebutted this criticism by arguing that the uncertainty and extreme costs of civil war would discourage the initiation of partition movements unless such movements are inevitable for domestic political reasons.[15] That position is also supported by a set of persuasive analyses of the "international spread of ethnic conflict," which has systematically proven that cross-country contagion effects of ethnic partition movements are rare.[16]

---

9. On ethnic diffusion cooperation, see Daniel L. Byman, "Divided They Stand: Lessons about Partition from Iraq and Lebanon," *Security Studies* 7 (Autumn 1997). On security guarantees and ethnic war termination, see Barbara F. Walter, "The Critical Barrier to Civil War Settlement," *International Organization* 51 (Summer 1997). Neither Byman nor Walter is a critic of partition theory (Byman in fact supports partition under certain conditions). Some of their arguments, however, can be read as indirect critiques of the theory.

10. Radha Kumar, "The Troubled History of Partition," *Foreign Affairs* 76 (January–February 1997).

11. Ibid.; see also Amitai Etzioni, "The Evils of Self-Determination," *Foreign Policy* 89 (Winter 1992–93); and Robert Schaeffer, *Warpaths: The Politics of Partition* (New York: Hill and Wang, 1990).

12. Byman (fn. 9).

13. Ibid.; and Schaeffer (fn. 11).

14. Etzioni (fn. 11); Allen Buchanan "Self-Determination and the Right to Secede," *Journal of International Affairs* 45 (Winter 1992).

15. Kaufman (fn. 1, 1998).

16. David A. Lake and Donald Rothchild, eds., *The International Spread of Ethnic Conflicts* (Princeton: Princeton University Press, 1998).

Successor States May Also Incorporate Ethnic Conflict

A CCORDING to partition theorists, the success of partition depends on the demographic reorganization of the new territories and on the absence of militarily significant minorities in the new states. However, successor states in most actual cases of partition are not ethnically pure. Hence, this core premise of partition theory may be unrealistic.[17] To quote Horowitz:

> The linchpin of all the arguments [for partition] is the assumption that the probable outcome of secession and partition will be more homogeneous states and, concomitantly, a lower ethnic conflict level. If the assumption were correct, the conclusion would follow. *But the assumption is wrong: the only thing secession and partition are unlikely to produce is ethnically homogeneous or harmonious states.*[18]

Furthermore, even if successor states were homogeneous, the mobilization perspective of ethnic conflict would suggest that, unless partition is accompanied by regime or leadership reform, there is no guarantee that ethnic groups in successor states will not be mobilized into another war against residual minorities.[19] So again the theory's claims depend critically on unrealistic premises about the ethnic composition and political institutions of successor and predecessor states.

This last point is related to the theory's dependence on the concept of the security dilemma, which ignores the fact that conflict is often due not to the defensive security needs of ethnic groups but rather to the "predatory" goals of their leaders. It is worth noting that even the "father" of the concept of the security dilemma—Robert Jervis—has acknowledged that in most contemporary civil conflicts there are not only security motives but also predatory ones. It follows that partition will not resolve the security dilemma of the partitioned ethnic groups if it exacerbates the "predatory" incentives of predecessor states. Yugoslavia's recurrent wars are a case in point.[20]

17. See Horowitz (fn. 2), 588–91 and chaps. 2, 6.
18. Ibid., 589, emphasis added.
19. See, among others, David A. Lake and Donald Rothchild, "Containing Fear: The Origins and Management of Ethnic Conflict," *International Security* 21 (Fall 1996); V. P. Gagnon, "Ethnic Nationalism and International Conflict: The Case of Serbia," *International Security* 19 (Winter 1995); Rui J. P. de Figueiredo and Barry R. Weingast, "The Rationality of Fear: Political Opportunism and Ethnic Conflict," in Barbara Walter and Jack Snyder, eds., *Civil Wars, Insecurity, and Intervention* (New York: Columbia University Press, 1999).
20. David Laitin, "Somalia: Civil War and International Intervention," in Walter and Snyder (fn. 19); and Jack Snyder and Robert Jervis "Civil War and the Security Dilemma," in Walter and Snyder (fn. 19), 19–24.

ETHNIC COOPERATION IS POSSIBLE WITHOUT PARTITION

THERE can be many ways to resolve the security dilemma.[21] Noncooperative game theory identifies a number of conditions under which a mutually beneficial Nash equilibrium can be achieved between parties whose preferences are, first, to cheat their opponent into cooperating while they defect and, second, to mutually cooperate rather than defect. Perspectives on international negotiation have also suggested that the parties can cooperate if they negotiate a solution to "delegate to neutral authorities."[22] If negotiation is a viable option, it may be possible to reach an internationally or regionally brokered agreement that addresses the conflict's underlying causes.[23]

The problem with these solutions is that they may not be credible, which reinforces the security dilemma.[24] Thus, argues Walter, civil wars tend not to end in negotiated settlements, and a settlement will hold only when external security guarantees are available.[25] However, it need not follow that all peace agreements and institutional solutions to ethnic conflict are noncredible. Only the warring parties can gauge ex ante whether an institutional framework designed to end the war will be successful because they know their opponents and can estimate the probability that the peace process will fail.[26] Also, partition, which is allegedly credible because it redraws national borders to resolve the minority's security dilemma, is as vulnerable to the credibility argument as any other solution, since only robust external security guarantees can credibly prevent predatory predecessor states from restarting the war against successor states.

What if there is no decisive end to the war (such as a military victory) and ethnic competition persists, threatening the possibility of new violence? The rationalist perspective on war would suggest that the war should have resolved any uncertainty about relative resolve and power that might have led to war in the first place. Thus, miscalculations would be less likely after the first war and rational parties would prefer not to start a new war regardless of

---

21. I do not develop a theory of ethnic cooperation in this paper. I only summarize relevant theoretical arguments to frame my empirical analysis. Thus, this section is not designed to resolve all doubt about the possibility of ethnic cooperation after civil war.

22. Snyder and Jervis (fn. 20), 18. On power sharing, see Timothy Sisk, *Power Sharing and International Mediation in Ethnic Conflicts* (Washington, D.C: United States Institute of Peace, 1996).

23. Lake and Rothschild (fn. 19).

24. Snyder and Jervis (fn. 20).

25. In Walter's (fn. 9) argument, the security dilemma depends on an asymmetry of power between the government and rebels. Walter notes that *credible* external security guarantees are effective, though difficult. The difficulty in proving the credibility of the third party's commitment amounts to indirect support for the partition thesis, though only if partition is proven to be more credible and less difficult to implement than a brokered settlement.

26. De Figuereido and Weingast (fn. 19).

the first war's outcome.[27] This could change, however, as the parties' relative capabilities change over time. So one way for the international community to enable stable peace is to preserve the military balance that follows the end of the war. An alternative, which could work better in some situations, is to create a regional hegemon responsible for regional peace.[28]

Finally, cooperation among ethnic groups may be possible if ethnic diffusion increases as a result of the war, that is, if the opposite of partition takes place. Byman has suggested that increased ethnic diffusion may mitigate the security dilemma, since it would reduce the probability that a single ethnic group could become politically and militarily dominant. His argument derives from the theoretical literature on international alliances and posits that ethnic "balancing" against threatening groups is both possible and stabilizing.[29] This hypothesis has yet to be tested, but it is relevant to note that a budding political economy literature on civil wars has identified a parabolic relationship between ethnic fragmentation and the probability of civil war; that is, the probability of civil war drops significantly at very high levels of ethnic diversity and it is greatest in ethnically polarized societies, which seems to support Byman's hypothesis.[30] The question that partition theorists raise is slightly different, however: can ethnic diversity reduce the risk of war recurrence after the first war ends? I answer this question in later sections.

TAKING SIDES: NEW DATA AND NEW EMPIRICAL TESTS
OF PARTITION THEORY

THE four most important questions in partition theory are still unresolved. (1) What are the main determinants of partition? (2) Does partition create democratic or undemocratic states? (3) Does partition prevent war recurrence?

27. The rationalist school is well represented by Geoffrey Blainey, *The Causes of War* (New York: Free Press, 1973); and James Fearon, "Rationalist Explanations for War," *International Organization* 49 (Summer 1995). War should reveal any private information about relative power and resolve, making it less rational for parties to resort to war again rather than to strike a more efficient bargain short of war. That said, we should also consider other explanations of war and weigh them against this argument.
28. Snyder and Jervis (fn. 20); and Laitin (fn. 20).
29. Byman (fn. 9). This argument can backfire. Ethnic balancing can also paralyze the state. For such an argument, see Harrison Wagner, "The Causes of Peace," in Roy Licklider, ed., *Stopping the Killing* (New York: New York University Press, 1993). Wagner argues that because military victory results in unitary political systems, it will be more stable than any peace agreement based on ethnic balancing. Indeed, the occurrence of an ethnic war suggests a precedent of failed ethnic balancing. In this paper, I present empirical results about the relationship of ethnicity to postwar violence, but that relationship also demands better theorizing.
30. See, e.g., Paul Collier, Ibrahim Elbadawi, and Nicholas Sambanis, "How Much War Will We See? Estimating the Probability of Civil War in 161 Countries" (Manuscript, World Bank, February 2000).

And (4) does partition end low-level ethnic violence (that is, violence short of war)?

To answer these questions, I have compiled a new cross-sectional data set of all civil wars since 1944. The unit of observation is a civil war. The analysis focuses on wars that have been over for at least two years at the time of writing, but also included are eight ongoing wars to capture the partition theorists' interest in partition as a way of ending ongoing wars.[31]

A civil war is defined as an armed conflict that has (1) caused more than one thousand deaths; (2) challenged the sovereignty of an internationally recognized state; (3) occurred within the recognized boundaries of that state; (4) involved the state as one of the principal combatants; (5) included rebels with the ability to mount an organized opposition; and (6) involved parties concerned with the prospect of living together in the same political unit after the end of the war.[32] This definition allows me to combine wars from several data sets.[33] Detailed documentation on my coding and sources for all the variables in the data set is available online.[34]

31. Dropping those cases did not affect any of the models estimated in later sections.
32. This definition is nearly identical to the definition of a civil war in J. David Singer and Melvin Small, *Correlates of War Project: International and Civil War Data, 1816-1992* (Ann Arbor, Mich.: ICPSR, 1994); idem, *Resort to Arms* (Beverly Hills, Calif.: Sage Publications, 1982); and Roy Licklider, "The Consequences of Negotiated Settlements in Civil Wars, 1945-1993," *American Political Science Review* 89 (September 1995). Unlike them, my coding of wars does not presume one thousand deaths per year, but rather uses the one thousand deaths as the threshold for the entire war. In fact, however, most of my cases have caused one thousand deaths annually. My coding decision was based on the arbitrariness of setting one thousand as the annual death criterion and on the lack of available data on annual deaths in the Correlates of War project. Indeed, the codebook of the ICPSR study, which includes the international and civil war data files for the Correlates of War Project, does not mention an annual death threshold and no annual death data are made available by the authors.
33. My sources for coding wars include Singer and Small (fn. 32, 1994); Licklider (fn. 32); idem (fn. 29); Peter Wallensteen and Margareta Sollenberg, "Armed Conflicts, Conflict Termination, and Peace Agreements, 1989–1996," *Journal of Peace Research* 34, no. 3 (1997); Daniel C. Esty et al., "The State Failure Project: Early Warning Research for US Foreign Policy Planning," in John L. Davies and Ted Robert Gurr, eds., *Preventive Measures: Building Risk Assessment and Crisis Early Warning Systems* (Boulder, Colo., and Totowa, N.J.: Rowman and Littlefield, 1998); David Mason and Patrick Fett, "How Civil Wars End: A Rational Choice Approach," *Journal of Conflict Resolution* 40 (December 1996); Patrick Regan, "Conditions for Successful Third Party Interventions," *Journal of Conflict Resolution* 40, no. 1 (1996); Walter (fn. 9); SIPRI, *SIPRI Yearbook* (http://editors.sipri.se/pubs/yearb.html); Human Rights Watch, *World Report* (New York and Washington, D.C.: Human Rights Watch, various years). Secondary texts consulted include Robert I. Rotberg, ed., *Burma: Prospects for a Democratic Future* (Washington, D.C.: Brookings Institution, 1998): Martin Stuart-Fox, *A History of Laos* (Cambridge: Cambridge University Press, 1998); David Callahan, *Unwinnable Wars* (New York: Hill and Wang, 1997); John O. Iatrides, "The Doomed Revolution: Communist Insurgency in Postwar Greece," in Licklider (fn. 29); Michael W. Doyle, Robert Orr. and Ian Johnstone, eds., *Keeping the Peace* (Cambridge: Cambridge University Press, 1997); Francis M. Deng, *War of Visions: Conflict of Identities in the Sudan* (Washington, D.C.: Brookings Institution, 1999); David McDowall, *A Modern History of the Kurds* (New York: St. Martin's Press, 1996); and Nicholas Sambanis, "United Nations

DEFINITION OF PARTITION

THE variable denoting partition, PART, is binary and equals 1 if an event of partition is observed and 0 otherwise. Partition is defined as a war outcome that involves border both adjustment and demographic changes. This is a broad definition that differs slightly from Kaufmann's. To justify a narrower definition of partition, Kaufmann wrote that "we should focus on partition rather than secession . . . to assess whether international intervention reduces or increases the costs of ethnic conflict."[35] He then defined partitions as "separations jointly decided upon by the responsible powers: either agreed between the two sides (and not under pressure of imminent military victory by one side), or imposed on both sides by a stronger third party . . . [and he defined] secessions as new states created by the unilateral action of a rebellious ethnic group."[36]

I do not find the narrow definition convincing or useful, given that the far-reaching implications of partition theory affect secessions and partitions equally in the minds of most policymakers and academics. Moreover, the narrow definition reclassifies as secessions certain cases that Kaufmann originally treated as partitions.[37] Finally, this definition does not justify the inclusion of some of the partitions included on Kaufmann's own list.[38] An example is Cyprus, which Kaufmann correctly—though for the wrong reasons—classifies as a de facto partition.[39] The 1974 partition of Cyprus was neither the outcome of an agreement nor an imposition by a third party, as the narrow definition would have it. Rather, it was the result of military victory by the Turkish side.[40]

Given these problems with the narrow definition, I use the broader definition, combining cases of partition and secession listed in Kaufmann's two

---

Peacekeeping in Theory and in Cyprus: New Conceptual Approaches and Interpretations" (Ph.D. diss., Princeton University, 1999). The most important difference between my coding and that of others concerns the periodization of wars. I have broken what is a single observation of war in other data sets into more than one observation; or, conversely, I have collapsed two or more observations in one by uniformly applying this rule: a war is coded as a single observation if the parties and issues are the same, if the war events are not separated by a substantial period of nonviolence, and/or if the parties sign a peace agreement or agree to a major truce.

34. The document can be downloaded from http: www.worldbank.org/research/conflict/....
    35. Kaufmann (fn.1, 1998), 125.
    36. See Kaufmann (fn.1, 1998), 125, fn. 21.
    37. Kaufmann (fn. 1, 1996).
    38. Kauffman (fn.1, 1998).
    39. Ibid.
    40. It is well known to scholars of the Cyprus problem that Turkey and the Turkish Cypriots constituted and acted as a single party both during the violent part of that conflict (1963–74) and during the subsequent negotiation phases; see Sambanis (fn. 33).

articles.[41] I also add cases that satisfy my definition but are not on Kaufmann's list.[42] Table 1 lists all civil wars and partitions in my data set, sorted by country name, war start/end dates, the type of war, war recurrence, and lower-level violence outcomes.[43]

In my analysis of democratization, war termination, and low-level political violence I use explanatory variables that other authors have identified as significant for those events. These variables are important both for the theory of partition and for use as controls in subsequent empirical tests. Table 2 presents summary statistics for all variables and explains what each one measures. Table 3 presents a correlation matrix with the most important variables used in the analysis.

I now turn to the question of the determinants of partition.

MAIN DETERMINANTS OF PARTITION

MY data set includes 125 civil wars, which produced 21 partitions.[44] Using the entire data set (which includes six right-truncated wars), I estimated probit models of the incidence of partition, selecting the explanatory variables on the basis of theory developed in the literature on civil war.[45] I want to test whether some of the same variables that either cause or terminate civil wars are also significant determinants of war-related partition.

41. Kaufmann (fn.1, 1996 and 1998). Other studies also use the broad definition, given that the distinction between secession and partition seems artificial. See, among others, Horowitz (fn. 2); and Alexis Heraclides, *The Self-Determination of Minorities in International Politics* (Portland: Frank Cass, 1991); both use the terms partition and secession interchangeably.

42. I consider only post-World War II cases because of the paucity of economic data from before 1945. Thus, I exclude the partition of Ireland. Cases of peaceful partition are also excluded, for example, Macedonia (1992), Czechoslovakia (1993), and Singapore (1965). I exclude one case (Iraq) that I believe was erroneously classified as a partition in Kaufmann (fn.1, 1998). I exclude Iraq (1991) because there is no recognized, functional, or even autonomous Iraqi Kurdistan and the territory and its population would have been within reach of the Iraqi military had it not been for the U.S.-enforced no-fly zone.

43. My coding of cases of partition incorporated suggestions made by anonymous referees.

44. One might argue that the "real" number of partitions is smaller, since several of them occurred in either the former Yugoslavia or the former USSR. This would imply that these partitions may not be independent of one another. Thus, I cluster all same-country observations in my statistical analysis, relaxing the assumption of independence for those observations and allowing for nonconstant variance within clusters.

45. See, for example, Paul Collier and Anke Hoeffler, "Justice-Seeking and Loot-Seeking in Civil War" (Manuscript, World Bank, February 1999); Michael W. Doyle and Nicholas Sambanis, "International Peacebuilding: A Theoretical and Quantitative Analysis" (Manuscript, Princeton University and the World Bank, February 2000); Paul Collier, "On the Economic Consequences of Civil War," *Oxford Economic Papers* 51 (1998); and Mason and Fett (fn. 33).

Table 1
CIVIL WARS BY YEAR AND TYPE, PARTITIONS, WAR RECURRENCE, AND
LOW-LEVEL VIOLENCE

Country Name Where Civil War Took Place	Year War Started	Year War Ended	Did War End for 2 Years?	Did Residual Violence End for 2 Years?	Was There a Partition?	Type of War (Identity or Not?)
Afghanistan	1978	1992	no	no	no	ideology/other
Afghanistan	1993	ongoing	no	no	no	ethnic/religious
Algeria	1962	1963	yes	yes	no	ideology/other
Algeria	1992	1997	no	no	no	ethnic/religious
Angola	1975	1991	no	no	no	ethnic/religious
Angola	1992	ongoing	no	no	no	ethnic/religious
Argentina	1955	1955	yes	yes	no	ideology/other
Azerbaijan	1988	1996	yes	yes	yes	ethnic/religious
Bangladesh	1973	1994	yes	yes	no	ethnic/religious
Bolivia	1952	1952	yes	yes	no	ideology/other
Burma	1948	1951	yes	no	no	ideology/other
Burma	1968	1982	no	no	no	ethnic/religious
Burma	1983	1995	yes	no	no	ethnic/religious
Burundi	1965	1969	yes	no	no	ethnic/religious
Burundi	1972	1973	yes	yes	no	ethnic/religious
Burundi	1988	1988	no	no	no	ethnic/religious
Burundi	1991	ongoing	no	no	no	ethnic/religious
Cambodia	1970	1975	yes	no	no	ideology/other
Cambodia	1979	1991	yes	yes	no	ideology/other
Central African Rep.	1995	1997	yes	yes	no	ideology/other
Chad	1965	1979	no	no	no	ethnic/religious
Chad	1980	1994	yes	yes	no	ethnic/religious
China	1967	1968	yes	no	no	ethnic/religious
China-Taiwan	1947	1947	yes	no	yes	ideology/other
China-Tibet	1950	1951	yes	no	no	ethnic/religious
Colombia	1948	1962	yes	yes	no	ideology/other
Colombia	1978	ongoing	no	no	no	ideology/other
Congo Brazzaville	1992	1996	no	no	no	ideology/other
Congo/Zaire	1967	1967	yes	yes	no	ethnic/religious
Congo/Zaire	1975	1979	yes	no	no	ethnic/religious
Congo/Zaire	1960	1965	no	no	no	ethnic/religious
Congo/Zaire	1996	1997	no	no	no	ethnic/religious
Costa Rica	1948	1948	yes	yes	no	ideology/other
Cuba	1958	1959	yes	no	no	ideology/other
Cyprus	1963	1964	no	no	yes	ethnic/religious
Cyprus	1974	1974	yes	yes	yes	ethnic/religious

Table 1
(CONTINUED)

Country Name Where Civil War Took Place	Year War Started	Year War Ended	Did War End for 2 Years?	Did Residual Violence End for 2 Years?	Was There a Partition?	Type of War (Identity or Not?)
Djibouti	1991	1995	yes	yes	no	ideology/other
Dominican Rep.	1965	1965	yes	yes	no	ideology/other
El Salvador	1979	1992	yes	yes	no	ideology/other
Eritrea	1974	1991	yes	yes	yes	ethnic/religious
Ethiopia	1977	1985	yes	no	no	ethnic/religious
Ethiopia	1974	1991	yes	yes	no	ideology/other
Georgia	1991	1993	yes	yes	yes	ethnic/religious
Georgia	1992	1994	yes	yes	yes	ethnic/religious
Greece	1944	1949	yes	yes	no	ideology/other
Guatemala	1954	1954	yes	yes	no	ideology/other
Guatemala	1966	1972	no	no	no	ethnic/religious
Guatemala	1974	1994	yes	yes	no	ethnic/religious
Haiti	1991	1994	no	no	no	ideology/other
Haiti	1995	1996	yes	yes	no	ideology/other
India	1946	1948	yes	yes	yes	ethnic/religious
India	1965	1965	yes	no	yes	ethnic/religious
India	1984	1994	yes	yes	no	ethnic/religious
India	1989	1994	yes	no	yes	ethnic/religious
Indonesia	1956	1960	yes	no	no	ideology/other
Indonesia	1986	1986	yes	yes	no	ethnic/religious
Indonesia	1950	1950	no	no	no	ethnic/religious
Indonesia	1953	1953	no	no	no	ethnic/religious
Indonesia	1975	1982	yes	no	no	ethnic/religious
Iran	1978	1979	no	no	no	ideology/other
Iran	1981	1982	yes	no	no	ethnic/religious
Iraq	1959	1959	no	no	no	ethnic/religious
Iraq	1961	1975	yes	no	no	ethnic/religious
Iraq	1988	1994	yes	no	no	ethnic/religious
Iraq	1991	1994	yes	no	no	ethnic/religious
Israel/Palestine	1947	1949	no	no	yes	ethnic/religious
Israel	1950	1994	yes	yes	no	ethnic/religious
Jordan	1971	1971	yes	yes	no	ethnic/religious
Kenya	1991	1993	yes	no	no	ethnic/religious
Korea	1950	1953	yes	yes	yes	ideology/other
Laos	1960	1975	yes	no	no	ideology/other
Lebanon	1958	1958	yes	yes	no	ethnic/religious
Lebanon	1975	1978	yes	no	no	ethnic/religious

Table 1
(CONTINUED)

Country Name Where Civil War Took Place	Year War Started	Year War Ended	Did War End for 2 Years?	Did Residual Violence End for 2 Years?	Was There a Partition?	Type of War (Identity or Not?)
Lebanon	1982	1992	yes	no	no	ethnic/religious
Liberia	1989	1992	no	no	no	ideology/other
Liberia	1993	1996	yes	no	no	ideology/other
Malaysia	1948	1959	yes	yes	no	ideology/other
Mali	1990	1995	yes	yes	no	ethnic/religious
Mexico	1992	1994	yes	yes	no	ethnic/religious
Moldova	1992	1994	yes	no	yes	ethnic/religious
Morocco/W. Sahara	1975	1989	yes	yes	no	ethnic/religious
Mozambique	1979	1992	yes	yes	no	ideology/other
Namibia	1965	1989	yes	yes	no	ethnic/religious
Nicaragua	1978	1979	no	no	no	ideology/other
Nicaragua	1981	1989	yes	yes	no	ideology/other
Nigeria	1967	1970	yes	yes	no	ethnic/religious
Nigeria	1980	1984	yes	no	no	ethnic/religious
Northern Ireland	1968	1994	yes	yes	no	ethnic/religious
Pakistan	1971	1971	yes	yes	yes	ethnic/religious
Pakistan	1973	1977	yes	no	no	ethnic/religious
Papua New Guinea	1988	1991	yes	no	no	ethnic/religious
Paraguay	1947	1947	yes	yes	no	ethnic/religious
Peru	1980	1996	yes	no	no	ideology/other
Philippines	1950	1952	yes	yes	no	ideology/other
Philippines	1972	1996	yes	no	no	ethnic/religious
Philippines	1972	1992	yes	no	no	ideology/other
Romania	1989	1989	yes	yes	no	ideology/other
Russia/Chechnya	1994	1996	no	no	yes	ethnic/religious
Rwanda	1963	1964	yes	no	no	ethnic/religious
Rwanda	1990	1994	yes	yes	no	ethnic/religious
Sierra Leone	1991	1996	no	no	no	ideology/other
Somalia	1988	1991	no	no	yes	ethnic/religious
Somalia	1992	ongoing	no	no	no	ethnic/religious
South Africa	1976	1994	yes	yes	no	ethnic/religious
Sri Lanka	1971	1971	yes	yes	no	ideology/other
Sri Lanka	1987	1989	yes	yes	no	ideology/other
Sri Lanka	1983	ongoing	no	no	no	ethnic/religious
Sudan	1963	1972	yes	yes	no	ethnic/religious
Sudan	1983	ongoing	no	no	no	ethnic/religious
Tajikistan	1992	1994	yes	no	yes	ethnic/religious

(CONTINUED)

Table 1
(CONTINUED)

Country Name Where Civil War Took Place	Year War Started	Year War Ended	Did War End for 2 Years?	Did Residual Violence End for 2 Years?	Was There a Partition?	Type of War (Identity or Not?)
Thailand	1967	1985	yes	yes	no	ethnic/religious
Turkey	1984	ongoing	no	no	no	ethnic/religious
Uganda	1966	1966	yes	yes	no	ethnic/religious
Uganda	1978	1979	no	no	no	ideology/other
Uganda	1980	1986	yes	no	no	ethnic/religious
Vietnam Rep.	1960	1975	yes	yes	yes	ideology/other
Yemen	1948	1948	yes	yes	no	ideology/other
Yemen	1994	1994	yes	yes	no	ideology/other
Yemen, North	1962	1969	yes	yes	no	ideology/other
Yemen, South	1986	1987	yes	yes	no	ideology/other
Yugoslavia/Bosnia	1992	1995	yes	yes	yes	ethnic/religious
Yugoslavia/Croatia	1991	1991	no	no	yes	ethnic/religious
Yugoslavia/Croatia	1995	1995	yes	yes	yes	ethnic/religious
Zimbabwe/Rhodesia	1972	1980	yes	no	no	ethnic/religious
Zimbabwe	1984	1984	yes	yes	no	ethnic/religious

I make the following testable hypotheses: Following the reasoning of partition theorists, I hypothesize that WARTYPE (ethnic/religious rather than ideological war) should be positively associated with partition.[46] Partition is not usually the goal of revolutions motivated by ideology, but it is often the stated goal of ethnic war. For the same reason, ethnic heterogeneity (EH) should be significantly associated with partition, especially if ethnic groups are large enough to constitute a politically and economically viable successor state. The human toll of the war (LOGCOST) should be positively correlated with partition. The intuition is that extremely violent wars can be settled only by partition and that the international community might be more supportive of such an outcome in those cases. The outcome of the war (OUTCOME2) should also be a significant determinant of partition, since we would not expect

46. The coding of the WARTYPE variable was not easy. There are substantial differences in the various sources and data sets I consulted. I used two main sources for this variable: Licklider (fn. 32); and Esty et al. (fn. 33). I coded the variables TYPELICK (Licklider's warissue variable) and TYPESTF (the State-Failure Project's war-type variable) to facilitate comparisons across cases. Where those two sources differed, I coded WARTYPE based on majority opinion in other data sets, including Regan (fn. 33); and Mason and Fett (fn. 33).

Table 2

SUMMARY STATISTICS OF VARIABLES USED IN THE ANALYSIS

Variable	Proxy for	Obs.	Mean	Std. Dev.	Min	Max
WAREND2	did the war end for 2 years?	125	0.744	0.438178	0	1
WAREND5	did the war end for 5 years?	114	0.745614	0.437438	0	1
NOVIOL2	2 years without low violence?	125	0.472	0.501224	0	1
NOVIOL5	5 years without low violence?	114	0.5	0.502208	0	1
PARTV2	is this a partitioned country?	125	0.168	0.375371	0	1
LOGCOST	log of deaths & displacements	124	11.93372	2.412293	6.907755	15.67181
LOGDEAD	log of deaths; battle & civilian	124	10.2669	2.093265	6.214608	14.91412
INTENSE	human cost per capita per month	124	0.005733	0.020525	4.83E-07	0.161202
OUTCOME2	how did the war end?	125	2.192	1.348213	0	4
TREATY	was a treaty signed?	125	0.28	0.450806	0	1
VREBEL	did the rebels win a victory?	125	0.216	0.41317	0	1
TRUCE	did the war end in a truce?	125	0.12	0.326269	0	1
MILOUT	was there a military outcome?	125	0.608	0.490161	0	1
WARDUR	duration of the war (months)	125	77.72	89.60987	1	528
GARM	size of gov't military (thousand)	124	402.729	957.5273	9	8256
ENERCAP	energy consumption per capita	124	0.000157	0.000413	−1.50e-07	0.00214
ELECTRIC	electricity consumption p/c (kwhrs)	123	586.8661	958.0384	10	5387
GDP	real GDP per capita (PPP)	124	1765.581	1789.364	130	10000
RGDPCH2	real GDP p.c.-no imputations	123	1556.398	1452.303	130	7741
PW10	was there a war in past 10 years?	125	0.48	0.50161	0	1
AIDGNP	foreign aid as % of GNP	116	8.731095	14.04966	0	83.8
ILLIT	percent illiterate population	118	43.23025	26.64874	1	85.5

(CONTINUED)

Table 2
(CONTINUED)

Variable	Proxy for	Obs.	Mean	Std. Dev.	Min	Max
GINI	income inequality index	125	40.3881	9.49447	19.29	62.88
LIFES	life expectancy at birth	125	52.15048	10.84891	32	73
EH	ethnic heterogeneity index	125	56.776	33.93563	0	144
EHLPOP	EH interacted w/log of population	125	935.8059	594.8487	0	2629.118
ELF	ethnolinguistic fractionalization	118	48.66102	30.61764	0	93
LOGPOP	log of population size	125	16.27787	1.535166	13.26733	20.53999
GEO	dummy for continent	125	3.592	1.289511	1	5
DECADE	decade in which war started	125	3.44	1.433471	1	6
WARTYPE	was it an ethnic/identity war?	125	0.64	0.481932	0	1
TYPELICK	Licklider's version of wartype	116	1.293103	0.45716	1	2
TYPESTF	state failure project wartype	108	0.722222	0.449991	0	1
GURR2	democracy—2 years after war	109	9.311927	6.37515	1	20
IGURR2	Gurr2 w/imputed missing cells	122	8.823376	6.310452	1	20
GPOL2	Freedom House political rights	88	4.840909	1.793259	1	7
GURRLAG5	5-yr mean democracy (prewar)	120	6.016667	5.680548	0	20
PEACEOP	third party peace operation type	125	1.056	1.477269	0	4
COLDWAR	dummy for the cold war period	125	.784	.4131703	0	1
PTEH	interaction term: $EH^{s}/$Partv2	125	9.6	26.57461	0	128
PTLCOST	interaction term: $Logcost^{s}/$Partv2	124	2.249478	5.031744	0	14.84513
PTARMY	interaction term: $Garm^{s}/$Partv2	124	140.6427	835.8922	0	8256
ETHPART	Interaction term: $Wartype^{s}/$Partv2	125	.144	.3525026	0	1

Table 3
CORRELATION MATRIX OF KEY VARIABLES (OBS. = 99)

	WAREND2	WAREND5	NOVIOL2	NOVIOL5	PARTV2	LOGCOST	OUTCOME2	TREATY	VREBEL	TRUCE
WAREND2	1									
WAREND5	0.8315	1								
NOVIOL2	0.551	0.5831	1							
NOVIOL5	0.5136	0.595	0.9395	1						
PARTV2	0.0639	−0.0592	0.078	0.0702	1					
LOGCOST	−0.2017	−0.238	−0.211	−0.183	0.2743	1				
OUTCOME2	0.2424	0.2034	0.2394	0.2375	0.2151	0.3133	1			
TREATY	0.0982	0.1234	0.2115	0.1997	−0.0281	0.3194	0.792	1		
VREBEL	0.0311	0.0575	−0.0874	−0.0527	0.1182	0.0104	−0.0591	−0.3469	1	
TRUCE	0	−0.1491	−0.0447	−0.0512	0.3972	0.0897	0.2126	−0.1887	−0.1838	1
MILOUT	−0.1308	−0.0617	−0.1909	−0.1764	−0.2227	−0.3245	−0.8978	−0.7768	0.4204	−0.4372
WARDUR	−0.0716	−0.0527	0.0394	0.0294	−0.1496	0.2662	0.2539	0.3623	−0.0807	−0.0859
GARM	0.1439	0.1139	−0.0655	−0.0736	0.2805	0.0658	−0.0682	−0.1726	−0.0372	0.2271
ENERCAP	0.1244	0.1206	0.2102	0.2033	0.2496	−0.0298	0.3037	0.2274	−0.1076	0.1899
GDP	0.0704	0.0963	0.1282	0.1147	0.0431	−0.1695	0.1574	0.1216	−0.0586	0.0899
EH	−0.0763	−0.1779	−0.0907	−0.156	0.1197	0.1456	0.0876	0.0899	−0.0022	−0.0051
EHLPOP	−0.0504	−0.1812	−0.102	−0.1631	0.1619	0.1371	0.0474	0.0378	−0.0195	0.0341
ELF	−0.0293	−0.0598	−0.0558	−0.1404	0.0767	−0.0178	0.0611	0.0744	−0.0843	0.0487
LOGPOP	0.0783	−0.044	−0.1768	−0.2017	0.2106	0.0433	−0.2587	−0.2654	−0.0579	0.0705
GEO	−0.0513	−0.0645	−0.1747	−0.2006	−0.1156	0.1143	−0.1046	−0.0138	−0.0949	−0.0405
DECADE	−0.191	−0.1595	−0.1097	−0.0985	0.0187	0.1561	0.0913	0.1472	−0.1039	0.0989
WARTYPE	−0.101	−0.1826	−0.1872	−0.2141	0.1074	0.0563	−0.0369	0.0694	−0.3339	0.093

(CONTINUED)

Table 3
(Continued)

	WAREND2	WAREND5	NOVIOL2	NOVIOL5	PARTV2	LOGCOST	OUTCOME2	TREATY	VREBEL	TRUCE
PW10	0.0054	−0.0414	−0.1923	−0.2129	0.1456	0.1777	−0.0558	−0.006	−0.0291	0.0319
IGURR2	0.1874	0.144	0.3281	0.358	0.1224	−0.0584	0.286	0.2708	−0.2439	0.18
GURRLAG5	0.0884	−0.0286	0.0744	0.036	−0.0184	−0.2111	0.0337	0.0341	−0.2133	0.1562
PEACEOP	0.0412	0.0733	0.1117	0.1255	0.2226	0.3622	0.4809	0.4213	−0.1693	0.3123
PTEH	0.0635	−0.1367	0.0285	0.0221	0.822	0.2579	0.2187	0.0405	0.037	0.32
PTLCOST	0.0648	−0.0545	0.0964	0.0886	0.9943	0.2937	0.218	−0.0182	0.1153	0.3833
PTARMY	0.0906	0.0422	0.0329	0.0294	0.4481	0.0962	0.0754	−0.0965	0.0302	0.3408
ETHPART	0.0179	−0.1233	0.0569	0.0502	0.8621	0.2541	0.2254	0.0285	0.0366	0.3604

	MILOUT	WARDUR	GARM	ENERCAP	GDP	EH	EHLPOP	ELF	LOGPOP	GEO
MILOUT	1									
WARDUR	−0.2824	1								
GARM	0.0131	−0.09	1							
ENERCAP	−0.3326	0.0801	−0.0723	1						
GDP	−0.1791	0.2231	−0.0532	0.5168	1					
EH	−0.076	0.1605	−0.153	−0.0741	−0.1648	1				
EHLPOP	−0.0529	0.1331	−0.0993	−0.1239	−0.1813	0.983	1			
ELF	−0.0776	0.1788	−0.1523	−0.0739	−0.067	0.6744	0.6919	1		
LOGPOP	0.1985	−0.0425	0.4709	−0.4209	−0.1725	0.219	0.3585	0.3016	1	
GEO	0.0608	0.1599	0.0757	−0.446	−0.576	0.2956	0.313	0.3914	0.2669	1
DECADE	−0.1687	0.0442	−0.2195	0.0152	0.1828	0.0667	0.0643	0.0425	−0.0308	0.0381

	MILOUT	WARDUR	GARM	ENERCAP	GDP	EH	EHLPOP	ELF	LOGPOP	GEO
WARTYPE	−0.1045	0.0594	−0.0225	0.1301	0.0432	0.3144	0.3221	0.3169	0.1356	0.3131
PW10	0.0073	0.1091	0.2128	−0.044	−0.1404	0.1435	0.1533	0.0553	0.2389	0.2513
IGURR2	−0.371	0.2454	−0.1826	0.2337	0.2378	−0.0007	0.0274	0.0583	−0.0277	−0.2358
GURRLAG5	−0.1377	0.0949	−0.047	0.1116	0.127	0.1147	0.1447	0.1075	0.0415	−0.0871
PEACEOP	−0.5503	0.0866	0.0266	0.2812	0.1221	0.0195	−0.0141	−0.008	−0.2631	−0.1399
PTEH	−0.2381	−0.1141	0.0102	0.1687	−0.0415	0.3518	0.4155	0.2268	0.28	−0.053
PTLCOST	−0.2234	−0.1415	0.266	0.2412	0.0353	0.1329	0.1742	0.0825	0.2018	−0.1079
PTARMY	−0.1206	−0.0929	0.8294	−0.0539	−0.1074	−0.1418	−0.1124	−0.1571	0.2031	0.0574
ETHPART	−0.2517	−0.1618	−0.0377	0.3132	0.0773	0.2611	0.2989	0.2046	0.1296	−0.161

	decade	wartype	pw10	igurr2	gurrlag5	peaceop	pteh	ptlcost	ptarmy	ethpart
DECADE	1									
WARTYPE	0.228	1								
PW10	0.2961	0.2596	1							
IGURR2	−0.033	−0.1643	−0.2346	1						
GURRLAG5	−0.1262	−0.0525	−0.165	0.5018	1					
PEACEOP	0.2453	0.0979	0.0839	0.2047	−0.0326	1				
PTEH	0.0903	0.2149	0.0621	0.2121	0.0784	0.1812	1			
PTLCOST	0.0163	0.1128	0.1342	0.1241	−0.0233	0.2248	0.835	1		
PTARMY	−0.2142	−0.1507	0.1349	−0.0866	−0.0511	0.1655	0.1181	0.4309	1	
ETHPART	0.1625	0.2534	0.0637	0.2335	0.0113	0.2277	0.9107	0.8668	0.0689	1

to see partition if the government wins a military victory, whereas partition would be more likely in the case of rebel victory. Population size (LOGPOP) should be positively associated with partition.[47] I also include as control variables a number of socioeconomic indicators of the country's overall level of development, since many studies have identified such variables as significant determinants of civil war.[48] However, it is harder to theorize about the nature of their association with the incidence of partition. I present the results of my estimations in Table 4.

A first important finding is that, as theorized, the type of the war is indeed a significant determinant of partition. Identity wars (ethnic and religious wars) are positively and significantly correlated with partition in model 1. This implies that the partition theorists correctly argue that ethnicity matters for the onset of partition. However, when I tested alternatively coded variables for the type of war in models 1b and 1c, I found a significant difference: both variables were significant, but Licklider's variable (TYPELICK in model 1a) is negatively correlated with the onset of partition whereas the State Failure Project variable (TYPESTF in model 1b) is positively correlated with partition. This implies that, while ethnicity seems important for partition, the direction of their association might be influenced by assumptions made in the coding of the WARTYPE variable.[49] At the same time, only small changes are observed in most of the other variables in models 1a and 1b, which suggests that the other variables are robust.

Ethnicity has a complicated relationship with partition. In models 1, 1a, and 1b, I found that as ethnic heterogeneity increases, the probability of a partition decreases significantly, suggesting that it may be difficult to coordinate and win in a secessionist war in extremely diverse societies.[50] However, as the size of ethnic groups increases, so does the probability of partition.[51] Large ethnic groups may be better able to overcome the coordination problems associated with mounting a rebellion and better able to defend their territory.

47. This hypothesis (with an emphasis on the proportion of young men) has been posited with reference to the causes of civil war by Collier and Hoeffler (fn. 45); and Robert H. Bates, "Ethnicity, Capital Formation, and Conflict," *CID Working Paper* no. 27 (Harvard University, October 1999).
48. For example, Collier and Hoeffler (fn. 45).
49. Given such problems, quantitative analysts of civil wars must be highly transparent in their coding of these variables. Moreover, it is necessary for those building data sets of civil war to coordinate their efforts and exchange information. I will use my WARTYPE variable in the rest of the analysis since I generated it with reference to as many sources as I could consult for each case. I tried to reflect majority opinion about the coding of each case, where there was disagreement between my main sources.
50. If we drop WARTYPE, then EH becomes nonsignificant but remains negative.
51. I proxy the size of ethnic groups by interacting the ethnic heterogeneity index EH with the log of population size (LOGPOP).

Table 4
PROBIT REGRESSION OF OCCURRENCE OF PARTITION[a]

Dep. Var.: Partition	Model 1	Model 1a	Model 1b	Model 2	Model 3
Constant	−4.53***	−2.09	−3.93*	−6.72*	−2.38
	(1.64)	(1.82)	(2.12)	(3.48)	(2.09)
WARTYPE (identity or ideology?)	1.65***	—	—	2.22***	1.59***
	(.553)	—	—	(.822)	(.547)
	.103	—	—	2.22	.032
LOGCOST (log of deaths & displacements	.358***	.471***	.338***	.441***	.396***
	(.118)	(.141)	(.138)	(.152)	(.138)
	.025	.025	.034	.44	.008
EH (Index of Ethnic Heterogeneity)	−.064**	−.068***	−.063**	−.049	−.075***
	(.026)	(.029)	(.027)	(.035)	(.027)
	−.005	−.004	−.006	−.049	−.0015
EHLPOP (EH * log of population size)	.003**	.0037**	.0034**	.003	.004***
	(.001)	(.002)	(.0015)	(.002)	(.0014)
	.0002	.0002	.0003	.003	.00008
TRUCE (war ended in an informal truce?)	1.69***	1.76***	1.71***	1.58***	1.75***
	(.348)	(.383)	(.342)	(.438)	(.414)
	.337	.313	.401	1.58	.183
VREBEL (war ended with a rebel victory?)	1.55***	1.59***	1.35***	1.91**	2.16***
	(.519)	(.578)	(.425)	(.778)	(.502)
	.247	.214	.256	1.91	.229
GEO (continent)	−.594***	−.644***	−.651***	−.514**	−.405*
	(.172)	(.205)	(.192)	(.207)	(.225)
	−.042	−.035	−.065	−.513	−.008
DECADE (decade in which war started)	−.175	−.204	−.167	−.019	−.023
	(.140)	(.161)	(.151)	(.181)	(.153)
	−.012	−.011	−.017	−.019	−.0005
TYPELICK (Licklider's wartype)	—	−2.07***	—	—	—
	—	(.591)	—	—	—
		−.113			
TYPESTF (State Failure Project wartype)	—	—	1.32**	—	—
	—	—	(.576)	—	—
			.094		
ILLIT (percentage population that is illiterate)	—	—	—	−.021	—
	—	—	—	(.016)	—
				−.02	
GDP (real GDP per capita, PPP)	—	—	—	2.17e-07	—
	—	—	—	(.0001)	—
				2.17e-07	

Table 4
(CONTINUED)

Dep. Var.: Partition	Model 1	Model 1a	Model 1b	Model 2	Model 3
LIFES				−.002	
(life expectancy	—	—	—	(.039)	—
at birth)				−.002	
GINI					−.113***
(income	—	—	—	—	(.029)
inequality index)					−.002
ENERGYS					.0003
(energy consumption	—	—	—	—	(.0002)
per capita)					5.72e-06
Observations	124	115	107	116	123
Log-likelihood	−30.365	−27.397	−29.242	−22.042	−21.529
Pseudo-R^2	0.4616	0.4844	0.4481	0.5597	0.6170
Correctly classified	87.20%	87.82%	86.91%	92.24%	93.49%
Reduction in error	23.80%	27.55%	22.08%	53.80%	61.25%

*significant at the .10 level (two-tailed tests).
**significant at the .05 level.
***significant at the .01 level.
[a] Reported are coefficients (robust standards errors) and marginals (dF/dx), in that order.

As expected, I found that partitions are positively and significantly correlated with the level of violence (LOGCOST). This variable is very robust, and since deaths and displacements chronologically precede the occurrence of partition, these results may be pointing to a causal relationship between high levels of violence and partition. At the same time, my data do not allow me to preclude the possibility that some of the observed violence may actually have been caused by partition (as, for example, in India and Cyprus).

War outcomes are also significant in model 1 and all its variants. Both rebel victory and truce are significantly and positively associated with the incidence of partition (although, these results should be interpreted with caution due to high collinearity among the regressors).

In model 2 I added several socioeconomic variables that may have been important causes of the previous war and I found them both individually insignificant. While I did not expect to find individual significance given their high level of collinearity, I did expect and did find joint significance (a joint test of ILLIT, LIFES, GDP, DECADE, and GEO yielded chi2(5) = 11.85 and Prob > chi2 = 0.0369). The fact that these variables are not individually significant allows me to use them as controls in my analytical models of war recurrence in the next section, since they are not significantly correlated with partition and I use partition as a core regressor in those models. The most important impact of these local capacity variables is that they make ethnicity (EH, EHLPOP) nonsignificant (although this may be due to the noise that they introduce in the equation).

Finally, in model 3 I controlled for income inequality (GINI) and replaced the socioeconomic controls of model 2 with a variable measuring the country's overall level of economic development (ENERGYS) at the start of the war.[52] Here I found a positive but nonsignificant relationship between economic development and partition. The opposite association is often found between development and the risk of onset of war, but my finding makes sense, since low levels of economic development often discourage ethnic minorities from seceding (although a more accurate result might have been obtained if I had data available on the regional concentration of natural resources and the geographic dispersion of industries within each country).[53] Income inequality is significant but negatively correlated with partition, which once again seems counterintuitive.[54] The control variables for geographical location and for the decade during which the war started pick up time- and place-specific effects. The DECADE variable is nonsignificant, but there seem to be important regional effects (which could be better studied in the context of a panel data set).

To summarize, I found that partition is significantly more likely to occur after an identity war than after an ideological war, after an informal truce or rebel victory following a very costly war, in a country with large ethnic groups and small levels of ethnic heterogeneity and a relatively higher level of economic development (compared to other war-torn states). Having identified

52. Measuring these variables at the start of the war not only prevents problems of reverse causality but also captures any impact that these variables might have had on causing the civil war in the first place. Thus, the inability to find significance for the economic variables in model 2 may be due to a selection effect (since all the countries in my sample are countries that experienced war and may therefore share the same socioeconomic background). Thus, the analysis of partition and war recurrence must focus here on war-related variables that would be expected to differ significantly across countries.

53. See Collier and Hoeffler (fn. 45). The precise relationship between partition and economic variables is undertheorized, so I will not explore this further, but this counterintuitive finding is worth further study. It may be that relatively richer countries can support partition, since the prospects of economic viability of the successor state will be greater.

54. These signs do not change if I drop the cases of ongoing war. The direction of this correlation, however, may result from measurement error or selection effects. Measurement error is possible because reliable data were often not available for the relevant years. Or it may be due to collinearity between income inequality and energy consumption, since I used GDP data to impute missing values of both of these variables.

these correlates of partition, I can now test the three critical hypotheses of partition theory: (1) that partitions create successor states that are at least as democratic as their predecessors, if not more so; (2) that partitions reduce the risk of war recurrence; and (3) that partitions reduce low-level ethnic violence after the war ends.

TESTING THE HYPOTHESES

DOES PARTITION CREATE UNDEMOCRATIC STATES?

Kaufmann has argued that successor states are generally no less democratic than their predecessors and that they can even be more democratic.[55] Although a full test of this hypothesis is not yet possible (see below), a first cut at such a test is provided in this section.

Using data on democracy and autocracy from the Polity 98 data set, I have created the variable GURR, measuring the level of democracy two years (GURR2) and five years (GURR5) after the end of the war for both predecessor and successor states.[56] Partitioned countries have a mean and standard deviation of GURR2 of 11.02 and 6.204, respectively. The corresponding values for nonpartitioned countries are 8.42 and 6.27, respectively. A score of 20 suggests a perfect democracy, whereas a score of 0, an extreme autocracy. The computed averages reveal that countries that have experienced a civil war—regardless of whether or not they have been partitioned—are generally nondemocratic two years after the end of the war. This may be due to the war itself or to a legacy of undemocratic institutions. These legacies can be measured by GURRLAG5—the mean level of democracy during the five years prior to the start of the war. Table 5 lists all partitioned countries and their GURR2 and GURRLAG5 indices. Thirteen cases broadly support Kaufmann's hypothesis that partitioned countries are no less democratic than their predecessors and six cases do not support that hypothesis.[57]

55. Kaufmann (fn. 1, 1998), 124.
56. The original data on democracy were compiled by Keith Jaggers and Ted Robert Gurr, *Polity 98 Project (http://www.bsos.umd.edu/cidcm/polity/)*. I added their democracy and autocracy scores as follows: GURR = [DEMOCRACY+ (10-AUTOCRACY)]. The resulting variable ranges from 0 to 20. The Polity3 data end in 1994, so I imputed thirty-five missing values using the political rights index of the Freedom House project after I established that there was a very close correlation between Gurr's democracy index and Freedom House's political rights index. See Freedom House, *Freedom in the World* (London: Freedom House, 1999).
57. This list includes not only ethnic partitions but also all other cases of partition in my data set. Subsequent analysis focuses directly on partitions that resulted from ethnic wars and therefore excludes a number of partitions (for example, the Koreas, Vietnam, and Taiwan). However, I test the robustness of my results by including all wars and partitions.

Table 5
PRE-WAR AND POST PARTITION POLITY INDICES[a]

Country Name	Five-Year Prewar Democracy Index (GURRLAG5)	Democracy Index Two Years after the War (IGURR2)
Azerbaijan	3	4
Yugoslavia-Bosnia	6	9
China-Taiwan	5	2
Yugoslavia-Croatia	6	11
Yugoslavia-Croatia	6	9
Cyprus	1	.
Cyprus	1	20
Ethiopia-Eritrea	1	11
Georgia-Abkhazia	11	15
Georgia Ossetia	11	15
India-Pakistan	1	16
India-Kashmir	19	17
India-Kashmir	18	18
Israel-Palestine	.	.
Korea (North-South)	1	3
Moldova	1	17
Pakistan-Bangladesh	3	18
Russia-Chechnya	11	14
Somalia-Somaliland	3	2*
Tajikistan	11	5
Vietnam, Republic of	7	3

[a] IGURR2 includes one imputed value (Somalia), denoted with an asterisk and rounded to the nearest integer. If the predecessor state was a colony or not a recognized state (e.g., Israel) 1-5 years before the war started, then we do not have a Polity score since these are only available for independent states. In those cases, I have entered an N/A and comparison of the polity index before and after the war is not possible. The same is true for cases where the country was created out of the civil war, as in Israel. A dot indicates no available information. The index is based on data from Polity 98 (see text).

An equality of means test for both GURRLAG5 and GURR2 reveals signs of significant differences between partitioned and nonpartitioned countries. Specifically, a t-test of the null hypothesis that there is no significant difference in the mean of GURR2 in partitioned and nonpartitioned countries can marginally be rejected with 120 degrees of freedom and a t-statistic of -1.6644 ($P > |t| = 0.098$). A two-sample t-test with equal variances only on cases of ethnic war does reveal that there is a significant difference and that partitioned countries have higher democracy averages (75 d.f.; t = −3.3842). However, this effect need not refer to the democratization effect of partition and may be due to the prewar level of democracy, which is on average higher among partitioned countries that have experienced war. A means test with respect to DEMCH—a variable that measures the difference of postwar and prewar levels of democracy—rejects equality with 73 degrees of freedom and t = −2.6597 (P > |t| = 0.0096). These results suggest that partitioned states fare slightly better in terms of postwar democratization.

I turn next to a multivariable OLS regression of GURR2 (and GURR5) using partition among the explanatory variables. A bivariate regression of democracy on partition shows no significance of partition at the 5 percent level if we use the entire data set but finds partition positive and significant among cases of ethnic war. A clearer picture emerges from multivariate models (see Table 6). In model 1 I regressed the postwar democracy index (with imputed missing values) on a number of explanatory variables, including partition.[58] Most of the variance in the dependent variable in this and the other models is explained by the country's democratic legacy (GURRLAG5), which is extremely robust and significantly increases postwar levels of democracy. There is a weak positive correlation between democratic postconflict states and the presence of third-party peace operations (PEACEOP). Given that this association is weak, I dropped PEACEOP from subsequent regressions. There is a negative, though not very robust relationship between the level of democracy and the size of the government's military, which suggests that troop demobilization and force reductions in postconflict states may be useful in promoting peace and democracy. War duration is significant and positively correlated with the level of democracy, lending support to the war-weariness hypothesis (that people tired of war will try harder to build peace). Real per capita GDP is positively correlated with democracy (as would be expected), but this association is not significant, possibly due to selection effects or measurement error.[59] Partition is positively correlated with democracy and it is significant at the 10 percent level. The type of war is also significant and the coefficient sign suggests that ethnic wars would reduce the postwar mean of democracy by 2.5 points as compared with nonethnic wars.

---

58. I selected these variables based on theoretical arguments regarding the determinants of the level of democratization after civil war, drawing on Doyle and Sambanis (fn. 45), among others. Also the relationship between economic variables and democracy has been the focus of numerous studies in the economics and political science literatures; see, e.g., Ross E. Burkhart and Michael S. Lewis-Beck, "Comparative Democracy: The Economic Development Thesis," *American Political Science Review* 88 (December 1994).

59. These regression results are robust for a large number of specifications.

Table 6

OLS AND 2SLS REGRESSIONS OF POSTWAR DEMOCRACY W/ROBUST STANDARD ERRORS AND CLUSTERED SAME-COUNTRY OBSERVATIONS[a]

Dependent Variable: Democracy 2 Years after End of the War (IGURR2)	Model 1 All wars	Model 2 Only Ethnic Wars	Model 3 Non-Imputed GURR2	Model 4[b] 2SLS Only Ethnic	Model 5[c] 2SLS Only Ethnic	Model 6[d] 2SLS Only Ethnic
Constant	4.56***	2.07	2.63*	1.46	1.11	1.57
	(1.42)	(1.26)	(1.33)	(1.33)	(1.20)	(1.18)
PARTITION did the war result in partition?	3.33*	5.72***	6.26***	7.53***	8.01***	6.01***
	(1.82)	(1.54)	(1.67)	(2.62)	(2.56)	(2.05)
WARTYPE was it an identity or nonidentity war?	−2.42** (1.13)	—	—	—	—	—
PEACEOP were there UN or other peace operations?	.66* (.36)	—	—	—	—	—
WARDUR duration of war in months	.015** (.006)	.02** (.007)	.023*** (.008)	.023*** (.008)	.024*** (.008)	.021*** (.007)
GARM * 1,000 size of the government military (in thousands)	−1.12*** (.27)	−.95* (.56)	−1.1* (.6)	−.77 (.58)	—	—
GDP * 1,000 real income per capita, PPP-adjusted	.5695 (.45)	.53 (.54)	.34 (.56)	.46 (.55)	.43 (.55)	.51(.55)
GURRLAG5 5-yr average prewar democracy score	.48*** (.08)	.47*** (.102)	.43*** (.11)	.46*** (.11)	.45*** (.11)	.46*** (.11)
Observations	116	74	64	73	74	74
Goodness-of-fit	$F_{(7, 61)}$ = 18.47 Prob > F = 0.0000	$F_{(5, 38)}$ = 12.24 Prob > F = 0.0000	$F_{(5, 33)}$ = 10.38 Prob > F = 0.0000	$F_{(5, 38)}$ = 10.22 Prob > F = 0.0000	$F_{(4, 39)}$ = 10.87 Prob > F = 0.0000	$F_{(4, 39)}$ = 4.80 Prob > F = 0.0000
R^2	0.4180	0.5010	0.5069	0.4924	0.4794	0.4963

*significant at the .10 level
**significant at the .05 level.
***significant at the .01 level.
[a] Coefficients and standards errors are reported in parentheses.
[b] Instrumented: partition; instruments: logcost outcome2 eh ehlpop geo.
[c] Instrumented: partition; instruments: logdead outcome2 eh ehlpop geo.
[d] Instrumented: partition; instruments: logcost truce vrebel eh ehlpop geo.

In model 2 I looked more closely at cases of ethnic war, and the results discussed previously are nearly identical, except for the significance and co-efficient of partition, which now more than doubles. In model 3 I regressed the same right-hand-side variables on the GURR2 variable without imput-ing missing values, and the results are robust. The democratic legacy variable (GURRLAG5) seems to be doing heavy lifting in these regressions. If we drop it from models 2–3, the R^2 drops by about 20 percentage points and the coefficient of partition increases by 20 percent.

Partition may also be endogenous or, rather, jointly determined with some of the other right-hand-side variables. Thus, I reestimated model 2 using a two-stage least squares (2SLS) estimator; no significant differences were observed (both the coefficient and standard error of partition were extremely volatile, but the t-test remained the same). In model 5 I estimated a different specification of this model again using 2SLS, dropping the now nonsignificant GARM variables, but again no major change occurred. In model 6 I changed two of the instrumental variables used in the first-stage regressions. Throughout these changes in specification and estimation method, the democratic legacy variable (GURRLAG5) was extremely robust, as was partition. The coefficient of the partition variable was positive and varied between 6 and 8.

Finally, testing the hypothesis that the instrumented 2SLS models might be more efficient than the OLS models, I found the OLS models more efficient. A Hausman test of the null hypothesis that the difference in coefficients be-tween the instrumented and OLS models is not systematic, estimated as: (b-B)' $[(V_b\text{-}V_B)^{-1}]$(b-B), yielded a chi-square statistic of 0.57 with 4 degrees of free-dom, so we cannot reject the null hypothesis that the instrumented models are less efficient and we should rely on the OLS estimates of models 1–3.[60]

Overall, these regression results seem to support partition theory. However, this is at best an incomplete picture, since we do not have comparable democ-racy data for successor states that are not internationally recognized. This therefore creates a problem of systematic bias in the coding of the dependent variable, which reduces the reliability of the findings just described. Successor states that are not internationally recognized may well have low democracy; contrast, for example, the political institutions of the Republic of Cyprus with those of the so-called Turkish Republic of Northern Cyprus or the democracy

60. J. Hausman, "Specification Tests in Econometrics," *Econometrica* 46 (1978), 1251–71. On the use of the Hausman test to test exogeneity, see B. H. Baltagi, *Econometrics* (New York: Springer-Verlag, 1998), 291; and Stata Corporation, *Stata Reference Manual: Release 6* (College Station, Tex.: Stata, 1999), 2:7–13. In the formula above b is the coefficient vector from the consistent estimator and B the coefficient vector from the efficient estimator and V_b, and V_B are their respective covariance matrices.

levels in Chechnya versus those in Russia or in Ossetia and Abkhazia versus those in Georgia. These comparisons are difficult, given that the Polity 98 project does not provide information on these territories. Thus, before making a judgment on the democratizing effects of partition, we need comparable data on democracy for all successor and predecessor states.[61] At this stage, I can neither reject nor accept the claims of the partition theorists with confidence. The link between partition and democratization must be studied further as high-quality data become available. At that time it would also be interesting to see whether high levels of GURRLAG5 tend to promote democracy in post-war successor states. At this stage the robustness of GURRLAG5 suggests that our focus should not be on designing democracy-friendly partitions but rather should be on strengthening democratic institutions in countries before they actually experience a civil war.

I now turn to the critical question of war recurrence.

DOES PARTITION PREVENT WAR RECURRENCE?

SEVERAL examples of wars following partitions provide support for the critics of partition theory: Croatia fought a second war with Serbia after it was partitioned in 1991. Ethiopia and Eritrea fought a bitter territorial war in 1999. The partition of Somaliland collapsed in a wave of new violence in 1992. India and Pakistan have fought three wars since their partition in 1947. Cyprus was at war again in 1974 after it was effectively partitioned into militarily defensible, self-administered enclaves between 1963 and 1967.[62] At the same

---

61. Given the paucity of data to answer this important question, a worthwhile project would be to conduct a comparative case study of the political institutions of all these successor states.

62. This is not a well-known case. In 1963 a "green line" was established in the capital city of Nicosia, partitioning the Greek Cypriot and Turkish Cypriot sectors. After 1964 the partition was expanded, and more than 30 percent of the Turkish Cypriot population moved to defensible, self-administered enclaves. These enclaves forcibly excluded the Greek Cypriot population and their demilitarization and defortification was part of the mandate given to a UN peacekeeping force—UNFICYP (see UN doc. S/5764, 15 June 1964, para. 61). The UN secretary-general often noted in his report that the enclaves gave the Turkish Cypriots "complete military and administrative control" of several areas (S/6228, para. 50). In 1965 the secretary-general noted that the enclave fortifications "contribute to maintaining tension at high pitch" and UNFICYP "insists on their removal" (S/6228, para. 51). Within six months in 1967, 52 new positions were built by the Greek Cypriot National Guard and 130 by the Turkish Cypriots (S/8286, December 8, 1967, para. 50). The secretary-general noted that "this ceaseless building of fortifications . . . [would] result in the Island being criss-crossed and honeycombed with defences [*sic*]" (S/8286, para. 49). On the Cyprus conflict during the critical years between 1963 and 1974, see Richard Patrick, *Political Geography and the Cyprus Conflict, 1963-1971* (Waterloo, Canada: Department of Geography, University of Waterloo, 1976); the work includes maps of the pre-1974 enclaves. See also Joseph, Joseph, *Cyprus: Ethnic Conflict and International Solution* (St. Martin's Press, 1997); and Sambanis (fn. 45).

Table 7
CROSS-TABS BETWEEN PARTITION, WAR RECURRENCE, AND RESIDUAL VIOLENCE
(TWO, FIVE, AND TEN YEARS AFTER THE WAR)

War Ended for	War Recurrence	Partition	No Partition	Total Cases	Pearson Chi-Square Test (1 Degree of Freedom)
2 years	war recurred	5	27	32	Pearson chi2(1) =
	no war	16	77	93	0.0425; Pr = 0.837
5 years	war recurred	5	24	29	Pearson chi2(1) =
	no war	14	71	85	0.0092; Pr = 0.923
10 years	war recurred	5	24	29	Pearson chi2(1) =
	no war	6	46	52	0.5159; Pr = 0.473

War Ended for	War Violence	Partition	No Partition	Total Cases	Pearson Chi-Square Test (1 Degree of Freedom)
2 years	low violence	10	56	66	Pearson chi2(1) =
	no violence	11	48	59	0.2719; Pr = 0.602
5 years	low violence	9	48	57	Pearson chi2(1) =
	no violence	10	47	57	0.0632; Pr = 0.802
10 years	low violence	8	38	46	Pearson chi2(1) =
	no violence	5	32	37	0.2334; Pr = 0.629

time, seemingly intractable conflicts and bloody ethnic wars have given way to peace without partition, as, for example, in South Africa, Guatemala, and Uganda.

These examples, however, do not constitute sufficient proof that the critics are right. To develop better insight into the relationship between partition and war recurrence, I present simple cross-tabulations of partition and war recurrence and low-level violence in Table 7.[63] No statistical association between partition and ending violence is evident either for the entire population of cases and or for ethnic wars.

A fuller test of the relationship between partition and war recurrence, conditional on the effects of several other variables, can be derived by estimating multivariable regressions (see Table 8). The dependent variable is WAREND

63. This table includes cases of nonethnic partition. I also ran these cross-tabs excluding nonidentity (ethnic/religious) wars, and the results were not significantly affected.

Table 8
MODELS OF CIVIL WAR RECURRENCE[a]

Dependent Variable: WAREND2 (Did the War End for Two Years?)	Model 1 Only Ethnic Wars Assume Exogeneity	Model 2 All Wars Assume Exogeneity	Model 3[b] 2SLS Linear Prob. Assume Endogeneity	Model 4[c] 2S Probit w/Rivers & Vuong Test	Model 5[d] Bivariate Probit rho-test for Exogeneity	Model 6 Probit w/Partition Interaction Only Ethnic Wars	Model 7 Same as Model 6, but for the 5-Year Period	Model 8 Probit w/Partition Interaction All Wars
PARTITION did the war result in partition?	-.068 (.461) -.021	.253 (.365) .066	-.025 (.204)	-.080 (.694)	-.260 (.675)	-4.72 (3.82) -.962	-2.25 (3.83) -.739	—
RES—residual to test for exogeneity	—	—	—	.122 (.956)	—	—	—	—
LOGCOST natural log of dead & displaced	-.164* (.087) -.051	-.185*** (.067) -.052	-.049* (.026)	-.152* (.086)	-.146* (.086)	-.162* (.096) -.049	-.185* (.097) -.058	-.17*** (.07) -.050
OUTCOME2 war outcome—four outcomes	.53*** (.147) .165	.37*** (.112) .104	.131*** (.036)	.406*** (.147)	.418*** (.142)	.578*** (.165) .178	.522*** (.145) .166	.35*** (.116) .097
WARDUR duration of war in months	.0015 (.002) .00047	.0028* (.0017) .0008	—	—	—	.0006 (.0021) .0002	.0016 (.002) .0005	.002(.002) .0005
GARM*1,000 size of the gov't military in '000s	.07 (.063) .22	.6557 (.52) .18	—	—	—	—	—	—
GDP* 1,000	-.0745	-.0733	-.0182	-.049	-.0435	-.00956	-.037	-.0241

(CONTINUED)

Table 8
(CONTINUED)

Dependent Variable: WAREND2 (Did the War End for Two Years?)	Model 1 Only Ethnic Wars Assume Exogeneity	Model 2 All Wars Assume Exogeneity	Model 3[b] 2SLS Linear Prob. Assume Endogeneity	Model 4[c] 2S Probit w/ Rivers & Vuong Test	Model 5[d] Bivariate Probit rho-test for Exogeneity	Model 6 Probit w/ Partition Interaction Only Ethnic Wars	Model 7 Same as Model 6, but for the 5-Year Period	Model 8 Probit w/ Partition Interaction All Wars
(real income per capita, PPP)	−.023 (.082)	−.02 (.069)	(.016)	(.06)	(.063)	−.0029 (.089)	−.01 (.09)	−.0068 (.082)
EH ethnic heterogeneity index	−.048 (.032)	−.045* (.025)	—	—	—	−.081*** (.029)	−.066*** (.022)	−.055** (.022)
EHLPOP	−.015	−.0127	—	—	—	−.025	−.021	−.015
EH interacted with log of population	.0027 (.0019)	.0024 (.0015)	—	—	—	.004** (.0018)	.003*** (.0013)	.003** (.0014)
WARTYPE	.00084	.0007	—	—	—	.0014	.0011	.0008
ethnic war or not?	—	−.265 (.34) −.072	—	—	—	—	—	—
PTEH	—	—	—	—	—	.013 (.012)	−.004 (.016)	.011 (.010)
interaction: partv2*eh	—	—	—	—	—	.0039	−.001	.003
PTLCOST	—	—	—	—	—	.311 (.283)	.22 (.311)	.244 (.265)
interaction: partv2*logcost	—	—	—	—	—	.0961	.069	.0687
PTARMY	—	—	—	—	—	−.0015	−.0025*	—

	(1)	(2)	(3)	(4)	(5)	(6)	(7)	(8)
interaction: partv2*garm	—	—	—	—	—	−.0004 (.001)	−.0008 (.001)	—
ETHPART								−3.82 (3.46)
interaction: partv2*wartype								−.91
CONSTANT	1.51 (1.07)	2.25** (.86)	1.06*** (.305)	1.69 (1.03)	1.62 (1.03)	1.75 (1.167)	2.36* (1.26)	2.29*** (.916)
Rho coefficient	—	—	—	—	.093 (.443)	—	—	—
Observations	78	122	78	78	78	78	73	123
Log-Likelihood	−35.955	−57.399	—	−40.916	−63.633	−35.895	−33.913	−59.211
Pseudo-R^2	0.2399	0.1824	0.1619	0.1350	—	0.2412	0.2409	0.1602
Correctly Classified	79.50%	81.14%	—	—	—	76.92%	78.08%	77.23%
Reduction in Error	37.56%	26.32%	—	—	—	19.72%	28.50%	11.05%

* significant at the .10 level.
** significant at the .05 level.
*** significant at the .01 level.

[a] Reported are coefficients, standards errors (in parentheses), and marginals (dF/dx), in that order.

[b] Marginals reported only for models 1 and 2 since they are the ones used for inferences. Model 3 goodness-of-fit: $F_{(4, 39)} = 4.61$. Instrumented: partition; Instruments: wardur garm gdp eh ehlpop.

[c] The first stage regression of model 4 has a Wald $chi2_{(7)} = 36.38$, a log-likelihood$= -2.727$, and a Pseudo-$R^2 = 0.4606$. All regressors except GARM are significant at the 5 percent level.

[d] Instruments as in models 3 and 4. All variables except GARM significant at the 5 percent level in the partition selection equation. The selection model's Wald $chi2_{(11)} = 50.02$.

(did the war end?) with the suffixes 2, 5, and 10 denoting that it is observed 2, 5, and 10 years after the end of the civil war. WAREND is coded 1 if there is no war recurrence and 0 otherwise.[64] The control variables in these regressions were selected on the basis of previous research on war termination. A regressor is used only if at least one other scholar has identified it as significant for war termination and peace building.[65]

The results of models 1 and 2 of Table 8 are quite robust to specification tests. A first interesting finding is that, though not significant in either model, partition is positively correlated with ethnic war recurrence in model 1 (it is negatively correlated with WAREND).[66] It is, however, positively correlated with WAREND if we look at the entire population of wars. In fact, among ideological nonethnic wars, partition is a significant determinant of war termination, which implies that nonethnic partitions are more stable and peaceful than ethnic partitions (although these results are driven by the very few cases of nonethnic partition).[67]

The human cost of the war in both models 1 and 2 is negatively correlated with war ending, confirming that the greater the number of people injured by the war, the harder it is to build peace.[68] War outcomes are the most significant

64. I estimate probit models with clustered same-country observations and robust standard errors. Since partition theory has focused on ethnic wars and since I found the type of war to be a significant determinant of partition, I dropped cases of nonidentity wars from my analysis, but I do report some results of interest as they apply to all civil wars.

65. Following are the explanatory variables and the researchers who identified their importance: war duration, Mason and Fett (fn. 33); size of the government's military, Mason and Fett (fn. 33); war outcomes, Licklider (fn. 32) and Walter (fn. 39); ethnic heterogeneity and population size, Collier and Hoeffler (fn. 45); deaths and displacements, Licklider (fn. 32) and Doyle and Sambanis (fn. 45); income per capita, Collier (fn. 45); major power involvement, Singer and Small (fn. 32); foreign intervention, Regan (fn. 33); third-party and UN peace operations, Doyle and Sambanis (fn. 45); democracy, Collier, Elbadawi, and Sambanis (fn. 30) and Håvard Hegre et al., "Towards a Democratic Civil Peace? Opportunity, Grievance, and Civil War, 1816-1992" (Paper presented at the World Bank Conference on the Economics of Political and Criminal Violence, Washington, D.C., February 16–22, 1999). I also controlled for the number of land borders, the decade the war started, and the cold war. I could not include too many of these variables together, given my small data set and the collinearity of these variables.

66. The Russia-Chechnya case causes the negative sign, and partition is positively correlated with WAREND if I drop that observation. The nonsignificance of partition, however, does not change by deleting that observation. I also sequentially deleted several other cases (e.g., Cyprus 1963/67, Somalia, Tajikistan, India), and the substantive results did not change. The results are also robust to using TYPELICK and TYPESTF instead of WARTYPE to identify ethnic wars.

67. The opposite argument (without much empirical support) is made in Chaim Kaufmann, "Intervention in Ethnic and Ideological Civil Wars: Why One Can Be Done and the Other Can't," *Security Studies 6* (Autumn 1997).

68. The sign of LOGCOST in models 1 and 2 is negative, indicating that the higher the human cost, the greater the probability of war recurrence. This may seem counterintuitive: why would more costly wars lead to new wars? Would not great human cost discourage war recurrence? That reasoning is correct and it is reflected in my findings on war duration (see below), which verify the war-weariness hypothesis. However, controlling for this finding, the

and robust variable, though the OUTCOME2 variable is hard to interpret (Table 9 below explains these effects more clearly).[69] Generally, the more conciliatory the outcome of the war, the greater the probability that the peace will last. War duration is positively correlated with no war recurrence, but it is only significant in model 2. This result is consistent with the findings of Mason and Fett and weakly supports the "war weariness" hypothesis.[70] The size of the government's military is also positive but nonsignificant (it is significant only at the 10 percent level in model 2).[71] Real GDP per capita is negatively correlated with war ending, though this association is not significant.[72]

The impact of ethnic heterogeneity on war recurrence is quite interesting. Ethnic heterogeneity (EH) and its interaction term with the log of population (EHLPOP) are not significant in models 1 and 2, despite the emphasis on ethnicity in the civil war literature. Moreover, EHLPOP has a positive sign, indicating that if the ethnic groups are large enough to protect themselves against domination, the risk of war recurrence is smaller. This result is consistent with Fearon and Laitin's analysis of the potential for interethnic cooperation and is robust to different measures of ethnic division (the ELF index) and different model specifications.[73] As I added several interaction terms between partition and other variables in models 6–8, I found a significant negative association between ethnicity and lasting peace but also a significant positive association between peace and larger ethnic groups. Other authors have found that ethnolinguistic and religious fractionalization is a significant determinant of the initiation of civil wars, but my findings suggest that civil war initiation and war

probability of war recurrence should be expected to be greater as the human costs of the war increase. These costs measure war-generated hostility and create grievances that may manifest themselves in future conflict. Further, the greater the human and economic cost of the war, the lower should be a country's human capital and the lower the state's capacity to resume normal operations.

69. OUTCOME2 is a categorical variable denoting whether the war ended in a truce, rebel victory, government victory, or peace settlement. It is highly significant in both models 1 and 2, though interpreting its sign is not straightforward. By disaggregating OUTCOME2, I found some of its components highly correlated with partition. Thus, entering them independently in the regression would increase collinearities. These correlations also generate sufficient concern over the possible endogeneity of partition when both OUTCOME2 and partition are included in the model.

70. Mason and Fett (fn. 33). I thank Russ Leng for pointing this out to me.

71. By contrast, Mason and Fett (fn. 33) find a significant negative correlation.

72. This finding may be due to selection effects, as I mentioned earlier, but it may also confirm the revenue-seeking economic model of civil war in Collier (fn. 45); and Collier and Hoeffler (fn. 45); the model looks at GDP per capita as a proxy for "lootable" resources, which would increase the risk of war.

73. James Fearon and David Laitin, "Explaining Interethnic Cooperation," *American Political Science Review 90* (December 1996).

Table 9
FIRST DIFFERENCES OF THE PROBABILITY OF WAR RECURRENCE FOR ETHNIC AND
ALL CIVIL WARS[a]

Only Ethnic Wars First Difference of	Estimate of Mean Change in Prob(warend2) = 1	Standard Deviation of Estimate	95% Confidence Interval	
PARTITION from 0 to 1	−.027	.174	−.374219	.3025837
EH from 25th to 75th percentile	−.601	.322	−.9731405	.2372383
EHLPOP & EH from 25th to 75th percentile	.002	.095	−.1844085	.1865729
OUTCOME2 from truce to treaty	.119	.027	.064833	.1706
LOGCOST from 25th to 75th percentile	−.182	.097	−.3737424	.0045121

All Civil Wars First Difference of	Estimate of Mean Change in Prob(warend2) = 1	Standard Deviation of Estimate	95% Confidence Interval	
PARTITION from 0 to 1	.088	.129	−.1755012	.3330738
EH from 25th to 75th percentile	−.621	.269	−.9458801	.1065577
EHLPOP & EH from 25th to 75th percentile	−.082	.067	−.2188984	.0452573
OUTCOME2 from truce to treaty	.098	.025	.0507963	.1499487
LOGCOST from 25th to 75th percentile	−.246	.088	−.416339	−.0723445
WARTYPE from ethnic to ideological	.094	.123	−.3369971	.1517012

[a] Changes in X-variables are noted in the first column. All other variables are held constant at their means.

recurrence are different phenomena with respect to the role of ethnicity and that ethnic diversity is not as detrimental to peace as many tend to assume.[74]

Models 1 and 2 present short-term results. To see if these results also hold in the medium term, I reestimated models 1 and 2 both five and ten years after the end of the war: the model's fit was roughly the same. However, while no major differences occur in the five-year model, in the ten-year model, war duration is no longer significant and partition is highly significant and negatively correlated with war termination.[75] In models 6–8, I added several interaction terms between partition and LOGCOST, WARTYPE, EH, and GARM, but no appreciably important associations emerged. In model 8, the coefficient of ETHPART—denoting ethnic partition—is negatively but not significantly correlated with war termination.

These findings build a strong case against partition theory. Before accepting them, I should address a methodological point with potentially substantive implications. My inferences may depend on the assumption that partition is exogenous to war recurrence, an assumption that makes sense, since war recurrence is observed after the occurrence of partition. It may be, however, that these two variables are jointly determined by a common set of explanatory variables. Thus, there is concern over the possible endogeneity of partition. I therefore estimated several models assuming partition is endogenous and I also tested its exogeneity (see the appendix for technical details and for an explanation of the statistical concept of endogeneity). I present the results of three models that address the issue of endogeneity in Table 8.

I estimate a parsimonious linear probability model treating partition as an endogenous variable (model 3). The model uses several variables that are not correlated with war recurrence (based on the previous estimations) as instruments for partition and reduces the number of exogenous variables in the structural equation to reduce noise in the system of equations. The model has good fit and is well specified. Despite this estimation adjustment, however, partition is not at all significant and continues to have a negative sign. The other key variables (LOGCOST, OUTCOME2, GDP) behave in much the same way as they did in the previous models.

In models 4 and 5 I formally tested (and could not reject) the null hypothesis that partition is exogenous. Model 4 is a two-stage probit model, estimated following Madalla and using the Rivers and Vuong exogeneity test (which was

---

74. See, e.g., Collier, Elbadawi, and Sambanis (fn. 30).
75. This could be due to missing observations. The ten-year model was estimated on fifty cases. The coefficient and robust standard error of partition were −1.137 and .627, respectively, yielding a z-statistic of −1.813 (P > |z| = 0.070) and a model log-likelihood = −23.460, with a Wald chi2(8) = 32.14 and a Pseudo R^2 = 0.3159.

originally designed for continuous endogenous explanatory variables).[76] The exogeneity consists of a t-test of the estimated coefficient of the predicted residual (RES) of the first-stage reduced form equation of partition. The estimated coefficient of RES is .122 and its standard error is .956, so we cannot reject the null hypothesis that partition is exogenous. To confirm this result, I estimated model 5—a bivariate probit model with sample selection (which is a full-information maximum likelihood model)—using the same instruments for partition and the same exogenous variables as in models 3 and 4.[77] The correlation coefficient rho (see Table 8) is .093 and its standard error is .443. A Wald test of the hypothesis that $rho = 0$ yields chi2(1) = .043, which does not allow us to reject the exogeneity of partitions at the 0.8346 level. Thus, more efficient estimates are obtained from Models 1 and 2 and we can rely on the previously discussed inferences.

Table 9 provides some easily interpretable results of the estimated change in the probability that there will be no war recurrence as a result of changes in key explanatory variables (these changes are also known as first differences). I reestimated models 1 and 2 from Table 8 and simulated (with one thousand repetitions) their parameter estimates using the CLARIFY software.[78] Using those estimates, I obtained the first differences reported.[79] I report the mean and standard deviation of the estimated change in probability (the standard deviation reflects the significance levels of the explanatory variables as in

76. G. S. Maddala, *Limited Dependent and Qualitative Variables in Econometrics* (Cambridge: Cambridge University Press, 1983); D. Rivers and Q. Vuong, "Limited Information Estimators and Exogeneity Tests for Simultaneous Probit Models," *Journal of Econometrics 39* (1988). This method is almost identical to Kenneth A. Bollen, D. K. Guilkey, and T. A. Mroz, "Binary Outcomes and Endogenous Explanatory Variables: Tests and Solutions with an Application to the Demand for Contraceptive Use in Tunisia," *Demography* 32 (February 1995). The two-stage probit model produces inefficient standard errors, though the efficiency loss is small. Rivers and Vuong derive the formula that gives the correct variance-covariance matrix, but their procedure is designed for continuous endogenous right-hand-side variables. A methodological discussion and Monte Carlo simulation results reporting the properties of this estimator in small samples are found in Michael Alvarez and Jennifer Glascow, "Two-Stage Estimation of Non-Recursive Choice Models," *Political Analysis* (forthcoming). For a political science application of this method, see Michael Alvarez and L. Butterfield, "The Resurgence of Nativism in California? The Case of Proposition 187 and Illegal Immigration," *Social Science Quarterly* (forthcoming). A discussion of the two binary variable case can be found in Madalla (p. 246).

77. For the case of two binary variables, this can be estimated as a seemingly unrelated bivariate probit model with a selection effect. The exogeneity test in this model consists of a Wald test of *rho*, the estimated coefficient of the correlation of the error terms in the structural and reduced-form ("first-stage") equations.

78. Michael Tomz, Jason Wittenberg, and Gary King, "Clarify: Software for Interpreting and Presenting Statistical Results," version 1.2.1 (June 1, 1999). See also idem, "Making the Most of Statistical Analyses: Improving Interpretations and Presentation" (Paper presented at the annual meeting of the American Political Science Association, Boston, 1999).

79. Note that these estimates may differ slightly in replications since I did not fix the number seed used to randomly select samples for the simulations.

Table 8). Note that the probability of no war recurrence (peace) is slightly reduced by a partition after an ethnic war, although it is increased by 8.8 percent when we use the entire population of civil wars (though this result is not statistically significant). Among the statistically significant effects, it is worth reporting that if the war ends in a treaty instead of a truce, the probability of no war recurrence increases by 11.9 percent in ethnic wars and 9.8 percent in all wars. Finally, the more costly the war. the less stable the peace. By varying LOGCOST from its 25th to its 75th percentile, the probability of no war recurrence drops by 18.2 percent in ethnic wars and 24.6 percent in all wars.

To conclude this section, the evidence does not support the assertion that partition significantly reduces the risk of war recurrence. Hence there is no support for partition as a policy option if the rationale advanced is that it will prevent future ethnic wars.

DOES PARTITION END ETHNIC VIOLENCE SHORT OF WAR?

THE third critical hypothesis in support of partition is that the physical separation of ethnic groups will reduce residual, low-level ethnic violence (that is, violence short of war). In this section I test this hypothesis empirically and find that only under carefully specified conditions does partition reduce lower-level violence. In most situations partition will have a negligible effect on residual violence.

The dependent variable in the models estimated in this section is NOVIOL, which takes the suffixes 2 and 5 when it is measured two and five years after the end of the war, respectively. NOVIOL is binary and it is coded 1 if there is no residual violence after the end of the war and 0 otherwise. It is coded based on available information and other data sets that code armed conflict short of war and/or politicides and genocides (a table with details on the coding of each case is included in the online data set). I use two versions of the dependent variable, NOVIOL2 and NOVIOL5, for two and five years after the end of the war.

I start by regressing NOVIOL2 on the explanatory variables from the war-recurrence model, which does not produce many significant results and has low explanatory power. Partition is positively but nonsignificantly associated with an end to lower-level violence (model 1 in Table 10). Given the model's low classification success, it appears that war recurrence and residual violence are substantially different phenomena, so I changed the model's specification in regressions 2–6. First, I disaggregated the OUTCOME2 variable and focused on the signing of treaties, which in model 2 increased the significance level of partitions by doubling its coefficient and reducing its standard error. Treaty

Table 10
Probit Regressions of No-Violence (part assumed exogenous)[a]

Dependent Variable: NOVIOL2 (No Violence for 2 Years?)	Model 1 Ethnic War	Model 2 Ethnic War	Model 3 Ethnic War	Model 4 Ethnic War	Model 5 Ethnic War	Model 6 Ethnic War
Constant	.783	1.37	1.14	1.55	.586	1.95**
	(.868)	(.924)	(.868)	(.987)	(.978)	(.93)
PART	.298	.668*	.632	.672	.272	.685
did the war result in	(.402)	(.387)	(.411)	(.418)	(.371)	(.441)
partition?	.116	.26	.248	.262	.106	.268
LOGCOST	−.144*	−.167*	−.125	−.195**	—	−.208**
natural log of deaths &	(.08)	(.087)	(.085)	(.094)	—	(.088)
displacements	−.055	−.064	−.048	−.075		−.080
INTENSE				16.14***	12.05***	21.47**
human cost per capita	—	—	—	(4.83)	(3.715)	(9.04)
per month				6.26	4.69	8.34
LOGDEAD					−.104	
natural log of deaths	—	—	—	—	(.097)	—
					−.04	
OUTCOME2	.276**					
outcome of the war—	(.123)	—	—	—	—	—
four outcomes	.106					
TREATY		.883*	.992**	.869	.756	.955*
was there a treaty	—	(.534)	(.482)	(.559)	(.526)	(.557)
signed?		.341	.380	.335	.294	.367
WARDUR	.0021	.0026	.0028	.004**	.0027	.0047**
duration of war in	(.0017)	(.0017)	(.0018)	(.002)	(.0019)	(.0022)
months	.0008	.0010	.0011	.0015	.0011	.0018
GARM*1,000	−.317	−.302	−.173	−.29	−.28	−.174
size of the government	(.27)	(.28)	(.22)	(.308)	(.26)	(.31)
military	−.1	−.1	−.067	−.11	−.11	−.067
ELECTRIC*1,000	.055	.009	−.040	−.053	−.0195	−.134
electricity consumption	(.117)	(.124)	(.13)	(.13)	(.15)	(.12)
p.c.; kilowatt hours	.02	.0036	−.015	−.02	−.0076	−.052
EH	−.017	−.02*	−.027*	−.032**	−.035**	−.024*
ethnic heterogeneity	(.013)	(.011)	(.015)	(.013)	(.014)	(.012)
Index	−.006	−.0077	−.011	−.012	−.013	−.0092
EHLPOP	.00097	.001*	.0013*	.0017***	.0019***	.0014**
ethnic heterogeneity	(.00069)	(.0005)	(.00074)	(.00068)	(.00073)	(.00062)
* log of population	.00037	.00042	.0005	.00068	.00074	.00055

Table 10
(CONTINUED)

Dependent Variable: NOVIOL2 (No Violence for 2 Years?)	Model 1 Ethnic War	Model 2 Ethnic War	Model 3 Ethnic War	Model 4 Ethnic War	Model 5 Ethnic War	Model 6 Ethnic War
PW10						−.85***
civil war in previous	—	—	—	—	—	(.34)
ten years?						−.323
Observations	77	77	72	77	77	77
Log-likelihood	−45.952	−45.608	−43.020	−43.713	−45.983	−40.606
Pseudo-R^2	0.1209	0.1274	0.1258	0.1637	0.1203	0.2231
Classification success	63.63%	61.03%	65.27%	67.53%	66.23%	71.42%
Reduction in error	20%	14.25%	46.79%	28.55%	25.69%	37.11%

*significant at the .10 level.
**significant at the .05 level.
***significant at the .01 level.
[a] Coefficients, standards errors reported (in parentheses), and marginals (dF/dx).

is also significant and positive, suggesting that treaties generally do signal the parties' intentions to reconcile their differences. We also find that EHLPOP is significant and positive.[80] Both results seem important. The first result seems to support partition theory, though the latter seems to contradict it. These

---

80. This result complements Bates's (fn. 47) findings on the relationship between ethnicity and political violence in Africa. Bates studies the relationship between ethnicity and economic modernization—urbanization, education, and the rise of per capita income, as well as political participation. Focusing on forty-six African countries from 1970 to 1995, he tests the relationship between ethnicity and political violence at several levels (not just wars). He measures the size distribution of ethnic groups, linguistic diversity, and the presence of an ethnic minority at risk, based on the work of a number of other researchers, and shows that the relationship between ethnicity and violence is complicated. Bates finds that "controlling for the impact of other variables, [linguistic diversity] associates with higher levels of violence . . . the size of the largest ethnic group enters quadratically; when the coefficient for the linear term is significant, so too is the coefficient for the quadratic. But as the size of the largest ethnic group grows, the level of violence initially decreases, but then increases; by contrast, the level of protest initially increases, but then falls" (p. 25). In Bates's analysis, it is extreme polarization that is most associated with violence. My finding that greater heterogeneity and more sizable ethnic groups reduces violence in postwar states is therefore compatible with Bates's result and complements it. I should note however, that Bates's results may not be generally applicable to non-African countries, given that African countries have a generally higher mean level of ethnic heterogeneity and this implies a selection effect *if the results are to be applied widely to non-African countries*. In my data set, for example, the mean and standard deviation of the ethnic heterogeneity index for African countries is 68.82 and 34.58, respectively, whereas for non-African countries it is 50.5 and 31.73. The ethnic heterogeneity index used was created by Tatu Vanhanen, "Domestic

results are essentially the same for the five-year period (NOVIOL5; see model 3 in Table 10).[81]

Models 3 and 4 are differently specified to facilitate sensitivity analysis of the previous results and to achieve higher classification success. Model 3—discussed previously—applies to the five-year period and has more than double the classification success of the two-year model. It shows that partition is not significant for ending residual violence. In model 4 I added the variable INTENSE, which measures the war's intensity and which is positive and extremely significant. Very intense wars seem either to provide no further appetite for violence or to eradicate all resistance early on, so no residual violence is necessary. The GARM variable is not significant in any of the regressions and neither is economic development (proxied by electricity consumption per capita).[82] In model 4 we find that residual violence is significantly reduced by long and bloody wars, but again partition is not significant. Further, the partition variable is extremely fragile to small specification changes. Contrast models 4 and 5, which differ only in that model 4 controls for LOGCOST and model 5 for LOGDEAD (that is, not for displaced persons). The coefficient of the partition variable drops from .67 to .27 (the marginal effect from .26 to .10). The other variables are much more stable.

Model 6 is the best-performing model specification; it controls for civil wars in the same country during the previous ten years. That variable is extremely significant and suggests that residual violence is much more likely if the country has had a history of civil war recurrence. This effect is mitigated, however, in the case of long and intense wars, which discourage residual violence. Model 6 has substantially higher classification success than the previous models, but, in general, the models of residual violence do not fit the data as well as the models of war recurrence discussed earlier. Thus, the lack of significance of the partition variable may be a function of omitted variables that could be identified in further theoretical research. At the same time model 6 confirms the results discussed earlier with respect to the positive impact of ethnic diversity, if ethnic groups are large (EHLPOP variable).

In sum, I can point to only very weak evidence in support of the hypothesis that partitions help end low-level ethnic violence (in model 2 and some vari-

---

Ethnic Conflict and Ethnic Nepostism: A Comparative Analysis," *Journal of Peace Research* 36, no. 1 (1999).

81. Ten years after the end of the war partition has a negative correlation with an end to low-grade violence, but this result may be an artifact of missing (right-censored) observations (only fifty-five observations are available for the ten-year period).

82. Thus, development levels and military strength are more relevant with respect to war recurrence than with respect to low-level violence.

ants). More importantly, the positive impact of partitions seems fragile and extremely dependent on whether or not the war ended in a treaty, on the war's intensity, on the number of people displaced by the war, and on the number and size of ethnic groups.

To confirm that these results are not influenced by the potential endogeneity of partitions to low-grade violence, I tested once again for exogeneity. I estimated model 4 using a 2SLS linear probability model using many different combinations of instrumental variables to see whether the coefficient of partition would become significant if endogeneity is assumed. I used as instruments only variables that were not significantly associated with low-level violence in the previous regressions. I could not, however, find any results that would increase my confidence in the significance of the partition variable.[83]

To summarize, I find only weak support for the hypothesis that partitions are significant for an end to low-grade ethnic violence after civil war. Models supporting that hypothesis are very sensitive to small specification changes. Models controlling for the potential endogeneity of partition are not robust, have poor fit to the data, and are quite sensitive to the choice of instrumental variables.

CONCLUSION

POPULATION movements to partition states during or after civil war are coerced, painful, and costly, and they may sow the seeds of future conflict. It is therefore imperative that international policy toward partition be informed by rigorous, empirically verified arguments, rather than by untested theory. In this paper, I have provided a host of empirical tests, starting with an empirical inquiry into the determinants of war-related partition. I have found that partitions are more likely after costly ethnic/religious wars, after rebel victory or truce, and in countries with better-than-average socioeconomic conditions. Partitions are more likely where ethnic groups are large; they are less likely to occur as the degree of ethnic heterogeneity increases.

---

83. Results are available from the author. Finding good instruments in this data set has proven notoriously difficult. I did not change the specification of model 4; rather I just added and dropped instruments and considered other variables as potentially endogenous (specifically, WARDUR, LOGCOST, TREATY, ENERCAP). The instruments I used in various combinations were GEO, BORDER, EH, GDP, URBST (urban population at the start of the conflict), GARM, INTERVEN (was there an external intervention?), MAJOR (was there a major power involved?). I found only one permutation that made partition significant, but when I estimated this model using a bivariate probit estimator, I found that the error terms of the structural and reduced-form first equation were perfectly correlated ($rho = 1$), which indicates either that there was too much noise in the system or that the distribution is not a bivariate normal.

My analysis has also shown that the differences between ethnic and nonethnic wars with respect to war termination and partition are small. The relationship between the degree of ethnic heterogeneity and the need for partition is not as straightforward as partition theorists assume.[84] The finding that partition does not significantly prevent war recurrence suggests, at the very least, that separating ethnic groups does not resolve the problem of violent ethnic antagonism.

These findings lead me to formulate a new hypothesis for future research: if border redefinition is in the cards after civil war (or before war), then the strategy of supporting ethnic diffusion by combining rather than partitioning large ethnic groups may be worth pursuing. Thinking along these lines could be very useful for Africa in particular, given the persistent concern about the "unnaturalness" of Africa's borders and the recent debate about redefining those borders in the hope of reducing the incidence of civil wars.[85] Partition theorists would argue for the partition of warring African states into a multitude of ministates each of which is composed of a single ethnicity group. Based on the empirical findings of this paper, I would put forth a rival hypothesis: if borders can be credibly and securely redrawn, then combining several large ethnic groups in a larger multiethnic state may reduce the probability of new wars. It would be useful for further research to try to clarify any threshold effects that may be associated with the size of ethnic groups as they affect the likelihood of violent secessionist activity.

No doubt this proposal is difficult, perhaps infeasible. Skeptics, however, should at least acknowledge that the political dangers of ethnic diversity are imperfectly understood and that, despite the practical difficulty of my proposal, it is at least based on a more nuanced understanding of the relationship between ethnicity and political violence. Indeed, much of the best recent research on political violence consistently points to the fact that ethnic diversity need not generate violence. Economic studies of the occurrence of civil war in a sample of 161 countries have found a parabolic relationship between ethnolinguistic and religious fractionalization and the onset and duration of civil wars.[86] Work in political science, too, has steadily reinforced this point.[87] Bates, for example, casts "doubt upon a . . . tenet of conventional wisdom: that ethnic

---

84. To cite Horowitz (fn. 2), 135: "Is there any reason to believe that the more pronounced the cultural differences that exist between groups, the greater the ethnic conflict? There has been no shortage of offhanded assertions that cultural differences engender ethnic conflict. But . . . systematic statements of the relationship are more difficult to find."
85. See, e.g., Jeffrey Herbst, "Responding to State Failure in Africa," *International Security* 21 (Winter 1996–97).
86. Collier, Elbadawi, and Sambanis (fn. 30).
87. Laitin and Fearon (fn. 73).

diversity promotes violence." He finds that the "red zone" for violent conflict occurs "when an ethnic bloc may be sufficient in size to permanently exclude others from the exercise of power."[88] Thus, enhancing ethnic diversity while strengthening political institutions can be beneficial. So why partition states to reduce ethnic diversity?

Perhaps there are other benefits to be derived from partition—democratization, for example. The jury is still out on this question. My empirical analysis shows that partitions may have such an effect, but this effect may be due to the prewar institutions of civil war–torn countries; such institutions may be at least as important as partition in determining the democratic future. And the process of democratization itself may harbor dangers and cause violence.[89] Thus, international policy aimed at preventing war recurrence should promote institution building and socioeconomic development before war occurs in the first place, rather than supporting partition after war occurs.

Partition, as we have seen, does not help reduce the risk of war recurrence. Partitions are in fact positively (though not significantly) associated with recurrence of ethnic war. The probability of a new war rises with the human toll of the previous war and with nondecisive outcomes to the war. War recurrence is also positively, though not significantly, associated with GDP per capita[90] and with ethnic heterogeneity, though as ethnic groups become larger, new wars tend to become less likely.[91] Negotiated settlements, a strong government army, and a lengthy previous war all reduce the probability of war recurrence. Thus, if the international community's interest lies in preventing new civil wars, it could manipulate some of these significant variables toward desirable goals. It could, for example, take steps to enhance the government's military and

88. My findings need not agree entirely with Bates's (fn. 47), since our samples and research questions differ. I have not measured the size of the largest ethnic group, which is critical in his argument, but I do find that greater ethnic heterogeneity within the context of a larger population reduces the risk of war recurrence and residual violence. This is consistent with Bates.

89. Bates (fn. 47), 28. Although the dangers of the process of democratization, as opposed to the end goal of democracy, should not be underestimated. On the potential of regime transitions, including democratic transitions, to create civil war, see Hegre et al. (fn. 65).

90. This correlation between GDP and war recurrence may seem counterintuitive since we saw that higher GDP is correlated with higher democracy, which is negatively correlated with civil war. The impact of GDP is ambiguous because GDP can be a proxy both for the country's overall development level, which should be positively associated with peace, and for "loot," inciting new wars; see Collier and Hoeffler (fn. 45).

91. Despite the fact that this study looks only at cases where war has already taken place, the results on the impact of ethnic heterogeneity are compatible with studies of initial war occurrence, in that ethnic heterogeneity seems to increase the risk of war at first, but as the degree of heterogeneity increases, that risk declines. In my analysis, however, this effect has not been statistically significant.

support decisive war outcomes.[92] Or it could support the negotiation of peace treaties, which reduce the threat of new violence. Again, what the international community should not do to prevent future wars is promote partition.

One benefit that can come from partition is the reduction of residual low-level ethnic violence. Certainly, it follows that if ethnic groups divide into ethnically homogeneous territorial units, the risk of ethnic conflict declines. I have found that this result depends critically on the number of displaced people, as well as on the way the previous war ended and on the country's longer war history. The probability of low-level violence is shaped by some of the same variables that influence war recurrence, but it also is a function of different determinants. The previous discussion of how to prevent war therefore applies to residual violence, but with some modifications. To reduce residual violence, it is important to prevent war recurrence, as patterns of large-scale violence over time seem to encourage lower-level violence.

Fine-tuning a war-to-peace transition is a difficult task because peace-building strategies can often backfire. For example, promoting economic growth may assist democratization and promote peace, but it can also lead to new wars by expanding the potential economic gains from a new rebellion. Strategies to support the government's prewar institutions and its military may also achieve peace, but they may do so at the expense of justice.

Muddling through this difficult terrain, I would propose an empirically derived strategy for resolving ethnic wars. This strategy demands action by the international community, which must promote democracy as its number one conflict-prevention strategy. If violence does erupt, its priority should be to facilitate a negotiated settlement, as well as to integrate and downsize the government's military. According to my empirical analysis, these strategies can be effective. If border redefinition is a viable option—and it should be an option only if it does not assist one party at the expense of another—then ethnic integration rather than ethnic partition may be a winning strategy. In addition to having the potential for greater success than partition, this strategy is also not loaded with subjective and arbitrary assumptions about the necessity for ethnically pure states and about the futility of interethnic cooperation. Only in extreme cases may partition be necessary, indeed inevitable. Those cases must be handpicked on the basis of political analysis of regional and global constraints, the history of the preceding war, and the special traits of the society in question. More research on this topic will help pinpoint the benefits and the dangers of partition under different conditions. What this study has suggested is that, on average, partition may be an impossible solution to ethnic civil war.

---

92. Such a strategy, however, might indirectly support political repression, so it must be carefully and selectively applied and militaries should integrate the rebel army if possible.

APPENDIX: TESTING FOR THE POSSIBLE ENDOGENEITY OF PARTITIONS

A number of explanatory variables are correlated with both partition and no war recurrence. This raises concerns about possible endogeneity of partition in models of war recurrence. This appendix explains the problem of endogeneity to which I refer in the text and explains how the problem can be addressed.

Endogeneity results if a system of simultaneous equations has correlated error terms. Here, we have a system of two equations of partition (P) and war recurrence (W):

$$P_i = \alpha + \beta_1 M_i + \beta_2 X_i + \varepsilon_i \tag{1}$$

$$W_i = \gamma + \beta_3 P_i + \beta_4 M_i + \beta_5 Z_i + \mu_i \tag{2}$$

where equation 1 determines the incidence of partition (P) and equation 2 determines war recurrence (W). M_i is a vector of common variables in the two equations and β_1 is the vector of coefficients of M_i; X_i is a vector of instrumental variables (correlated with partition but not with war recurrence) and β_2 is a vector of their coefficients; Z_i is a vector of variables that are correlated with war recurrence and β_5 is a vector of their coefficients. Endogeneity stems from the possible correlation between ε_i and μ_i (both of them disturbance terms with mean zero and no correlation to the other explanatory variables). The presence of common explanatory variables in equations 1 and 2 (that is, the variables in M_i) implies that ε_i and μ_i may be correlated, in which case, a simple probit regression would produce biased parameter estimates.

To resolve this problem, we must first test for endogeneity, and if we detect it, we must estimate a model that corrects for it as in the two-stage least squares model for linear regression. This problem is harder when the dependent variable is binary. The two-state probit used by Bollen, Guilkey, and Mroz, following Rivers and Vuong, is a model that has been shown to generate consistent parameter estimates with small efficiency loss. This model has attractive properties.[93] The procedure is similar to 2SLS: first, estimate the reduced form of equation 1 using a probit regression, obtaining predicted values (PHAT) of the dependent variable (PART).[94] Then, compute the error of that prediction

93. The choice of estimator depends on the number of observations, the degree of identification of the model, the number of potentially endogenous variables, and the goodness of fit of the first-stage equation. See Bollen, Guilkey, and Mroz (fn. 76).

94. Use of this method is strictly based on attaining an R^2 no smaller than 10 percent in equation 1. In my case, the R^2 was higher than 30 percent. Further, Bollen, Guilkey and Mroz (fn. 76) discuss evidence from Monte Carlo simulations that suggest that the models' identification

(RES) and plug the PHAT into equation 2, replacing PART. PHAT is un-correlated with the disturbance term in equation 1. Then, estimate equation 2 using a probit regression with robust standard errors. The resulting coefficient estimates are consistent asymptotically inefficient.[95] However, evidence from small-sample Monte Carlo simulations has shown that the efficiency loss is very small.[96]

To determine whether this process should be used, a simple exogeneity test can be applied. This involves a t-test of the estimated coefficient of the prediction error (RES), added as a regressor along with the actual value of PART in equation 2 in the model of war recurrence.[97] If RES is nonsignificant, we cannot reject the null hypothesis of exogeneity of partitions and we should rely on the simple probit estimates. Applying this method to the no-war-recurrence model, I find that more efficient results are reached by models that assume exogeneity. This is confirmed by estimating a bivariate probit model of war recurrence that provides efficient standard errors (estimated by maximum likelihood) and a different test of exogeneity.

---

must be less than 75 percent for the two-step probit estimator to be preferable to the simple probit (i.e., the overlapping variables in the two equations must be fewer than three-fourths of the total number of right-hand-side variables in the structural equation).

95. T. Amemiya. "The Maximum Likelihood and the Nonlinear Three-Stage Least Squares Estimator in the General Nonlinear Simultaneous Equation Model," *Econometrica* 45 (1978).

96. See Bollen, Guilkey, and Mroz (fn. 76); and G. Tauchen, "Diagnostic Testing and Evaluation of Maximum Likelihood Models," *Journal of Econometrics* 30 (1985). Formulas to compute efficient standard errors can be found in Maddala (fn. 76), and a method to estimate the asymptotically efficient covariance matrix when the model is overidentified has been developed by Amemiya (fn. 95). Alvarez and Butterfield (fn. 76) use bootstrapping to obtain estimates of the correct standard errors.

97. Bollen, Guilkey and Mroz (fn. 76) find this to be the best-performing exogeneity test.

THE PROBLEM WITH NEGOTIATED SETTLEMENTS
TO ETHNIC CIVIL WARS

ALEXANDER B. DOWNES

A burgeoning literature has emerged on the utility of negotiated settlements as a method of terminating civil wars.[1] Negotiated settlements comprise less than one quarter of all civil war endings,[2] but garner the

Alexander B. Downes is assistant professor of political science at Duke University.

Previous versions of this paper were presented at the conference on Living Together After Ethnic Killing at Rutgers University in New Brunswick, N.J. (October 2000); and the annual meeting of the International Studies Association in Portland, OR, February 2003. For helpful comments and suggestions, the author wishes to thank Jasen Castillo, David Edelstein, Kelly Greenhill, John Mearsheimer, Will Moore, Sebastian Rosato, Paul Yingling, and two anonymous *Security Studies* reviewers. Research for this article was conducted while the author was a graduate student at the University of Chicago; it was revised while he was a visiting fellow at the Olin Institute for Strategic Studies, Harvard University, and the Center for International Security and Cooperation, Stanford University. He is grateful to each of these programs for financial and institutional support.

1. Examples from a vast and growing literature include Roy Licklider, ed., *Stopping the Killing: How Civil Wars End* (New York: New York University Press, 1993); Licklider, "The Consequences of Negotiated Settlements in Civil Wars, 1945–1993," *American Political Science Review* 89, no. 3 (September 1995): 681–90; T. David Mason and Patrick J. Fett, "How Civil Wars End: A Rational Choice Approach," *Journal of Conflict Resolution* 40, no. 4 (December 1996): 546–68; Stephen John Stedman, "Negotiation and Mediation in Internal Conflict," in *The International Dimensions of Internal Conflict*, ed. Michael E. Brown (Cambridge: MIT Press, 1996), 341–76; Stedman, Donald Rothchild, and Elizabeth M. Cousens, ed., *Ending Civil Wars: The Implementation of Peace Agreements* (Boulder: Lynne Rienner, 2002); Charles King, *Ending Civil Wars*, Adelphi Paper 308 (Oxford: International Institute for Strategic Studies [IISS]/Oxford University Press, 1997); Barbara F. Walter, "The Critical Barrier to Civil War Settlement," *International Organization* 51, no. 3 (summer 1997): 335–64; Walter, "Designing Transitions from Civil War: Demobilization, Democratization, and Commitments to Peace," *International Security* 24, no. 1 (summer 1999): 127–55; Walter, *Committing to Peace: The Successful Settlement of Civil Wars* (Princeton: Princeton University Press, 2002); Caroline Hartzell, "Explaining the Stability of Negotiated Settlements to Intrastate Wars," *Journal of Conflict Resolution* 43, no. 1 (February 1999): 3–22; Hartzell, Matthew Hoddie, and Donald Rothchild, "Stabilizing the Peace After Civil War: An Investigation of Some Key Variables," *International Organization* 55, no. 1 (winter 2001): 183–208; Nicholas Sambanis, "Partition as a Solution to Ethnic War: An Empirical Critique of the Theoretical Literature," *World Politics* 49, no. 4 (July 2000): 437–83; and Mark Peceny and William Stanley, "Liberal Social Reconstruction and the Resolution of Civil Wars in Central America," *International Organization* 55, no. 1 (winter 2001): 149–82. This focus on civil wars makes sense given that they compose the vast majority of current armed conflicts: intrastate wars of one kind or another accounted for 30 of 31 ongoing armed conflicts in 2002. See Mikael Eriksson, Peter Wallensteen, Margareta Sollenberg, "Armed Conflict, 1989–2002," *Journal of Peace Research* 40, no. 5 (September 2003): 594.

2. Of ethnic civil wars that end, 20 to 25 percent terminate in negotiated settlements. See the datasets in Licklider, "Consequences of Negotiated Settlements in Civil Wars"; Mason and

majority of the scholarly attention. Most analysts try to answer questions such as: which factors facilitate negotiated settlements to civil wars? How can such agreements be made to stick once implemented? What types of institutions tend to prevent a reoccurrence of hostilities? How best can third parties assist former combatants to reconcile and share power? Are wars fought over identity issues more or less susceptible to termination by negotiated agreement than those fought over ideological or economic differences?

Ethnic civil wars in particular appear to be difficult to resolve with negotiated settlements. While this type of war is no less likely than wars fought over ideological issues to end in a negotiated agreement, hardly any ideological wars resume after a settlement is implemented, whereas such agreements fail as often as two-thirds of the time in identity wars.[3] The conventional wisdom in both academic and policy circles on how best to end ethnic wars contends that secessionist conflicts are best managed by giving regional autonomy to restive ethnic groups, while contests for control of the state should be contained by sharing power. According to Ted Robert Gurr, a leading scholar of ethnic conflict, the "essential principles" of this new regime "are that threats to divide a country should be managed by the devolution of state power and that communal fighting about access to the state's power and resources should be restrained by recognizing group rights and sharing power."[4] That this new conventional wisdom has found its way into the policy community is evidenced by the international community's preference for autonomy, power sharing, or

---

Fett, "How Civil Wars End"; Walter, *Committing to Peace* and "Critical Barrier"; and Sambanis, "Partition as a Solution to Ethnic War." One scholar puts this rate as low as 15 percent (Stephen John Stedman, *Peacemaking in Civil Wars: International Mediation in Zimbabwe, 1974–1980* [Boulder: Lynne Rienner, 1991], 4–9). Others, using a more liberal definition of negotiated settlement, find that 40–45 percent of civil wars end in such agreements (Hartzell, "Explaining the Stability of Negotiated Settlements to Intrastate Wars," 12; and Hartzell, Hoddie, and Rothchild, "Stabilizing the Peace After Civil War," 194).

3. Licklider, "Consequences of Negotiated Settlements in Civil Wars," 686.

4. See Ted Robert Gurr, "Ethnic Warfare on the Wane," *Foreign Affairs* 79, no. 3 (May/June 2000): 52. For further elaboration, see Gurr, *Peoples versus States: Minorities at Risk in the New Century* (Washington, D.C.: United States Institute of Peace Press, 2000); and Gurr, *Minorities at Risk: A Global View of Ethnopolitical Conflicts* (Washington, D.C.: United States Institute of Peace Press, 1993). Other prominent works include Graham Smith, ed., *Federalism: The Multiethnic Challenge* (London: Longman, 1995); Timothy D. Sisk, *Power Sharing and International Mediation in Ethnic Conflicts* (Washington, D.C.: United States Institute of Peace Press, 1996); Ruth Lapidoth, *Autonomy: Flexible Solutions to Ethnic Conflict* (Washington, D.C.: United States Institute of Peace Press, 1997); and Yash Ghai, ed., *Autonomy and Ethnicity: Negotiating Competing Claims in Multiethnic States* (Cambridge: Cambridge University Press, 2000). Of course, arguments for power sharing and autonomy as solutions to ethnic conflict have been around for a long time. For early works on the former, see Arend Lijphart, "Consociational Democracy," *World Politics* 21, no. 2 (January 1969): 207–25; and Lijphart, *Democracy in Plural Societies: A Comparative Exploration* (New Haven: Yale University Press, 1977); on the latter, see Donald L. Horowitz, *Ethnic Groups in Conflict* (Berkeley: University of California Press, 1985), 601–28. What is new is the acceptance and promotion of these policies by third party interveners in ethnic wars.

some combination of the two in countries where it has intervened or mediated, such as Angola, Bosnia, Sierra Leone, Kosovo, Macedonia, and most recently Afghanistan and Iraq.[5] In addition, many countries have either federalized their political systems (Spain, Ethiopia), created new federal units if already a federation (India), granted regional autonomy (Sudan, Sri Lanka, Israel, Nicaragua, Moldova, the Philippines, Russia, Bangladesh), or instituted power sharing (Lebanon in 1958 and 1976, Chad, Northern Ireland) to curb ethnic rebellions.

Despite the appearance of this new regime, lasting solutions to ethnic civil wars remain elusive. Since 1945, power sharing governments instituted after ethnic wars have collapsed into renewed conflict (Lebanon 1958 and 1976, Chad 1979, Angola 1994, and Sierra Leone 1999), other power sharing deals agreed to were abrogated before they could be implemented (Uganda 1985 and Rwanda 1993), while the success of still others recently negotiated remains unclear (Bosnia 1995, Northern Ireland 1998, Burundi 2000, and Macedonia 2001).[6] Furthermore, agreements that provided regional autonomy for rebellious ethnic groups usually either failed to end the conflict (Moros in the Philippines, Ethiopia's Afars, Somalis, and Oromo, Sri Lankan Tamils, India's Assamese and Bodos), saw serious conflict resume sometime after the agreement was implemented (India's Kashmiri Muslims, Nagas, and Tripuras, Sudan's Southerners, Palestinians in the West Bank and Gaza, and Russia's Chechens), or could not prevent the onset of a serious armed conflict after autonomy was agreed upon (India's Sikhs and Pakistan's Baluchis). Overall, despite a few recent apparent successes in relatively mild conflicts (India's Mizos, Nicaragua's Miskito Indians, Moldova's Gagauz, and Mali's Tuaregs), the record of negotiated settlements to ethnic wars which share or divide power is far from stellar.[7]

This article has three goals: (1) to explain why negotiated solutions to all types of civil wars are relatively rare; (2) to investigate why agreements specifically in ethnic wars involving power sharing or territorial autonomy are so hard to sustain; and (3) to suggest that ending such wars with partition or military victory may be more stable than agreements to share or diffuse power within the confines of a single state.

---

5. Ghai, "Ethnicity and Autonomy: A Framework for Analysis," in Ghai, *Autonomy and Ethnicity*, 15–16. There was also a sharp increase in the number of civil wars settled via negotiations in the 1990s. Monica Toft observed that negotiated settlements outnumbered decisive military victories as methods of civil war termination in the 1990s for the first time. See Monica Duffy Toft, "Peace Through Victory?" (paper presented at the annual meeting of the American Political Science Association, Philadelphia, PA, 27–31 August 2003), 10.

6. Dates given indicate the year when settlements were agreed upon.

7. This data is summarized in Alexander B. Downes, "The Holy Land Divided: Defending Partition as a Solution to Ethnic Wars," *Security Studies* 10, no. 4 (summer 2001): 89–97.

I argue that the experience of warfare provides combatants with ample evidence of their adversary's malign intentions. Although the enemy appears willing to settle now, the war just fought gives each side little reason to be sanguine about the other's future intentions. Negotiated settlements to civil wars, however, require that groups forsake their armed forces—and hence their ability to protect themselves and enforce the terms of any agreement negotiated—in order to unify the country. How, though, can they be sure that their former adversary will not cheat on the deal and attack when they are most vulnerable?

Structural realism traditionally has argued that states' inability to know whether other states' present or future intentions are malign or benign inhibits cooperation in a world without a sovereign authority to provide protection or enforce contracts. States wishing only to protect themselves amass military power that threatens other states, which then arm themselves in self-defense. This process of competitive arming can cause states to infer malign intentions and lead to conflict and war. Should war actually occur, a state may not always be able to change its enemy's intentions—although this does happen, by changing its regime, for example—but it can at least reduce its foe's capability to act on those malign intentions. Most importantly, after a war between them, states retain their own armies and institutions, and thus their ability to defend themselves in the future.

Civil war combatants, however, do not have this luxury. Forced to surrender their arms and share the same state, groups legitimately fear cooperating while the other cheats, or that their opponent's intentions will turn malign again in the future. Given the high stakes involved—group survival—and the recent history of hostility, combatants are understandably reluctant to take the risk of settling. Militarily, therefore, negotiated single-state solutions founder on the issue of disarmament.

Politically, uncertainty regarding an adversary's future intentions undercuts the functioning of institutions designed to share or diffuse power after the war. Both the government and the rebellious group(s) are uncertain as to how political institutions will work, and distrust that their recent adversary will sincerely abide by the rules of the game. In power sharing arrangements, each side fears that the other will attempt to capture the state, exclude them from power and resources, and use the instruments of state power to repress them. In a federal or autonomous arrangement, the government fears groups will use autonomy to prepare for secession while groups suspect that the government may curtail or revoke their liberties.

Ironically, although ethnic civil wars in theory have a greater number of possible solutions owing to the territorial concentration of most ethnic groups, the military and political problems engendered by uncertainty regarding intentions are particularly problematic in ethnic civil wars. First of all, many ethnic wars are secessionist, raising the possibility that groups will not share one state after the war. Furthermore, warfare heightens ethnicity as the relevant line of cleavage in society, but negotiated settlements leave intact groups' infrastructure and organizations, leaving them able to continue the struggle at a future time. Moreover, because most ethnic groups are deeply attached to territory, viewing it as integral to their identity and security, they are highly sensitive to encroachments on the autonomy they have gained in a peace settlement.

Taken together, concern over the future intentions of former adversaries and the specific properties of ethnic wars discourage solutions to ethnic wars short of military victory for one side or partition, and undermine the success of negotiated settlements if implemented. These difficulties hold even if the parties are largely segregated on the ground or if a third party intervenes temporarily to keep the peace. For the former, if a state is to exist, there must be some form of central government, in which case uncertainty regarding intentions will inhibit cooperation. In the latter, the parties to the conflict know that interveners will eventually depart; the security they bring, therefore, is temporary, which forces the parties to worry about each other's intentions and their future security.

My conclusion is that once a full-scale ethnic war breaks out, solutions predicated on autonomy or power sharing are unlikely to settle the conflict: the more stable solutions are partition, that is, separation *plus* independence, or a decisive military victory for one side over the other.[8] Partition has potential because it minimizes the degree to which groups must cooperate with and trust one another; does not require them to disarm or merge their militaries; limits the level of external military intervention required and allows it to be used to better effect; and, by satisfying nationalism and the need for physical security, allows passions to cool between formerly hostile groups. Military victory, on the other hand, renders a decisive verdict to the struggle for power in favor of one side, thus leaving its opponent less willing and less able to renew the contest. Thus, the international community (IC) should perhaps be more circumspect about its ability to engineer negotiated single-state solutions to ethnic wars, and more willing to consider facilitating partition or military victory.

The remainder of the paper is divided into three parts. The first section discusses my argument in greater detail, delineates the military and political

8. Stability in this context means solely that the likelihood of renewed warfare is minimized. I do not mean to imply that ethnic domination or separation is normatively superior or desirable.

difficulties that hinder negotiated single-state solutions to ethnic wars, and briefly evaluates the empirical evidence regarding the success of such solutions. The second section presents a pair of case studies to illustrate my argument. Bosnia and Kosovo should be strong cases for other arguments: the Dayton Peace Agreement established a federal state with extensive power sharing provisions in the former, while the latter stands to gain substantial autonomy. Furthermore, the IC is strongly committed in both areas, providing robust civil administration and military occupation forces. Moreover, war produced three ethnically homogeneous regions in Bosnia, and a nearly homogeneous Albanian population in Kosovo, thereby reducing incentives for ethnic cleansing. These conditions notwithstanding, the legacies of large-scale interethnic armed conflict stymie solutions based on autonomy and power sharing. I draw out four observable propositions for likely behavior, including reluctance to disarm and merge armies, popular support for nationalist politicians, gridlock in political institutions, and opposition to refugee return, and test these propositions against evidence from Bosnia and Kosovo. The third section concludes by addressing potential objections to my argument.

REALISM AND CIVIL WAR

PRESENT AND FUTURE INTENTIONS OF THE ADVERSARY

Existing realist literature on civil conflict uses the security dilemma to explain the causes, conduct, and endings of internal wars. Realists have mainly focused on ethnic civil wars, arguing that ethnic intermingling gives rise to a security dilemma which can both cause ethnic wars and prevent them from ending short of ethnic separation.[9] My argument, on the other hand, focuses

---

9. On the ethnic security dilemma as a cause of war, see Barry R. Posen, "The Security Dilemma and Ethnic Conflict," *Survival* 35, no. 1 (spring 1993): 27–47; William Rose, "The Security Dilemma and Ethnic Conflict: Some New Hypotheses," *Security Studies* 9, no. 4 (summer 2000): 1–51; Jack Snyder and Robert Jervis, "Civil War and the Security Dilemma," in *Civil Wars, Insecurity, and Intervention*, ed. Barbara F. Walter and Jack Snyder (New York: Columbia University Press, 1999), 15–37; and Flemming Splidsboel-Hansen, "The Outbreak and Settlement of Civil War: Neorealism and the Case of Tajikistan," *Civil Wars* 2, no. 4 (winter 1999): 1–22. On the security dilemma as preventing wars from ending, see Chaim D. Kaufmann, "Possible and Impossible Solutions to Ethnic Civil Wars," *International Security* 20, no. 4 (spring 1996): 136–75; and Kaufmann, "When All Else Fails: Ethnic Population Transfers and Partitions in the Twentieth Century," *International Security* 23, no. 2 (fall 1998): 120–56. Closely related to the security dilemma are arguments that focus on commitment problems: the inability of a majority group to do anything credible to commit itself not to use the power of the state to exploit the minority in the future. See Walter, "Critical Barrier" and *Committing to Peace*; and James D. Fearon, "Commitment Problems and the Spread of Ethnic Conflict," in *The International Spread of Ethnic Conflict: Fear, Diffusion, and Escalation*, ed. David A. Lake and Donald Rothchild

on another important realist variable: the impact that fighting the war has on each side's estimate of the other's intentions and thus their ability to trust each other enough in the future to share a state.[10] Barbara Walter was the first to observe that civil war combatants face a particularly severe dilemma. Unlike negotiated settlements to wars between states, implementation of such agreements within states requires groups to disarm and merge their militaries. Disarming, however, increases their vulnerability and reduces their ability to enforce compliance with the agreement by the other side. Civil war combatants, therefore, face an unappealing choice should they decide to terminate the conflict via negotiations. "As groups send their soldiers home, hand in their weapons, and surrender occupied territory," writes Walter, "they become increasingly vulnerable to a surprise attack. And once they surrender arms and cede control of territory, their rival can more easily seize control of the state and permanently exclude them from power."[11] The non-trivial risk of betrayal, combined with the enormous costs of being cheated, inhibits groups from gambling on a settlement.

A structural realist approach argues that uncertainty regarding an adversary's present and future intentions fuels the security dilemma in international politics and thwarts negotiated settlements to intrastate wars. In the international realm, although realism assumes that states seek only to survive (and hence attempt to maximize their security), security competition still occurs because "[t]here are many possible causes of aggression, and no state can be sure that another state is not motivated by one of them."[12] In other words, knowledge about state type is not public, but only indirectly observable via state behavior. Uncertainty about current intentions inhibits cooperation because of the possibility that the other side is motivated by goals beyond simple security that

---

(Princeton: Princeton University Press, 1998), 107–26. Other authors have adjusted the security dilemma concept to include the state, arguing that if "the state cannot protect the interests of all ethnic groups, then each group will seek to control the state, decreasing the security of other groups and decreasing the ability of the state to provide security for any group." See Stephen M. Saideman, "The Dual Dynamics of Disintegration: Ethnic Politics and Security Dilemmas in Eastern Europe," *Nationalism and Ethnic Politics* 2, no. 1 (spring 1996): 23; and Saideman, "Is Pandora's Box Half-Empty or Half-Full? The Limited Virulence of Secession and the Domestic Sources of Disintegration," in Lake and Rothchild, *The International Spread of Ethnic Conflict*, 127–50.

10. I accept as given that ethnic war tends to cause ethnic separation, and that solutions to such wars should be based on separation; as Stathis Kalyvas puts it, "civil wars tend to produce segregation even when the intention is not to 'cleanse'" (Stathis Kalyvas, "The Logic of Violence in Civil War," unpub. ms., University of Chicago, April 2003, 25). Intermingling by itself, however, does not cause ethnic wars in the first place; it is the effect of the war that makes intermingling dangerous.

11. Walter, *Committing to Peace*, 21.

12. John J. Mearsheimer, *The Tragedy of Great Power Politics* (New York: Norton, 2001), 31. See also Kenneth N. Waltz, *Theory of International Politics* (New York: McGraw-Hill, 1979), 105–6.

will lead it to cheat on the agreement. Moreover, a state's intentions are never fixed, but are subject to change with little advance notice, making it dangerous to cooperate too closely because today's ally might be tomorrow's enemy: "No matter how much decision makers are committed to the status quo, they cannot bind themselves and their successors to the same path. Minds can be changed, new leaders can come to power, values can shift, new opportunities and dangers can arise."[13]

In a civil conflict, each of these problems is more severe because the requirements for settling an internal war—disarmament and demobilization of military forces—make the penalty for being wrong about the other side's intentions far worse than in relations between sovereign states.[14] In a civil war, each side knows for a fact that the other has malign intentions; after all, both "have been killing one another with considerable skill and enthusiasm" for some time.[15] Even if one party wants to end the war, it may be prevented from doing so by the belief that it cannot trust the other side. "Whatever the obstacles to an arrangement that would have prevented war," remarks Fred Iklé in the context of interstate war termination, "the use of violence itself engenders new obstacles to the reestablishment of peace. Fighting sharpens feelings of hostility. It creates fears that an opponent might again resort to violence, and thus adds to the skepticism about a compromise peace."[16] As Joanna Spear puts it, "where violence has been extreme and the conflict long-running, confidence and mutual trust will be more difficult to build between the erstwhile enemies."[17]

Should its enemy appear willing to strike a bargain, however, how can a group be sure that its opponent is not trying to deceive them and that the adversary's seemingly benign attitude is a façade behind which malign

13. Robert Jervis, "Cooperation Under the Security Dilemma," *World Politics* 30, no. 2 (January 1978): 168. See also Dale C. Copeland, "The Constructivist Challenge to Structural Realism," *International Security* 25, no. 2 (fall 2000): 202–03. Jervis and other defensive realists argue, however, that when offensive and defensive military technologies are distinguishable, and the balance between them favors defense, not only is the security dilemma likely to be less intense, but states can signal their type (security-seeker or revisionist) by the types of weapons they procure (Jervis, "Cooperation Under the Security Dilemma," 190; and Charles L. Glaser, "Realists as Optimists: Cooperation as Self-Help," *International Security* 19, no. 3 [winter 1994/95]: 67–70).
14. Jervis, "Cooperation Under the Security Dilemma," 172; Walter, "Critical Barrier," 338; and Thomas Hobbes, *Leviathan*, ed. J. C. A. Gaskin (Oxford: Oxford University Press, 1996), 85.
15. Roy Licklider, "Early Returns: Results of the First Wave of Statistical Studies of Civil War Termination," *Civil Wars* 1, no. 3 (autumn 1998): 122.
16. Fred Charles Iklé, *Every War Must End*, rev. ed. (New York: Columbia University Press, 1991), 107. Put another way, "no matter what a civil war may initially have been about, once antagonists have set about killing one another they are likely to be concerned about their future security" (Hartzell, Hoddie, and Rothchild, "Stabilizing the Peace After Civil War," 203).
17. Joanna Spear, "The Disarmament and Demobilization of Warring Factions in the Aftermath of Civil Wars: Key Implementation Issues," *Civil Wars* 2, no. 2 (summer 1999): 12.

intentions lurk? Combatants in the face of such uncertainty often choose to continue fighting rather than take that risk. Moreover, even if each side is nearly certain that the other's present intentions are benign, both also worry that those intentions could change in the future. Nothing prevents either party to the agreement from changing its mind at a later date, for example if the current group leadership is flanked or replaced by hard-liners.

The "problem of other minds" is bad enough in international politics, in which uncertainty regarding other states' present and future intentions inhibits potentially beneficial cooperation, fuels security competition, and sometimes leads to war. It is nearly intractable in intrastate conflict, however, in which combatants are not allowed to retain their military forces and retreat behind fortified frontiers. I sketch the deleterious effect of uncertainty about the other side's intentions on the military and political aspects of negotiated settlements to civil wars below.

MILITARY OBSTACLES: DISARMING AND INTEGRATING ARMIES

If a negotiated settlement to a civil war is to succeed, the rebellious group(s) must relinquish its arms and permit its soldiers to be integrated into the government army or returned to civilian life. Such groups, however, are reluctant to part with their weapons because to do so removes both their ability to defend themselves and their ability to threaten or use violence to enforce the agreement should the other side cheat. By the very act of disarming a group forfeits its leverage over its rival, thereby making itself vulnerable. An attack at this crucial time would be devastating, perhaps decisive. Unfortunately, in this case the consequence of cooperation could be destruction, a disaster few groups are willing to risk. Thus, even if the payoff for continuing to fight is negative, it often appears the more attractive option.[18]

A second military issue that must be overcome if a single state is to be preserved is how to integrate the former combatants' military forces. Negotiations must invent some formula acceptable to both sides of how to create a united army. If separate armies are allowed to exist, any political disagreement can quickly become militarized, leading to the resumption of hostilities. In some cases military units retain their ethnic or regional loyalties even years after they have supposedly been integrated into the government army, and

18. Walter, "Critical Barrier," 338. On the difficulties inherent in disarming and demobilizing, see Mats R. Berdal, *Disarmament and Demobilization after Civil Wars*, Adelphi Paper no. 303 (Oxford: IISS/Oxford University Press, 1996); and Joanna Spear, "Disarmament and Demobilization," in Stedman, Rothchild, and Cousens, *Ending Civil Wars*, 141–82.

can form the nucleus of a renewed rebel force.[19] Moreover, separate armies prevent the central government from exercising any real authority in parts of the country controlled by different ethnic groups. This situation can easily drift toward de facto partition, or war if the central state attempts to impose its will on the area it does not control.[20]

Most students of civil war termination focus on measures to reassure the combatants about each other's present intentions and preventing (or lowering the costs of) immediate betrayal. Settlement optimists argue that independent monitoring and verification or third party security guarantees can mitigate fears of cheating, but this is not always the case.[21] Even a sizable military occupation force—and peacekeeping detachments are often far from robust—cannot prevent combatants from simply stashing their weapons in secret locations rather than turning them in, or giving up only old, relatively useless guns. It is widely acknowledged by observers, for example, that Albanian fighters in Kosovo relinquished only a small fraction of their arms in 1999.[22] Moreover, third parties rarely have incentives to remain involved for extended periods of time. Knowing that the outsiders will eventually leave, parties to the settlement wish to keep their weapons as insurance against renewed attack in the future.

POLITICAL OBSTACLES: WHY SETTLEMENTS ARE HARDER TO SUSTAIN
IN ETHNIC WARS

Settlement optimists contend that institutions that "seek to balance, divide, or share power among competing groups" using power sharing, proportional representation, regional autonomy, or federalism can solve the security dilemma by constraining the use of force, and distributing political power and material resources.[23] Properly designed institutions, according to this view, allow all parties to participate in the exercise of state power at the national or regional level, permitting groups to protect their core interests and prevent them from being shut out of power.

19. This was the case in Sudan, where Southern units in the army rebelled in 1983 (eleven years after they were integrated) when president Jaafar al-Nimeiri attempted to transfer them to the north in response to increasing tension between the two regions. See Nelson Kasfir, "Peacemaking and Social Cleavages in Sudan," in *Conflict and Peacemaking in Multiethnic Societies*, ed. Joseph V. Montville (Lexington, Mass.: D.C. Heath, 1990), 363–87.

20. These twin problems contributed to the failure of three negotiated settlements in Angola (1989, 1991, and 1994). See Human Rights Watch, *Angola Unravels: The Rise and Fall of the Lusaka Peace Process*, at http://www.hrw.org/reports/1999/angola.

21. On the former, see Spear, "Disarmament and Demobilization of Warring Factions," 17–19; on the latter, see Walter, "Critical Barrier."

22. See the case study of Kosovo below.

23. Hartzell, "Explaining the Stability of Negotiated Settlements," 6. See also Hartzell, Hoddie, and Rothchild, "Stabilizing the Peace After Civil War," and Walter, *Committing to Peace*.

By contrast, I argue that uncertainty regarding the present and future intentions of one's negotiating partner exacerbates the difficulty of implementing political institutions after ethnic civil wars and regularly causes them to fail. Most generally, the lack of trust between groups in a post-conflict situation handicaps the likelihood that democracy will survive. As columnist Thomas Friedman has argued, "democracy means the willingness to have your group or party be outvoted and have power go to the competing group or party . . . To do that, though, the party or group that loses has to trust the new majority and believe that its basic interests will still be protected and that there is nothing to fear from a change in power."[24] Some new data, however, suggests that "democratic" solutions to civil wars do not result in democratic outcomes over the long term. States that have civil wars ended by negotiated settlement receive a short term boost in their level of democracy, but 20–30 years after the agreement these same states tend to be less democratic than those which had a civil war end with a decisive victory.[25]

Problems specific to ethnic wars. More specifically, skepticism regarding intentions induced by civil war, combined with several unique features of ethnic conflicts, handicaps the mechanisms proposed by the conventional wisdom for stemming ethnic disputes. The theory as described thus far applies to all types of civil wars. Indeed, both the ethnic and ideological varieties are about equally likely to end in a negotiated settlement. The difference between the two only emerges after an agreement is implemented: hardly any ideological civil wars begin anew, but at least half of the ethnic wars start again. I argue that several distinctive properties of identity-based conflicts render negotiated settlements in these wars especially difficult to sustain.[26]

First, as opposed to ideological civil wars, which are almost always fought for control of an existing state, and which thus may be won outright or settled by power sharing between the various factions, ethnic wars are often fought to break away from an existing state and form a new political unit. Political independence, although often not a goal when the war began, can become an

---

24. Thomas L. Friedman, "Not Happening," *New York Times*, 23 January 2001, A21.

25. Using the Polity IV dataset, Toft finds that twenty years later, states that had a civil war end with a negotiated settlement are on average five points less democratic (on a 21-point scale) than they were before the war. After thirty years, such states are nearly seven points less democratic (Toft, "Peace Through Victory?" 23). These results are preliminary, however, and should be viewed with caution: because there are few negotiated settlements, one or two bad outcomes could wreck an otherwise positive trend.

26. Other scholars have found some support for the argument that the *causes* of the two types of civil wars are different. See Nicholas Sambanis, "Do Ethnic and Nonethnic Civil Wars Have the Same Causes? A Theoretical and Empirical Inquiry (Part 1)," *Journal of Conflict Resolution* 45, no. 3 (June 2001): 259–82.

objective during the course of the fighting. As Yash Ghai and Anthony Regan observe regarding the conflict in Papau New Guinea, "the conflict certainly intensified Bougainvillean ethnic identity and the depth of ethnic division, and, as a result, the degree of autonomy that might be acceptable to accommodate ethnic identity is now far greater than it was in the 1990s."[27] Ethnic groups that reach full-scale rebellion, furthermore, typically have a deep attachment to a homeland, viewing it as an essential piece of their identity and a key to their cultural and physical security.[28] These features of ethnic wars lend to them an indivisible quality that not only makes them harder to settle in the framework of a single state, but also tends to undermine the variety of possible territorial outcomes below the level of independence, such as regional autonomy or federalism.[29]

Second, ethnic wars tend to polarize societies more severely than do wars in which civilian loyalties are viewed as more malleable. In the prototypical ideological insurgency, guerrillas and government forces alike compete to draw support from the same underlying population. In ethnic wars, on the other hand, each party to the conflict tends (at least initially) to recruit and draw support almost exclusively from members of its own group.[30] Suffering extensive violence at the hands of another group increases peoples' identification with their own ethnic group (often referred to as "hardening" ethnic identity). The ability to make cross-ethnic appeals is lost as people are forced by violence to choose sides, sometimes against their will.[31] Invariably, however, they choose their own ethnic kin, and violence increasingly polarizes society. "The trauma of the wars [in the Balkans]," argues the Independent

27. Yash Ghai and Anthony Regan, "Bougainville and the Dialectics of Ethnicity, Autonomy and Separation," in Ghai, *Autonomy and Ethnicity*, 264.
28. Monica Duffy Toft, "Indivisible Territory, Geographic Concentration, and Ethnic War," *Security Studies* 12, no. 2 (winter 2002/3): 81–118; and Toft, *The Geography of Ethnic Violence: Identity, Interests, and Territory* (Princeton: Princeton University Press, 2003).
29. Because most ethnic groups have a territorial base, regional autonomy or federalism are applicable, whereas those solutions usually do not pertain to ideological wars. Some form of regional autonomy has been implemented after a few ideological civil wars, such as the twenty-three development zones allocated to the Contras by the Nicaraguan peace accords in 1990. According to a study of the role of territorial autonomy in divided societies, however, "These zones were chosen not because the Contras controlled that territory or represented a majority group within those areas, but because the land was available for settlement" (Donald Rothchild and Caroline Hartzell, "Security in Deeply Divided Societies: The Role of Territorial Autonomy," *Nationalism and Ethnic Politics* 5, nos. 3–4 [autumn/winter 1999]: 261).
30. Incumbents in a subset of ethnic wars—typically colonial wars—attempt to recruit from the "enemy" ethnic group. This practice tends to reduce the reliability of ethnicity as a marker of loyalty over time (Kalyvas, "The Logic of Violence in Civil War").
31. John Mueller points out that people often face the choice of "being dominated by vicious bigots of one's own ethnic group or by vicious bigots of another ethnic group: Given that range of alternatives, the choice was easy" (John Mueller, "The Banality of Ethnic War," *International Security* 25, no. 1 [summer 2000]: 56).

International Commission on Kosovo, "has left a trail of fear and insecurity, guilt and mistrust—emotions that cannot be easily allayed but which seek reassurance in the apparent certainties of ethnic identification."[32] "The result [of violence]," two scholars remark, "is a deeply divided society whose members may withdraw temporarily into their communal containers for life support."[33]

A final problem with negotiated settlements to civil conflicts that may be worse in ethnic wars is that the factor which, according to many analysts, is the prerequisite for a negotiated settlement—a "mutually hurting stalemate" or a balance of power—also makes a resumption of armed conflict more likely.[34] According to Robert Wagner, "because no combatant is able to disarm its adversaries, a settlement requires that all the adversaries retain some semblance of their organizational identities after the war, even if they are disarmed."[35] Ethnic groups are relatively enduring social formations, and thus can function as built-in organizations, especially in the wake of large-scale violence with an out-group that reinforces in-group identification. This ethnic organization is always available, and hence the start-up costs for returning to war may be lower when the conflict is ethnic in nature.[36]

How institutions for sharing and diffusing power are undermined. Power sharing, as proposed by Arend Lijphart (who terms it "consociational democracy"), calls for government by a cartel of elites from a country's ethnic groups in which power is exercised jointly, ministries and government funds are parceled out proportionally, groups have autonomy on ethnic issues, and all groups possess a minority veto on issues they deem threatening to their vital interests.[37]

32. The Independent International Commission on Kosovo (IICK), *The Follow-Up: Why Conditional Independence?* (November 2001), 4. This document updates and restates the findings of the commission's original publication, *The Kosovo Report* (October 2000), found at http://www.reliefweb.int/library/documents/thekosovoreport.htm.

33. Rothchild and Hartzell, "Security in Deeply Divided Societies," 256. The polarization of identity induced by violence, as these authors point out, declines over time: wartime levels of hostility do not remain constant forever. As discussed in the case studies below, however, uncertainty regarding the future political arrangements of the state and fear of what one's former adversary will do when unconstrained by a third party provides a rational reason for continuing to identify with ethnic kin.

34. The term is Zartman's; see, for example, I. William Zartman, "The Unfinished Agenda: Negotiating Internal Conflicts," in Licklider, *Stopping the Killing*, 24.

35. Robert Harrison Wagner, "The Causes of Peace," in ibid., 261.

36. For an explanation of ethnic competition along similar lines, see Robert H. Bates, "Modernization, Ethnic Competition, and the Rationality of Politics in Contemporary Africa," in *State Versus Ethnic Claims: African Policy Dilemmas*, ed. Donald Rothchild and Victor A. Olorunsola (Boulder: Westview Press, 1983), 152–71.

37. Lijphart, "Consociational Democracy," and Lijphart, "The Power-Sharing Approach," in Montville, *Conflict and Peacemaking in Multiethnic Societies*, 491–509. See also Sisk, *Power Sharing and International Mediation*.

After an ethnic civil war, however, the more trust and cooperation a political system demands from former adversaries after ethnic wars, the more likely it is to fail. The hostility and mistrust that pervade relations between groups after they have fought a war cause power sharing institutions to be gripped by gridlock. Moreover, power sharing systems often apportion power based on each group's percentage of the population, which makes them extraordinarily sensitive to demographic changes over time.

Regional autonomy is also increasingly recommended as a solution for ethnic conflict because it seemingly satisfies everybody: the ethnic group obtains greater self-rule and the state retains its unity. "The popularity of autonomy as a solution," writes Svante Cornell, "undoubtedly stems from its being one of the few conceivable compromise solutions in conflicts over the administrative control of a specific territory."[38] Unfortunately, this promise is not borne out in practice, as doubts about intentions hinder the implementation of regional autonomy and federalism following ethnic civil wars. From the perspective of the rebellious group, although the government is making concessions now, what prevents it from going back on its word in the future? Authoritarian governments have routinely impinged upon the prerogatives of autonomous regions,[39] but this problem is not unknown in democracies.[40] Moreover, distrust of the government among the rebellious group is often so pervasive that some group leaders reject even generous autonomy arrangements in favor of fighting on for full independence.[41] From the government's perspective,

---

38. Svante E. Cornell, "Autonomy as a Source of Conflict: Caucasian Conflicts in Theoretical Perspective," *World Politics* 54, no. 2 (January 2002): 247. See also Hartzell, Hoddie, and Rothchild, "Stabilizing the Peace After Civil War," 191. In an autonomous or federal solution, an ethnic group gains control of governmental structures that have both symbolic and practical power, fulfilling group aspirations for greater independence and providing members with tangible benefits, such as the ability to conduct business and education in the native tongue, keep more tax revenue at home, and access to expanded job opportunities in the regional bureaucracy that were previously unavailable. The difference between the two is that regional autonomy grants these powers only to the particular region in question whereas the rest of the state remains unitary, while in a federal solution all regions of the state are given substantial powers of self-government, a bicameral legislature is created at the center having an upper house in which the regions are represented equally regardless of population, and a judiciary is established to adjudicate disputes between the federal and regional authorities.

39. Sudanese president Jaafar al-Nimeiri frequently violated the details of the autonomy agreement that ended his government's civil war with the country's Christian South in 1972, finally provoking a new war by re-dividing the region into three provinces in 1983. See Kasfir, "Peacemaking and Social Cleavages in Sudan." Other examples of autocracies revoking autonomy agreements include Pakistan (Baluchistan, 1973) and Yugoslavia (Kosovo and Vojvodina, 1989).

40. India provides an example, as central authorities have repeatedly dissolved regional governments and instituted presidential rule to crack down on ethnic unrest. Thus, regional governments in India ultimately serve at the pleasure of New Delhi.

41. Stedman has coined the term spoilers to describe such actors: Stephen John Stedman, "Spoiler Problems in Peace Processes," *International Security* 22, no. 2 (fall 1997): 5–53.

state leaders fear that their ethnic opponent will use autonomy as a platform to make further demands, up to and including the right to secede,[42] and that granting autonomy to one group may prompt others to demand it as well, possibly provoking additional protests or armed rebellions.[43] Finally, autonomy provides an institutional base for ethnic groups that increases their ability and motivation to make further demands or launch a rebellion.[44]

Federalism, although institutionalized to a greater extent than a regional autonomy agreement, is sensitive to changes in the initial conditions of the federal bargain, problems that are made worse by the fear and uncertainty that follow a civil war. Should the majority group's demographic dominance in the region appear to be threatened by immigration of other ethnic groups, the chance increases that the majority group will either attack the minorities to drive them out, or try to secede from the state and hence gain control of its

42. See Alicia Levine, "Political Accommodation and the Prevention of Secessionist Violence," in Brown, *International Dimensions of Internal Conflict*, 332. Gurr ("Ethnic Warfare on the Wane," 56) argues that autonomy rarely leads groups to make greater demands, and is thus not a slippery slope toward independence.

43. Toft, *Geography of Ethnic Violence*, 26–29. For statistical support for this finding, see R. William Ayres and Stephen Saideman, "Is Separatism as Contagious as the Common Cold or as Cancer?" *Nationalism & Ethnic Politics* 6, no. 3 (autumn 2000): 91–113. State leaders thus usually prefer to oppose rebel groups militarily to discourage other secession-minded groups that might view the government's cutting a deal as a sign of weakness. Offers of autonomy to groups in traditionally unitary states can also provoke conflict within the government over the appropriateness of autonomy as a solution. See Keith B. Richburg, "France Split on Self-Rule for Corsica," *Washington Post*, 1 October 2000, A23.

44. As one scholar puts it, "The institution of autonomous regions is conducive to secessionism because institutionalizing and promoting the separate identity of a titular group increases that group's cohesion and *willingness* to act, and establishing political institutions increases the *capacity* of that group to act" (Cornell, "Autonomy as a Source of Conflict," 252, emphasis in original). Following the collapse of communism in Eastern Europe, for example, the only states to undergo partition were federal ones: Yugoslavia, Czechoslovakia, and the Soviet Union. See Valerie Bunce, "Subversive Institutions: The End of the Soviet State in Comparative Perspective," *Post-Soviet Affairs* 14, no. 4 (October–December 1998): 323–54; Bunce, "Peaceful versus Violent State Dismemberment: A Comparison of the Soviet Union, Yugoslavia, and Czechoslovakia," *Politics & Society* 27, no. 2 (June 1999): 217–37; and Philip G. Roeder, "Soviet Federalism and Ethnic Mobilization," *World Politics* 43, no. 2 (January 1991): 196–232. This is because federal structures in those countries "provid[ed] an excellent organizational base for political leaders to exploit with nationalist appeals once the center began to weaken" (Robert H. Dorff, "Federalism in Eastern Europe: Part of the Solution or Part of the Problem?" *Publius* 24, no. 2 [spring 1994]: 104). Within the former Soviet republics in the Caucasus, moreover, regional autonomy was an excellent predictor of ethnic rebellion as those states became independent in the late 1980s/early 1990s (Cornell, "Autonomy as a Source of Conflict"). Regional autonomy also supplies the group with the experience of self-government, which by itself can be significant, and opens up "multiple, competing political arenas rather than a common political space" when states democratize. On the former, see Gail W. Lapidus and Edward W. Walker, "Nationalism, Regionalism, and Federalism: Center-Periphery Relations in Post-Communist Russia," in *The New Russia: Troubled Transformation*, ed. Gail W. Lapidus (Boulder: Westview, 1995), 87. For the latter, see Carol Skalnik Leff, "Democratization and Disintegration in Multinational States: The Breakup of the Communist Federations," *World Politics* 51, no. 2 (January 1999): 207.

immigration policy. Furthermore, conflict over the distribution of revenues within a federal system can induce grievances in both advanced and backward groups, advanced groups because they believe they are being forced to support backward regions, and deprived groups because they feel discriminated against or left behind.[45]

NEGOTIATED SETTLEMENTS IN ETHNIC CIVIL WARS: EMPIRICAL EVIDENCE

Negotiated settlements in general. Uncertainty regarding the intentions of one's adversary in the particularly dangerous environment of an internal armed conflict is responsible for the fact that military victories provide more stable endings to civil wars than do negotiated settlements.[46] The most current research on civil war termination finds that 77 percent of such conflicts that reach a conclusion end in decisive victory, compared to 23 percent that end in negotiated settlements.[47] Of these two types of war termination, decisive victories are more stable: only 12 percent of wars (4 of 42) ended in this way reignited, whereas 23 percent of negotiated settlements (3 of 13) broke down into renewed warfare.[48] Each of the three failures occurred in an ethnic civil war, however, and fully one-half (three of six) of the identity-based wars settled by negotiated agreements in Walter's dataset experienced further fighting.[49] This is similar

45. These dynamics were documented in the disintegration of the former Yugoslavia and Soviet Union. In Yugoslavia, Slovenia and Croatia were the more advanced republics, while the Baltic and Caucasian republics were relatively advanced in the Soviet Union. For details on Yugoslavia, see Susan L. Woodward, *Balkan Tragedy: Chaos and Dissolution After the Cold War* (Washington, D.C.: Brookings Institution, 1995); for the USSR, see Roeder, "Soviet Federalism and Ethnic Mobilization."

46. As Charles King puts it, "such attempts run against the tide of history" (King, *Ending Civil Wars*, 25).

47. Twenty-two percent remain unresolved. When these conflicts are included, decisive victories account for 60 percent and negotiated settlements 18 percent (Walter, *Committing to Peace*, 169–70).

48. Walter's full dataset may be found at http://www-irps.ucsd.edu/irps/faculty/bfwalter/data.html. I coded a war as having resumed if fighting broke out again between the same combatants over the same issues, whether within the five year limit generally used to define successful settlements or after. These codings were based on Licklider, "Consequences of Negotiated Settlements in Civil Wars," and Sambanis, "Partition as a Solution to Ethnic War." Monica Toft's work produces similar results: 60 percent of civil wars end in victory, 18 percent in negotiated agreements, and 9 percent in cease-fires or stalemates. Of these types of termination, 12 percent of the victories experienced renewed warfare whereas 29 percent of negotiated settlements broke down into war (as did 33 percent of cease-fires; Toft, "Peace Through Victory?" 9, 11).

49. The three failures are Lebanon (1958), Sudan (1972), Croatia (1992), while the three successes are Zimbabwe (1979), Mozambique (1992), and Bosnia (1995). Zimbabwe experienced a war (1982–87) after its negotiated settlement, but it was between former allies who turned against each other after settling with their common enemy. For more on such cases, see Pierre M. Atlas and Roy Licklider, "Conflict Among Former Allies After Civil War Settlement: Sudan, Zimbabwe, Chad, and Lebanon," *Journal of Peace Research* 36, no. 1 (January 1999): 35–54.

to Licklider's earlier finding that half of all negotiated settlements to civil wars broke down as compared to 15 percent of military victories. Again, however, every instance of a civil war starting again after a settlement was negotiated occurred in an ethnic war: two-thirds of negotiated settlements in ethnic wars failed to endure, compared to a failure rate of only 21 percent for decisive victories.[50]

Power sharing. Unsurprisingly, power sharing governments instituted after ethnic wars have generally failed eventually: agreements in Lebanon (1958 and 1978), Angola (1994), Chad (1979), and Sierra Leone (1999) all collapsed into renewed warfare between the same parties over the same issues.[51] The Arusha agreement in Rwanda (1993) failed before it could be implemented, as did the Nairobi agreement in Uganda (1985), while the success of deals in Bosnia (1995), Northern Ireland (1998), Burundi (2000), and Macedonia (2001) remains to be seen.

Autonomy and federalism. Nor does the empirical record support the assertion that autonomy or federalism lead to ethnic peace after civil wars. Kaufmann claimed eight successes for autonomy, but seven of these cases remain unresolved or experienced violence after autonomy was implemented.[52] Ted Gurr presents a more comprehensive dataset that documents 24 cases in which states granted autonomy to ethnically defined regions.[53] Examples of all three methods of self-government are present: autonomy for one region in a unitary state, creating a new federal region within a federation, or federalizing a unitary state. Of these 24 cases, however, only four resulted in a clear and lasting cessation of hostilities, and these four were mostly low-casualty cases, which is consistent with my argument that full-scale ethnic war makes negotiated single-state solutions unlikely.[54]

50. The failures in Licklider's dataset are Cyprus (1964), India (1948, 1965), Lebanon (1958, 1976), and Sudan (1972); the successes are Chad (1987), Cyprus (1974), and Zimbabwe (1984). No ideological civil wars re-started no matter how they were settled (Licklider, "Consequences of Negotiated Settlements in Civil Wars," 688–89, 686). The failure rates for negotiated settlements in ethnic wars in Walter's and Licklider's data roughly coincide with the 58 percent rate I found in a previous work (Downes, "Holy Land Divided," 90). Although the codings of each particular analyst are somewhat different, the fact that they tend to converge in the same range gives us greater confidence in the finding (for a similar conclusion, see King, *Ending Civil Wars*, 25).
51. Walter (*Committing to Peace*, 94–95) found that unless accompanied by a third-party guarantee, power sharing failed to end civil wars in eight of ten cases.
52. Kaufmann, "Possible and Impossible Solutions," 160. Cases with violence continuing after autonomy are the Nagas and Tripuras vs. India, Basques vs. Spain, Palestinians vs. Israel, Moros vs. Philippines, Chittagong vs. Bangladesh, and Abkhazians vs. Georgia. The sole success is the Miskito Indians vs. Nicaragua.
53. Gurr, *Peoples versus States*, 198–202.
54. The four successes are Mizos vs. India, Miskitos vs. Nicaragua, Gagauz vs. Moldova, and Tuaregs vs. Mali. Chittagong vs. Bangladesh (1997, different from the 1989 agreement

Statistical analyses have produced conflicting results regarding the efficacy of federalism as a means of conflict prevention. Two studies using the Minorities at Risk (MAR) dataset found that countries with federal systems experienced greater levels of non-violent protest but lesser intensities of violent rebellion.[55] A third study, however—also using the MAR data—found federalism to have no significant impact on rebellion, a finding confirmed by a fourth study using states rather than groups as the unit of analysis and civil war onset as the dependent variable.[56] Considering the known issues of selection bias in the MAR dataset,[57] and the fact that no study has specifically examined the impact of federalism instituted after a civil war, this debate should be considered as yet unresolved.

---

cited in note 52) was originally counted as a success, but I recoded it as a failure owing to the fact that the government has failed to implement the autonomy provisions of the peace agreement, which has sparked renewed violence. See Sharier Khan, "Hill Violence Threatens Bangladesh Peace Treaty," *OneWorld.net* at http://www.oneworld.net/article/view/76728/1. Of the 20 non-successes, low-level conflict continued in three; serious conflict erupted after autonomy was granted in two; serious conflict resumed after a period of inactivity in six; and serious conflict continued with no cessation in seven. Two others were suppressed by third party occupation, hence no judgment is possible (Downes, "Holy Land Divided," 94–96). Several studies, however, have found that the inclusion of autonomy in a negotiated settlement reduces the likelihood of the country experiencing another conflict (Hartzell, "Explaining the Stability of Negotiated Settlements," 15–18, Rothchild and Hartzell, "Security in Deeply Divided Societies," 266–67, and Hartzell, Hoddie, and Rothchild, "Stabilizing the Peace After Civil War," 196–201). These datasets, however, are flawed for two reasons. First, they include far more negotiated settlements than previous studies because they code any war that ended after a process of negotiations as a negotiated settlement no matter what the battlefield outcome. This problem leads the authors to code several stalemates or military victories as negotiated settlements, which in turn causes a number of false positives for autonomy as these victories or deadlocks have proven stable (examples include Azerbaijan 1994 [Nagorno-Karabakh], Croatia 1995, and Georgia 1992 and 1994 [South Ossetia and Abkhazia]). Second, the coding rules are biased in favor of agreement success: negotiated settlements that broke down into war after more than five years are excluded, as are settlements in which the parties did not fully implement the agreement (the 1993 Arusha Accords in Rwanda are excluded, for example).

55. Frank S. Cohen, "Proportional Versus Majoritarian Ethnic Conflict Management in Democracies," *Comparative Political Studies* 30, no. 5 (October 1997): 625; and Stephen M. Saideman et al., "Democratization, Political Institutions, and Ethnic Conflict: A Pooled Time-Series Analysis," *Comparative Political Studies* 35, no. 1 (February 2002): 118–20. The first of these studies examined only democracies and did not control for wealth. The second study controlled for income but found that federalism in democracies had no significant effect on rebellion, contradicting the earlier analysis. Moreover, the authors of the second study note that federalism was sensitive to changes in other variables in the model (ibid., 120n34).

56. Alexander B. Downes, "Federalism and Ethnic Rebellion: A Quantitative Analysis" (unpub. ms., University of Chicago, May 2000); and James D. Fearon and David D. Laitin, "Ethnicity, Insurgency, and War," (unpub. ms., Stanford University, 30 March 2000), 30.

57. The unit of analysis in the MAR dataset is the ethnic group, but not all ethnic groups are included, and the sample that is included is not random. Groups must have suffered or benefited from discrimination in the past or present, or be politically mobilized to make it into the study (Gurr, *Minorities at Risk*, 6–7). These criteria probably bias the sample toward higher levels of conflict.

IMPLICATIONS

Clearly negotiated settlements to civil wars are rare, and such agreements in ethnic civil wars seem quite prone to failure. Power sharing, regional autonomy, and federalism succeed only rarely in preventing the recurrence of ethnic wars. Decisive military victories in ethnic civil wars, on the other hand, almost never result in a recurrence of serious armed conflict. This evidence suggests solutions to identity wars based on decisive victory for one group, leading either to the consolidation of control over the original state—or a new state created by partition—are likely to be more stable than those based on efforts to divide or disperse power among formerly warring groups in one state.

This study, therefore, implies a very different intervention strategy by international actors. If the IC values stability—defined as the absence of war—it should allow or assist governments or rebels to win civil wars decisively.[58] Depending on the objective of the group, military victory can result in one state or two. In the former case, victory is more stable because it resolves uncertainty regarding the relative strength of the contending parties and establishes the dominance of one over the other.[59] "An unpleasant truth often overlooked," remarks Edward Luttwak, "is that although war is a great evil, it does have a great virtue: it can resolve political conflicts and lead to peace."[60] Unlike a negotiated settlement, which preserves both parties and leaves uncertain the true balance of power between them, when one side conclusively overwhelms its opponent, there is little room for uncertainty about their relative strength. This outcome makes a renewed challenge unlikely.

Should the goal of the victorious group be secession, on the other hand, decisive victory will result in multiple states. In this case, partition should provide independence for relatively homogeneous states and attempt to draw defensible borders and establish a balance of power between them. Independence eliminates the military and political uncertainties that plague solutions to ethnic war short of partition (detailed below), does not require the parties to trust each other, and satisfies nationalist desires and desires for security induced by war.[61] Moreover, working to draw defensible borders and ensure a

58. I defend this controversial recommendation further in the article's conclusion.

59. Wagner, "Causes of Peace," in Licklider, ed., *Stopping the Killing*, 260-63; and Toft, "Peace Through Victory?" 31–32.

60. Edward N. Luttwak, "Give War a Chance," *Foreign Affairs* 78, no. 4 (July/August 1999): 36.

61. While Kaufmann agrees that formal partition will often accompany demographic separation in practice, he does not prefer independent states, arguing instead that autonomy is sufficient once separation is achieved (Kaufmann, "Possible and Impossible Solutions," 162; and "When All Else Fails," 123n7). Kaufmann offers no theoretical basis for this assertion, however; his argument is grounded solely in demography, not institutions.

balance of power reduces the danger should one side repudiate the agreement by making it harder for each party to mount a successful attack and reverse the verdict of partition.[62]

WILL THEY SUCCEED? CASE STUDIES OF NEGOTIATED SETTLEMENTS IN BOSNIA AND KOSOVO

The remainder of the article demonstrates the plausibility of my argument by focusing on two prominent recent cases in which the IC implemented or is trying to implement single-state negotiated solutions to ethnic civil wars: Bosnia and Kosovo. I chose these cases because they represent easy cases for other arguments. Bosnia's civil war ended in a negotiated settlement that established a highly institutionalized framework including both federal and extensive power sharing provisions, is enforced by a robust third-party military presence, and came at a time when both parties knew they could not decisively win the war. The Kosovo war ended when Serbia agreed to pull its military forces out of the embattled province following NATO's airborne intervention. The alliance, however, never unambiguously endorsed the population's separatist aspirations, and has sought since the war to retain the province as an autonomous unit in Serbia.[63] Intervention in both cases, therefore, took place to bring about negotiated settlements. Finally, ethnic intermingling was largely eliminated by war in both Bosnia and Kosovo, thus fulfilling Kaufmann's criteria for post-war stability. To the extent that we observe problems even in these post-conflict situations, my argument gains strength.[64]

Four observable propositions for behavior flow from the uncertainty about intentions and concerns for physical and political security described above that I trace through the cases. First, groups will prove recalcitrant when it comes time to lay down their arms. Even if separated from each other and with a third party present, groups want to keep an insurance policy to protect themselves when the intervener departs because that is when they will be most vulnerable. This security fear is compounded by uncertainty regarding how political institutions will function and whether they will protect the group's vital interests.

---

62. For a more detailed exposition of the argument for partition, see Downes, "Holy Land Divided," 74–77.

63. Technically, Kosovo would be part of the "Union of Serbia and Montenegro," as of February 2003 the successor to Yugoslavia.

64. It should be noted, however, that the length and intensity of the Bosnian war, and the long history of Albanian dissent and Serb repression in Kosovo, makes these cases relatively strong ones for my argument as well.

Second, past experiences of war and uncertainty regarding future military and political security solidifies support for nationalism, ensuring that nationalist politicians and parties will dominate the political dialogue. Even if they did not enter the war bent on secession, groups often come to believe that the only way they can assure their survival is by acquiring their own state. Furthermore, compared to the dangers inherent in placing its safety in the hands of a former adversary, or the uncertainty of how power will be divided in a state of autonomies, an ethnic group may find its own state attractive.

Third, fears about the future increase the likelihood that statewide institutions will devolve into deadlock. Both sides will be suspicious that autonomy agreements will not be respected, while power sharing, which requires far more trust and cooperation, is even more susceptible to the effects of mistrust. Ironically, international intervention and administration only exacerbates this problem because the institutions established by the agreement will never have had to function. Thus, no one knows if they will actually work.

Finally, groups will oppose the return to their territory of members of the enemy group displaced by the fighting. These returnees are the object of war-generated hatred and are liable to have their return blocked by protests or be attacked once they come home. Moreover, minority returns are particularly difficult because the houses of those who fled are often occupied by members other ethnic groups (usually the locally dominant one) who have been turned out of their homes in other regions of the country. Minority returns also increase competition for employment and economic resources and, if they occur in large numbers, can threaten the local majority's demographic dominance. Lastly, returnees are vulnerable to re-cleansing should the agreement break down or its international enforcers depart. A return to a true multiethnic society after the war, therefore, is unlikely.

BOSNIA

The problems inherent to, and in the implementation of, the Dayton Peace Agreement (DPA) that ended the Bosnian War have been amply documented.[65] The DPA is an agreement at war with itself: unable to avoid a deal based on

---

65. See, for example, Ivo H. Daalder, "Bosnia After SFOR: Options for Continued US Engagement," *Survival* 39, no. 4 (winter 1997/98): 5–18; Jane M.O. Sharp, "Dayton Report Card," *International Security* 22, no. 3 (winter 1997/98): 101–37; Charles G. Boyd, "Making Bosnia Work," *Foreign Affairs* 77, no. 1 (January/February 1998): 42–55; Gideon Rose, "The Exit Strategy Delusion," *Foreign Affairs* 77, no. 1 (January/February 1998): 56–67; Warren Bass, "The Triage of Dayton," *Foreign Affairs* 77, no. 5 (September/October, 1998): 95–108; Michael O'Hanlon, "Turning the Bosnia Cease-Fire into Peace," *Brookings Review* 16, no. 1 (winter 1998): 41–44; Gary Dempsey, *Rethinking the Dayton Agreement: Bosnia Three Years Later* (Washington, D.C.: Cato Institute, 1998); Ivo H. Daalder and Michael B.G. Froman, "Dayton's Incomplete Peace," *Foreign*

ethnically-defined entities, but unwilling to abandon the ideal of a multiethnic Bosnia, Western negotiators incorporated aspects of both into the final settlement. Thus, the DPA accepted the verdict of the war—partition and ethnic cleansing—but at the same time sought to reverse it through power sharing and refugee return. The result has been gridlock: a large portion of the Croats in Herzegovina have left for Croatia;[66] most Bosnian Croats and Serbs do not wish for their regions to remain part of Bosnia;[67] nationalist parties dominate the electoral process; and federal institutions function poorly, with Bosnia's international administrators repeatedly stepping in to dictate contentious decisions. Three separate military forces exist on Bosnian soil, and hundreds of thousands of Bosnian refugees and internally displaced persons remain dislocated from their homes. Returns to areas where the returnees would be in the minority have been especially slow; although the pace has quickened lately, it mainly comprises old people returning to destroyed villages in isolated areas. In sum, according to David Chandler, "The extended mandates of the international implementation of the Dayton settlement, which have undermined all the main parties, have not created a political basis for a unitary Bosnian state, except in so far as it is one artificially imposed by the international community."[68] "It thus remains the case," agrees the International Crisis Group (ICG), "that were it not for the significant international presence in Bosnia, and especially the NATO presence, the Dayton Peace Accords would rapidly unravel."[69] After nine years under international tutelage, peace in Bosnia is still not self-sustaining.

The Dayton framework. The initialing of the DPA in November 1995 officially ended three and a half years of war.[70] The agreement created a federal state

Affairs 78, no. 6 (November/December 1999): 106–13; Elizabeth M. Cousens and Charles K. Cater, *Toward Peace in Bosnia: Implementing the Dayton Accords* (Boulder: Lynne Rienner Publishers, 2001); and Sumantra Bose, *Bosnia After Dayton: Nationalist Partition and International Intervention* (New York: Oxford University Press, 2002).

66. The Croat share of Bosnia's population, approximately 17 percent before the war, was estimated in 1999 at 8 percent and falling. See International Crisis Group (ICG), *Preventing Minority Return in Bosnia and Herzegovina: The Anatomy of Hate and Fear* (Sarajevo: August 1999), 3. All of the ICG reports referenced in this article are available at ICG's website, http://www.crisisweb.org.

67. A survey of Serb university students in 2000 found that 74 percent preferred either independence for the Serb region of Bosnia or union with Serbia. See ICG, *Bosnia's November Elections: Dayton Stumbles* (Sarajevo: December 2000), 19. Similarly, in a referendum in November 2000, 99 percent of the Bosnian Croats who voted (turnout was 71 percent) supported the creation of a "third entity" that would be dominated by Bosnian Croats and which eventually might join Croatia proper (Bose, *Bosnia After Dayton*, 29).

68. David Chandler, *Bosnia: Faking Democracy After Dayton*, 2nd ed. (London: Pluto, 2000), 197.

69. ICG, *Bosnia's November Elections*, ii.

70. The best work on the war's origins, conduct, and endgame is Steven L. Burg and Paul S. Shoup, *The War in Bosnia-Herzegovina: Ethnic Conflict and International Intervention* (Armonk, N.Y.: M. E. Sharpe, 1999).

composed of two autonomous entities—a Bosniak/Croat Federation (FBIH) and a Serb republic (Republika Srpska, or RS)—under a weak central government. The presidency consists of one member from each of the three ethnic groups, and each group can exercise a minority veto in the presidency or the legislature if it deems a measure harmful to its vital interests. Most ambitiously, Annex 7 of the DPA calls for all refugees displaced by the war to have the right to return to their former homes in areas where they would now comprise an ethnic minority. It is this provision that is at the heart of the IC's vision for Bosnia, since returning refugees to their pre-war homes will reintegrate the ethnically homogeneous regions that emerged from the war, thereby recreating a multiethnic state and preventing the *de facto* ethnic partition of Bosnia.

NATO, led by the United States, sent a 60,000-strong military implementation force (IFOR) to implement the terms of the agreement, initially intended to complete its work and withdraw after one year. IFOR metamorphosized into SFOR (Stabilization Force) in November 1996 as little progress toward integration occurred. Originally scheduled to pull out after eighteen months, SFOR's mandate was extended indefinitely in June 1998. SFOR was replaced by a 7,000-stong European Union force (EUFOR) in December 2004.[71]

The civilian implementation of Dayton is presided over by the Office of the High Representative (OHR). Annex 10 to the agreement grants OHR a sweeping mandate as the "final authority in theater regarding interpretation of this Agreement on the civilian implementation of the peace settlement."[72] Originally scheduled to give way to a Bosnian government after elections in September 1996, OHR's mandate was extended from one to three years in November of that year, and later (June 1998) prolonged indefinitely. The High Representative, initially empowered only to coordinate international activities, facilitate the efforts of the parties, and promote compliance with the agreement, was granted vastly increased authority in 1997 by the Peace Implementation Council (PIC) to recommend and, later, even formulate policy on his own when the parties could not agree, and to dismiss officials deemed to be obstructing implementation of the agreement.[73]

Reluctance to disarm. Despite this robust security and institutional environment, anxiety about the future has led each of Bosnia's ethnic groups to refrain from dismantling and integrating their armies. Bosnia's military is now legally integrated at the top as a result of reforms in 2003 and 2004, but in

---

71. See http://www.euforbih.org.
72. *The Dayton Peace Accords: General Framework Agreement for Peace in Bosnia and Herzegovina,* Annex 10, Article V, available at OHR's website, http://www.ohr.int.
73. The PIC is the international body, composed of representatives of the major Western countries, that oversees implementation of the DPA.

reality remains divided into the Army of the Federation of BiH (the VF, with, 13,200 troops) and the Army of the Republika Srpska (VRS, 6,600 troops). The Federation Army is further divided into a Bosniak component (VF-B) and a Bosnian-Croat component (VF-H). Bosniaks and Croats serve in separate corps and "only at the headquarters is the VF [Federation Army] manned with officers and soldiers of the two components."[74]

Establishing a single, integrated Bosnian military is a crucial aspect of unifying Bosnia, but progress toward this objective has been slow. In 1998, the PIC noted with displeasure the "lack of real progress toward improving the level of co-operation and confidence between the Entity Armed Forces (and within the Federation army)," and warned that "it is important to do everything possible to minimize the instability that is inherent in having two—and in practice three—armies present in one country."[75] Reports in 2000 indicated that the Bosnian Serbs remained implacably opposed to unifying their army with that of the Federation. "Talk of creating a single Bosnian army," said the *Economist*, "wins a hearing from some Muslims, but from few Croats or Serbs."[76] Despite formally integrating its command structure with that of the Federation army in 2004, the VRS remains largely independent and opposed to a real merger.[77] The VRS, for example, apparently kept its former leader and fugitive war criminal Ratko Mladić on the payroll until 2002, and sheltered him at a military facility as late as 2004.[78] This lack of military integration—and the failure of the VRS to cooperate with the International Criminal Tribunal for the former Yugoslavia in handing over wanted war criminals—caused NATO to reject Bosnia's application to join the Partnership for Peace program in December 2004 for the second time.

Underscoring the division within FBiH forces, in late March 2001 virtually all of Bosnia's Croat soldiers walked out of their barracks in support of the revolt for Croat self-rule then underway.[79] Although most eventually returned, this

74. Sgt. Peter Fitzgerald, "The Armed Forces in Bosnia and Herzegovina," SFOR *Informer On-line* no. 127, 28 November 2001 http://www.nato.int.sfor/indexinf/127/content.htm. The VF and VRS are in the process of reducing their numbers to 8,000 and 4,000, respectively (SFOR, *Main News Summary*, 4 February 2004, at http://www.nato.int/sfor/media/2004/ms040204.htm).
75. Peace Implementation Council, "Part VII: Military and Security Issues," *Annex to the Madrid Declaration of the Peace Implementation Council* (Madrid, Spain: 16 December 1998), at http://www.ohr.int/pic/default.asp?content_id=5191.
76. "The Delicate Balkan Balance," *The Economist*, 19 August 2000, 42.
77. Nicholas Wood, "Bosnian Serb Premier Quits, Criticizing West," *New York Times*, 18 December 2004, A5.
78. OHR Press Release, "High Representative Maps Out Process to Tackle War Criminal Networks and to Reform BiH's Security Institutions," at http://www.ohr.int/ohr-dept/presso/pressr/default.asp?content_id=33742.
79. Nick Thorpe, "Croatian Soldiers Mutiny in Bosnia," *The Guardian* (London), 29 March 2001, 17.

protest highlights the fragility of Bosnia's armed forces and the widespread sympathy of the Croat component for Croat nationalism. "Six years after the end of the war in BiH and seven and a half years after the end of the Muslim-Croat armed conflict," remarks Sumantra Bose, "the Federation's armed forces are formally integrated, with a standard uniform for personnel and insignia reflecting the national symbols of both Croats and Bosniacs. In practice, however, erstwhile HVO [Croatian Defense Council] and Armija BiH units exist more or less separately within this nominally unified force, and despite the appearance of a 'joint command', there is little scope for illusions."[80]

The fact that each of Bosnia's ethnic groups remains armed increases the probability that the internationals leave, the political gridlock that is likely to grip Bosnia will be backed up by force. Bosniaks, Croats, and Serbs fear disarming because of their political insecurity, but the fact of their separate armies makes it clear that no Bosnian government will be able to enforce its will over the state's territory. This de facto partition would become formal as soon as a political dispute leads to disagreement between the groups. Refugees who have returned under the DPA's auspices to areas where they constitute minorities may be re-cleansed. Thus, the DPA's autonomous solution could relapse into war should EUFOR ever leave.

Support for nationalist parties. Support for nationalist parties is fed by fears for security and uncertainty regarding the intentions of other groups. Even though separation is largely a fact and the country is occupied by foreign soldiers, state institutions are weak and the autonomy of Serb and Croat areas questionable: "Political insecurities are still rife as to the political autonomy of the Serb entity and the Croat areas of the Federation, and the central political authority of the state remains very weak with state authority as reliant on outside support as when Bosnian recognition was called for in 1991."[81] This political insecurity, and doubts about the future viability of the state's political institutions, lead people to cast their lot with nationalist parties and the hope of ethnically homogeneous states: "The overwhelming concern for Bosnian people is security, the two entities and the state itself have been established on very weak foundations and there is little guarantee that current arrangements, as they stand, will last past international withdrawal. The lack of political security has, in effect, guaranteed continuing support for the three main nationalist parties despite disillusionment with their leaderships."[82]

80. Bose, *Bosnia After Dayton*, 77–78.
81. Chandler, *Bosnia*, 160.
82. Ibid., 195.

Unsurprisingly, nationalist parties have performed strongly in Bosnia's post-war elections. The DPA decreed that elections would take place within nine months of the agreement entering into force, a provision driven by the scheduled withdrawal of IFOR after one year.[83] The results of the voting were a severe setback for the IC's vision of a multiethnic Bosnia. In the balloting for the Parliamentary Assembly, the three principal nationalist parties—the Muslim Party for Democratic Action (SDA), led by wartime president Alija Izetbegović, the Croatian Democratic Union (HDZ), and the Serb Democratic Party (SDS), headed by indicted war criminal Radovan Karadžić—captured 86 percent (36 of 42) of the seats.[84] These three parties also dominated the entity assemblies.[85] Rather than pave the way for a return to a multiethnic Bosnia, the 1996 elections "turned into a glorified ethnic head count ... As in 1990 [Bosnia's first elections], Croats voted for Croats, Serbs for Serbs, and Bosniaks for Bosniaks."[86] Two analysts of Bosnia describe the results as follows:

> As [OSCE chairman] Cotti and others had noted, indicted war criminals still dominated political life, opposition politician figures had been targets of attack, freedom of media and of movement was minimal, civilians who belonged to minority communities were subject to systematic violence and intimidation by authorities, and brute uncertainty prevailed among Bosnia's residents and its refugees about whether their country could be rebuilt as one or would be split into three. In short, Bosnia's climate was one of such manifest insecurity that the rational vote for people to cast was for the nationalist parties, which most reliably, if narrowly, had always promised to protect their interests.[87]

The dominance of ethnic parties changed little in the municipal elections of September 1997: nationalist parties won 129 out of the 136 municipalities that their group controlled militarily, and took 90 percent of the vote

83. The Organization for Security and Cooperation in Europe (OSCE) was designated to organize and oversee the balloting, but it was "overwhelmed" by and "unprepared" for the task. Moreover, conditions in the country were far from ideal: refugee return had not yet begun, intimidation and fraud were rampant, and nationalist propaganda dominated the airwaves. See Paul Shoup, "The Elections in Bosnia and Herzegovina: The End of an Illusion," *Problems of Post-Communism* 44, no. 1 (January-February 1997), 7, 10. OSCE chair Flavio Cotti initially refused to certify that free and fair elections were possible. Under heavy pressure from the US, though, Cotti reversed himself and the elections went forward (Cousens and Cater, *Toward Peace in Bosnia*, 113–14).
84. Chandler, *Bosnia*, 70.
85. Between them, the SDA and HDZ garnered 80.7 percent of the votes for the FBiH Parliament, while the SDA, SDS, and SRS (Serb Radical Party, an ultra-nationalist party led by Vojislav Šešelj), took 78.3 percent of the votes for the RS Assembly (ibid., 72, 75).
86. ICG, *Is Dayton Failing?: Bosnia Four Years After the Peace Agreement* (Sarajevo: 28 October 1999), 13.
87. Cousens and Cater, *Toward Peace in Bosnia*, 115.

country-wide.[88] The ethnic parties that wanted to preserve the homogeneity of their territory—the SDS and HDZ—pressured their Serb and Croat displaced voters to register where they currently lived, or in towns where a large absentee Bosniak vote was expected, while the party that had the most to gain from refugee return—the SDA—pressured displaced Bosniaks to vote in their pre-war places of residence.[89] Responding to these pressures, displaced Serbs voted overwhelmingly in their new municipalities, whereas Bosniaks voted where they used to live.[90]

The IC's hopes for Bosnia received another setback in the general elections of September 1998. International officials had swung their support behind "moderate" RS president Biljana Plavšić after her split with the SDS's hard-line leadership in Pale.[91] Unfortunately, Plavšić went down to defeat at the hands of the Serb Radical Party's Nikola Poplasen, a wartime paramilitary leader. IC support for Plavšić was reported to be a significant factor in her defeat.[92] Together the nationalist parties (including the SRS) won 69 percent of the votes for the BiH House of Representatives. At the entity level, nationalist parties won 57 percent of the ballots for the RS Assembly and 69 percent for the FBiH Assembly. In addition, opinion polling done in 1998 by the United States Information Agency (USIA) showed that 92 percent of Serbs in the RS believed that their region should leave Bosnia, while 74 percent of Bosnian Croats held the same preference.[93]

The year 2000 was supposed to be the year in which non-ethnic parties would break through in Bosnia. Although the non-nationalist Social Democratic Party (SDP) did make significant gains in the Federation, elections in 2000 also

88. ICG, *Is Dayton Failing?*, 14; and Michael Pugh and Margaret Cobble, "Non-Nationalist Voting in the Bosnian Municipal Elections: Implications for Democracy and Peacebuilding," *Journal of Peace Research* 38, no. 1 (January 2001): 34.
89. ICG, *Is Dayton Failing?*, 13–14.
90. Pugh and Cobble, "Non-Nationalist Voting in the Bosnian Municipal Elections," 31, 39.
91. A special election took place in the RS in November 1997 after president Biljana Plavšić dissolved the RS Assembly. Owing to the split in the SDS caused by Plavšić's defection and subsequent formation of the Serb People's Alliance (SNS), the SDS lost its parliamentary majority. In the ensuing struggle to form a government, Plavšić—with the connivance of the IC—succeeded in excluding the SDS and SRS. Plavšić proposed Milorad Dodik for prime minister, head of the Independent Social Democrats (SNSD), which had garnered only two seats. When the nationalist parties adjourned the session for the night on 17 January 1998 and walked out, those remaining reconvened the session, and SFOR intercepted a legislator who had headed home but who was needed to provide a majority for Dodik.
92. ICG, *Is Dayton Failing?*, 15. Although she was embraced by the West and trumpeted as a moderate, Plavšić was later indicted and convicted of war crimes by ICTY and is currently serving an eleven-year sentence. Poplasen, who defeated her in the 1998 balloting, was removed from office by High Representative Carlos Westendorp for obstructing the DPA's implementation in March 1999.
93. United States Information Agency, *Public Opinion in Bosnia and Herzegovina*, Vol. V (Washington, D.C.: Office of Research and Media Reaction, 1998), 35–37.

showed the resilience of the nationalist parties in general and the resurgence of the SDS in particular. In the municipal elections, held in April, the SDS captured forty-nine out of sixty-one municipalities in the RS, whereas the "moderate" Serb parties, Dodik's SNSD and Plavšić's SNS, took a total of but seven.[94] In Croat areas of the Federation, although voter turnout was down, the HDZ took majorities in all municipalities except Zepce (where it boycotted) and Glamoč (where it only gained a plurality due to high levels of Bosniak absentee voting). Elsewhere in the Federation, the moderate SDP took the most votes in eighteen municipalities, but the SDA, alone or in combination with wartime prime minister Haris Silajdžić's Party for Bosnia and Herzegovina (SBiH, a moderate ethnic party), won in thirty-nine.[95] Thus, nationalist parties dominated in both Serb and Croat areas, and retained significant strength in Bosniak areas, winning two-thirds of those municipalities.[96]

In the general elections held in November 2000, the main ethnic parties again dominated Serb and Croat regions, and remained strong among Bosniaks. In the RS, the SDS won the races for RS president and vice-president and formed the largest party in the Assembly, where it later came to power as part of a coalition with new prime minister Mladen Ivanić's Party of Democratic Progress (PDP). The HDZ again obtained an absolute majority among Croat voters, while the Bosniaks split their support among three parties: the SDA, SDP, and the SBiH.[97] The more moderate parties in Parliament (the Alliance for Change, led by the SDP and SBiH), however, were eventually able to form a coalition government that excluded the SDA and HDZ.[98] While the results of this election showed that the Bosniaks had retreated somewhat from their support for hard-line nationalists, it also demonstrated the continuing commitment of Bosnian Croats and Serbs to nationalist parties, democratic changes in Croatia and Serbia notwithstanding. As ICG put it, "The elections highlighted once again the near complete failure—in the face of determined nationalist extremism—of an international approach that places emphasis on hopes

94. ICG, *Bosnia's Municipal Elections 2000: Winners and Losers* (Sarajevo: April 2000), 14. This strong nationalist showing is even more notable given that the OSCE barred the SRS from participating.
95. The SDA won alone in twenty-four municipalities, and in coalition with SBiH in fifteen others.
96. It should be noted that the SDP's appeal is limited to the Bosniak area of the federation; the party did not obtain a significant percentage of votes in any municipality where Bosnian Croats or Serbs constituted a majority.
97. The SDA and SDP finished neck-and-neck in both the Bosnian and Federation Assemblies with the SBiH trailing about ten points behind.
98. This coalition, which included ten moderate parties, fell apart in June 2002 and did not contest the October election as a group.

that moderate, co-operative Bosnian partners will come to power through elections."[99]

A strong resurgence of nationalist parties—especially the SDA among Bosniaks—and the consequent decline of non-nationalist parties characterized the October 2002 elections. Despite open support for "moderate" parties from Bosnia's international sponsors, and grave warnings regarding the consequences of voting nationalist,[100] Bosnian voters handed all of the country's major offices to nationalists, and made nationalist parties the largest in the state's various representative bodies. The SDA candidate for the Bosniak member of the presidency, Sulejman Tihić, upset the favored Silajdžić of the SBiH; the SDA obtained as many votes for the state and entity-level House of Representatives as the SBiH and SDP combined; and the SDA won more seats than its two competitors in eight of the nine cantonal assemblies in which Bosniak parties obtained seats.[101] The SDA's rise came mostly at the expense of the SDP, which saw its vote share decline significantly from its performance in 2000.[102] The HDZ continued its dominance of the Bosnian Croat electorate, easily winning the presidency and receiving by far the largest share of Croat votes for the two Parliaments.[103] Finally, the SDS swept the Serb high offices, winning the RS presidency, the Serb slot on the state presidency, and the largest number of seats in the state House of Representatives and the RS National Assembly.[104] None of this changed in the October 2004 municipal elections: the three nationalist parties won control over 99 of the country's 122 municipalities.[105]

---

99. ICG, *Bosnia's November Elections*, ii.

100. US Secretary of State Colin Powell, for example, warned on the eve of the election that Bosnians could vote for reform and integration into Europe, or "elect to go back down the dark and dangerous road to ethnic division, economic stagnation and international isolation." Quoted in Nicholas Wood, "Nationalists Take Lead in Bosnian Elections," *Washington Post*, 8 October 2002, A17. The US then refused to work with the nationalist government.

101. Election results for 2002 may be accessed at http://www.izbori.ba.

102. The SDP candidate for the state presidency, for example, came in a distant third behind the SDA's Tihić and Silajdžić of the SBiH with about 17.5 percent of the vote, and the SDP now ranks third among parties which draw their primary support from the Bosniak population.

103. The HDZ's Dragan Čović won the presidency slot with 61.5 percent of the vote, while the party formed the second largest bloc in both the state and entity House of Representatives with five and sixteen seats, respectively.

104. Dragan Cavić became the RS president, and Mirko Sarović won the Serb spot on the country's presidency, although he was forced to resign in 2003 after a scandal over selling weapons to Iraq. Overall, the nationalist parties combined obtained about 45 percent of the vote. See OSCE Office for Democratic Institutions and Human Rights, *Bosnia and Herzegovina: General Elections, 5 October 2002, Final Report* (Warsaw: 9 January 2003), 20, at http://www.osce.org/documents/odihr/2003/01/1188_en.pdf. Former RS prime minister Milorad Dodik's more moderate party, the SNSD, did make a comeback, however, and is now the second largest party after the SDS among Serbs after polling about 22 percent in the various races.

105. See the European Forum for Democracy and Solidarity web page on Bosnia, at http://www.europeanforum.net/country_updates/bosnia_herzegovina_update.

Clearly, support for nationalist parties remains strong almost ten years after the war's end. In fact, there are essentially no parties in Bosnia today with a cross-ethnic base, a crucial integrating factor deemed necessary by many analysts for multiethnic democracies to be successful. The closest contender for such status is the SDP, but, as Sumantra Bose points out, "90% of the total SDP vote [in the November 2000 election] came from the five predominantly Bosniac cantons of the Muslim-Croat federation ... the conclusion is inescapable that the vast majority of SDP supporters are Bosniacs."[106] Even worse, all efforts by the IC to foster cross-ethnic voting have failed. Minority returns, although increasing, will never restore meaningful ethnic heterogeneity to the RS, for example, which means that incentives for Serb parties to appeal to voters of other ethnicities to defeat rival Serb parties are absent.

Moreover, attempts to engineer cross-ethnic voting through electoral mechanisms, such as the preferential voting system installed for the 2000 RS presidential election, have backfired. This system was meant to encourage Bosniak voters to indicate the moderate Serb candidate, Milorad Dodik, as their second or third choice for the office, thereby staving off a victory by the SDS slate. Unfortunately, it appears that Serbs voted in larger numbers for the SDS ticket as their first preference—58.5 percent of Serb voters in the RS chose the SDS, whereas the party obtained only 44 percent of the votes in the simultaneous parliamentary elections—in order to prevent a moderate Serb party from winning with the support of Bosniaks. Additionally, hardly any Bosniaks voted for Dodik as a secondary preference: almost all of them supported other Bosniak parties which, of course, stood no chance of winning.[107] Not only did the RS electorate strategically adapt to the altered voting environment, but Bosniak voters proved unwilling to select a Serb as even a secondary or tertiary choice. These two factors, combined with the segregated post-war demographic situation, render the prospects for cross-ethnic voting in Bosnia rather bleak.

Shared institutions or stalemate machines? Dayton established an intricate system of political institutions designed to share power at the state level, and also within the Bosniak/Croat Federation.[108] Unfortunately, these byzantine arrangements more often lead to stalemate than compromise, as exemplified by the frequency with which the High Representative must break decision-making deadlocks, such as on the design of a new currency, a national flag and anthem, automobile license plates, or passports.[109]

---

106. Bose, *Bosnia After Dayton*, 209.
107. See ibid., 220–38, for an excellent analysis of this issue.
108. For a full description of Bosnia's institutional structure, see ibid., 60–89.
109. See "A Survey of the Balkans," *The Economist*, 7, Chandler, *Bosnia*, 64; and the OHR web page on the decisions of the High Representative in the area of state symbols and state-level matters, http://www.ohr.int/decisions/statemattersdec/archive.asp.

In fact, the only reason such squabbling has not derailed Dayton completely is that Bosnians themselves wield little actual power: the ultimate authority is OHR. Consider the following statement by former High Representative Wolfgang Petritsch in 2000: "Last fall I took two important measures designed to accelerate the return process. First, I imposed a package of reforms to the legislation governing property return in the two Entities . . . And second, I dismissed 22 public officials from across the country, who had a proven track record of obstructionism, particularly of Annex 7 of Dayton, the Annex governing refugee return."[110] This tendency to rule by decree has increased rather than decreased over time: the number of decisions imposed by High Representative Paddy Ashdown in 2004 was 158, up from 86 handed down by Petritsch in 2000.[111] Ashdown fired 59 RS officials in June 2004 (and 85 individuals overall)—including the interior minister and the president of the SDS—for failing to turn over suspected war criminals to ICTY.[112] A similar purge by Ashdown in December 2004 caused RS premier Dragan Mikerevic to resign rather than "accept and implement threats and ultimatums of the high representative."[113] Actions like these have led some analysts to conclude that "democratization" in Bosnia is not leading to actual democracy because "state and entity institutions exist largely on paper, with policy preparation and implementation in the hands of external agencies."[114] Ashdown, in his November 2004 report to the UN, acknowledged that state-level institutions lacked sufficient capacity to govern the country and needed to be strengthened "if the High Representative's executive powers are to be phased out and the transition to full domestic ownership completed."[115]

Clearly, Bosnia's political institutions are fragile, dependent on mutual trust, respect, and a cooperative spirit. Unfortunately, these qualities are largely absent in Bosnia, and thus these institutions regularly yield an ethnic stalemate. Moreover, when the international occupation and administration of Bosnia

---

110. *Speech by the High Representative, Wolfgang Petritsch, to the United Nations Security Council*, New York, 9 May 2000 (http://www.ohr.int/ohr-dept/presso/presssp/default.asp?content_id=3236).

111. See http://www.ohr.int/decisions/archive.asp.

112. Paddy Ashdown, *26th Report of the High Representative for Implementation of the Peace Agreement to the Secretary-General of the United Nations*, 18 November 2004, at http://www.ohr.int/other-doc/hr-reports/default.asp?content_id=33537.

113. Wood, "Bosnian Serb Premier Quits, Criticizing West."

114. Chandler, *Bosnia*, 204. Petritsch basically conceded this point in 1999: "But our presence here has inadvertently absolved them [Bosnian politicians] of their responsibilities as democratically elected leaders. We enable the local politicians to fight their tribalistic battles, and then to place the blame for potentially unpopular compromises squarely on the shoulders of foreigners. I call this the 'dependency syndrome'." Wolfgang Petritsch, "The Future of Bosnia Lies with its People," *Wall Street Journal Europe*, 17 September 1999, at http://www.ohr.int/ohr-dept/presso/pressa/default.asp?content_id=3188.

115. Ashdown, *26th Report of the High Representative*.

ends, these institutions stand a slim chance of functioning as planned because they have never had to. OHR has always intervened to impose a solution when the parties could not agree, a tendency that—as we have seen—has become more prevalent over time. Without this higher authority to break recurrent impasses, a tradition of collective problem solving, or extensive trust between community leaders, this system may collapse. Bosnia thus presents a clear example of the paradoxical effect that extensive intervention can have on local capacity: "On the one hand, in the name of efficiency it may make sense for the implementing agents to take over many of the functions of the state and play a pivotal role in the country. On the other hand, however, such actions may undermine the (already weak) capacity of the state, when one of the eventual aims of the peace process is capacity building."[116]

The contradiction of refugee returns. The four-year Bosnian war drove an estimated 2.1 million people from their homes—about half of the country's pre-war population—and resulted in near total ethnic segregation.[117] As the ICG has observed, "The key to the successful implementation of the DPA is the ability of refugees to return to their pre-war place of occupancy."[118] Reconstructing a multiethnic Bosnia, and preventing the solidification of ethnic partition, requires that people be encouraged to return to areas where they would now be an ethnic minority.[119] The record of returns, however, shows that refugees have not gone back to their old homes in large numbers, and those who have are mostly the elderly spontaneously returning to abandoned or destroyed villages. Those who go back have done so largely in spite of the IC's efforts, and face difficult conditions owing to massive unemployment, a dearth of financial support to rebuild destroyed homes, and local hostility.

The story of refugee and displaced person (DP) returns through August 1999 can be quickly summarized. A total of 610,920 people returned to municipalities in Bosnia: 340,919 refugees and 270,001 DPs.[120] The bulk of these individuals did not return to their pre-war homes, but instead settled in areas

116. Spear, "Disarmament and Demobilization of Warring Factions," 12.
117. The percentage of Serbs in the territory that now comprises the RS, for example, rose from 54 percent in 1991 to 97 percent in 1997, while the proportion of Serbs in the FBiH dropped from 18 to 2 percent. Robert M. Hayden, "Bosnia Ten Years After 'Independence': The Dictatorship of the Protectariate Under Civicist Self-Management," *EES Special Report*, May 2002, 4.
118. ICG, *Is Dayton Failing?*, 32.
119. See Catherine Phuong, "Freely to Return: Reversing Ethnic Cleansing in Bosnia-Herzegovina," *Journal of Refugee Studies* 13, no. 2 (June 2000): 165–83. For a skeptical view of the priority placed on minority returns, see Richard Black, "Return and Reconstruction in Bosnia-Herzegovina: Missing Link or Mistaken Priority?" *SAIS Review* 21, no. 2 (summer-fall 2001): 177–99.
120. These figures can be found in ICG, *Is Dayton Failing?*, 32–33.

controlled by their own ethnic group (these are called "majority returns"). In fact, only 100,714 people—about 5 percent of all those displaced by the war, and only 16 percent of all returnees—returned to areas where their group was in the minority. The situation was particularly bad in the RS, where a mere 13,586 Bosniaks and Croats had been allowed back since the war's end.[121] As ICG gloomily argued in 1999, "The single greatest area of failure in implementing the DPA has been Annex 7. The numbers speak for themselves. Minority return in bih has more or less failed."[122]

In 2000, however, minority returns—often spontaneous—began to increase. Whereas annual figures for minority returns hovered around 40,000 in 1998 and 1999, in 2000 the figure jumped to a new high of 67,000. This new high was surpassed by the numbers for 2001 and 2002 of 92,000 and 102,000, respectively, although this figure fell to 45,000 in 2003, and dwindled to 13,000 through October 2004. This makes for a total of about 447,000 minority returns since the war ended, or nearly 45 percent of the 1,004,000 total returns of refugees and displaced persons overall.[123]

This movement sparked renewed optimism among Bosnia's international administrators and others that a self-sustaining multiethnic Bosnia is in sight.[124] A closer look at these returns, however, shows this not to be the case. The pattern of minority returns largely conforms to the logic of my argument: the age, ethnicity, and location to which people have been allowed to return is such

121. Most minority returns (64.7 percent, or 65,159 people) took place in Bosniak-dominated municipalities (ibid., 33). OHR's Reconstruction and Return Task Force characterized the pattern of returns as follows in March 1998: "Few people have returned to areas where they would be ethnic minorities, and such 'minority returns' are often localized in the Zone of Separation, and correspond to elderly individuals or large groups with strong international back up" (OHR Reconstruction and Return Task Force, *Report* [March 1998], "Executive Summary," at http://www.ohr.int/ohr-dept/rrtf/key-docs/reports/default.asp?content_id=5612).
122. ICG, *Is Dayton Failing?*, 34. Inadequate housing made increasing the rate of returns extremely difficult, since many homes were damaged or destroyed during the war, or are now occupied by members of another ethnic group driven from elsewhere in Bosnia. ICG estimated that "up to 50% of the entire housing stock was destroyed during the war" (ibid., 37). Moreover, the war accelerated the process of urbanization already underway in Bosnia, and made residents of remote villages dependent on agriculture for a living reluctant to go back. See OHR Reconstruction and Return Task Force, *Report* (March 1998), "Current Situation."
123. All of these figures are updated through the end of October 2004, and may be found at UNHCR's Bosnia website, http://www.unhcr.ba, under the heading "statistics."
124. See, for example, *Speech by the High Representative, Wolfgang Petritsch, to the United Nations Security Council*, New York, 9 May 2000 http://www.ohr.int/ohr-dept/presso/pressa/default.asp?content_id=3236; Wolfgang Petritsch, "Don't Abandon the Balkans," *New York Times*, 25 March 2001, section 4, 15; Petritsch, "We Must Stay the Course in BiH," *Wall Street Journal Europe*, 12 June 2001 http://www.ohr.int/ohr-dept/presso/pressa/default.asp?content_id=3153; Petritsch, "Islam is Part of the West, Too," *New York Times*, 20 November 2001, A19; Joseph Biden, "Nation Building? Yes," *New York Times*, 25 January 2001, A23; Lord Robertson, "The Work Ahead in Bosnia," *New York Times*, 25 November 2000, A19.

that they pose the least threat to local majorities. To Bosnian Serbs in the RS, for example, "the return of Bosniaks . . . means the return of Muslim fighting men who could kill Serbs in the next war." Unsurprisingly, then, the "substantial majority of all minority returns to Republika Srpska have been elderly people to destroyed rural villages." Old people returning to isolated villages do not constitute a threat; young Bosniaks do, though, and hence their return to urban areas of the RS has been "non-negotiable."[125] Similarly, Bosnian Croats have been far more reluctant to allow minority returns to western Herzegovina than to central Bosnia. The difference is that the Croats could never hope to control central Bosnia militarily in a future war, whereas western Herzegovina is the heartland of Croat secessionism and thus important to keep ethnically pure. If some returnees must be accepted in this region, however, better they be Serbs—who, isolated from the RS, do not represent a strategic threat—than Bosniaks, who do.

Most of the recent minority returns are "spontaneous," meaning that they were undertaken without IC assistance. People simply got fed up with waiting for the IC's efforts to produce results and went back on their own. Most returnees continue to be retirement-age people who have nowhere else to go: "A large proportion of returnees consist of elderly persons and couples. Relatively few families with children, and even fewer young individuals, tend to return, raising questions of how 'sustainable' these returns will prove to be in the longer run."[126] True reintegration, however, is not occurring, as the new return strategy targets "areas of least resistance . . . remote, unoccupied, burned out villages deep within 'enemy' territory, where there is little or no presence of the majority group . . . This policy of reoccupying remote or empty regions, is responsible for most of spontaneous returns."[127]

Minority returnees face three major problems once they reclaim their former homes. First, returnees are sometimes attacked by hostile members of other ethnic groups opposed to their return to the neighborhood. The UN, for example, counted 385 violent incidents in the 2001 return season (April to September), the highlight of which came when Serb rioters prevented the laying of foundation stones for the rebuilding of mosques destroyed during the war in the RS cities of Trebinje and Banja Luka on 5 and 7 May.[128] In

125. ICG, *Is Dayton Failing?*, 36.
126. Bose, *Bosnia After Dayton*, 35–36.
127. ICG, *Bosnia's Refugee Logjam Breaks: Is the International Community Ready?* (Sarajevo: May 2000), 3. Some younger people have returned to urban areas, taking advantage of new property laws instituted by OHR in 1998 that allow authorities to evict current residents and let homeowners reclaim their property.
128. Figures are from ICG, *The Wages of Sin: Confronting Bosnia's Republika Srpska* (Sarajevo: October 2001), 38. In Banja Luka, one man was killed, a minimum of 34 were injured, and

2002, return-related crimes numbered over 400.[129] Incidents occurred all over Bosnia, but the problem was worst in Serb-controlled eastern Bosnia where, according to ICG, "a Bosniak returnee to Bijeljina or Prijedor is ten times more likely to become a victim of violent crime ... than a local Serb."[130] Return-related incidents declined to 277 in 2003 and 135 in 2004, but returns also declined in both these years.[131]

Second, the economic situation is bleak. Unemployment among Bosnians able to work is about 50 percent, one quarter of the population lives in absolute poverty, and nearly half lack the right to public health care.[132] For returnees, the economic situation is even more austere: unemployment among returnees is nearly 100 percent and they face institutional discrimination as employment laws favor locally dominant groups. In fact, local and international officials argued that "economic stagnation was the single greatest obstacle to return" in 2002.[133] Again, this should surprise no one: the majority group seeks to keep scarce jobs for its own members, and is reluctant to employ unwanted outsiders.

Finally, for all its emphasis on minority returns, the spontaneity and magnitude of the recent movements caught OHR off-guard: the IC lacks the funding necessary to assist the returnees to reconstruct their destroyed homes. In the year 2000, the IC faced a funding gap of as much as 90 percent. Many returnees were living in the rubble of their old houses, awaiting international assistance to begin rebuilding.[134] By late 2002, this state of affairs had not improved: the funding gap for reconstruction of some 66,500 housing units stood at €599 million, and many refugees "continue to shelter in tent villages or to cram together in partially reconstructed houses, waiting for building materials and other assistance."[135]

Because of the inhospitable environment for minority returnees, many Bosnians are opting to sell or rent their reclaimed properties and relocate to areas where their group comprises a majority rather than re-occupy

---

hundreds of international officials and Bosniaks visiting for the ceremony were trapped inside the local Islamic Community Center (ibid., 33–36).

129. UNHCR, "Update on Conditions for Return to Bosnia and Herzegovina," January 2005, at http://www.unhcr.ba/publications/B&HRET0105.pdf.

130. ICG, *The Continuing Challenge of Refugee Return in Bosnia & Herzegovina* (Sarajevo: December 2002), 18.

131. UNHCR, "Update on Conditions for Return to Bosnia and Herzegovina."

132. Ibid. More than half of all Bosnians reported in mid-2002 that they did not earn enough money to meet their own needs or those of their families (ICG, *Continuing Challenge of Refugee Return*, 15).

133. Ibid., 15.

134. For details on this problem, see ICG, *Bosnia's Refugee Logjam Breaks*, 7–11.

135. ICG, *Continuing Challenge of Refugee Return*, 7.

their pre-war dwellings and face the hardships and hostility of minority life. When people do choose to go back, it is common for "only older family members to return permanently and for school-age children to remain in or be sent back to their 'majority' areas."[136] An important factor retarding the return of young people to minority areas is discrimination in education. "Despite the thousands of registered Serb returns to Sanski Most," for example, "only fifteen Serb primary school pupils were reported to have signed up for classes in the municipality this autumn [2002]."[137] Most students, rather than endure the national curriculum of another group and have few teachers of their own ethnicity, attend school in other areas or do not go at all.

Not only is minority return questionable from a security perspective, but even if it goes ahead it is unlikely to result in a true multiethnic Bosnia.[138] The majority of returnees are elderly people going back to remote rural areas, creating isolated, unobtrusive pockets of one ethnic group dwelling in the territory of another. There are no jobs in these areas, and hence little opportunity or attraction for young people. Many young or educated people have chosen not to return to the country at all, seeking brighter futures elsewhere.[139] Needless to say, if few young people return to minority areas, not only will the repatriated community be smaller than it was before the war, but it will dwindle over time as its elderly members pass away. It is thus hard to disagree with Sumantra Bose's assessment of refugee return: "Bosnia's demographic map has probably been changed forever. Even if substantial minority returns occur during 2001 and 2002, what will emerge are minority enclaves within areas otherwise solidly dominated by the majority, rather than a restoration of the pre-war leopard-spot mix."[140]

Conclusion. Bosnia, despite robust third-party intervention and extensive institutionalization, stands little chance of surviving the departure of its international patrons as a unified state. Bosnia should have been partitioned in 1995, but partitioning it now could still remove many of the obstacles to peace identified in this article by eliminating the fears for future security

136. Ibid., 11.
137. Ibid., 20.
138. In addition, the political-territorial structure set up by the DPA, combined with refugee return, raises the danger that the majority populations of each entity may perceive their dominant status to be under threat by minority returns. As outlined earlier, this is one of two mechanisms that can lead to majority-group violence in a federal state. The dangers of this process argue strongly for limiting minority returns to a small percentage of each entity's population, such that the majority group will not feel its power under siege.
139. Five hundred thousand of Bosnia's 1.3 million refugees had found "durable solutions" outside the country by 1998, and 62 percent of young people surveyed in 2000 "expressed the desire to leave the country if they could" (Bose, *Bosnia After Dayton*, 37).
140. Ibid., 36.

produced by uncertainty about Bosnia's political future. Western Herzegovina should be allowed to merge with Croatia, and a reduced RS should join Serbia, with a Bosniak state in between. The border between Serbs and Bosniaks in northern Bosnia should be straightened by transferring the bulge of Serb-held land southwest of Banja Luka to Bosniak control. The Serbs would retain the land north of the line roughly demarcated by Prijedor, Banja Luka, Doboj, and Bijeljina, gaining control of Brčko, although the two northern Federation enclaves would join Croatia. This adjustment rationalizes the border, corresponds to the natural terrain of the area, and minimizes the number of people who would be displaced.[141]

A partition of Bosnia along these lines would have several benefits. First, by giving each group its own largely homogeneous state, partition obviates much of the rationale for nationalist parties. Second, Bosniaks, Croats, and Serbs would not need to disarm and merge their militaries, but could maintain separate armies. Third, partition ends the refugee return process, and hence eliminates fears regarding groups' demographic majorities. Fourth, because these states would be composed mainly of one ethnic group, they would need much simpler institutions than those currently in place to bridge Bosnia's ethnic divides. Finally, partition reduces the magnitude and scope of international intervention required. Turning over governance to local parties obviates the need for OHR, and creating states changes the military mission from nation-building and law enforcement to deterrence, which requires fewer forces and for which military power is better suited.

Most commentators reject partition in Bosnia, arguing that it would lead to renewed ethnic cleansing and war, reward ethnic cleansers, and set a bad precedent for other secession-minded groups in the region.[142] These criticisms miss the mark. For one, partition would not precipitate violent ethnic cleansing; on the contrary, it would plan for ethnic unmixing and ensure that it took place peacefully and as humanely as possible. Furthermore, far from causing a new war, partitioning Bosnia would remove Croat and Serb motives for war. Moreover, partition does not so much reward ethnic cleansing as acknowledge how difficult it is to reverse. The time to stop ethnic cleansing is before it happens, not afterwards. If the IC opposes ethnic cleansing, then it should

---

141. A similar plan advocated by Robert Pape would displace about 200,000 Serbs and some tens of thousands of Bosniaks. See Robert A. Pape, "Partition: An Exit Strategy for Bosnia," *Survival* 39, no. 4 (winter 1997/98): 25–28. An alternative plan—to amputate the western half of the RS—would drastically shorten the Serb-Bosniak border, but would force the Serbs to abandon their capital city and require two-thirds of the RS population to leave. See Daalder, "Bosnia After SFOR."

142. Besides warnings from the various High Representatives, see Carl Bildt, "There is no Alternative to Dayton," *Survival* 39, no. 4 (winter 1997): 19–21.

intervene to prevent it instead of allowing it to occur and in some cases facilitating it, then trying to reverse it later. Finally, the precedent argument gets it backwards: despite keeping Bosnia firmly unified, secessionism is alive and well elsewhere in the Balkans. Montenegro and Kosovo are likely to become independent regardless of what happens in Bosnia, and whether Macedonia descends into full-scale war depends on whether or not Albanian grievances are satisfied by the Macedonian government, not whether or not Bosnia is partitioned.

KOSOVO

A humanitarian disaster in the tiny Yugoslav province of Kosovo provided the unlikely occasion for NATO's first shooting war. NATO mounted a 78-day bombing campaign to stop and reverse Serb leader Slobodan Milošević's attempt to expel Kosovo's ethnic Albanian population. Milošević's forces succeeded in driving about 800,000 ethnic Albanians into neighboring countries (and internally displacing nearly 500,000 more within Kosovo) before he finally agreed to a peace deal that allowed the refugees to return and placed the embattled province under NATO military occupation.[143]

Since the war ended in June 1999, KFOR (NATO's Kosovo Force) and UNMIK (the United Nations Interim Administration Mission in Kosovo) have presided over an ethnically divided province. While the expelled Albanians poured back into Kosovo, many of the remaining Serbs fled to Serbia, fearing for their lives at the hands of vengeful Albanians.[144] Indeed, many Albanians took their revenge, not only on Serbs, but on Roma and Albanian collaborators as well. Hundreds died. Tim Judah comments that "just as most Serbs had so recently been either indifferent to the fate of the Albanians, or thought they deserved to be expelled for 'asking for NATO air strikes,' now most Kosovars were indifferent to the fate of the Serbs. Indeed, many thought they deserved to be expelled, for having tried to expel them." The flight of the Serbs also served a larger political purpose because "with every Serb that left, Serbia's claim to the

143. For these numbers, see Ivo H. Daalder and Michael O'Hanlon, *Winning Ugly: NATO's War to Save Kosovo* (Washington, D.C.: Brookings Institution, 2000), 151. On the origins and conduct of the war, see Tim Judah, *Kosovo: War and Revenge* (New Haven, Conn.: Yale University Press, 2000), Kelly M. Greenhill, "The Use of Refugees as Political and Military Weapons in the Kosovo Conflict," in *Yugoslavia Unraveled: Sovereignty, Self-Determination, Intervention*, ed. Raju G.C. Thomas (Lanham, MD: Lexington Books, 2003), 205–42; and Wesley K. Clark, *Waging Modern War* (New York: PublicAffairs, 2001).
144. UNMIK reported that 211,000 people, "mostly Serbs," fled Kosovo after the war ended. See UNMIK, "UNMIK 1st Anniversary Backgrounder—Returns—5 June 2000," at http://www.unmikonline.org/1styear/returnees.htm. The Yugoslav Red Cross registered 247,391 people who had fled or been expelled from Kosovo by November 1999 (Judah, *Kosovo*, 287).

province for any but legal and historical reasons became that much weaker."[145] Those Serbs who did not perish or flee are now concentrated mainly in the areas bordering Serbia and Montenegro north of the Ibar River, starting in the divided town of Mitrovica, and in isolated pockets in Albanian-majority areas. As of mid-2004, less than 11,000 minorities had returned to their pre-war places of residence in Kosovo out of a total displaced population of about 230,000.[146]

Kosovo is plagued by the same dynamics that operate in Bosnia. First, the massive violence against civilians that characterized Serb counterinsurgency operations against the KLA, and particularly the attempt to expel the entire Albanian population of the province, increased the ethnic identification and nationalism of the Albanians. This legacy has made support for independence unanimous among Albanians: there are no non-nationalist parties in Kosovo. Second, the war and its aftermath have made it impossible for both Albanians and Serbs in Kosovo to trust the future intentions of the other: "The violent means used by the Albanian guerrilla, and the counter-violence, have undermined the basic elements of trust needed, precisely for the viability of a state based on the coexistence of two separate communities."[147] This lack of trust, combined with the pervasive uncertainty regarding the political future of the province has caused both sides to be reluctant to disarm. Serbs have taken their security into their own hands, hunkering down in northern Kosovo and preparing for a possible partition. Emboldened by NATO's intervention, and interpreting it as an endorsement of their demands, Albanians took up arms to join the Presevo Valley—an Albanian-majority area just over the border in Serbia proper—to Kosovo, and also in western Macedonia, where the Albanian minority aspires to greater rights. The IC's attempt to put the conflict on ice by postponing the determination of Kosovo's final status, however, far from cooling passions and bringing calm to the embattled province, has angered the Albanian population and made their calls for independence ever more strident. This frustration burst forth in a storm of anti-Serb—and anti-UN—violence in March 2004, which dealt the death-blow to the IC's vision of a multiethnic, autonomous Kosovo within Serbia.

Reluctance to disarm. Uncertainty regarding the future political status of Kosovo makes both sides hesitant to turn over all their weapons. Both ethnic Serbs and Albanians know that the artificial stability provided by UNMIK and

145. Ibid., 294.
146. UNHCR Briefing Notes, "Kosovo Minorities Still need International Protection, says UNHCR," 24 August 2004, at http://www.unhcr.ch/cgi-bin/texis/vtx/country?iso=yug&expand=news.
147. IICK, *The Follow-Up*, 6.

KFOR will not last because neither of those institutions can stay forever. Should the internationals leave, both communities will be forced to rely on self-help for their security, and the side that disarms makes itself vulnerable, perhaps disastrously so. "As long as Albanian fears and Serb hopes of Kosovo's eventual re-incorporation into Yugoslavia are left unanswered," the ICG argues, "efforts to develop normal, constructive relations between the two communities, either within Kosovo or between Kosovo and Serbia, are unlikely to bear fruit. While the issue remains open, each side will continue to regard the other as a threat . . . leaving the matter unresolved perpetuates mistrust between the communities and may encourage extremists who continue to see violence as a means of achieving their aims."[148]

If the West continues to press autonomy as its preferred solution, the Albanians have two powerful reasons not to disarm. First, Serbia is likely to attempt to re-impose its authority in Kosovo, a terrifying thought to all Albanians (even without Milošević in power). Second, the Albanians will need arms to turn autonomy into statehood. Thus, even though Kosovo is occupied by 17,000 troops, and the province's Serbs currently number perhaps 130,000,[149] who are largely confined to a few areas, ethnic Albanians are reluctant to disarm completely. Recent surveys estimate the number of small arms in civilian hands in Kosovo at between 250,000 and half a million despite several UN-sponsored drives to collect illegal weapons.[150] According to one Albanian resident of Cernica, a village in eastern Kosovo, "You can't depend on KFOR to protect you . . . There were KFOR troops just up the street when the [grocery] store was grenaded, and they didn't stop it from happening. The only protection is to have your own gun and shoot back."[151]

Most of the KLA was demilitarized after the war and partially reconstituted in September 1999 as the 3,000-member Kosovo Protection Corps (KPC), supposedly a civilian emergency service. Although the KLA turned in over 10,000 weapons to KFOR, it is widely known that they retained the bulk of their arsenal.[152] KFOR, for example, has repeatedly seized large Albanian weapons stockpiles in Kosovo.[153] Moreover, according to Daalder and O'Hanlon, "Critics

---

148. ICG, *A Kosovo Roadmap (I): Addressing Final Status* (Pristina: March 2002), 6.

149. ICG, *Return to Uncertainty: Kosovo's Internally Displaced and the Return Process* (Pristina: December 2002), 1.

150. These drives have largely failed, the last one in fall 2003 collecting a paltry 155 guns. See "Geneva-Based Organization Says Kosovo Weapons Collection Drive Has Failed," *BBC Monitoring Europe*, 6 December 2003.

151. Quoted in Arie Farnam, "Gun Culture Stymies the UN in Kosovo," *Christian Science Monitor*, 26 September 2003, 8.

152. Judah, *Kosovo*, 299.

153. KFOR troops seized weapons stockpiles in March, May, and June of 2000, the last of these yielding a haul of some 70 tons. See Philip Shenon, "U.S. Troops Seize Weapons from Albanians

rightly saw this [the conversion of the KLA into the KPC] as camouflage for the KLA's real intention of retaining some type of military organization and, in addition, of establishing political control in Kosovo."[154] Former KLA men and weapons played a substantial role in the Albanian uprising in the Presevo Valley (located in the security zone between Kosovo and Serbia) and the 2001 uprising by Albanians in neighboring western Macedonia.[155]

On the other side, Kosovo's remaining Serbs are greatly outnumbered and believe they need weapons to protect themselves from Albanian revenge attacks, which KFOR has proved unable—and unwilling—to prevent.[156] As a joint report by UNHCR and OSCE declared in March 2003, "Notwithstanding the stabilization of the security situation, the fear of harassment, intimidation and provocation remains part of everyday experience for members of minority communities throughout Kosovo."[157] Given this atmosphere of hostility, regularly punctuated by violence,[158] and the overwhelming desire for an independent Kosovo among ethnic Albanians, for the Serbs to remain armed is a rational response. "The international community is not protecting us," said Oliver Ivanović, a Serb representative from the northern Kosovo town of Mitrovica, "and we have to do it ourselves."[159]

Nationalism. As long as the IC insists on autonomy for Kosovo, support for nationalist parties is guaranteed because the war has convinced ethnic

---

in Kosovo," *New York Times*, 16 March 2000, A1; Shennon, "U.S. Soldiers Seize Weapons in Kosovo," ibid., 20 May 2000, A8; and Steven Erlanger, "Aide Takes Stock of U.N. in Kosovo," ibid., 17 July 2000, A1. Arms seizures continued in 2001, primarily of weapons moving from Kosovo to Albanian rebels in Macedonia, but did not end with the dampening of that conflict. See "KFOR Discovers Large Arms Cache in Southern Kosovo," *BBC Monitoring Europe*, 28 August 2002; and "KFOR Seizes 'Large' Arms Cache in Areas Populated 'Solely' by Kosovo Albanians," *Global News Wire*, 9 April 2003.

154. Daalder and O'Hanlon, *Winning Ugly*, 178. "To all intents and purposes," comments Judah, "the KPC is the KLA in mothballs" (Judah, *Kosovo*, 300).

155. See Tim Judah, "Greater Albania?" and Alexander Yannis, "Kosovo Under International Administration," *Survival* 43, no. 2 (summer 2001): 11 and 39, respectively, as well as Steven Erlanger, "Adrift in the Balkans," *New York Times*, 12 March 2001, A1.

156. See Steven Erlanger, "Torn Mitrovica Reflects West's Trials in Kosovo," *New York Times*, 27 February 2000, 16. It is widely believed among Serbs that Kosovo's international administrators are biased in favor of the majority Albanians. See, for example, Daniel Simpson, "A Restive Kosovo, Officially Still Serbian, Squirms Under the Status Quo," *New York Times*, 29 December 2002, 14.

157. OSCE/UNHCR, *Tenth Assessment of the Situation of Ethnic Minorities in Kosovo* (March 2003), 12, at http://www.unmikonline.org/press/reports/MinorityAssessmentReport10ENG.pdf.

158. For examples from the last quarter of 2002, see ibid., 14–26. Notable violent incidents in 2003 included the shooting of two young Serb men while swimming in the Bistrica River and an incident in which local Serbs threw stones at the Kosovar prime minister. See "New Violence Feared in Kosovo After Death of 2 Serbian Youths," *New York Times*, 15 August 2003, A4; and "Rocks Thrown at Kosovan PM," *The Gazette* (Montreal), 7 December 2003, A12.

159. Irena Guzelova, "Mitrovica Arms Hunt Sparks Attack on KFOR," *Financial Times*, 21 February 2000, 6.

Albanians that they can never be safe under Serb governance. Indeed, even before Milošević's army ethnically cleansed Kosovo beginning in late March 1999, support for independence among the Albanians was virtually unanimous. For example, a 1995 survey indicated that 43 percent of Kosovo's ethnic Albanians wanted Kosovo to join Albania, while 57 percent wanted the province to become an independent state. Not a single respondent preferred autonomy within Serbia.[160] Some commentators, however, opined that an autonomy agreement and de-escalation of the conflict was still possible as late as March 1998: "The local population still supported its elected 'president,' Ibrahim Rugova, including his nonviolent policies of civil disobedience. The KLA was little more than a small, unorganized, ragtag band of rebels that would most likely have disappeared once a serious political dialogue aimed at granting greater autonomy had started. Therefore a solution well short of independence may still have been possible and would have satisfied most of Milošević's immediate concerns."[161]

While the possibility of such a solution at that time is open to debate, what is certain now is that the harsh Serb repression made independence for Kosovo the only option. The Report of the Independent International Commission on Kosovo declared that "[a]ny remaining support for a political future involving autonomy within the FRY [Federal Republic of Yugoslavia] vanished in March 1999 when FRY forces began expelling the entire Kosovar Albanian population. Even a substantial exercise of autonomous self-government is now regarded as insufficient."[162] As one member of the commission put it, "To suggest that Serbian police or government officials could be allowed to return is a dangerous delusion. To imagine that after all that has happened, the Kosovo Albanians will be willing and able to live in the same state as Serbs, that they will even pay taxes to Belgrade . . . or to seek passports from a state that has expelled half of them, destroying their identity papers to make sure the bond is severed, is utterly unrealistic."[163]

Kosovo's international governors point to the participation of Serbs and the success of moderate Albanians in elections in the province as support for their optimistic view that autonomy within Yugoslavia can work. Although Serbs largely boycotted the municipal elections—Kosovo's first ever—in October

160. Julie A. Mertus, *Kosovo: How Myths and Truths Started a War* (Berkeley: University of California Press, 1999), 319. The same survey reported that 65 percent of Albanians did not believe the two populations could live together in one state, while the same percentage believed that Serbs wanted all Albanians to leave Kosovo (ibid., 319–20).

161. Daalder and O'Hanlon, *Winning Ugly*, 186–87.

162. IICK, *The Kosovo Report*, 264–65.

163. Jacques Rupnik, "Yugoslavia After Milosevic," *Survival* 43, no. 2 (summer 2001): 25.

2000,[164] Serb turnout for the November 2001 provincial assembly elections was 46 percent, and Serbs won 22 places in the 120-seat chamber.[165] Moreover, in both elections—as well as the 2002 municipal elections—Ibrahim Rugova's moderate Democratic League of Kosovo triumphed over parties led by former KLA commanders.[166]

The optimists, however, neglect a critical point: all Albanians, regardless of where they fall on the political spectrum, favor independence for Kosovo. "Despite their differences on the means," observes Jacques Rupnik, "all Kosovo Albanian parties are united over the goal of independence . . . Any attempt to ignore this assertion and to return Kosovo to 'substantial autonomy' within 'Yugoslavia' is bound to fail, to discredit Kosovar Albanian moderates and to prepare the ground for new violence."[167] Indeed, Rugova, Kosovo's informal president in the 1990s who advocated non-violent resistance to Serb rule, irritated international officials immediately after his election by stating that he intended to move the province quickly toward independence.[168] Thus, the fact that Albanians favor moderate politicians over those advocating violence does not mean they are any less committed to independence for Kosovo. Finally, the Serbs boycotted the last parliamentary elections in October 2004 in the wake of the anti-minority riots the previous March.

Political institutions. Although Kosovo's ethnic Albanians have long sought independence, the West has remained ambivalent toward this goal. For example, during the course of negotiations in 1998 with president Milošević, Secretary of State Madeleine Albright warned that "[w]e have made it clear to Milošević and Kosovars that we do not support independence for Kosovo, that we want Serbia out of Kosovo, not Kosovo out of Serbia."[169] In addition

---

164. Carlotta Gall, "As Albanians Flock to Polls, Serbs Lie Low," *New York Times*, 29 October 2000, A1.

165. Melinda Henneberger, "Serb Turnout in Kosovo Vote Seen as an Encouraging Step," *New York Times*, 20 November 2001, A8. Ten of these seats were guaranteed by the electoral laws. I thank an anonymous reviewer for pointing this out. The OSCE's Kosovo division has the election results on its website at http://www.osce.org/kosovo/elections.

166. Melinda Henneberger, "Albanian Moderate's Party Wins Peaceful Kosovo Election," *New York Times*, 18 November 2001, A14.

167. Rupnik, "Yugoslavia After Milosevic," 22–23.

168. Henneberger, "Serb Turnout in Kosovo Vote Seen as an Encouraging Step."

169. Quoted in Roger Cohen, "In Balkans Again, Promises, Promises," *New York Times*, 14 October 1998, A1. Prominent international officials also expressed support for autonomy after the war. As Carlos Westendorp, High Representative in Bosnia at the time, put it, "The only possible solution for Kosovo, once those ethnically-cleansed have been returned to their homes, is the eventual establishment of an autonomous state within Serbia (or Yugoslavia). Autonomy is a necessary condition for a lasting peace, though it cannot bring peace on its own." Carlos Westendorp, "Lessons Bosnia Taught Us," *Wall Street Journal*, 19 May 1999 http://www.ohr.int/ohr-dept/presso/pressa/default.asp?content_id=3182.

to the destabilizing effect advocating Kosovo's independence might have had on the rest of the region (especially Macedonia, which contains a large Albanian minority), the West feared it would also "set a precedent for Bosnia, where Bosnian Serb and Croat claims for independence—or for merger with Oneighboring states—were at least as strong as those of the Kosovar Albanians."[170] The Rambouillet agreement, however, contained a provision that in effect allowed for a referendum on independence to be held after three years. That said, the "will of the people" would be only one of four factors influencing the final status of Kosovo, so that even a vote for independence would not guarantee such an outcome.[171]

Unfortunately, Western ambivalence over the final status for Kosovo has led to contradictions. As Michael Mandelbaum pointed out, the air war against Serbia neither prevented the purging of the Kosovars nor fully supported their aims: "While insisting that Kosovo be granted autonomy, NATO asserted that it must remain part of Yugoslavia. The alliance had therefore intervened in a civil war and defeated one side, but embraced the position of the party it had defeated on the issue over which the war had been fought."[172]

The dilemma in Kosovo is spelled out in UN Security Council Resolution 1244, which calls for the establishment of "an international civil presence in Kosovo in order to provide an interim administration for Kosovo under which the people of Kosovo can enjoy substantial autonomy within the Federal Republic of Yugoslavia." Unfortunately, as Michael Ignatieff comments, "[t]he problem is that 1244 . . . is political science fiction. It reaffirms the sovereignty of Yugoslavia over Kosovo, and it also calls for the Kosovars to enjoy 'substantial autonomy and self-government.' Which sounds fine, except that no Kosovar will ever accept Belgrade's sovereignty and no Serb in Kosovo wants to accept Kosovar majority rule."[173] This dilemma is aptly captured by the phrase "Catch 1244."[174]

The Kosovars unanimously desire independence, and believe that the IC is going to give it to them. The Constitutional Framework for Provisional

---

170. Daalder and O'Hanlon, *Winning Ugly*, 25.

171. The other three factors would be the opinions of "relevant authorities," the efforts of the parties to implement Rambouillet, and the Helsinki Final Act (which guarantees the territorial integrity of states; ibid., 82; and Judah, *Kosovo*, 213–14).

172. Michael Mandelbaum, "A Perfect Failure: NATO's War Against Yugoslavia," *Foreign Affairs* 78, no. 5 (September/October 1999): 5.

173. Michael Ignatieff, "The Reluctant Imperialist," *New York Times Magazine*, 6 August 2000, 47.

174. Christian Jennings, "War-Ravaged Kosovo Caught in Catch 1244 Situation," *Scotland on Sunday*, 9 February 2003, 24.

Self-Government, announced in May 2001 by then-High Representative Hans Haekkerup, although providing for an elected assembly and an executive, leaves significant powers in the IC's hands. In fact, the "extensive powers accorded to the SRSG mean that, instead of the substantial self-government promised the Kosovars under Resolution 1244, they will instead get very limited autonomy. They will have the illusion of self-rule rather than the reality."[175] This situation has caused substantial bitterness in the Albanian community, exemplified by prime minister Bajram Rexhepi's comment in October 2003: "Being ruled 5,000 miles away from New York is simply not working ... With no road maps, or political deadlines, or sense of resolving their unclear international status as a non-state entity, Kosovars are fast losing hope ... People voted me into office and instead I find myself with my hands tied behind my back. It's a total contradiction."[176]

Refugee returns and violence. The Serb exodus that followed the war's end has made Kosovo even more ethnically homogeneous than it was before. As Albanians returned to the province, Serbs fled or were driven out. Perhaps as few as 100,000 remain, most of whom (55,000) are concentrated north of Mitrovica. Violence gradually declined, partially owing to the increased efforts of KFOR and UNMIK's international police force, but mainly because of "the virtual segregation of the Serbs, who either continued their exodus or regrouped in mainly rural enclaves within Kosovo."[177] One Serb woman who returned to Kosovo Polje commented that conditions had improved for Serbs "but only because most were not here anymore. 'There are fewer Serbs, so there are fewer problems.'"[178] Indeed, the main threat to peace in Kosovo today is caused by the continued presence of some Serbs in Albanian-majority areas, and the attempt to reintegrate the two populations by returning ethnic Albanians to their former homes in Serb-dominated areas.

In such a tense environment, trying to return refugees to areas in which they are a minority simply makes them targets for the other group's hostility. The repeated attempts to bring ethnic Albanians back to the north side of Mitrovica demonstrate this point. UNMIK and the Albanians remain committed to

---

175. IICK, *The Follow-Up*, 7.
176. Quoted in Helena Smith, "Angry Kosovars Call on 'Colonial' UN Occupying Force to Leave," *The Observer*, 19 October 2003, 21.
177. Yannis, "Kosovo Under International Administration," 37.
178. Quoted in Melinda Henneberger, "Dose of Tolerance in a Kosovo Town," *New York Times*, 2 December 2001, A12. Daalder and O'Hanlon are quick to point out the "silver lining" in this emigration and segregation: it "has reduced the likelihood of interethnic violence by physically separating those who would commit it from their potential victims" (Daalder and O'Hanlon, *Winning Ugly*, 177).

breaking down the division of the town, but even former Special Representative Kouchner warned "[y]ou have to think of the Serb reaction. The only place they feel protected is in the north—that's simply the fact."[179] After an early attempt to escort Albanians over the Ibar River that divides Mitrovica led to Serb resistance and riots in September 1999,[180] serious violence erupted in the town the following February, including one incident in which seven Albanians were killed.[181] Further attacks against UN personnel followed in June 2000, prompting UNHCR to suspend its activities in Mitrovica for a week. The continued atmosphere of violence caused many Albanians to flee the northern, Serb-dominated section of the town.[182] The persistent refusal of Serbs to allow Albanians to return to their former homes in northern Mitrovica set off several days of riots in early February 2001 when a fifteen-year-old Albanian boy was killed in a grenade attack.[183] On 8 April 2002, twenty-six UNMIK police were injured in a violent clash with local Serbs when officers set up a traffic checkpoint just across the bridge in north Mitrovica.[184]

The massive Albanian attacks on Serbs that occurred in March 2004 should dispel any lingering illusions that Kosovo can be reconstructed as a multiethnic society. In response to the drowning deaths of three Albanian children in the Ibar after local Serbs allegedly set dogs on them, Albanian mobs went on a rampage that left nineteen dead, 900 wounded, created 4,500 refugees, and damaged or destroyed 700 homes and 30 religious sites.[185] NATO was forced to rush extra troops to the region to help quell the violence. The apparent orchestration of the attacks led international officials to denounce the violence as an Albanian attempt to complete the ethnic cleansing of the province in

179. Kouchner adds that he opposes a permanent division of Mitrovica. See Steven Erlanger, "Fears Grow Over the De Facto Partition of Kosovo," *New York Times*, 14 November 1999, 1. A Serb teacher, Zoran Virijevic, commented in the same article, "Only a suicidal Serb would go to the other side [of Mitrovica]."

180. The Associated Press reported that the September violence in Mitrovica resulted in 184 wounded and 1 dead (an ethnic Albanian). See "K.L.A. Calms Ethnic Riots in Tense Town in Kosovo," *New York Times*, 12 September 1999, 6. Violence also occurred in October as Albanians clashed with French peacekeepers who barred them from crossing the Ibar. See "French Clash With Albanians in Kosovo Town," *New York Times*, 16 October 1999, A5.

181. Carlotta Gall, "7 Killed and 9 Hurt in Kosovo Rampage, Worst Since War," *New York Times*, 5 February 2000, A3; and Gall, "In Riot-Torn Kosovo City, Serbs Force Albanians From Homes," ibid., 12 February 2000, A6.

182. 1,700 Albanians, Turks, and Bosniaks fled the northern section of Mitrovica between 2 and 20 February due to renewed violence. See UNHCR/OSCE, *Update on the Situation of Ethnic Minorities in Kosovo* (February-May 2000), 6, at http://www.osce.org/kosovo/documents/reports/minorities).

183. Irena Guzelova, "Kosovo's Albanians Grow Impatient for Self-Rule," *Financial Times*, 8 February 2001, 3. This episode set off further unrest throughout Kosovo, peaking with the Albanian attack on the "Nis Express" bus convoy that killed 10 Serbs on 16 February.

184. ICG, *UNMIK's Kosovo Albatross: Tackling Division in Mitrovica* (Pristina: June 2002), 4–5.

185. ICG, *Collapse in Kosovo* (Pristina: April 2004), 1.

anticipation of eventual talks on Kosovo's final status.[186] This is certainly the lesson drawn by Kosovo's Serb population: "It is very difficult to look at the future of Kosovo, but one thing's for sure—there's no more talk about multicultural life. This is rubbish no one here even thinks about any more."[187]

Why partition is better. Three solutions are possible for Kosovo, all based on independence for all or part of the province.[188] One scenario is simply to partition all of Kosovo from Yugoslavia and allow the Albanians to deal with the Serbs as they choose, which would probably result in their forcible expulsion. Alternatively, those Serbs who desired to leave could be transferred peacefully to Serbia. A second option would also partition the entirety of Kosovo from Yugoslavia, but would make independence conditional on minority populations being given extensive rights—such as the right to government services and education in their own language and freedom of religion. Kosovo's internal minority rights and external security would be guaranteed by the IC.[189] The third option would grant Kosovo independence, but would partition the province along the Ibar River: the land north of this line, where most of Kosovo's Serbs live, would go to Serbia, while the area to the south would become an independent state. Kosovo would be compensated for this territorial loss by gaining the districts of Presevo, Medveja, and Bujanovac, the Albanian-majority areas along Kosovo's southeast border.[190] In this scenario, rather than design minority rights provisions, remaining minority populations would be exchanged: the Serb enclaves in the south would leave Kosovo, and Albanians north of the Ibar would go south. A reduced KFOR would remain to police Kosovo's borders.

Each of these plans has its plusses and minuses, but on the whole option three is preferable.[191] Full independence (option one) would cause further violent ethnic cleansing, while conditional independence (option two) looks a lot like the status quo, and begs the question of how long the IC is to protect Kosovo's minorities. The major objection to partitioning Kosovo is that the

186. See, for example, the comments of the Under-Secretary of UN for Peacekeeping Operations Jean-Marie Guéhenno to the Security Council at http://www.unmikonline.org/news.htm#1304.

187. Oliver Ivanović, quoted in Adam LeBor, "Troops Pour in as Serbs Flee Kosovo Homes," *The Times* (London), 20 March 2004, 14.

188. I reject two other options—continued protectorate and autonomy within Yugoslavia—as undesirable and unworkable.

189. For further details on this and other plans for Kosovo's future status, see IICK, *The Kosovo Report*, chap. 9, Rupnik, "Yugoslavia After Milosevic," and ICG, *A Kosovo Roadmap*.

190. These territories were taken from Kosovo and added to Serbia shortly after the Second World War, and Serb-majority districts added to northern Kosovo in compensation.

191. It should be noted that in simulated negotiations conducted under the auspices of the United States Institute for Peace, local Serb and Albanian officials also repeatedly chose partition (Simpson, "A Restive Kosovo").

Albanians would reject the loss of northern Kosovo because it would deprive them of the Trepče mines, Kosovo's main economic asset, thus creating a permanent grievance that could lead to future conflict. The loss of the Trepče complex, however, would be made much more palatable if compensated with the gain of the Presevo Valley, the sight of a recent armed uprising by ethnic Albanians. Another objection to partition, that it would require forced relocations of populations, is made less significant by the fact that full independence would cause expulsions, while conditional independence would probably see most Serbs leave anyway, when the IC no longer remained to protect them. The final objection to partition, that it would spark a domino effect in the region, has it backwards: arguably it is the uncertainty caused by the IC's refusal to grant Kosovo independence that has contributed to armed Albanian rebellions in Presevo and Macedonia. Thus, on balance, a partition plan that gives northern Kosovo to Serbia and the Presevo region to Kosovo seems the most sensible option.[192]

POLICY IMPLICATIONS AND RESPONSES TO COUNTERARGUMENTS

Negotiated settlements to ethnic civil wars, while not impossible, face grave difficulties. The process of fighting imbues the combatants with mutual fear and a deep sense of mistrust. The inability to trust in the adversary's future benign intentions sharply limits the amount of military and political cooperation forthcoming after the war. Rebels fear disarming lest the government betray them in their moment of greatest vulnerability. Politically, both power sharing and regional autonomy agreements are difficult to implement and apt to fail if tried. Nationalist parties dominate politics, institutions become gridlocked, and refugees returning to their old homes face a violent reception. Neither ethnic separation nor international intervention truly surmounts these obstacles.

The policy implication of this argument is that international actors should re-think their strategies for intervening in civil conflicts. If the IC is interested in minimizing the recurrence of ethnic wars, then it may wish to facilitate military victories or partitions. At the very least, the IC should realize that there is likely to be a trade-off between its preferred method of conflict resolution— negotiated settlements—and stability. Where partition is feasible, such as when groups have an attachment to territory, are mostly separated, and capable of

---

192. Moreover, combining the partition of Bosnia and Kosovo into a single deal, in which the RS acceded to Yugoslavia, would perhaps gain Belgrade's acquiescence in the loss of Kosovo.

holding their own militarily, a settlement which creates multiple states rather than one may be preferable.[193] Otherwise, it may be wiser to help one side or the other win, or simply let these wars burn themselves out.[194]

Critics argue that these solutions have flaws of their own. For partition, the most serious criticisms contend that it fails to end violence or prevent future wars; causes a domino effect that leads other minorities in the same (or nearby) states to seek self-determination; creates economically unviable and undemocratic successor states; and is unnecessary because it is possible to foster benign ethnic identities.[195] To rebut these objections fully demands more space than I am allowed here,[196] so a few comments will have to suffice. Taking these criticisms in reverse order, partition would be unnecessary if identities could be re-engineered or if single-state solutions provided lasting solutions to ethnic violence. Although identity is changeable in theory, once mobilized it is difficult to manipulate in practice, especially after large-scale violence has occurred.[197] As shown, single-state solutions, such as power sharing or autonomy, as shown do not provide a viable alternative. Partition does not produce undemocratic successor states,[198] and economic viability is a non-issue, as no state has ever "failed" for economic reasons as a consequence of being too small.[199] The weakness of the domino argument is demonstrated by recent Balkan history: holding Bosnia together did not prevent secessionism in Kosovo, and maintaining Kosovo as part of Yugoslavia has not kept Montenegro from moving toward independence or armed conflict by ethnic Albanians in search of greater rights in Macedonia. Nor have these policies discouraged secessionists in other parts of the world, such as Chechnya, Palestine, or Sudan. In fact, the failure to resolve the final status of Kosovo has arguably

193. In the words of the IICK: "It is better, in our view, that the international community develop procedures to accord self-government to these groups under appropriate and justifiable conditions than to maintain an obsolete regime of unalterable state sovereignty . . . In such cases . . . the international community must not shrink from its responsibility to devise rules for secession and independence which allow persecuted groups to find a constitutional order which grants them security and self-government" (IICK, *The Kosovo Report*, 277–78).

194. Luttwak, "Give War a Chance," 37.

195. Prominent critiques include Robert Schaeffer, *Warpaths: The Politics of Partition* (New York: Hill and Wang, 1990); Radha Kumar, "The Troubled History of Partition," *Foreign Affairs* 76, no. 1 (January/February 1997): 22–34; and Sambanis, "Partition as a Solution to Ethnic War." For others, see Downes, "Holy Land Divided," 59-60 nn5-8; and 78-89 passim.

196. For a more complete response, see ibid., 77–89.

197. Daniel Byman, "Forever Enemies? The Manipulation of Ethnic Identities to End Ethnic Wars," *Security Studies* 9, no. 3 (spring 2000): 149–90.

198. Sambanis, "Partition as a Solution to Ethnic War," 459–64.

199. Moreover, this argument ignores the existence and prosperity of many micro-states, and is an argument against all small states, whether ethnically homogeneous or multiethnic. See Michael Lind, "In Defense of Liberal Nationalism," *Foreign Affairs* 73, no. 3 (May/June 1994): 94.

encouraged assertiveness by Albanians in Yugoslavia's Presevo valley and western Macedonia.[200] Finally, with regard to violence, partition does not stop or prevent future violence when ethnic separation does not also occur.[201] Where separation was incomplete, violence festered and wars occurred (Northern Ireland, Cyprus before 1974, Kashmir), but where separation reduced the minority population to insignificant numbers, violence ended (Republic of Ireland, Cyprus post-1974, Greece, Turkey, and Bulgaria after the population exchanges of the early 1920s). This evidence simply demonstrates that ethnic separation must be an integral part of partition.

The major criticism of facilitating a military victory is that it entails more bloodshed than a negotiated settlement.[202] This is only true, however, if the war does not resume some time after the agreement is implemented. Moreover, if it is true that a "mutually hurting stalemate" is required to facilitate a negotiated settlement, it is equally true that such standoffs often drag on for years after it has become apparent that neither side can prevail. Thus, the conditions that make such conflicts "ripe for resolution" do not always translate into fewer casualties.[203]

International actors, of course, value things other than stability, such as promoting democracy and preventing genocide. States that implement negotiated settlements to civil wars, however, may become less democratic (on average) over the long term. Military victories, on the other hand, have no effect on a state's level of democracy, while partition may increase it slightly.[204] A serious drawback of supporting a policy of victory could be that decisive victories in civil wars are more likely to be followed by mass killing than are negotiated settlements.[205] Unfortunately, civil wars tend to kill a greater proportion of civilians than interstate wars, and civil war involvement is a powerful predictor

200. As the IICK has commented, "Far from Kosovar independence acting as a domino . . . the uncertainty about the future means that there is still everything to play for and that southern Serbia and parts of Macedonia could still enter the equation through changing the facts on the ground. In other words, the recent conflicts could be treated as a consequence of uncertainty, which provides an incentive to try to change the facts on the ground before a final settlement is reached" (IICK, *The Follow-Up*, 8).

201. Kaufmann, "When All Else Fails."

202. Licklider, "Consequences of Negotiated Settlements in Civil Wars," 686–87; Stedman, "Negotiation and Mediation," 375–76; and King, *Ending Civil Wars*, 12–13.

203. Wagner, "Causes of Peace," in Licklider, *Stopping the Killing*, 260; and Walter, "Critical Barrier," 362.

204. Toft, "Peace Through Victory?" 23; and Sambanis, "Partition as a Solution to Ethnic War," 459–64.

205. Nineteen percent of victories in identity wars were followed by genocide, 7 percent of victories in ideological wars had such an outcome, but no genocides occurred after negotiated settlements (Licklider, "Consequences of Negotiated Settlements in Civil Wars," 686–87). Neither of the first two relationships was statistically significant.

of mass killing by states.[206] International interveners, therefore, should think long and hard before encouraging such a policy; it could be that the costs in terms of other values would be too high. At the very least, policymakers should be aware of the trade-offs involved.

206. Matthew Krain, "State-Sponsored Mass Murder: The Onset and Severity of Genocides and Politicides," *Journal of Conflict Resolution* 41, no. 3 (June 1997): 331–60.

WHICH SECURITY DILEMMA? MITIGATING ETHNIC CONFLICT: THE CASE OF CROATIA

PAUL ROE

Since the beginning of the cold war, the concept of the security dilemma has been fundamental to International Relations (IR) literature. Although often contested, the basic nature of the concept, according to Barry Posen, rests upon the notion that the actions of a state to enhance its own security produce reactions that, can make another less secure.[1] This action-reaction dynamic is predicated on an "inadvertency" of the first state's behavior. Hence, Robert Jervis remark that "most of the ways in which a country seeks to increase its security have the *unintended* effect of decreasing the security of others."[2] "Unintended consequences" implies that decision makers find themselves in security predicaments that are not of their own making. In this regard, Charles Glaser identifies the concept as "the key to understanding how in an anarchical international system states with *fundamentally compatible goals still end up in competition and war.*[3]

The traditional (inter-state) formulation of the security dilemma has been employed to explain the outbreak of the First World War[4] as well as the superpower competition between the Soviet Union and the United States.[5] Since the end of the cold war, however, the concept has departed from its traditional inter-state use in seeking to explain conflict at the intra-state level. Now the security dilemma has arguably become the favored tool for Realist/neor-Ralist approaches to the questions surrounding ethnic violence and war. Indeed, perusing the literature may well leave the impression that the security dilemma is at work in most, if not all, such cases. My contention in this respect is that

Paul Roe is assistant professor in the Department of International Relations and European Studies (IRES), at Central European University (CEU), Budapest.

1. Barry Posen, "The Security Dilemma and Ethnic Conflict," *Survival* 35, no. 1 (spring 1993): 28.
2. Robert Jervis, "Realism, Game Theory and Cooperation," *World Politics* 40, no. 3 (April 1988): 317 (emphasis added).
3. Charles Glaser, "The Security Dilemma Revisited," *World Politics* 50, no. 1 (October 1997): 171 (emphasis added).
4. See Jack Snyder, "Perceptions of the Security Dilemma in 1914," in *Psychology and Deterrence,* ed. Robert Jervis, Richard Ned Lebow, and Janice Gross Stein (Baltimore: Johns Hopkins University Press, 1985), 153–179.
5. See Robert Jervis, "Was the Cold War a Security Dilemma?" *Journal of Cold War Studies* 3, no. 1 (winter 2001): 36–60.

the security dilemma concept has thus tended to group together what may be disparate conflicts; different instances of violence and war might well have been mistakenly conflated by virtue of carrying the security dilemma label.

In addressing this, I divide the security dilemma into three categories: "tight," "regular," and "loose."[6] This categorization derives from refocusing the security dilemma from the fundamental compatibility of "goals" to the fundamental compatibility of "security requirements." That is, I shift the emphasis of enquiry from the general consideration of whether security is being sought, to the specific consideration of the means through which security is being sought. The value in doing so is not simply academic: the security dilemma not only explains why ethnic conflict erupts, it also informs effective means of conflict resolution.[7] In this regard, Chaim Kaufmann writes, "The only stable solution to an ethnic civil war is separation of the warring communities into distinct, defensible regions, because only this can eliminate the security dilemma faced by both sides."[8] In this article, I argue that the security dilemma faced by both sides is not so much *the* security dilemma as *a* security dilemma, and the means of conflict resolution—Kaufmann's "possible and impossible solutions"—derive from a particular interpretation of which security dilemma is at work.

My intention here is not to take issue with Kaufmann but to put in place a conceptual framework that can be used to evaluate his work[9] by bringing into focus Kaufmann's (apparent) assumptions concerning the security dilemma and ethnic conflict. In this sense, the tight, regular, and loose interpretations of the concept simply reflect the range of the existing security dilemma literature. In the first part of the article, I lay out the basic elements of the security dilemma. I then discuss my tight, regular, and loose formulations. Subsequently, I show how different interpretations of the security dilemma result in different means of conflict resolution.

The second part of the article deals with my case study: the August 1990 outbreak of ethnic violence between Serbs and Croats in Croatia. Here I argue that the Croatian case can be identified as a regular security dilemma. This differs from Kaufmann's interpretation of the conflict in the former Yugoslavia, which, I suggest, interprets the dilemma as a loose formulation. Again, my purpose is not to criticize Kaufmann's work, but to put forward a

6. See Paul Roe, "Actors' Responsibility in 'Tight,' 'Regular,' or 'Loose' Security Dilemmas," *Security Dialogue* 32, no. 1 (March 2001): 103–116.
7. See Barbara F. Walter and Jack Snyder, eds., *Civil Wars Insecurity and Intervention* (New York: Columbia University Press, 1999).
8. Chaim Kaufmann, "Intervention in Ethnic and Ideological Civil Wars: Why One Can Be Done and the Other Can't," *Security Studies* 6, no. 1 (autumn 1996): 68.
9. I am grateful to one of the anonymous referees for drawing my attention to this point.

different version of the violence in the Republic of Croatia, thereby offering different implications for conflict resolution.

THE SECURITY DILEMMA: CONSTITUTIVE ELEMENTS

THE starting point for the security dilemma concept is usually seen as the ambiguity inherent to military preparations. States try to increase their security by building up their arms. However, most arms used for defensive purposes, can also be employed for offensive purposes. Consequently, as Nick Wheeler and Ken Booth point out, one state's military preparations can cause an "unresolvable uncertainty" for another as to whether those preparations are for offensive or defensive purposes.[10] Robert Jervis sums up this basic point well by stating, "Unless the requirements for offense and defense differ in kind or amount, a status quo power will require a military posture that resembles that of an aggressor."[11] This situation is referred to as the indistinguishability between offense and defense. In this situation of uncertainty, decision makers must try to distinguish between so-called status quo and revisionist states.

Factors that can exacerbate uncertainty may readily be located within International Relations' three, traditional levels of analysis: the individual, the state, and the international system. In keeping with the Classical Realist tradition, Herbert Butterfield concentrates on how uncertainty manifests itself at the individual level through the assumption of humans as inherently fearful:

> You yourself may vividly feel the terrible fear that you have of the other party but you cannot enter the other man's counterfear.... As this operates on both sides ... neither sees the nature of the predicament that he is in, for each only imagines that the other party is being hostile and unreasonable.[12]

Other explanations can be found at the level of the state, those propounded by mostly liberal and constructivist thinkers. Perceptions concerning state behavior derive from several considerations: whether or not the other is democratic, national culture and identity,[13] and a specific focus on domestic

---

10. Nick Wheeler and Ken Booth, "The Security Dilemma," in, *Dilemmas of World Politics: International Issues in a Changing World*, ed. John Baylis and Nick Rengger (Oxford: Clarendon Press, 1992), 64.

11. Robert Jervis, *Perception and Misperception in International Politics* (Princeton: Princeton University Press, 1976), 64.

12. Herbert Butterfield, *History and Human Relations* (London: Collins, 1951), 21.

(bureaucratic) political processes—what Glaser refers to as "national evalu-ative capabilities."[14] Neo-Realism, however, with its emphasis on structural considerations, has been predominant. Because the context of international anarchy gives rise to self-help conditions, states tend to assume the worst. In-tentions are equated with capabilities: what others can do, they will do, given the chance.[15] Moreover, uncertainty concerning current intentions can be sep-arated from uncertainty as a more general product of the system; neighbors that are friendly today might just as well be enemies tomorrow.

The propensity for assuming a worst-case scenario can also be affected by the advantage of offense over defense. According to Jervis, the advantage of offense over defense holds when "it is easier to destroy the other's army and take its territory than to defend one's own."[16] As such, the uncertainty which derives from the indistinguishability between offense and defense resolves itself through the advantage of offensive measures: in addition to being un-sure as to the nature of my neighbors preparations, I also see they may have something to gain by striking first.

The logic of the security dilemma assumes a worst-case scenario which provokes an action-reaction dynamic between the parties involved. Coun-termeasures are required to deter/defend against an apparently aggressive neighbor. This process manifests itself as arms racing: the more you increase your arms, the more I have to increase mine if I am to maintain at least the same level of security. The action-reaction dynamic is certainly an element crucial to the security dilemma concept as it seeks to explain how an existing conflict can escalate to actual hostilities.

In trying to remove themselves from the action-reaction dynamic, actors may choose to launch a pre-emptive strike: as I believe that you will attack me, I can counteract and attack you first. Hence, Erik Melander's asserts, "A specific precondition of any security dilemma is that in the case of confrontation

13. See Peter J. Katzenstein, ed., *The Culture of National Security: Norms and Identity in World Politics* (New York: Columbia University Press, 1996).

14. Charles Glaser discusses the role of certain institutions within the state (units within the government, think-tanks, and so on) charged with evaluating others' policies. Perceptions, he notes, can be affected not only by the quality of the information these institutions provide, but also by the strong political influence that particular organizations have. In other words, states might misinterpret others' behavior because evaluative capabilities are poor or certain institutions which are dominant in the policy-making process provide misleading information. See Glaser, "The Political Consequences of Military Strategy: Expanding and Refining the Spiral and Deterrence Models," *World Politics* 44, no. 1 (July 1992): 514–518.

15. Jervis, *Perception and Misperception*, 64–65.

16. Jervis, "Cooperation Under the Security Dilemma," in, *Conflict After the Cold War: Arguments on Causes of War and Peace*, ed. Richard K. Betts (New York: Macmillan, 1994), 315.

it is better to move first than to wait for the adversary to make ... [its] move."[17] In other words, when offense has the advantage the security dilemma is likely to manifest itself in violence and war.

As previously mentioned, the security dilemma is marked by what is often referred to as unintended consequences, where the parties involved "inadvertently" reduce the security of others by the actions they take to increase their own. The following sections will show that in the existing security dilemma literature the notion of inadvertency is apparent to greater and lesser degrees.

A TIGHT SECURITY DILEMMA

A tight security dilemma occurs when two or more actors with compatible security requirements misperceive the nature of their relationship and thus employ countermeasures based on an illusory incompatibility. That is to say, what each party believes it needs to be secure does not, in fact, conflict with what is required by its neighbor.[18] In this sense, actors can be divided into those with compatible security requirements and those with incompatible security requirements. Incompatibility exists when security for both sides cannot be realized. By contrast, illusory incompatibility refers to a situation where security for both sides is possible if only they understand that this is the case.

Butterfield writes that "the greatest war in history could be produced without the intervention of any great criminals who might be out to do deliberate harm to the world," but with two actors each "desperately anxious to avoid conflict of any sort.[19] In this way, Butterfield's interpretation of the security dilemma rests upon the importance of states' intentions; the actors involved harbor no expansionist (revisionist) desires. Butterfield, therefore, characterizes the situation as a "tragedy" since neither party to the conflict originally intended to harm the other. Similarly, John Herz comments, "[I]t is one of the *tragic implications* of the security dilemma, that mutual fear of

17. Erik Melander, *Anarchy Within: The Security Dilemma Between Ethnic Groups in an Emerging Anarchy* (Uppsala: Department of Peace and Conflict Research, Uppsala University, Report no. 52, 1999), 21.

18. This borrows from what Kenneth Boulding describes as "two very different kinds of incompatibility.... 'real' incompatibility, where we have two images of the future in which realization of one would prevent realization of the other," and "'illusory' incompatibility, in which there exists a condition of compatibility which would satisfy the real interests of the two parties but in which the dynamics of the situation or illusions of the parties create a situation of ... misunderstandings, which increase hostility simply as a result of the reactions of the parties to each other, not as a result of any basic differences of interests" (Boulding, "National Images and International Systems," in *International Politics and Foreign Policy: A Reader in Research Theory*, ed. James N. Rosenau [New York: Free Press, 1969], 429–430).

19. Butterfield, *History and Human Relations*, 19–20.

what may never have existed may subsequently bring about what is feared the most."[20]

The work of Robert Jervis also embodies Butterfield's and Herz's tragedy. Jervis distinguishes between what he terms the "spiral model" and the "deterrence model." While both models describe a process of action and reaction between the parties involved, their core dynamic differs. Jervis explains the deterrence model:

> the aggressor, of course, is hostile because its expansion is blocked ... and the increase of the arms and tensions can continue for several cycles as each matches the other's belligerence. But this process resembles that explained by the spiral model only superficially.... The heightening of the conflict does not represent, as it does in the spiral theory, the creation of an *illusory incompatibility*, but only the real incompatibility that were there from the beginning.[21]

In the deterrence model, the second state employs the correct countermeasures to deter a real aggressor by arming itself. By contrast, in the spiral model, the actors are non-expansionist; the hostility of the first state is merely apparent, not real. Thus, according to Jervis, only spiral model dynamics equate to a security dilemma.

Jervis demonstrates how "historians have seen a number of cases which fit the spiral model," by citing the Anglo-German Naval Race prior to the First World War:

> In 1904 President Roosevelt noted that the Kaiser 'sincerely believes that the English are planning to attack him and to smash his fleet, and perhaps join in a war to the death against him. As a matter of fact, the English harbour no such intentions, but are themselves in a condition of panic terror lest the Kaiser secretly intend to form an alliance against them with France or Russia, or both, to destroy their fleet .... It is as funny a case as I have ever seen of mutual distrust and fear bringing two peoples to the verge of war.'[22]

This fits well with a tight security dilemma formulation. Both actors, Great Britain and Germany, misperceive a situation of compatible security requirements. Security for Great Britain—at least according to Roosevelt—does not necessitate attacking the German fleet, and security for Germany does not require destroying the British Navy in possible alliance with France or Russia. Likewise, Jervis points towards an illusory incompatibility when asserting that

20. John Herz, *International Politics in the Atomic Age* (New York: Columbia University Press, 1966), 241 (emphasis added).
21. Jervis, *Perception and Misperception*, 80.
22. Ibid., 74.

if the cold war was indeed a security dilemma "[n]o one was to blame and everyone was to blame. "[23]

In the same way, Randall Schweller writes that the security dilemma is "always real," not apparent, and if states are arming for reasons other than security, "then it is no longer a security dilemma but rather an example of a state . . . mobilizing for the purposes of expansion . . . . "[24] Therefore, such actors must be treated as aggressors, but what, about actors who arm for reasons of security? Shifting the focus in this way from goals to security requirements, the question, Is this actor interested in security? becomes, In what way—through what means—is this actor interested in security? This becomes clearer when comparing a regular security dilemma with this tight one.

A REGULAR SECURITY DILEMMA

In keeping with Schweller, Jervis notes "the tendency to assume that a desire for security, rather than expansion, is the prime goal of most states."[25] The corollary of this is that actors can be neatly split into two types: security seekers and power seekers. These two types equate more or less to status quo states and revisionist states, respectively. Security seekers have no desire to expand, while power seekers do. Similarly, Glaser labels states as "greedy" and "not greedy." He uses "the term greedy for a state willing to incur the costs or risks for non-security expansion; [while] by contrast a not greedy state is unwilling to run the risks for non-security expansion."[26]

Glaser goes on to qualify his classification. He duly notes the difference between *intentions* and *motives*. He further divides security seekers into "secure not greedy" and "potentially insecure not greedy."[27] The importance of this division lies in Glaser noting that not all security seekers are status quo actors: if not greedy states become insecure, aggression might be the solution to their insecurity. Glaser writes, "As . . . insecurity increases, expansion becomes more attractive if acquiring additional territory would provide a buffer zone against invasion or additional resources for defence and/or would deny those resources to the defender."[28] That is to say, states' security may sometimes require hostile actions, such as occupying neighboring territory and/or seizing

23. Jervis, "Was the Cold War a Security Dilemma?" *Journal of Cold War Studies* 3, no. 1 (winter 2001): 38.
24. Randall L. Schweller, "Neorealism's Status Quo Bias: What Security Dilemma?" *Security Studies* 5, no. 3 (spring 1996): 117.
25. Jervis, *Perception and Misperception*, 75.
26. Glaser, "The Political Consequences of Military Strategy," 501.
27. Ibid., 503–505.
28. Ibid., 504.

others' resources. Jeffrey Taliaferro notes, "The historical record abounds with cases of states that pursued security-driven expansion or preventive war."[29] I refer to this situation as "required insecurity" in that my security necessitates your insecurity.

The presence of required insecurity has significance inasmuch as it precludes the compatibility of actors' security requirements. In a tight security dilemma, security seekers behave according to an illusory incompatibility concerning their security requirements. In a regular security dilemma, security seekers act in accordance with a real incompatibility; regular security dilemmas are not marked by misperception. This seems to place regular security dilemmas somewhere between Jervis' spiral and deterrence models. Although still dealing with security seekers, a second state, in assuming the worst, correctly interprets the security requirements of the first (expansion). Thus, by employing countermeasures, the second state is taking the correct course of action.

The belief that security might be achieved through military aggression can often be the result of the state's strategic situation. Indeed, Jervis stresses this particular factor. He notes how before the First World War a status quo Germany might have been compelled to attack its neighbors.[30] Given the presence of less-than-friendly powers, France and Russia, on either side, strategic necessity dictated that one be defeated quickly, whether or not either country intended to attack Germany. Thus, as Jervis writes, "The security dilemma is at its most vicious when commitments, strategy, or technology dictate that the only route to security lies through expansion. Status quo powers must them act like aggressors."[31]

All in all, Snyder articulates the essential nature of a regular formulation when he defines the security dilemma as "a situation in which each state believed that its security *required the insecurity of others.*"[32]

---

29. Jeffrey W. Taliaferro, "Security Seeking Under Anarchy," *International Security* 25, no. 3, (winter 2000/01): 145.

30. Jervis, "Cooperation Under the Security Dilemma," 315.

31. Ibid., 316. Jack Snyder and Charles Reynolds also talk of the security dilemma in terms of expansionist states (although they both prefer to use the term "imperialist state"). Reynolds argues that imperialist states will pursue expansionist policies in order to counter their vulnerability to changes in the relative power of their neighbors. Charles Reynolds, *Modes of Imperialism*, (Oxford: Oxford University Press, 1981), 24. Similarly, Snyder argues that while an aggressor (imperialist state) might well begin with the intention of attacking another, because this second state employs countervailing measures, what can then ensue between the two is "a testing of will and capabilities." Snyder claims that in such a situation the fear of being taken advantage of is experienced by both sides. As such, the expansionist state further arms for both defensive (to deter the other) and offensive (a preemptive strike) purposes. Snyder, "Perceptions of the Security Dilemma in 1914," 165.

32. Snyder, 155 (emphasis added).

A Loose Security Dilemma

In tight security dilemmas, security seekers have compatible security requirements. In regular security dilemmas, matters are complicated by security seekers having incompatible security requirements. In loose security dilemmas, however, whether actors are security seekers at all may be inconsequential.

In "The Security Dilemma Revisited," Glaser builds upon his earlier work concerning greedy and not greedy states. Glaser first discusses the ways in which security seekers generate unintended consequences. He then focuses, however, on the relevance of power seekers to the security dilemma: "The importance of the security dilemma does not become unimportant in a world with greedy states."[33] It does seem to depend, though, on the level of greed. The greedier the actor, the less relevant the security dilemma is in explaining state behavior. Glaser is not clear in defining "more greedy" and "less greedy," although he is clear in his claim that greedy states and the security dilemma can go together. Glaser contends that "Schweller's conclusions are somewhat exaggerated, because Schweller believes incorrectly that greedy states rob the security dilemma of all its explanatory value."[34]

Glaser's argument in this respect is that "with greedy states, offense-defense variables still play a role in explaining war."[35] In essence, Glaser argues that power seekers will be either encouraged or discouraged from employing (intended) aggressive policies depending on whether offense or defense has the advantage. In other words, the benefits of going to war are influenced by offense-defense variables. This resembles what Jan Angstrom and Isabelle Duyvesteyn refer to as the "declining-prize dilemma." Rather than actions from fear of being harmed by others, "... incentives to win ... compel the actors to initiate violence or maintain fighting."[36] Angstrom and Duyvesteyn continue:

33. Glaser, "The Security Dilemma Revisited," 190.
34. Ibid. I recognize the debate over greedy and non-greedy states might be considered a false one. This is because for some Realists security dilemmas are generated regardless of states' intentionality. Rather, it is structural characteristics and not actors' attributes which culminate in the "tragedy." In this respect, Realists point to the possible scenario of today's friendly neighbors becoming tomorrow's enemies. I certainly cannot dismiss this point, and I am grateful to Ben Frankel for drawing my attention to it. However my own categorization of the security dilemma, however, rests not so much with benign/malign intentions but with compatible/incompatible security requirements. In addition, I argue that decision makers who do play it safe with today's friends behave in accordance with what can be called a projected intentionality, where probabilities concerning what the other's attributes will likely be next year, five years hence, and so forth are considered.
35. Ibid., 191.
36. Jan Angstrom and Isabelle Duyvesteyn, "Evaluating Realist Explanations of Internal Conflict: The Case of Liberia," *Security Studies* 10, no. 3 (spring 2001): 199.

Actors are thus *not necessarily mere security seekers*, but rather power- maxi-mizers. The declining-prize dilemma suggests that under anarchy ... and, crucially, under suddenly reduced resources, it becomes rational for any actor to try to win, because even ... [some] prize is better than none. This can explain why actors are prepared to accept huge costs, that is, war.... This results in a dilemma, because as one group strives to win the prize, the violence decreases the prize further, thereby inviting others to try to win it.[37]

Here actors engage in and continue fighting not necessarily because of strate-gic considerations—whether or not offense has the advantage—but simply to secure the ever-decreasing spoils. Nevertheless, in both the loose secu-rity dilemma and the declining-prize dilemma power considerations lie at the core.

KAUFMANN'S AND POSEN'S INTERPRETATION

Kaufmann's approach to the security dilemma is similar to that of Glaser, inasmuch as the predominant focus is on offense-defense considerations. In its application of the concept to ethnic conflicts, Kaufmann's work draws much from Barry Posen's scholarship.

Using the security dilemma to explain conflict in the former Yugoslavia, in particular the 1991 Serb-Croat war, Posen begins by characterizing the situation as an "emerging anarchy." The collapse of central government meant that Yugoslavia's various ethnic groups—Croatia's Serb and Croat populations— had to provide for their own security: "The competition will continue to a point at which the competing entities have amassed more power than needed for security and, thus, consequently begin to threaten others. Those threatened will begin to respond in turn."[38]

Set against this action-reaction process, Posen's employment of the security dilemma is premised on the following three elements: "the indistinguishability of offence over defence," "the superiority of offensive over defensive action," and "windows of vulnerability and opportunity."

Concerning the indistinguishability of offense and defense, Posen argues that newly independent groups must try to determine their neighbors' in-tentions, and that they will often do so by examining one another's military capabilities. Clear distinctions between offensive and defensive capabilities are usually difficult to make, especially in terms of lightly armed, irregular forces. As Posen points out, "The weaponry available to such groups will

---

37. Ibid.
38. Posen, "Security Dilemma and Ethnic Conflict," 28.

often be quite rudimentary, their offensive military capabilities will be as much a function of the quantity . . . of the soldiers as the particular characteristic of the weapons they control."[39]

Posen then considers circumstances in which offensive action is likely to be preferable to some form of defense. Here, Posen is keen to stress the importance of what he calls "ethnic islands," where [i]slands of one group's population are stranded in the sea of another."[40] The protection of ethnic islands can be difficult. "[T]hese islands may not be able to help one another; they may be subject to blockade or siege, and by virtue of their numbers relative to the surrounding population and because of topography, they may be militarily indefensible."[41] As such, groups will have incentives to rescue these islands before the other side is able to take advantage of the islands' relative vulnerability. Thus, the presence of ethnic islands makes preventive war more likely.

Lastly Posen considers windows of vulnerability and opportunity. He notes how the "relative rate of state formation" has an effect on the incentives for preventive war. When central authority is dissolving, "[t]he material remnants of the old state . . . will be unevenly distributed across the territories of the old empire. Some groups may well have held a privileged position in the old system. Others will be less well placed."[42]

Where preventive war might be desirable, calculations must be made as to the relative power of one side against the other. If the other is militarily weak, but over time is expected to become stronger, then the move to strike sooner rather than later is desirable. Moreover, whether the other has potential allies (and, if so, how soon could their armed forces be mobilized) will also influence the timing of an armed attack.[43]

Citing to the 1991 Serb-Croat war, Posen writes that on Serbia's part, offense appeared to have the advantage in terms of rescuing fellow nationals in

---

39. Ibid., 29. In such circumstances, Posen continues, intentionality is ascertained largely by reference to the historical record. Posen describes how the historical views taken by ethnic groups often turn out to be inaccurate and misleading. First, regimes in multi-ethnic states may well have suppressed or manipulated the historical record in order to consolidate their own position. Second, within the groups themselves old rivalries will have been preserved more in stories, poems, and myths than in codified history, and will thereby have been "magnified in . . . [their] telling." Third, because of this each group will have difficulty in adhering to another's view of the past. Finally, actors are likely to assume the worst: "as central authority begins to collapse and local politicians begin to struggle for power, they will begin to write down their versions of history in political speeches. Yet stories are likely to be emotionally charged" (ibid., 31).
40. Ibid., 32.
41. Ibid.
42. Ibid., 34.
43. Ibid., 34–35.

Croatia. Given this and Serbia's relative power advantage over the Croatian republic, "[p]reventive war incentives were relatively high."[44] Serbs living in Croatia were "scattered in a number of vulnerable islands," and thus required rescuing by Serbia. Although Serbia held military superiority over Croatia— Serbia commanding the majority of resources of the Yugoslav national army (JNA)—in time Croatia was likely to increase its own armed forces. Thus, a window of opportunity existed for Serbian forces to strike Croatia first.

As Posen does, Kaufmann also emphasizes the advantage of offense over defense: "Offense has the advantage over defence in inter-community conflict, especially when settlement patterns are inter-mingled, because isolated pockets are harder to hold than take."[45] He continues, "The more mixed the opposing groups, the stronger the offense in relation to the defense; the more separated they are, the stronger the defense in relation to the offense."[46]

In keeping with a loose security dilemma formulation, Kaufmann considers whether the parties to the conflict are seen in terms of security seekers or power seekers as largely beside the point. Fundamentally, actors are driven by offense-defense considerations. Vulnerable ethnic islands make defense difficult (as in the case of Croatia's ethnic Serbs), thus providing strong incentives for pre-emptive action.

From this tight, regular, and loose security dilemma categorization, I now want to make the claim that each type of security dilemma corresponds to a particular type of conflict. I label them "resolvable short of war," "difficult to resolve short of war," and "irresolvable short of war."[47]

THE SECURITY DILEMMA AND CONFLICT RESOLUTION

The categorization of the security dilemma into its tight, regular, and loose formulations is not merely of conceptual value. It is also of importance to policy-making. In the context of ethnic conflict, Snyder and Jervis recognise that the security dilemma is an indispensable tool for third parties considering intervention. They argue that in order to fully grasp how security fears cause and perpetuate ethnic war, observers must have a knowledge not only of the anarchical situation facing the belligerents, but also of "the participants' perceptions of that situation and their expectations of each others' likely behavior

44. Ibid.
45. Kaufmann, "Possible and Impossible Solutions to Ethnic Civil Wars," *International Security* 20, no. 4 (spring 1996): 148.
46. Ibid.
47. See Roe, "Former Yugoslavia: The Security Dilemma That Never Was?" *European Journal of International Relations* 6, no. 3 (2000): 373–393.

in that situation." As such, "Interveners must confront not only the circumstances that constitute the security dilemma . . . but also the ideas and social
forces that produced the dilemma in the first place and that may reproduce it
unless the interveners can neutralize them."[48] Snyder and Jervis continue by
pointing out that nearly every conflict is marked with a mixture of "security
fears" and "predatory goals," which are difficult to separate; yet, if possible,
interveners must do exactly that: separating security fears and predatory goals
enables policymakers to discern what kind of actors are involved, what type of
conflict they are dealing with, and thus, what intervention strategies are best
employed.

According to Snyder and Jervis, the security dilemma informs three "general types of prescription." The first is to "establish a sovereign authority
capable of enforcing hegemonic peace upon all fearfully contending parties";
that is to say, get the new regime in place, and quickly. The second is to
"devise a situation in which the parties can provide for their own security
through strictly defensive measures"; in other words, give defense the advantage and first-strike incentives disappear. And finally, the third prescription
is "for the contending parties to lock themselves into an institutional framework that guarantees their mutual self-restraint once they lay their weapons
down."[49]

Like Snyder and Jervis, my formulation of the security dilemma informs
three different kinds of policy prescriptions.

RESOLVABLE SHORT OF WAR (TIGHT SECURITY DILEMMA)

Conflicts that are resolvable short of war equate to the existence of a tight
security dilemma. In this regard, relations can be enhanced through mechanisms that can reveal misperception to both sides. Amongst such measures,
"power sharing enables . . . ethnic groups to influence or determine policy,
[because] this reduces their uncertainty concerning the policies' likely impact
on their ethnicity."[50] Other confidence-building measures (CBMs) may also be
applicable: clearer information and more effective methods of communication
can reduce the ambiguity of actors' intentions. Reference to CBMs is nothing
new: within the literature, CBMs are discussed at length when referring to the
possibility of mitigating or ameliorating the security dilemma. Still, in cases

---

48. Jack Snyder and Robert Jervis, "Civil War and the Security Dilemma," in *Civil Wars,
Insecurity and Intervention*, ed. Barbara Walter and Jack Snyder (New York: Columbia University
Press, 1999), 10.
49. Ibid., 18.
50. Alan Collins, *The Security Dilemmas of Southeast Asia* (London: Macmillan, 2000), 179.

where the incompatibility between actors is real, CBMs on their own will likely be ineffective, thus other policy prescriptions will also be needed.

DIFFICULT TO RESOLVE SHORT OF WAR (REGULAR SECURITY DILEMMA)

Conflicts that are difficult to resolve short of war are informed by a regular security dilemma situation. In this scenario, CBMs are largely inapplicable as there is simply no misperception to be revealed. Although the situation may not be so easy to overcome peaceably, the actors may still be induced to change their security requirements. As Alan Collins points out:

> [I]n some instances it is not possible to mitigate a security dilemma via spiral prescriptions such as confidence-building measures. In other words, simply reducing statesmen's uncertainty is not enough, [as] the goal [of the state] ... is the cause of the neighbour's insecurity. In this instance it is only possible for all to be secure if the ... [state] *reinterprets its criteria for achieving security*.[51]

Appropriate strategies here may include positive sanctions, or, perhaps more accurately, incentives.

Han Dorussen notes how incentives are usually treated as being in opposition to sanctions, since they are largely rewards while sanctions are seen as punishment. Referring to the work of David Cortright, Dorussen defines incentives as "the granting of a political *or* economic benefit in exchange for a specific policy adjustment by the recipient nation."[52] Thus, incentives may be an effective mechanism for inducing change in security requirements. Incentives provide possible means for prompting some shifts in policy. The fact that the recipient state is not seen to be punished is also important, since, after all, it is a security seeker. Dorussen subsequently notes how "incentives are much less likely to lead to 'rallying around the flag'."[53]

IRRESOLVABLE SHORT OF WAR (LOOSE SECURITY DILEMMA)

With a loose security dilemma, the situation is irresolvable short of war Given that the parties (or at least one of the parties) are power seekers and wish to fight it out between themselves, third parties will require some degree of military force to resolve the conflict. As such, loose security dilemmas must

---

51. Ibid., 25.
52. Han Dorussen, "Mixing Carrots with Sticks: Evaluating the Effectiveness of Positive Incentives," *Journal of Peace Research* 38, no. 2 (2001): 252.
53. Ibid., 253.

be clearly distinguished from tight and regular formulations: tight and regular security dilemmas may be addressed through peaceable, economic, political or legal means, but loose security dilemmas invariably warrant a military solution.

In keeping with conflict that is irresolvable short of war, partition reflects a military solution. Kaufmann advocates partition by addressing the strategic necessity of giving defense the advantage: incentives for preemptive strikes are dampened, and although an action-reaction dynamic might well continue, further military confrontations seem unlikely. As Kaufmann writes:

> [A]ny attempt to seize more territory requires a major conventional offensive. Thus the conflict changes from one of mutual pre-emptive ethnic cleansing to something approaching conventional interstate war in which normal deterrence dynamics apply. Mutual deterrence does not guarantee that there will be no further violence, but it reduces the probability of outbreaks, as well as the likely aims and intensity of those that do occur.[54]

For Kaufmann, population transfer is crucial for conflict resolution in this regard. If partition takes place without ethnic separation, conflict may increase. This is because, as Kaufmann describes it, "stay behind minorities are completely exposed," creating incentives for rescue and ethnic cleansing.[55] Often third parties must intervene militarily in order to draw the line of separation and to enable the transfer of populations from one entity to another.

In this first part of the article, my purpose was to show how the existing security dilemma literature might be interpreted according to three different formulations: tight, regular, and loose. In turn, I showed how each of these formulations informs a different type of conflict: resolvable short of war, difficult to resolve short of war, and irresolvable short of war. Accordingly, I have placed Kaufmann's interpretation of the security dilemma into the loose category, thereby characterizing his approach in the context of ethnic conflicts that are irresolvable short of war. The second part now employs the tight, regular, and loose security dilemma categorization in an actual case. Here, my interpretation of the security dilemma in the Serb-Croat conflict in the Republic of Croatia is largely regular, and thus implies a method of conflict resolution different from that of Kaufmann.

---

54. Kaufmann, "Possible and Impossible Solutions," 150.
55. Ibid., 162.

CROATIA: WHICH SECURITY DILEMMA?

F ollowing the establishment of the first (Royal) Yugoslav State at the end of the First World War, antagonisms between Croatia and Serbia over the nature of the new country were soon apparent. Many Croats resented that Royal Yugoslavia was centralized and Serb-dominated. Most Serbs saw themselves as the natural and deserving hegemony of the South Slav people; without their great sacrifice in the two Balkan Wars and the First World War, Yugoslavia would not have been possible. However, not until the onset of the Second World War, did such antagonisms turn into bloodshed.

Under the guidance of Vladko Macek in the 1930s, Croatia pursued its goal of greater autonomy within a re-worked state structure. In August 1939. the new Yugoslav Prime Minister, Dragoljub Cvetkovic, offered Croatia what amounted to federal status and more territory. On 26 August, the *Sporazumen* (Compromise), also known as the Cvetkovic-Macek Agreement, was signed. The new autonomous Croatian *banovina* created by this agreement encompassed a population of nearly four and a half million.

On 10 April 1941, four days after Nazi Germany invaded Yugoslavia, the *Nezavisna Drzava Hrvatska* (NDH), or Independent State of Croatia, was established under a puppet regime. The NDH, now also encompassing all of Bosnia and Herzegovina, contained almost two million (Orthodox) Serbs.[56] The new Croatian state was run by the fascist Ustashe party, under the leadership of Ante Pavelic. Pavelic's goal was to create an ethnically pure (Catholic) "Greater Croatia, and the Ustashe set about their task with an intense religious hatred for Serbs. Serbs were slaughtered in their tens, if not hundreds, of thousand."[57] John Lampe refers to the Serb-populated areas of NDH as having been the "Krajina Killing Fields."[58] The most feared among the killing fields of the NDH was the concentration camp at Jasenovac where some 700,000 men, women, and children were detained. According to Robert Fisk, "Many of them . . . were hacked to death with axes, or beheaded with saws. The women were often handed over to professional butchers who hacked them to death with knives."[59]

---

56. Out of a total population of some 6.3 million, the NDH was home to 1.9 million ethnic Serbs. Noel Malcolm, *Bosnia: A Short History* (London: Macmillan, 1994), 176.
57. The number of Serbs (and others) killed by the Ustashe during the Second World War is still keenly contested; however, total Serb casualties between 1941 and 1945—including fatalities inflicted by the Partisans and the German army—was likely 500,000.
58. John R. Lampe, *Yugoslavia as History: There Was Twice a Country* (Cambridge: Cambridge University Press, 1996), 205.
59. Robert Fisk, "Croatian Death Camp Gives Hate a New Twist," *The Independent*, 20 June 1994.

The genocidal policies of the NDH provoked tens of thousands of Serbs to enlist in either the Chetniks or the Partisans resistance movements. Under the leadership of Draza Mihailovic, the Chetniks fought for the restoration of royal power and for the creation of a "Greater Serbia." The establishment of the Chetniks and the Partisans as effective resistance movements to the Ustashe served to create a vicious circle of atrocities and counter-atrocities against the NDH Serb and Croat populations. "Acting in the name of preserving their faiths, Serbs and Croats conducted a holy war trying to exterminate each other."[60] The Partisans wanted to create a new Yugoslavia along socialist lines. Their leader was Josip Broz, better known as Tito. Thus, between the Chetniks and the partisans there also developed a conflict as to whether the post-war Yugoslav state should be monarchist or communist.

When the Second World War, and with it the Yugoslav civil war, came to an end in 1945, victory for the Partisans enabled Tito to take over the leadership of the country. Yugoslavia's new federal structure, together with the personal strength of Tito's leadership, managed to keep further hostilities between Serbs and Croats at bay.[61] This lasted some forty-five years, until the onset of democratization.

FROM DEMOCRATIZATION TO VIOLENCE

Throughout 1990, multi-party elections were held in all of Yugoslavia's six republics. In the Croatian republic, victory went to the Croatian Democratic Union (HDZ) under the leadership of Franjo Tudjman. When the election results were announced on 25 and 26 April, Tudjman's party had won an overall majority, securing fifty-eight percent of the seats in the Croatian parliament (*Sabor*).[62]

The election campaign officially began on 24 February, the very same day Tudjman was elected as HDZ president. Tudjman pursued a political program based on the notion of Croatian sovereignty. In doing so, however,

---

60. Dusko Doder, "Yugoslavia: New War, Old Hatreds," *Foreign Policy*, no. 91 (summer 1993): 10.

61. During the mid-1960s there was, however, a revival of Croatian national consciousness. In 1967, a body of Croatian intellectuals demanded constitutional recognition of a separate Croatian language. The language declaration sparked a mass movement known as Maspok, and the concomitant revival of Croat nationalism was accompanied by the reappearance of some symbols last seen during the period of the NDH. The so-called Croatian Spring lasted until 1972, when it was finally suppressed by Tito.

62. Out of the 356 seats in the Sabor, the HDZ won 205 of them outright and gained a further four in coalition with other parties, this despite having received just over 40 percent of the total vote.

he was keen to point out that the party was not advocating an independent Croatia.

Tudjman's biggest concern in this respect was the republic's Serb population, especially those living in the *Krajina*, or frontier, region. The Krajina constituted a series of thirteen administrative districts running from northern Dalmatia to western Slavonia. At the time of the elections, Serbs formed an absolute majority in eleven and a relative majority in two of the districts. Those in the Krajina made up roughly thirty percent of all Croatia's Serb inhabitants,[63] but their regional concentration and strong ethnic consciousness made them a significant factor in Croatian politics.[64] Krajina's major town, Knin, was the stronghold of Serbian nationalism, and even before Tudjman's election victory, serious tensions had manifested themselves in the town.[65] Rather than calming rising tensions in Krajina following his election success, however, Tudjman only served to agitate the nascent sense of hostility between Croatia's Serb and Croat communities. "Once in power," Robert Hislope writes, "the Tudjman regime initiated a policy agenda that sought to secure the unconditional right of Croatians to exercise political priority over their own republic."[66] I refer to this policy agenda as "Croatization."

Croatization was both symbolic and pragmatic. Many markers of Croatia's independent (often fascist) past were restored, including the checkerboard flag (*Sahovnica*) and the Croatian coat of arms.[67] Streets and squares were renamed: the Square of the Victims of Fascism in Zagreb was changed to the Square of the Great Croats. Tudjman's government also proposed certain amendments to the Croatian Constitution. For example, Section 1 of the new Draft Constitution established the Republic of Croatia as "the national state of the Croatian nation and the state of the members of *other nations and minorities* that live within it." For many Serbs, this, in effect, seemed to be saying, "Croatia

63. The majority of Croatia's 600,000 ethnic Serbs were urbanized, living in the republic's major towns and cities.

64. Serb communities had been in Krajina mainly since the period of Ottoman rule in the Balkans. During this time, many Serb families driven out of the Serbian Kingdom by the Turks came to settle in the region. In return for pledging their allegiance to Vienna, Serbs were granted religious freedom and a measure of self-government.

65. For example, in July 1989 Serbs in Knin demonstrated in support of their fellow nationals in Kosovo. Their outburst of nationalist sentiment sparked a major confrontation between local Serb leaders and the nationally sensitive communist government in Zagreb. See Leonard J. Cohen, *Broken Bonds: Yugoslavia's Disintegration and Balkan Politics in Transition* (Oxford: Westview Press, 1995), 130.

66. Robert Hislope, "Intra-Ethnic Conflict in Croatia and Serbia: Flanking and the Consequences for Democracy," *East European Quarterly* 30, no .4 (1997): 476.

67. The checkerboard pattern, which appears on many of Croatia's symbols, is, in fact, slightly different with the red and white checks reversed from the wartime symbols. Again, I am grateful to one of the anonymous referees for pointing this out.

for the Croats." Indeed, the Draft Constitution referred to the Croatian nation (*Hrvatski narod*), but it no longer referred to Serbs in the same respect. Previously a constituent nation in the Republic of Croatia and enjoying equal constitutional status alongside the Croats, the Serbs were now relegated to the category of "other nations and minorities." Moreover, in the first paragraph of Article 12, the official language and alphabet of Croatia was specified as "the Croatian language and alphabet." Dual-language road signs were torn down, even in Serb majority areas. Furthermore, numbers of Serbs were removed from the bureaucracies and the police and duly replaced with ethnic Croats.

The Serbian Democratic Party (SDS) represented the interests of ethnic Serbs in Croatia. In May 1990, the party's leader, Jovan Raskovic, met with Tudjman on several occasions. During their meetings, Raskovic is said to have articulated two primary objectives. First, he wanted the Draft Constitution to define Serbs on equal footing with Croats. Second, he asked Tudjman to grant the Krajina Serbs some form of autonomy within the republic. But the two leaders, failed to reach an agreement.

When the revised Draft Constitution appeared on 25 July, it said nothing about the Serbs as a constituent nation. Not surprisingly, the SDS rejected it. At a mass rally held in the town of Srb on 25 July—which was attended by 120,000 Serbs from all over Yugoslavia-Raskovic announced that a referendum was to be held on 18 August concerning the status of Croatia's Serb population. The referendum was to legitimate the newly-formed Serbian National Council's "Declaration on the Sovereignty and Autonomy of the Serbian People." According to leading SDS figures, if Croatia were to remain part of the Yugoslav Federation, the declaration mainly advocated the provision of cultural autonomy. If, though, the republic were to move towards secession from Yugoslavia, the document instead demanded political autonomy.[68] The Croat leadership was alarmed, warning that the referendum threatened to create "a state within a state."[69]

As the date for the referendum approached, some Serbian leaders met in Belgrade with Yugoslav Federal President Borisav Jovic, to ask for protection.[70]

---

68. Cultural autonomy entails the granting of certain rights in relation to the means of cultural production: control of one's schools, museums, newspapers, religious institutions, even one's own television and radio broadcasts. Ethnic autonomy is more territorially based and involves self-government along a wider range of issues. This can be manifest in some kind of autonomous region within the state, or, in its most extreme representation, in independence outside the existing state structure.
69. See Cohen, *Broken Bonds*, 132.
70. Jovic is said to have told the Serbian leadership in Croatia that in his role as Federal President he would be unable to help them in any "official" capacity. Instead, he directed them to Slobodan Milosevic who, Jovic assured them, would be able to offer assistance.

To thwart possible Croat interference at this time, log barricades were set up in some of Krajina's predominantly Serb districts, thus beginning the so-called log revolution. On 17 August, the day before the referendum, the Croatian Ministry for Internal Affairs sent several helicopters to the Knin region. They were met by jet fighters from the Yugoslav Air Force and forced to turn back. Milan Martic, chief of the Knin police force, ordered his men to take over the police station. Meanwhile, Knin Radio announced that the town's mayor, Milan Babic, had declared a state of war in the region.[71] There were widely confirmed reports that the Serbs had set up roadblocks throughout the area. It was "indicated that about 120 active and reserve policemen had mutinied, distributing weapons and joining civil brigades. Groups of civilians, including some military reservists, also broke into civil defense storage depots and seized arms."[72] The Split daily newspaper, *Slobodna Dalmacija*, warned that the Croatian government would be unable to stop the referendum without causing bloodshed.

The referendum went ahead as scheduled and the declaration of the Serbian National Council was reported as having been accepted unanimously.[73] Then Croatian Prime Minister Stipe Mesic angrily voiced his concerns:

> What kind of referendum in Croatia is this when Croats are not taking part in it, only Serbs and nobody else. . . . They are not a God-given nation, they are equal to everybody else, not more equal. If there are problems we should discuss them. . . . Who gave them the right to go to [Federal President] Jovic, to speak on behalf of the Serbs of Croatia? Who authorized Jovic to have talks with them without representatives of the republic of Croatia . . .? These people in this country think that everything should be measured with criteria that suits the Serbs.[74]

The day before the referendum, 17 August 1990, was certainly crucial as it signaled the beginning of the log revolution, where Serb communities in Krajina effectively began to separate themselves from the rest of Croatia. Also at this point, relations deteriorated sufficiently to produce the first significant hostile encounters between the two parties.

The period from the election campaign to the log-revolution is marked by certain security dilemma dynamics. In the following sections I argue that the Croatian case can be viewed most profitably through the concept's regular

71. Silber and Little, 106.
72. Milan Andrejevich, "Croatia Between Stability and Civil War (Part 1)," RFE/RL *Report on Eastern Europe*, 14 September 1990, 42–43.
73. According to the referendum, every Serb over the age of 18 who was a resident living in Croatia or held Croatian citizenship while living outside the republic was entitled to vote.
74. Quoted in Silber and Little, 135.

formulation where both sides are security seekers, but security requirements are marked by a real incompatibility.

CROAT SECURITY REQUIREMENTS/SERB (MIS)PERCEPTIONS

D etermining security requirements is problematic. What any state, nation, or ethnic group feels it needs to be secure is invariably internally contested. This is certainly the case with the Croatian republic. Here, however, Croatian security requirements can arguably be taken as those articulated through the policies of Franjo Tudjman's HDZ government. Tudjman certainly enjoyed the support of the majority of Croats in the Croatian republic while acknowledging that the HDZ was not representative of the Croatian community as a whole. The HDZ came to power characterizing itself as "the most Croatian party." Indeed, according to Robert Hislope the HDZ was "[m]ore than a broad base mass movement than a political party," which aspired to represent the interests of the entire Croatian nation."[75] In the main government, policy reflected the sentiment of the majority, and there was thus a marked absence of dissension among ethnic Croats toward Tudjman's program of Croatization.

CROAT GOALS

Initially, Tudjman articulated his intentions in further demands for greater decentralization in Yugoslavia. However, it is arguably the case, that although maintaining an apparently (con)federalist approach, Tudjman's ultimate wish was for a sovereign Croatia, and for the republic to thus secede from the Yugoslav State.[76] Dusko Doder is particularly clear about this: "Although they [the Tudjman government] professed to be advocating a confederal arrangement, the Croats in fact were determined to destroy Yugoslavia."[77] Doder's vehemence aside, Tudjman sought at least an arrangement whereby Croatia be free of perceived Serbian domination.

More specifically, Tudjman's desire was create a Croatian state that would be the home of the Croatian nation. Robert Hayden points out that in a Croatia for the Croats, "minorities are foreign to the bodies political and social.

---

75. Hislope, 475.
76. See Andrejevich, "Croatia Goes to the Polls," RFE/RL *Report on Eastern Europe*, 4 May 1990, 36.
77. Dusko Doder, "Yugoslavia: New War, Old Hatreds," *Foreign Policy*, no. 91 (summer 1993): 18.

Thus, for the majority to obtain its primary goal of the nation-state, only two choices are possible: 'the territorial truncation of the state, or the expulsion of disloyal minorities.'"[78] Of these two choices, territorial truncation was out of the question.[79] Indeed, territorial integrity was particularly important with regard to Krajina, and especially Knin. "Knin is sacred, Knin is sacred,"[80] he reportedly told Stipe Mesic.

In economic terms, Knin was vital to the Tudjman government. The central communications junction between Zagreb to the north and the Dalmatian coastline to the south was responsible for generating much of Croatia's wealth. As Misha Glenny notes, "With Knin outside of its control, Croatia faces unsurmountable difficulties in developing its tourist industries. Without Knin, Croatia is an economic cripple."[81] Culturally, Knin is also of great significance in that it is the site where kings of the medieval Croatian State were crowned in the tenth and eleventh centuries.

Given Knin's economic and cultural importance, as Haakan Wiberg explains, the inviolability of state borders "ruled out the territorial compromise necessary to get a Croatian state that was also ethnically Croatian, leaving forced ethnic cleansing or Croatization as [the] only possibilities."[82] The expulsion of disloyal minorities was both extreme and undesirable. This left Croatization.

Glenny outlines the relationship between Tudjman's nationalism and the program of Croatization:

> His [Tudjman's] obsession was with the Croatian of a state which would be identified with the Croatian people.... Croats in Yugoslavia now wanted a state which they could call their own in every respect. In Tudjman's eyes that meant hanging the red and white chequered shield, the sahovnica ... from every building; it meant demoting the Serbs from their status ... as a majority Yugoslav nation to that of a minority within Croatia; it

78. Robert Hayden, "Constitutional Nationalism in the Formerly Yugoslav Republics," *Slavic Review* 51, no. 4 (winter 1992): 672.
79. Essentially, there were three different visions of an independent Croatia: the Yugoslav republic of Croatia, the Banovina Hrvatska (the Croatia created by the 1939 Sporazumen), and the NDH (the 1941–45 Pavelic state). The NDH vision represented the extreme nationalist view, one held by Dobroslav Paraga's Hrvatska Stranka Prava (HSP), or "Croatian Party of [State] Right." The Yugoslav republic of Croatia vision was the least Tudjman could ask for and still get away with; anything less would have likely cost him the presidency, given the degree of Croat nationalist sentiment.
80. Quoted in Misha Glenny, *The Fall of Yugoslavia: The Third Balkan War* (London: Penguin, 1992), 14.
81. Ibid., 2.
82. Haakan Wiberg, "Divided Nations and Divided States as a Security Problem; The Case of Yugoslavia," *Copenhagen Peace Research Institute (COPRI)* Working Paper, no. 14 (1992): 17.

meant pronouncing literary Croat as the only language of administration and dismissing the Serb's Cyrillic script as well.[83]

Vis-à-vis the republic's ethnic Serbs, Croatization, then, was the predominant means with which to achieve the goal of "a state which they could call their own in every respect."

The fundamental question still to be addressed, however, is whether the Croatization program can be equated to security seeking or power seeking behavior on the part of the Croatian president. This is difficult, although there is some weight of opinion to suggest the largely security seeking behavior of the HDZ government.

Glenny argues that the nature of Croatization was predicated, at least in part, on Tudjman's serious misjudgment over the nature of the republic's Serb communities. More so than elsewhere, Krajina is where the Serbs had been shaped by their particular historical experiences. Krajina is where the memory of civil war atrocities was most vivid. As such, amongst these rural Serbs any perceived manifestation of Croatian nationalism was likely to be seen in terms of the fascist NDH. This set them apart somewhat from urban Serbs living in Zagreb and Croatia's other major cities who had settled in Croatia after the Second World War, and had thus been more or less unscathed by the experience of the Ustashe. Set against this, Glenny notes that "Tudjman's ability to recognise the complexity of Serbian society within Croatia was probably the costliest mistake that he ever made in his life."[84] He goes on to suggest that the president was ill-informed by his political advisors, who were well acquainted with the more sophisticated Serbs living in cities such as Zagreb but knew almost nothing as to the nature of those living in the countryside.[85]

Glenny's view is partly upheld by Mario Nobilo, one of Tudjman's foreign policy advisors. Nobilo notes that tensions and hostilities might have been significantly reduced if "we [the Croatian government] had taken better account of their [the Krajina Serbs'] reaction to our emotional explosion when we won the election," and importantly, that "[t]his wasn't directed against anyone, it was just an explosion, which the Serbs took as being directed against them."[86]

83. Glenny, *The Fall of Yugoslavia*, 12.
84. Ibid., 3.
85. Rural Serbs in living in Krajina and other parts of the Croatian countryside often referred to their fellow nationals in the major cities as Hrbi, a mix of Hrvati (Croats) and Srbi (Serbs).

Nobilo's remarks suggest that while the HDZ may well have been both reckless and provocative, Tudjman's actions were not expressly intended to suppress the Serbs—either physically or in identity.

Although perhaps security seeking, Tudjman's government was often erratic and at times sent contradictory signals to the Krajina Serbs: "Persistent efforts by Tudjman and his more moderate colleagues to reassure the republic's Serbs that their rights would be protected were deeply distrusted in the Serbian community."[87] Tudjman failed to distance the HDZ government from the wartime, Pavelic regime. The president insisted that Croatia be free from blame for past events. Tudjman refused to renounce what happened at the Jasenovac concentration camp. "If he had done so," Michael Ignatieff suggests, "Serbs and Croats might have begun the process of ending the past, instead of living it over and over. "[88]

SERB REACTIONS

To the HDZ, the distinction between the positive side of its symbolism—being Croatian—and the negative side—being fascist—were not ambiguous; it was self-evident that those symbols taken or copied from the 1941–45 period were only meant to represent the positive.[89] To the Krajina Serbs, however, it was anything but self-evident. As was noted, most of their families had been subjected to the horrors of the Ustashe. Thus, Croatization had a far greater resonance amongst these rural Serbs than amongst those in urban areas, who were less exposed, personally, to the traumas of the Yugoslav civil war.[90]

The following story told by Milan Babic is indicative of this:

> In 1990 my closest neighbours were the most active in forming the HDZ party branch in my village. Their father in 1941 was the head of the Ustashe government of the village. In the summer of 1941 he brought a group of Ustashe killers to slaughter my family. My father was 12 years

86. Quoted in Mark Almond, *Europe's Backyard War: The War in the Balkans* (London: Mandarin, 1994), 216.

87. Cohen, 131.

88. Michael Ignatieff, Blood and Belonging: Journeys into the New Nationalism (London: Chatto and Windus, 1993), 23.

89. For example, Slaven Letica points out that the key Ustashe symbol, the letter "U," was absent from Croatization, and that most symbols—such as the flag, coat of arms, and national anthem—are merely traditional expressions of Croatian statehood, which date back long before the NDH. See Letica, "The Genesis of the Current Balkan War," in *Genocide After Emotion*, ed. Stepjan G. Mestrovics (London: Routledge, 1996), 111.

90. Many Serbs in Žagreb did see the symbolism of HDZ as threatening. These, however, were mostly Serbs from Serbia proper who had moved to Croatia's major cities after the Second World War in search of work.

old at the time, and only escaped because his family had fled from this home.

When this man came to kill the family and found no one at home, he took a great carving knife from house. He used it to make a gash in the bark of the mulberry tree in our garden. The tree has since grown large, but the scar remained. And we children that were born after the war were shown that tree, and that scar.[91]

Just as the scar on the mulberry tree remained, so too did he suffering of the Krajina Serbs, passed down from grandparents to parents, from parents to children.

More so than other Serb communities in the Croatian republic, the Krajina Serbs seemed largely disinterested in or mostly unaware of the great economic potential of Croatia.[92] For example, on 5 May, in an attempt to calm rising tensions in Krajina over the removal of Serb policemen from their jobs, the Croatian Interior Minister, Josip Boljkovac, along with his deputy, Petrica Juric, and the commander of the Sibenik police, Ante Bujas, under whose authority Knin fell, addressed ninety members of the town's overwhelmingly Serb police force. They stressed how all p0olicemen would be much better off economically under the Tudjman regime. By way of reply, Milan Martic at first accepted that staying in the Croatian republic certainly meant the chance of providing for a better life for the policemen and their families. Nonetheless, he went on: "What cannot be bought is our Serb dignity. We would rather go hungry, as long as we are together with our Serb people. We will eat [only] potatoes . . . but we will be on the side of our people."[93] Hence, Glenny's asserts that "the economic horizons of the rural Serbs are limited, but the . . . concepts of land and home are central to their thinking and sense of security."[94]

Although in Croatia as a whole ethnic Serbs were indeed over-represented in the Croatian bureaucracies and police force, dismissal from his or her position was not recognized by a Serb in these terms. Instead, this represented aggressive behavior by a government that was far from democratic. Indeed, attempts by the Tudjman government to "start addressing the imbalance in the police force where rural Serbs dominated . . . [this] was able to invoke their worst nightmare: the return of the Ustasha, the Croat fascists."[95]

---

91. Quoted in Silber and Little, 106.
92. Glenny, The Fall of Yugoslavia, 3.
93. Quoted in Silber & Little, 106.
94. Glenny, The Fall of Yugoslavia, 3.
95. Ibid., 13–14.

Tudjman failed to take into account that these Serbs, inexplicably deprived of their livelihood, may well be unaware that they had only been appointed to these positions because of their nationality.

To sum up briefly: Croat security requirements seemingly derived from Franjo Tudjman's strong nationalist convictions concerning the achievement of a sovereign Croatia. The variety of nationalism this brought with it, however, seemed potentially at odds with the well being of the republic's Serb community. The achievement of Croatia as the homeland for all Croats was pursued through the program of Croatization. Croatization represented the primacy of a separate—from the Serbian—Croatian identity based on (re)expressions of Croatia's historical past, together with other measures such as ensuring the predominance within the republic of a distinct Croatian language in the Latin script. The often provocative symbolism of the program, together with dismissals from the bureaucracies and the police, convinced many Serbs that at best they would be second-class citizens in the new Croatia and at worst physically threatened as they had been under the Second World War, Pavelic regime.

The regime in Zagreb was arguably revisionist (power seeker) in its general stance toward the maintenance of the Yugoslav Federation. Still, in the specific context of relations with the republic's ethnic Serbs, there is some weight of opinion to suggest that Tudjman was security seeking; he simply misjudged the reaction of the Krajina Serbs to Croatization, rather than deliberately attempting to suppress the Serb community. At the same time, though, contradictory statements by the HDZ served to create uncertainty amongst many Serbs as to the degree of inclusion they might be afforded in a future Croatian State.

SERB SECURITY REQUIREMENTS/CROAT (MIS)PERCEPTIONS

As with the Croats, security requirements for the Serbs were also subject to internal contestation. However, as the dominant political voice amongst the Krajina Serbs, SDS leader Jovan Raskovic articulated and defined security requirements. The SDS leader represented the desires of the majority of ethnic Serbs in the Krajina region until the Serbian National Council's "Declaration on the Sovereignty and Autonomy of the Serbian People" on 19 August 1990, when Raskovic's status in the party became marginalized.

SERB GOALS

Raskovic was essentially a moderate, wishing, to avoid any kind of hostilities between the republic's Serb and Croat populations. During his meetings with

Tudjman in May, Raskovic expressed two primary concerns. The first dealt with the general goal of preserving the Yugoslav State. Raskovic explained why Croatia's potential secession from the federation was a frightening prospect for a great deal of Serbs:

> For the Serb, Yugoslavism is something identical with Serbianism. For other peoples, this . . . does not exist and therefore this is one of the greatest divisions in the political and psychological life of Yugoslavia. One people identify with Yugoslavia, but other people accept it conditionally. . . . Federalism is something tied to the ideas of the Serbian people. . . . As regards a confederation, nobody in the world knows what a confederation is.[96]

The perpetuation of Yugoslavia was therefore synonymous with the maintenance of Serbian national identity: Yugoslavia was the only entity in which all Serbs resided. Any moves toward greater decentralziation, a confederation, or, even worse, an actual break-up of the state, was tantamount to a loosening or severing of those structures that bound Serbs together.

Raskovic's second concern dealt with the more specific task of protecting the status of Croatia's Serbs. With regard to the Tudjman-Raskovic meetings, Leonard Cohen writes that disagreement arose over Raskovic's claim for "for some kind of 'ethnic sovereignty [ethnic autonomy]'."[97] According to Cohen, Tudjman's main problem in the talks was allowing the Serbs some degree of regional (territorial) control within Croatia. Indeed, Mark Thompson remarks as to the Croatian government's undertaking "never to cede 'as much as a millimetre' of the republic to any Serbs."[98]

Different from Cohen, Glenny argues that during the meetings Raskovic more than anything wanted local control over the school system in Serb majority areas.[99] This is reflected in a June 1990 address made by Raskovic in the ethnically mixed town of Petrinja, to the south of Zagreb. Belgrade Radio reported that the SDS leader said the following:

> [T]he Serbs admit the Croatian people the right to their sovereign state, but they demand in that state an equal position for the Serbian and other people. The Serbs do not want a second state in Croatia, but they demand autonomy. . . . The Serbian people in Croatia should be enabled to speak their language, to write their script, to have their schools . . . to have their education programmes, their publishing houses, their newspapers.[100]

96. Quoted in Cohen, 130.
97. Ibid., 132.
98. Mark Thompson, *A Paper House: The Ending of Yugoslavia* (London: Vintage, 1992), 260.
99. Ibid., 19.
100. Quoted in Cohen, 131.

Glenny continues, "At no point did Raskovic express an interest in taking Serb areas out of Croatia. The autonomy he demanded would be realised in a Croatian state, whether part of Yugoslavia or not."[101] Laura Silber and Alan Little are of the same view:

> He [Raskovic] wanted autonomy for the Serbs, but this had no explicit territorial dimension. There was to be no specific autonomous region; the Serbs were to enjoy national rights, as individuals and collectively as a nation, wherever they lived in Croatia.[102]

In keeping with the declaration of the Serbian National Council, Serb security requirements were defined very much in terms of cultural autonomy.

SECURITY SEEKING?

Security seeking on the part of the SDS leadership is easier to establish than for the HDZ government. Raskovic, unlike some of his more radical colleagues in the party, was an essentially moderate voice in the republic's Serb community. Raskovic was not opposed to Croatia's secession per se, but he required some kind of Serbian autonomy—whether in the context of a more confederal Yugoslavia or in an independent Croatia.

Given that Raskovic's intentions were devoid of any clear territorial (ethnic autonomy) element, vis-à-vis the Croatian republic, the SDS leader may thus be described as a status-quo actor. Raskovic's demands for control over local education and other mechanisms of cultural reproduction in Serb majority areas neither compromised Croatia's territorial integrity, nor created a state within a state. Nevertheless, for many Croats, Serbian autonomy within Croatia raised the prospect of territorial revision, where Belgrade would wrest Krajina from Zagreb's control as part of the Greater Serbia project.

CROAT REACTIONS

Raskovic's demands were seen by Tudjman and other leading HDZ figures in terms of the danger of future territorial compromises. For the Croatian government, the granting of cultural autonomy might well make the achievement of ethnic autonomy just a matter of time. In turn, the fear that ethnic autonomy would surely enable Krajina's eventual unification with Serbia was somewhat justified: at this time, Belgrade was continuing to churn out anti-Croat propaganda, and Milosevic's support for the more extreme elements in the SDS was

---

101. Glenny, *The Fall of Yugoslavia*, p. 19.
102. Silber and Little, 103.

becoming more apparent. On 25 July, in an address to the Sabor, Tudjman warned of a possible "scenario of Kosovization and destablization" in Croatia; the Serbian minority provoked outside military intervention on their behalf by falsely claiming persecution at the hands of the Croat majority.[103]

In much the same way as many Serbs saw any expression of Croatian nationalism as a revival of Second World War fascism, many Croats viewed nascent Serbian nationalism in terms of the civil war experience: Serbian nationalism was portrayed throughout Croatia as the return of the Chetniks. Serbian nationalism per se was invariably conflated with the Greater Serbia project, Belgrade's apparent desire to carve-out an ethnically sure nation-state from those territories inhabited by Serbs. Raskovic's demands for cultural/ethnic autonomy were therefore tied to the dual threat of Chetnick revival and the territorial dismemberment of the Croatian republic.

Again, to sum up briefly: Serb security requirements, as articulated by Raskovic in his meetings with President Tudjman, equate to the provision of cultural autonomy to include control over mechanisms for cultural reproduction, such as local education. However, Serbian nationalists, were able to convince that HDZ policies and pronouncements alike marked the presence of a neo-Ustashe regime bent on the suppression—or, indeed, elimination— of Croatia's Serbs in much the same way that Croatians saw SDS demands as made easily to fit with Milosevic's Greater Serbia nationalism. This was made possible given demands leveled by the more extreme elements in the party; Milan Babic, for example, advocated outright secession from the new Croatia and, at least within Knin, received some significant support.

REAL OR ILUSORY INCOMPATIBILITY?

FRANJO TUDJMAN's goal of a sovereign Croatia had two major implications. First, the inviolability of republican borders ruled out any territorial compromises. Second, the very "Croatness" of the republic challenged the strong "Serbness" of the Krajina Serbs. On the other side, Raskovic desired to secure equal constitutional (national) status in Croatia alongside ethnic Croats and to gain some measure of cultural autonomy for the Krajina Serbs who posed a challenge to Croatian national consciousness as they sought to bolster Serbian identity within Croatia.

Evidently, Raskovic was prepared to accept either a more autonomous Croatian republic within a looser, confederal Yugoslavia, or, indeed, an inde-

---

103. Quoted in Cohen, p. 132.

pendent Croatia outside any Yugoslav structures. But the crux of the matter is whether or not Tudjman was ready to grant Serbian cultural autonomy and equal constitutional status.

CULTURAL AUTONOMY

Cohen writes:

> Although Croatian leaders appeared willing to guarantee the rights of the Serbian community (e.g. the use of Cyrillic in predominant Serbian localities, provisions for Serbian cultural association and media), they were opposed to any arrangements for "autonomy" that would compromise the republic's authority over Serbian majority [areas] . . . .[104]

In other words, cultural autonomy was indeed acceptable to Tudjman. This is backed up by Milan Andrejevich:

> The lengthy text [of the Tudjman-Raskovic meetings reported by *Danas*] revealed the tension between the leaders. But far more significantly, it showed both leaders' tolerance and willingness to come to . . . [an] agreement. During the meeting Tudjman guaranteed that Croatia's Serbs would have cultural autonomy.[105]

According to Andrejevich both Tudjman and Prime Minister Mesic said that "they did not see any reason not to grant Croatia's Serbs cultural autonomy, but . . . stopped short of granting the Serbs political [ethnic] autonom."[106] Silber and Little disagree, though. They argue that cultural autonomy alone was unacceptable to the HDZ government, which saw in it "the negation of their overriding objective: the founding of the Croatian nation-state."[107]

Given these interpretations concerning the provision of cultural autonomy within the framework of the Tudjman-Raskovic meetings, it is difficult to come to conclusions with any great degree of certainty. Nonetheless, if the major preoccupation for the Krajina Serbs was local control over schools and the like in Serb majority areas, then there is certainly some grounds to suggest that the HDZ government was indeed willing to allow this. This being the case, incompatibility between the two groups will have been illusory; the security requirements of the Krajina Serbs would not have been in conflict with those of the Croatian republic after all. However, there is some weight of opinion, to suggest that this was not the fundamental source of conflict.

104. Cohen, 132.
105. Andrejevich, "Croatia Between Stability and Civil War (Part I)," 41.
106. Ibid.
107. Silber and Little, 103.

CONSTITUTIONAL STATUS

Mark Thompson highlights the key insecurity for the Krajina Serbs as their constitutional status. Thompson quotes Lazar Macura, press officer for what became Serbian Krajina: "We want to be people in Croatia . . . as we always were until now. The new constitution has eliminated us as people."[108] Disagreement in this respect centered specifically on Section 1 of the Croatian Constitution, which labeled Serbs among "other nations and minorities." Set against this, questions pertaining to the use of the Cyrillic alphabet and other cultural provisions were largely of secondary importance. Indeed, it was the vast majority of Serbs in Krajina who wrote with the Latin script and spoke the Croatian (western) version of Serbo-Croat.

In this sense, security requirements for the Krajina Serbs were defined in terms of majority rights, that is, the same constitutional status in the republic as ethnic Croats. As Thompson points out, anything less than majority rights was not worth having in Croatia: "Zagreb could have promised its Serbs heaven and earth as individuals, and they still would have reacted hostilely to any hint that their collective status would be downgraded."[109]

Tudjman's vision of a sovereign Croatia equated, amongst other things, to a Croatia for the Croats: a country in which ethnic Croats dominated culturally to the exclusion of all others, especially Serbs. That is to say, Croatia could not be a true Croat homeland as long as ethnic Serbs enjoyed anything more than minority status. Thompson notes how the Croats' "emotional explosion" after Tudjman's election victory "was directed against someone: nor could it have been otherwise. Croat self-assertion was against Yugoslavia and, in concrete terms, this meant against Serbia, above all the Serbs within Croatian borders'.[110] In other words, this was a case of required insecurity.

Croatia's security requirements—cultural, and indeed political, predominance in the new Croatia—were only to be achieved at the expense of Serbs' status within the Croatian republic. This meant the HDZ implementing political-legal measures (in the Croatian Constitution) designed to categorize Serbs as second-class citizens. Indeed, that the language of the Croatian Constitution provides a propitious source with which to determine security requirements is given weight by Hayden:

> Constitutions are among the most effective subjects for the study of the implementation of nationalist ideologies . . . providing not only the conceptual framework for the state, but also to make the state conform to

108. Quoted in Thompson, 271.
109. Ibid.
110. Ibid., 280.

that model. When the states envisioned by the constitution exclude many residents from the bodies political and social ... the seemingly blood-less media of constitutions and laws are socially violent and often induce bloodshed.[111]

The security dilemma that existed between the two groups was in this respect arguably regular. The SDS rejected the Draft Constitution on 25 July and subsequently announced the 18 August referendum concerning the state of the republic's Serb population predicated on a real incompatibility in the means (requirements) by which both sides sought their goals. The outbreak of violence in many parts of Krajina on 17 August was predominantly the consequence of Serb resistance to a Croatian government that was not willing to afford ethnic Serbs equal constitutional status in the republic. The Tudjman government was aware of the potential reaction of the Serb community to the Draft Constitution, but the HDZ clearly sought to suppress Serb culture and identity, and this proved contentious. Glenny describes the relationship between Tudjman and the Krajina Serbs as a confused account of "real and perceived discrimination."[112] Thompson arrives at much the same conclusion when labeling the actions of HDZ as "reckless" more than anything else.[113] Thus, while elements of power seeking behavior may have been apparent, the intentions of the Tudjman government were sufficiently ambiguous to justify the downplaying of a looser security dilemma interpretation.

CONCLUSION: MITIGATING CROATIA'S SECURITY DILEMMA

The violence that broke out between Serbs on 17 August 1990 was a direct result of Croatian President Franjo Tudjman's obduracy concerning the new Draft Constitution. In meetings with SDS leader Jovan Raskovic, Tudjman made no concessions concerning the constitutional status of Serbs within the republic, despite warnings from Raskovic that the Serbs' relegation to "other nations and minorities" was almost certainly the harbinger of troubles. However, for Tudjman and his governing HDZ, Croatian security entailed the predominance of ethnic Croats, a Croatia for the Croats. Croat security necessitated Serb insecurity.

Given the presence of a regular security dilemma between the two parties, mechanisms designed to reveal misperception would likely have been ineffective. In simple terms, this is because there was no misperception to reveal. To

111. Hayden, 785.
112. Glenny, *The Fall of Yugoslavia*, 11.
113. Thompson, 264.

be sure, relations between the Serb and Croat communities were marked by uncertainty, and confidence-building measures (CBMs) in some way may have addressed this. Nevertheless, the Tudjman-Raskovic meetings provided an unambiguous context in which goals were clearly articulated. Thus, a worst-case scenario cannot be attributed to a lack of transparency, information failures, and the like.

In the end, the conflict might have been resolved had the Croatian government been induced to change its security requirements. In other words, the log revolution may well have been averted had Tudjman agreed to Serb demands in amending the new constitution. His failure to do so not only created the pretext for violence between the two parties but also led to a radicalization of the SDS when the moderate Raskovic was marginalized, and the more nationalist mayor of Kinin, Milan Babic, took over party leadership.

As a regular security dilemma implies, some package of incentives would likely have been effective in Krajina. When third party intervention eventually came, it was too late. The period between the log revolution and the June 1991 Serb-Croat war arguably saw a shift from a regular security dilemma to a loose one: Federal Yugoslavia, headed by Serbia and Slobodan Milosevic, was intent on war to prevent Croatia's secession and in maintaining Belgrade's (Serbia's) control over the breakaway republic. The time for incentives had gone, and the time for military action had come.

I have conceived the tight, regular, and loose security dilemma formulations as representing points on a scale, ideal-type categories constructed for the purpose of mapping out the body of the security dilemma scholarship.

*	*	*
Tight Security Dilemma	Regular	Loose
Security Seeking	Security	Power
Compatible Security Requirements	Incompatible	
Resolvable Short of War	Difficult to Resolve	Irresolvable
Reveal Misperception	Change Security Requirements	Intervention

What I argued here places Croatia closest to being a regular security dilemma—although the more accurate location is somewhere between the regular and loose interpretations—and thus suggests that the conflict might have been resolved if the actors had been induced to change their security requirements. My intention in this respect was to highlight the presence of a security dilemma that operates before the outbreak of violence and war: to view the security dilemma as an instigator of ethnic conflict. This is set against Kaufmann's work, which utilizes a predominantly loose interpretation. Kaufmann's security dilemma operates after the outbreak of hostilities; it is thus an exacerbator and not an instigator.[114]

Different security dilemmas bring different solutions, both possible and impossible, to conflict resolution. It is therefore of great importance that policymakers have a framework within which to establish which security dilemma. Furthermore, not all security dilemmas are best mitigated through partition and ethnic separation.

114. For a discussion of security dilemmas that instigate or exacerbate ethnic conflict, see Roe, "Former Yugoslavia: The Security Dilemma That Never Was?"

IS PARTITION REALLY THE ONLY HOPE? RECONCILING CONTRADICTORY FINDINGS ABOUT ETHNIC CIVIL WARS

ALAN J. KUPERMAN

A FTER decades of statistical studies on interstate wars,[1] political scientists more recently have turned to the question of civil wars. A spate of high-profile internal conflicts during the 1990s—including those in Bosnia and Rwanda—led some scholars to narrow their focus still further to ethnic civil wars.[2] In this context, a sharp debate has arisen over the prospects for resolving violent ethnic conflicts through negotiated, power-sharing settlements. In particular, two prominent articles reach opposing conclusions. Chaim Kaufmann adduces statistics to support his contention that ethnic (in contrast to ideological) civil wars are virtually impossible to resolve through such power-sharing settlements and can be resolved only by physical separation of the opposing ethnic groups into politically autonomous, ethnically homogenous zones.[3] A subsequent statistical study by David Mason and Patrick Fett, however, finds that ethnic conflicts are

Alan J. Kuperman is resident assistant professor of international relations at the School of Advanced International Studies (SAIS), Johns Hopkins University, Bologna Center.

The original version of this article was written in 1997. An initially revised version was presented at the 96th annual meeting of the American Political Science Association, Washington, D.C. August 31–September 3, 2000. That version has been further substantially revised for publication in the current special issue of the journal *Security Studies* on "Living Together After Ethnic Killing." The author gratefully acknowledges past financial support from the MIT Department of Political Science, the U.S. Institute of Peace, Harvard University's Belfer Center for Science and International Affairs, the Institute for the Study of World Politics, the Harvard-MIT MacArthur Transnational Security Fellowship, the Brookings Institution, and the Federation of American Scientists. The author also would like to thank Jim Alt and Chaim Kaufmann, and two anonymous *Security Studies* reviewers for their comments on earlier versions of this article.

1. For a brief overview of the generally inconclusive and contradictory findings of such large-N studies, see Edward D. Mansfield, "The Distribution of Wars Over Time," *World Politics* 41, no. 1 (October 1988): 21–51. For a longer and broader discussion, see Jack S. Levy, "The Causes of War: A Review of Theories and Evidence," in *Behavior, Society, and Nuclear War*, ed. Philip E. Tetlock et al. (New York and Oxford: Oxford University Press, 1989), 209–333.
2. "Ethnic civil war" is a term used commonly, including in this article, in a sense broader than its actual meaning, to include any internal war that pits groups divided by ascriptive characteristics such as race, religion, ethnicity, or clan—in contrast with ideology or political affiliation.
3. Chaim Kaufmann, "Possible and Impossible Solutions to Ethnic Civil Wars," *International Security* 20, no. 4 (spring 1996): 136–75.

no more difficult to resolve through negotiated settlements than other civil wars.[4]

As in the earlier literature on inter-state conflicts, such divergent conclusions may result in part from the authors' methodological choices.[5] For example, differing operational definitions of "ethnic civil war" cause these authors to rely on two very different universes of cases. Although both studies claim to base their conclusions on all ethnic civil wars resolved since the Second World War, and rely on databases with an almost identical number of cases (twenty-seven and twenty-eight, respectively), remarkably few cases (six) overlap in the two databases (see table 1). Other differences in operational definitions— most fundamentally, whether negotiated agreements that provide for some degree of regional autonomy should be categorized as "power-sharing" or "ethnic separation"—further contribute to the divergent conclusions. Finally, some of the apparent discrepancy between the two studies may result from the authors rhetorically exaggerating the significance of their statistical findings.

One means of resolving such discrepancies—indeed, the most common response in political science—would be to construct a "better" database and set of operational definitions that would yield more robust conclusions. In many cases, however, such additional research is conducted without a firm understanding of the shortcomings of existing research, or the reasons for past discrepant findings. To lay the proper groundwork for such future research, this article instead attempts to explain how and why these two prominent studies reached such incompatible findings and to explore whether their findings may in fact be reconcilable based on a more nuanced analysis. Resolving these discrepancies has great practical significance for international efforts to reduce ethnic civil war, because it will determine whether such efforts are most usefully directed towards power-sharing settlements or ethnic partitions.

This article first summarizes the methodology, findings, and conclusions of the two previous studies, drawing attention to their possible shortcomings and speculating about possible reasons for their discrepant conclusions. Second, it examines the degree to which the discrepant conclusions result from divergent operational definitions of two terms—that of "civil war," which leads to different databases, and that of "negotiated agreement," which leads

---

4. T. David Mason and Patrick J. Fett, "How Civil Wars End: A Rational Choice Approach," *Journal of Conflict Resolution* 40, no. 4 (December 1996): 546–68.

5. For an illustration of how differing methodologies and definitions can yield contradictory results, even when relying on the same database, see John Vasquez, "The Steps to War: Toward a Scientific Explanation of the Correlates of War Findings," *World Politics* 40, no. 1 (October 1987): 108–45.

Table 1
LITTLE OVERLAP IN TWO DATABASES OF "ALL" RESOLVED ETHNIC CIVIL WARS,
1944–94*

State	Ethnic Group	Mason-Fett	Kaufmann	Overlapping Cases
Angola	Ovimbundu	1975–91		
Azerbaijan	Armenians		1988–	
Bangladesh	Chittagong		1975–89	
Burma	Karens		1945–	
Burundi	Hutu	1972		
Burundi	Hutu	1988		
Chad	Various	1980–88		
China	Tibetans	1950–51		
China	Tibetans	1956–59	1959–89	1 case for each
China	Uighurs, etc.		1980	
Ethiopia	Tigreans/Eritreans	1974–91	1961–91	2 cases for Kaufmann
Georgia	Abkhazians		1992–93	
India	Nagas		1952–75	
India	Tripuras		1967–89	
India-Hyderabad	Hyderabadis	1948		
Indonesia	Acehnese	1953		
Indonesia	Acehnese		1975–80s	
Indonesia	Papuans		1964–86	
Indonesia	Timorese	1975–77	1974–80s	1 case for each
Iran	Kurds		1945–80s	
Iraq	Kurds	1959, 1961–75	1960–	2 cases for M&F
Iraq	Shiites		1991	
Israel	Palestinians		1968–93	
Jordan	Palestinians	1970		
Lebanon	Various	1958		
Lebanon	Various		1975–90	
Liberia	Various	1989–92		
Mozambique	Ndau/Shona	1979–92		
Nicaragua	Miskitos		1981–88	
Nigeria	Ibo	1967–70	1967–70	1 case for each
Nigeria	Maitatsine	1980–84		
Pakistan	Bengalis	1971		
Pakistan	Baluchis	1973–77		

Table 1 (Continued)

State	Ethnic Group	Mason-Fett	Kaufmann	Overlapping Cases
Papua New Guinea	Bougainville		1988	
Philippines	Moros		1972–87	
Rwanda	Tutsi	1963–64		
Rwanda	Tutsi		1990–94	
Somalia	Northern clans		1988–	
Spain	Basques		1959–80s	
Sri Lanka	JVP**	1971		
Sudan	Various	1963–72		
Uganda	Baganda	1966		
Uganda	Various	1980–88		
USSR	Lithuanians		1945–52	
USSR	Ukrainians		1944–50s	
Western Sahara	Saharawi	1975–83		
Zaire	Katangans	1960–65		
Zimbabwe	Blacks	1972–79		

*Kaufmann's database spans 1944–94; Mason and Fett's 1945–92.
**JVP was neither an ethnic, religious nor other identity group, so this case is recoded as ideological for the remaining calculations in this article.

to different categorization of outcomes. It explores this question, in part, by applying each study's methodology to the other's database. Third, a hypothesis is proposed to reconcile the two studies' findings, and preliminary tests of this hypothesis are conducted. Fourth, the article explores in greater depth those cases of ethnic civil war resolved by negotiated agreement to determine if they are reconcilable with Kaufmann's theory. Fifth, it summarizes these findings and proposes an improved research design to help resolve the differences. The article concludes by discussing the theoretical implications of this and other recently published research.

KAUFMANN: THE HUMPTY-DUMPTY THEORY OF ETHNIC CONFLICT

CHAIM KAUFMANN argues that once ethnic civil wars reach a threshold level of violence (a standard which, unfortunately, he does not define) opposing ethnic groups lose the ability to live peacefully intermingled under a common political authority. The root cause, he argues, is a security dilemma between individuals of opposing ethnic groups, which is exacerbated by the war. Following a peace agreement, if members of these groups find themselves living side-by-side, absent the clear ethnic power hierarchy that results from one side's victory, they inevitably will lash out against each other—in self-defense, if not in anger—reigniting the civil war.[6] Kaufmann argues that such security dilemmas are much worse following *ethnic* civil wars, because identities cannot be hidden or changed as they can after *ideological* civil wars. He concludes that this security dilemma, and therefore ethnic civil wars, can be ended in only three ways: (1) military victory by one side to establish a clear ethnic hierarchy; (2) suppression of the conflict by a third-party military occupation; or (3) physical separation of ethnic groups into defensible enclaves. To put it crudely, because of the persistent security dilemma after ethnic civil wars, a multi-ethnic Humpty-Dumpty cannot be put back together again. Accordingly, Kaufmann offers a radical prescription to the international community: not only should it stop seeking power-sharing agreements to resolve violent ethnic conflicts, it should instead facilitate population exchanges to achieve ethnic separation, as a means to lasting peace.

Kaufmann defends his theory with an analysis of all "ethnic civil wars resolved from 1944–94," based on databases assembled by Ted Robert Gurr.[7] Of the twenty-seven such wars completed in this period (see table 3), he finds that twelve ended by military victory, five by de facto or de jure partition, two by outside military occupation, and eight by negotiated agreements other than partition. On initial inspection, the last group of eight appear at odds with Kaufmann's theory, because they are peace settlements achieved without partition. Kaufmann, however, argues that all eight of these settlements depended on grants of full or partial autonomy to a regionally concentrated ethnic group, so that—like partition—they are essentially based on physical separation of ethnic groups. Apparently relying on Gurr's coding of regional concentration, he states:

> The data supports the argument that separation of groups is the key to ending ethnic civil wars. Every case in which the state was preserved by agreement involved a regionally concentrated minority, and in every case the solution reinforced the ethnic role in politics by allowing the regional

---

6. Kaufmann suggests that a minimal level of residual ethnic intermingling, following population exchanges, will not necessarily trigger renewal of war, although he does not define this threshold.

7. See Ted Robert Gurr, *Minorities at Risk: A Global View of Ethnopolitical Conflicts* (Washington, D.C.: U.S. Institute of Peace, 1993); and Gurr, "Peoples Against States: Ethnopolitical Conflict and the Changing World System," *International Studies Quarterly* 38, no. 3 (September 1994): 347–77.

minority group to control its own destiny through regional autonomy for the areas where it forms a majority of the population.[8]

Kaufmann's logic suggests combining his cases of partition and regional autonomy into a single category. Such a re-categorization yields twelve ethnic civil wars resolved by military victory, thirteen by grants of sovereignty or political autonomy to regionally concentrated ethnic groups, and two by outside military occupation. Accordingly, Kaufmann states:

> There is not a single case where non-ethnic civil politics were created or restored by reconstruction of ethnic identities, power-sharing coalitions, or state-building. . . . Finally, it should be noted that all eight of the cases resolved through autonomy involve groups that were largely demographically separated even at the beginning of the conflict . . . [9]

There are, however, several problems with Kaufmann's theory, methodology, and conclusions. First, Kaufmann's own data belie his claim that physical separation, rather than political separation, is the key to ending violence through partition. He writes: "Stable resolutions of ethnic civil wars are possible, but only when the opposing groups are demographically separated into defensible enclaves. . . . Sovereignty is secondary: defensible ethnic enclaves reduce violence with or without independent sovereignty . . . "[10] In all eight of his cases of ethnic civil war resolved by negotiated agreement, however, the ethnic groups already were largely physically separated prior to the outbreak of violence. This pre-existing physical separation proved insufficient, by itself, to prevent the outbreak of violence or to end it once started. Rather, civil war ended only after the ethnic groups also were granted some degree of political autonomy. This suggests a minor clarification of Kaufmann's theory:

At a minimum, this clarification implies that negotiated agreements of ethnic civil wars cannot succeed if they have any of three characteristics: (1) opposing

---

8. Kaufmann, "Possible and Impossible," 161. He does not explicitly cite the source of this data, but relies on Gurr's database throughout the article.

9. Kaufmann, "Possible and Impossible," 161. The full quote is:

> "Further, deaths in these cases [of negotiated agreement based on ethnic regional autonomy] average an order of magnitude lower than in the wars which ended either in suppression or partition: less than 13,000, compared [to] about 250,000. This lends support to the proposition that the more extreme the violence, the less the chances for any form of reconciliation. Finally, it should be noted that all eight of the cases resolved through autonomy involve groups that were largely demographically separated even at the beginning of the conflict, which may help explain why there were fewer deaths."

10. Ibid., 137.

Figure 1
CLARIFICATION OF KAUFMANN'S THEORY

A negotiated settlement of an ethnic civil war cannot succeed unless ethnic groups
are physically separated into ethnically homogenous, politically autonomous, militarily defensible zones.

ethnic groups remain physically intermingled; (2) common political authority
is retained over physically separated ethnic groups; or (3) at least one physically
separated group cannot defend its zone.

A second problem is that Kaufmann does not clearly distinguish which
of two potential causal mechanisms he is proposing to explain the observed
absence of successful, negotiated power-sharing agreements. (See figure 2.)
Primarily, he argues that when such agreements are reached, their implementation fails. He does not, however, test this version of the theory. Such a
test would involve dividing all settlements reached in ethnic conflicts into two
categories—(1) those based on ethnic intermingling and/or common political
authority, and (2) those based on ethnic separation and regional autonomy—
and then comparing their relative rates of success in implementation. (Such a
comparison would be bedeviled by selection effects, in any case, because the
pool of ethnic conflicts is not randomly divided into the two treatment groups,
so that relative rates of success might be determined by something other than

Figure 2
TWO POSSIBLE CAUSAL MECHANISMS FOR KAUFMANN'S FINDING OF NO SUCCESSFUL
NEGOTIATED AGREEMENTS BASED ON COMMON POLITICAL AUTHORITY AND/OR
ETHNIC INTERMINGLING

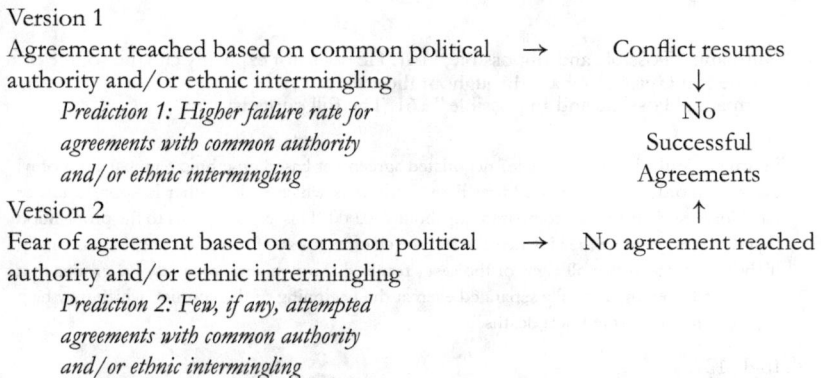

Version 1
Agreement reached based on common political   →   Conflict resumes
authority and/or ethnic intermingling   ↓
   Prediction 1: Higher failure rate for   No
   agreements with common authority   Successful
   and/or ethnic intermingling   Agreements
Version 2   ↑
Fear of agreement based on common political   →   No agreement reached
authority and/or ethnic intrermingling
   Prediction 2: Few, if any, attempted
   agreements with common authority
   and/or ethnic intermingling

the nature of the settlement.) At other times, however, Kaufmann implies that ethnic groups actually *anticipate* the failure of any potential settlement involving common political authority or ethnic intermingling, so that they are unwilling even to contemplate them, preferring to fight on. This version of his theory would predict that no such power-sharing settlements ever are agreed upon, even temporarily.

Moreover, neither of these versions of Kaufmann's theory is proved by his statistical evidence, which essentially consists of two findings. First, he finds that out of twenty-seven completed ethnic civil wars, none was resolved by a negotiated power-sharing agreement—that is, common political authority over all ethnic groups and regions. This finding would support the first version of Kaufmann's theory, but only if he also found a significant number of power-sharing settlements had been attempted and failed—a question he leaves un-addressed. Alternately, if the reason that no power-sharing settlement has suc-ceeded is because none has been attempted, that would support the second ver-sion of Kaufmann's theory. No evidence is adduced, however, for this version either. Nor would such evidence, if it existed, lead inexorably to Kaufmann's prescription for the international community to eschew power-sharing agree-ments. Even if contending ethnic groups had been unwilling to accept such settlements voluntarily in the past, that would not mean such settlements nec-essarily would fail if adopted under coercion by the international community.

While this attempt to clarify the causal mechanism of Kaufmann's theory may be criticized as hair-splitting, it is crucial in light of the draconian pol-icy prescription he infers from his theory: that the international community should eschew negotiated settlements and instead facilitate population trans-fers to resolve civil wars. If Kaufmann's finding results from the fact that many negotiated settlements have been attempted, but all failed, his prescrip-tion merits immediate consideration. If instead his finding results from the fact that few negotiated settlements even have been attempted, it might be prudent for the international community first to focus its energies on fostering such negotiated settlements.

Kaufmann's second finding is that out of eight negotiated settlements not based on partition, all involved regionally concentrated ethnic groups. This finding suggests a corollary—that conflicts with regionally concentrated ethnic groups are more likely than other ethnic conflicts to be resolved by negotiated agreement (even excluding formal partitions), because the ethnic groups al-ready are physically separated. He does not test this corollary. Doing so would involve dividing all ethnic civil wars (preferably not just ones that have ended) into those with and without regionally concentrated ethnic groups, and testing for a significant difference in the rate of settlement.

Figure 3
KAUFMANN'S IMPLICIT COROLLARY

Regional concentration → Greater chance of lasting peace agreement
of ethnic groups   (even without formal partition)

*Prediction: Ethnic civil wars between regionally concentrated ethnic groups should
be more likely than other ethnic civil wars to end in a peace agreement
(even excluding formal partitions)*

MASON AND FETT: THE APPARENT IRRELEVANCE OF ETHNICITY IN RESOLVING CIVIL WARS

MASON AND FETT's primary objective is to determine which factors in completed civil wars—not limited to ethnic wars—are correlated with the outcome of negotiated settlement as opposed to some other outcome. In the process, however, they reach a finding that contradicts a key aspect of Kaufmann's theory. According to their statistics, ethnic civil wars are no less likely than ideological civil wars to end in negotiated settlements. As they observe: "The finding of no relationship between the ethnic basis of the conflict and the likelihood of a settlement is . . . at odds with most of the literature."[11]

The universe of cases that Mason and Fett explore is derived from the well-known Correlates of War project, with some minor adjustments.[12] Based on this universe, they perform a series of logistic regressions to explore if peace is associated with any of six variables, including whether or not the conflict is ethnic. Interestingly, in a regression of all six putative causal variables, the authors find the coefficient for the ethnic variable to be zero. Only two of their putative variables turn out to have significant (at the .10 level), non-zero coefficients in any of the regressions. They find that the smaller the government's army, and the longer the civil war, the more likely it is to have ended in negotiated settlement.[13]

---

11. Mason and Fett, "How Civil Wars End," 563.
12. For an explanation of their manipulation of the original data in the Correlates of War database, see Mason and Fett, "How Civil Wars End," 556–58.
13. After running a series of logistic regressions, the authors find only two variables significantly associated with peaceful negotiated outcomes: the duration of the war is positively correlated, and the size of the government's army is negatively correlated. Using these two variables, their model correctly predicts the outcome of completed civil wars 87.7 percent of the time, as opposed to 77.2 percent in the naive model (which always predicts the war was not resolved by negotiated agreement). The other putative variables, found not to be significantly associated, are battle death rate, ethnic-basis (yes or no), war-type (revolutionary or separatist), and foreign intervention (yes or no).

In at least one manner, Mason and Fett's methodology is sounder than that of Kaufmann, because they start from a database of *all* completed civil wars, not just ethnic ones, allowing them to test for the impact of the ethnic factor on outcome. Their results, however, are still vulnerable to a selection bias because they ignore *ongoing* civil wars. Presumably, this discarded subset of civil wars ultimately will have a longer average duration (when eventually they do end) than the included civil wars, which suggests they also may be more likely to end in negotiated settlement, assuming the authors' general findings hold. To determine whether this selection bias is likely to have affected the authors' findings, a first step would be to explore the total universe of both ongoing and completed civil wars, checking to see if any of the other variables— the ethnic factor, for example—is significantly correlated with wars that are ongoing as opposed to completed. Unfortunately, the authors do not explore this question.

EXPLAINING DIVERGENT FINDINGS: THE ROLE OF DEFINITIONS

PERHAPS THE most obvious cause of divergence in the two studies' findings is their opposite coding of cases of negotiated agreements involving grants of regional autonomy to at least one ethnic group. Kaufmann dismisses such agreements as based on ethnic separation, and thus not true power-sharing settlements, leaving him a null set in the latter category. Mason and Fett, by contrast, include such agreements in their category of negotiated settlements, as opposed to their other category that includes military victories and formal partitions.

Underlying this stark semantic difference is a more subtle and interesting theoretical disagreement between the two studies—the question of whether negotiated settlements of ethnic civil wars must be based on granting re-gional autonomy to ethnically concentrated ethnic groups. Clearly, Kaufmann believes this to be the case. Mason and Fett at first glance appear to agree, stating:

> In an ethnically fragmented society, no settlement can resolve the deeply held and culturally grounded beliefs that are the source of ethnic identity and, therefore, ethnic conflict. Hence ethnic conflicts are subject to set-tlement only by formulae that guarantee or at least enhance the autonomy and security of the contending ethnic groups in a society.[14]

---

14. Mason and Fett, "How Civil Wars End," 554. Their first assertion actually is questionable. In some cases, it appears that ethnic conflict is based not on culturally grounded beliefs or ethnic

Mason and Fett, however, hold out the possibility that such negotiated agreements need not be based on either ethnic separation or regional autonomy, stating that "settlement formulae can take the form of ... consociational arrangements."[15]

To help resolve this theoretical disagreement, it would be necessary to re-code the outcomes of ethnic civil wars into three categories: (1) negotiated settlements based on regional autonomy for concentrated ethnic groups; (2) negotiated settlements leaving ethnic groups intermingled or not granting regional autonomy; and (3) other outcomes, including victory for one side, partition, or third-party occupation. One decisive test between the two theories would be to see whether the second category truly is a null set as Kaufmann contends—a question that is explored further below.

Another cause of divergence in the two studies' findings is their reliance on two remarkably different universes of cases, as highlighted in table 1. Although each study claims to examine all cases of ethnic civil war completed since the Second World War, there are only six overlapping cases among Mason and Fett's twenty-eight and Kaufmann's twenty-seven. The only cases found in both databases (noted in the final column of table 1) are Chinese repression in Tibet, the Ethiopian civil war, Indonesia's occupation of East Timor, Iraqi suppression of Kurds, and the Ibo secession from Nigeria. Both studies also include civil wars in Lebanon, Rwanda, and the Aceh region of Indonesia, but the dates differ in each pair of cases by at least seventeen years, so these cannot be considered the same. Remarkably, each study excludes the majority of the other's cases.

In some instances, Mason and Fett may have justifiable—or at least understandable—reasons for excluding cases that are in Kaufmann's database, including: the conflict was resolved after their 1992 cut-off date (for example, Georgia, Rwanda, Somalia); the case is coded as non-ethnic, because ethnicity was not the prime cause of the war (for example, Nicaragua); the number of dead was too small to qualify as a war by their methodology (for example, Israel, Papua, Spain); the case is viewed as internal repression, rather than civil war (for example, USSR vs. Ukrainians and Lithuanians); or the conflict is regarded as ongoing. In a number of other cases, however, their omissions are hard to justify. Additionally, in one case they err by coding as ethnic what was clearly an ideological civil war, Sri Lanka-1971, an ill-fated

---

identity, but rather political power struggles, sometimes within a single ethnic group. See, for example, Alan J. Kuperman, "The Other Lesson of Rwanda: Mediators Sometimes Do More Damage Than Good," *SAIS Review* 16, no. 1 (winter-spring, 1996): 221–40. This does not imply necessarily that their conclusion is wrong.

15. Mason and Fett, "How Civil Wars End," 554 (emphasis added).

uprising by a youth-based Sinhalese Maoist group against the Sinhalese government.[16] Accordingly, in the calculations below, this case is re-coded as ideological.

Kaufmann's likely reasons for excluding cases in Mason and Fett's database are that he regards them either as unresolved (for example, Angola, Burundi, Sudan) or not primarily ethnic (for example, Liberia, Uganda, Zaire). In a number of other cases, however, his omissions are hard to justify. Moreover, it is strange that Kaufmann chooses to include several cases with relatively low death levels (for example, Israel, Papua, and Spain) considering that his theory is based on the effects of high levels of inter-ethnic violence.[17]

One way to test for how much of the divergence in the two studies' findings stems from their having relied on different databases is to apply each study's methodology to the other's cases. Applying Kaufmann's method to the ethnic civil wars in Mason and Fett's database, we find initially (see table 5) that seven of their twenty-seven such wars (26 percent) were resolved by negotiated agreement (excluding de jure or de facto partition). This proportion is quite similar to that in Kaufmann's own database, in which eight of twenty-seven completed ethnic civil wars (30 percent) were so resolved. Kaufmann, as noted, dismisses all eight in his own database as not true power-sharing settlements, because they relied on grants of autonomy to regionally concentrated ethnic groups.

In Mason and Fett's collection of negotiated settlements of ethnic civil wars, however, there are at least two that involved neither regionally concentrated ethnic groups nor grants of autonomy: Lebanon-1958 and Zimbabwe-1979. These two cases are incompatible with Kaufmann's theory that power-sharing settlements of ethnic civil wars are impossible unless they grant autonomy to regionally concentrated ethnic groups. This observation also suggests that reliance on different databases contributed significantly to the divergence in findings and conclusions between the two studies. (These and other cases that defy Kaufmann's theory are explored in greater detail below.)

Turning the tables, it is impossible to replicate Mason and Fett's logistic regression using Kaufmann's database, because he provides neither a list of ideological wars nor the requisite data on ethnic wars. Kaufmann's database, however, can be used to explore Mason and Fett's finding that ethnic wars are no less likely than ideological wars to be resolved by negotiated agreement, by

16. See, for example, http://www.geocities.com/HotSprings/6774/zaini.html (accessed 11 March 2004).
17. It appears that Kaufmann selected the cases for his database with a concept in mind but without formal selection criteria. Kaufmann, pers. comm., 17 October 1997.

Table 2

PERCENTAGE OF CIVIL WARS RESOLVED BY NEGOTIATED AGREEMENT (USING
MASON AND FETT'S DEFINITION WHICH INCLUDES AGREEMENTS BASED ON GRANTS
OF REGIONAL AUTONOMY)

	Mason/Fett	Kaufmann
Ethnic	26% (7/27)	30% (8/27)
Ideological	21% (6/29)	NA

comparing his findings with Mason and Fett's raw data for ideological wars. Mason and Fett find that six of twenty-nine completed ideological civil wars (21 percent) were resolved by negotiated agreement.

As indicated in table 2, when Mason and Fett's definition of negotiated agreement is applied, Kaufmann's database appears to support Mason and Fett's finding that ethnic civil wars are not less likely to be resolved by negotiated agreement than ideological civil wars. Indeed, ethnic conflicts appear slightly more likely to be so resolved, though the difference is not statistically significant.[18] This indicates that divergence in this aspect of the two studies' findings results not from reliance on different databases, but rather from their employing different operational definitions.

RECONCILING THE DIFFERENCES

ALTHOUGH ON initial inspection the two studies reach incompatible conclusions, it is worth exploring to what extent they can be reconciled. In this regard, it is important to observe that Kaufmann implies that ethnic civil wars may be both harder and easier than ideological civil wars to resolve by

18. The difference in the rate of negotiated settlements between Kaufmann's sample of ethnic civil wars and Mason and Fett's sample of ideological civil wars, or $p_1 - p_2$, is 30% − 21% = 9%, or .09. To determine if this difference is statistically significant, we explore whether we can reject the null hypothesis that the two populations from which the samples were drawn have the same likelihood of negotiated settlement. The variance of the estimate of the difference between the two sample percentages, $p_1 - p_2$, is determined by the formula:

$$s^2 = [p_1(1 - p_1)/n_1] + [p_2(1 - p_2)/n_2] = [.3(.7)/27 + .21(.79)/29] = .0135. \text{ Or, } s = .116.$$

A 95% confidence interval for the true difference in the rate of negotiated settlement between the two populations is $p_1 - p_2 + /- (s*2) = .09 +/- .23 = [-.14 \longleftrightarrow +.32] = [-14\% \longleftrightarrow +32\%]$. This interval includes the value zero, so we cannot reject the null hypothesis that the two populations have the same probability of negotiated agreement.

Figure 4
PROPOSED TWO-PART HYPOTHESIS TO RECONCILE THE TWO STUDIES' FINDINGS

1. Ethnic civil wars involving regionally concentrated ethnic groups are more amenable to negotiated agreement than ideological civil wars; and
2. Ethnic civil wars involving intermingled ethnic groups are less amenable to negotiated agreement than ideological civil wars.

negotiated agreement. On the one hand, ethnic wars are harder to resolve peacefully, he argues, because power-sharing agreements are impossible. On the other hand, one can infer that ethnic wars may be easier to resolve because they are subject to regional autonomy agreements—at least in cases where ethnic groups are regionally concentrated—a solution generally unsuitable in ideological civil wars.

Thus, one can conceive a hypothesis under which both studies could be correct, if the degree of regional concentration of groups determines whether ethnic civil wars are more—or less—susceptible to negotiated agreement than ideological civil wars (see figure 4). If both parts of the hypothesis were true, we might find that when ethnic civil wars were measured without differentiating group concentration, they would appear roughly equally as amenable to negotiated agreement as ideological civil wars.

To test this hypothesis, we reexamine Kaufmann's corollary, that ethnic conflicts with concentrated ethnic groups are more likely to be resolved by negotiated agreement than other ethnic conflicts. As noted above, a true test of this corollary would start from a universe of all ethnic civil wars, both ongoing and completed, but Kaufmann provides no data for the former category. Nevertheless, unless there is a significant bias created by ignoring ongoing wars, Kaufmann's corollary also has a testable prediction for the universe of completed civil wars: namely, those involving concentrated ethnic groups should be more likely to have been resolved by negotiated agreement. Although Kaufmann asserts this to be the case, he does not adduce raw data enabling it to be confirmed by a rigorous test. To facilitate such a test, we have constructed table 3, including a coding for whether the ethnic group is regionally concentrated in the state. In most cases, this coding was available in the Minorities at Risk dataset, Phase IV (2000).[19] In two cases from the former

---

19. An ethnic group is coded as having a "regional base" if there is "a spatially contiguous region larger than an urban area that is part of the country, in which 25 percent or more of the minority resides and in which the minority constitutes the predominant proportion of

Table 3
VERIFYING KAUFMANN'S COROLLARY WITH KAUFMANN'S DATABASE

State (by Outcome)	Ethnic Group	Dates	Concentrated?
Military Victory			
Burma	Karens	1945–	No
China	Tibetans	1959–89	Yes
China	Uighurs, etc.	1980	Yes
Ethiopia	Tigreans	1975–91	Yes
Indonesia	Acehnese	1975–80s	Yes
Indonesia	Papuans	1964–86	Yes
Indonesia	Timorese	1974–80s	Yes
Iran	Kurds	1945–80s	Yes
Iraq	Shiites	1991	Yes
Nigeria	Ibo	1967–70	Yes
Papua New Guinea	Bougainville	1988	Yes
Rwanda	Tutsi	1990–94	No
Outside Military Occupation by 3rd Party			
Iraq	Kurds	1960–	Yes
Lebanon	Various	1975–90	No
			(Sunni, Palestinian)
De Facto or De Jure Partition			
Azerbaijan	Armenians	1988–	Yes
Ethiopia	Eritreans	1961–91	Yes
Somalia	Northern clans	1988–	Yes (Issaq)
USSR	Lithuanians	1945–52	Yes*
USSR	Ukrainians	1944–50s	Yes*
Negotiated Settlement (Other than Partition)			
Bangladesh	Chittagong	1975–89	Yes
Georgia	Abkhazians	1992–93	Yes
India	Nagas	1952–75	Yes
India	Tripuras	1967–89	Yes
Israel	Palestinians	1968–93	Yes
Nicaragua	Miskitos	1981–88	Yes
Philippines	Moros	1972–87	Yes
Spain	Basques	1959–80s	Yes

*These two codings are from Gurr 1993.

Table 4
POSSIBLE EFFECT OF REGIONAL CONCENTRATION ON SETTLEMENT LIKELIHOOD IN
KAUFMANN DATABASE

| | *Ethnic Group Concentrated in One Region?* | |
	Yes	No
Number of ethnic civil wars	24	3
Number of negotiated settlements	8	0
Percent of negotiated settlements	33% (8/24)	0% (0/3)

Soviet Union, concentration values were taken from an earlier, 1993 version of the dataset.[20]

As summarized in table 4, of the twenty-seven completed ethnic civil wars in Kaufmann's database, twenty-four involve ethnic groups that are regionally concentrated, while three do not. Of the twenty-four cases involving highly concentrated ethnic groups, eight (or 33 percent) were resolved by negotiated settlement. By contrast, of the three cases involving ethnic groups that were not highly concentrated, none (or 0 percent) were resolved by negotiated settlement. Thus, as Kaufmann stated, all cases resolved by "negotiated agreement other than partition" involved highly concentrated ethnic groups. This finding, although not statistically significant,[21] is supportive of Kaufmann's corollary—that among ethnic civil wars, those with highly concentrated ethnic groups are more likely than others to be resolved by negotiated agreement. Moreover, when combined with Mason and Fett's finding that 21 percent of completed ideological civil wars were resolved by negotiated agreement, the data also appears to support the two-part hypothesis proposed at the start of this section (see table 7). Unfortunately, the small number of cases (three) in which ethnic groups were not highly concentrated makes it less than cautious

---

the population." See Ted Robert Gurr, Monty G. Marshall, Christian Davenport, *Minorities at Risk: Dataset Users Manual.1002* (College Park: University of Maryland, Integrated Network for Societal Conflict Research, Center for International Development and Conflict Management, 2002), 27.

20. Gurr, *Minorities at Risk.*

21. In a random draw of eight balls (without replacement) from a pool of 24 black and 3 red balls, the probability of drawing all black balls is $(24/27) * (23/26) * \ldots (17/20) = (24!/16!)/(27!/19!) = 33$ percent. Thus, we cannot reject the possibility that this outcome occurred solely by chance. That is, even if regional concentration of ethnic groups has no impact on the prospects for negotiated settlement of ethnic civil wars, we might well find by chance that eight out of eight negotiated settlements involved regionally concentrated ethnic groups.

to rely on conclusions drawn from this subset. Likewise, it would be imprudent to rely on a comparison of statistics from one database with those of another that employs a different operational definition of civil war.

It is important to apply the same methodology to Mason and Fett's database. Accordingly, table 5 has been constructed, again utilizing values for ethnic concentration from the Minorities at Risk dataset, Phase IV (except for six groups not coded in the database, which were coded by this author).

As summarized in table 6, of the twenty-seven completed ethnic conflicts in Mason and Fett's database, twenty-one involved ethnic groups that were regionally concentrated, of which five (or 24 percent) were resolved by negotiated settlement. Of the remaining six cases where ethnic groups were not regionally concentrated, two (or 33 percent) were resolved by negotiated settlement. Thus, Mason and Fett's database does not support Kaufmann's corollary, nor our proposed two-part hypothesis. This indicates that even when utilizing identical operational definitions, we get different results from the two databases because of their divergent selection of cases, as reflected in table 7.

POWER SHARING AFTER ETHNIC WAR

THE CRUX of the difference between the two studies is whether ethnic groups can share political power over the same territory after fighting a civil war against each other. Kaufmann declares that such power sharing is not merely difficult or unlikely but "impossible," as per the title of his article. The reality, however, is that a handful of ethnic civil wars—including several in Mason and Fett's database, and others more recently—have been settled by power-sharing agreements. To salvage Kaufmann's thesis in his absolutist form, it would be necessary to show that none of these was actually an ethnic civil war resolved through power sharing. There are five grounds on which such cases could be rejected:

1. Regional Autonomy: A negotiated agreement based on substantial regional autonomy could be characterized as tantamount to partition and therefore not power sharing. To be consistent with Kaufmann's theory, however, such a settlement also would require defensible borders and regional control over security forces.
2. Peace Enforcement: If outside forces ensure order after the signing of a power-sharing accord, the peace could be attributed to enforcement

Table 5
TESTING KAUFMANN'S COROLLARY WITH MASON AND FETT'S DATABASE

State (by outcome)	Ethnic Group	Dates	Concentrated?
Not Negotiated Settlement			
Burundi	Hutu	1972	No
Burundi	Hutu	1988	No
China	Tibetans	1950–51	Yes
China	Tibetans	1956–59	Yes
Ethiopia	Eritrean	1974–91	Yes
India-Hyderabad	Hyderabadis	1948	Yes*
Indonesia	Acehnese	1953	Yes
Indonesia	Timorese	1975–77	Yes
Iraq	Kurds	1959	Yes
Iraq	Kurds	1961–75	Yes
Jordan	Palestinians	1970	Yes
Liberia	Various	1989–92	Yes*
Nigeria	Ibo	1967–70	Yes
Nigeria	Maitatsine	1980–84	No*
Pakistan	Bengalis	1971	Yes*
Pakistan	Baluchis	1973–77	Yes
Rwanda	Tutsi	1963–64	No
Uganda	Baganda	1966	Yes
Uganda	Various	1980–88	Yes
Zaire	Katangans	1960–65	Yes*
Negotiated Settlement (Other than Partition)			
Angola	Ovimbundu	1975–91	Yes
Chad	Various	1980–88	Yes
Lebanon	Various	1958	No (Sunni, Palestinian)
Mozambique	Ndau/Shona	1979–92	Yes*
Sudan	Various	1963–72	Yes
Western Sahara	Saharawi	1975–83	Yes
Zimbabwe	Blacks	1972–79	No

*These cases were coded by author.

rather than power-sharing.[22] In such cases, the true test of power sharing would be whether peace persists after withdrawal of outside forces.

22. Barbara F. Walter, *Committing to Peace: The Successful Settlement of Civil Wars* (Princeton: Princeton University Press, 2002).

Table 6
REGIONAL CONCENTRATION DOES NOT INCREASE SETTLEMENT LIKELIHOOD
IN MASON AND FETT DATABASE

| | Ethnic Group Concentrated in One Region? | |
	Yes	No
Number of Ethnic Civil Wars	21	6
Number of Negotiated Settlements	5	2
Percent of Negotiated Settlements	24% (5/21)	33% (2/6)

3. Disguised Victory: If the side that is losing a civil war signs a power-sharing agreement, the peace could be attributed to negotiated surrender, rather than power-sharing.[23] In such a case, the test would be whether the stronger side actually shared any significant power during implementation of the agreement.

4. Non-Ethnic: If a civil war divides members of at least one of the ethnic groups, the war could be ideological rather than ethnic, in which case its resolution by power-sharing would not contradict Kaufmann's theory. Because some intra-group conflict occurs in all ethnic civil wars, however, the determining factor would be whether the main schism in the war runs between or across ethnic groups.[24]

5. Pause in Fighting: If civil war resumes after a period of post-war power sharing, the original war may never have been resolved. On the other hand, a substantial period of peace—five years is the typical test—would be hard to reconcile with Kaufmann's theory. Moreover, if the new war is between different combatants than the original, it would not vitiate the success of power-sharing at resolving the initial conflict.[25]

As detailed below, there are at least six civil war settlements since the Second World War that pass all these tests, thereby defying Kaufmann's theory. Two are the cases already noted in Mason and Fett's database, which will be examined first and in greatest depth. Two others are cases in their database in which ethnic civil war between regionally concentrated ethnic groups was settled

23. Thomas C. Schelling, *Arms and Influence* (New Haven: Yale University Press, 1966).
24. Pierre M. Atlas and Roy Licklider, "Conflict among Former Allies After Civil War Settlement: Sudan, Zimbabwe, Chad, and Lebanon," *Journal of Peace Research* 36, no. 1 (January 1999): 40.
25. Atlas and Licklider, "Conflict among Former Allies."

Table 7
TWO DATABASES YIELD CONFLICTING RESULTS ON EFFECT OF GROUP
CONCENTRATION

	Percent of Negotiated Settlements (including autonomy)	
Type of Completed Civil War	*Kaufmann*	*Mason/Fett*
Ethnic: Group Regionally Concentrated	33% (8/24)	24% (5/21)
Ideological	NA	21% (6/29)
Ethnic: Group Intermingled	0% (0/3)	33% (2/6)

without de facto partition.[26] None of these four is in Kaufmann's database. The last two cases occurred too recently for consideration by either study.

LEBANON-1958

Lebanon's 1958 civil war arose when the pro-Western, Christian-led government was opposed by a coalition of Arab nationalists, Muslim militants, and Christian political challengers to the president. The country quickly divided along sectarian lines, however, and violence occurred between rather than within these ethnic groups. After an estimated 1,300 to 2,500 deaths, an agreement was struck to resume power sharing between Lebanon's three primary sectarian groups—Maronite Christians, Sunni Muslims, and Shiite Muslims. The Sunni were not regionally concentrated, and the agreement did not involve regional autonomy, but rather a consociational sharing of central authority. Although U.S. troops intervened for three months, they did not engage the combatants, and there was no other outside peace enforcement.[27] The agreement did not represent the surrender of any group, because each retained its pre-war share of political power. As before, the president would be Christian, the prime minister Sunni, and the speaker of parliament Shiite. The president had a veto, could dissolve parliament, and could fire or appoint the premier, who had the power to form a cabinet but only with the support of parliament, which had seats reserved 6:5 in favor of the Christians (based roughly on the 1932 census). In addition, civil service posts and budgetary allocations were doled out by quota.[28]

26. Of the three remaining cases that Mason and Fett code as negotiated settlement of ethnic civil war, two were merely pauses in fighting (Chad-1988 and Angola-1991), while one was a disguised victory (Western Sahara-1983).
27. Erika Alin, "U.S. Policy and Military Intervention in the 1958 Lebanon Crisis," in David W. Lesch, *The Middle East and the United States: A Historical and Political Reassessment*, 3rd ed. (Boulder: Westview, 2003), 149–67.

There are two grounds on which this case could be questioned as power-sharing resolution of ethnic civil war: (1) whether the fighting actually was ethnic; and (2) whether peace was more than just a pause in fighting. Ideological factors, including pan-Arabism fed by the temporary unification of Egypt and Syria and revolution in Iraq, both in 1958, helped motivate the outbreak of fighting and the subsequent intervention, so the war is often characterized not as sectarian, but rather pro-Western vs. pro-Arab.[29] As Cobban writes, however: "In Beirut, the city was divided along largely sectarian lines, with the Sunni-dominated areas held by the rebels and the Christian-dominated areas in the hands of the loyalists." She adds that by September 1958, "which saw many of the bloodiest incidents, ... many regions of the country became polarized along sectarian lines."[30] Likewise, Meo writes, "the great majority of Muslims, who constituted almost half of the population, sympathized with and supported the objectives of the revolution. The other half of the population, the Christians, however, were overwhelmingly in favor of the regime."[31] Similarly, Salibi explains, "the insurrection had spread to nearly all Moslem and Druze districts," driven by a combination of pan-Arabism and Muslim resentment of perceived Christian advantage, both inflamed by political aspirants. [32] A recent detailed study by Attié also notes the "predominance of the confessional nature of the Lebanese crisis," and reports that "the divisions were almost totally along sectarian lines."[33] As in virtually all ethnic wars, a fraction of each group, notably in the elite, crossed over to ally with another for ideological, political or personal reasons, but this does not invalidate the main sectarian divide.

Peace from renewed power-sharing was only temporary, but it did endure for a remarkable seventeen years in a region of intense instability. In addition, the eventual breakdown of peace resulted mainly from an exogenous factor—Palestinian refugee militias being armed by external supporters—rather than a security dilemma between the parties of the original war. As Seaver writes about the eventual renewal of war in 1975: "Although both the Maronite leaders ... and the Sunni oligarchs ... agreed that the Sunni-Maronite ruling

28. Brenda M. Seaver, "The Regional Sources of Power-Sharing Failure: The Case of Lebanon," *Political Science Quarterly* 115, no. 2 (summer 2000): 254–55.

29. Michael Hudson, "Trying Again: Power-Sharing in Post-Civil War Lebanon," *International Negotiation* 2, no. 1 (January 1997): 108.

30. Helena Cobban, *The Making of Modern Lebanon* (London: Hutchinson, 1985), 88, 91.

31. Leila M. T. Meo, *Lebanon: Improbable Nation* (Bloomington: Indiana University Press, 1965), 169.

32. K.S. Salibi, *The Modern History of Lebanon* (New York: Praeger, 1965), 201.

33. Caroline Attié, *Struggle in the Levant: Lebanon in the 1950s* (London: I.B. Tauris, 2004), 171, 228.

formula should not be altered, the Palestinian issue ultimately proved fatally divisive."[34] Finally, Kaufmann's exclusion of the case from his database cannot be justified by the relatively low level of deaths, because his database includes ethnic conflicts with even lower totals: Nicaragua-Miskitos from 1981 to 1988; Spain-Basques from 1959 to 1980s; and Bougainville-Papua in 1988.[35]

ZIMBABWE-1979

The civil war in Zimbabwe (Southern Rhodesia) from 1972 to 1979 pitted the ruling white minority against a coalition of black rebels, resulting in 12,000 battle deaths. A power-sharing agreement, including integration of the opposing armed forces, was signed in late 1979, after both sides faced a series of sticks and carrots from external supporters.[36] The white minority government agreed to accept black majority rule, and in turn the blacks agreed to reserve white seats in parliament for seven years, honor pension obligations to white officials, and not seize white lands without payment. In the first years after the agreement, the black coalition splintered along ethnic lines, as Matabele supporters of Joshua Nkomo's ZAPU party were marginalized by Robert Mugabe's Shona-dominated ruling ZANU party. In 1982, frustrated Matabele rebels began to seize white lands. Remarkably, Mugabe's black government did not acquiesce to the seizures, but rather fought a war against erstwhile black allies in order to defend the rights of erstwhile white enemies. The government successfully quashed the Matabele insurgency by 1987, thereby sustaining the core of the original black-white, power-sharing agreement. [37]

The case of Zimbabwe-1979 stands up to all five potential objections as a successful resolution of ethnic civil war through power sharing. The peace agreement did not grant regional autonomy. The British-led monitoring force had neither the size nor the mandate to conduct enforcement and withdrew

34. Seaver, "The Regional Sources of Power-Sharing Failure," 266.
35. Mason and Fett, "How Civil Wars End"; Kaufmann, "Possible and Impossible."
36. Each side was told by its historical sponsor (the United Kingdom for the whites; neighboring frontline states for the blacks) that support would be cut off if they did not negotiate in good faith, but would be sustained if the other side rejected a negotiated settlement. The United Kingdom also agreed, in response to rebel demands, to deploy more than one-thousand British-led Commonwealth monitors during the transition and to permit the rebel forces to be cantoned near supportive frontline states where they felt less vulnerable in case the white government reneged. See Stephen John Stedman, *Peacemaking in Civil War: International Mediation in Zimbabwe, 1974–1980* (Lynne Rienner, 1991). See also Walter, *Committing to Peace*, 131–42, who emphasizes the monitors, although the location of cantonment areas seems to have been more decisive. The death total is from Mason and Fett, "How Civil Wars End."
37. Atlas and Licklider, "Conflict among Former Allies," 40–43.

within three months.[38] The agreement did not disguise a victory by the blacks because the whites were nowhere near defeat on the battlefield and the power-sharing agreement was fully implemented after the war, preserving white economic dominance. The conflict clearly was ethnic, as the main divide was black-white. Admittedly, the black rebel coalition during the war masked an internal divide, but ethnic wars typically subsume other societal divides temporarily. Though low-level violence resumed shortly after the peace agreement, it was power struggle among blacks, not resumption of the original ethnic war. The most remarkable fact about Zimbabwe was noted aptly two decades after the peace agreement: "There has been no renewed violence between whites and blacks to date."[39] Admittedly, a few years later, economic failure and Mugabe's faltering political support led to a temporary renewal of violent seizures of white farms, which triggered some white emigration.[40] Even if this low-level violence represented the demise of the 1979 agreement, which is an exaggeration, it would not invalidate the achievement of twenty years of peace.

SUDAN-1972

Following a nine-year civil war that produced 250,000 battlefield deaths, Sudan's 1972 agreement brought more than a decade of peace between northern Arabs and southern Christians and animists, until another civil war broke out in 1983. This peace cannot be rejected as a mere pause in fighting because the second war arose from distinct northern political dynamics rather than an unresolved security dilemma with the south.[41] The agreement did grant a degree of regional autonomy and thus might be dismissed by Kaufmann as de facto partition. The agreement, however, did not establish a defensible border or full regional control over security forces, two factors he insists are essential to resolving an ethnic civil war by partition. Thus, his theory cannot account for how this ethnic civil war was resolved for eleven years by power sharing.

MOZAMBIQUE-1992

Mozambique's thirteen-year civil war, which entailed 200,000 battlefield deaths, is sometimes coded as ideological because it pitted the communist

---

38. All of the monitors withdrew by 16 March 1980, leaving behind only forty British officers to help train the Zimbabwean army, http://www.britains-smallwars.com/RRGP/Agila/Sunset.jtm (accessed 6 March 2004).

39. Atlas and Licklider, "Conflict Among Former Allies," 40.

40. R. W. Johnson, "Mugabe, Mbeki, and Mandela's Shadow," *The National Interest*, no. 63 (spring 2001): 59–75.

41. Atlas and Licklider, "conflict among Former Allies," 38, summarize: "the settlement seems to collapse as an unanticipated consequence of internal political tensions within the northern elite."

FRELIMO government against RENAMO rebels supported by anti-communist Rhodesia and South Africa. RENAMO, however, drew its leadership from the Ndau people in the geographic center of the state, while the FRELIMO government was led and supported mostly by ethnic groups in the south. Because RENAMO never relied exclusively on one ethnic group nor received unanimous support from any ethnic group, and did receive external support, Michel Cahen has concluded that, "while ethnic factors were undoubtedly a factor in the war, it cannot be defined as an interethnic conflict."[42] By contrast, many others including Mason and Fett code the war as ethnic. Labels aside, the fact is that opposing ethnic groups killed each other for years, leading to sharp polarization of identity. According to Kaufmann's theory, therefore, the groups should not have been able to achieve peace by sharing central authority. Yet, that is precisely what they have done for more than a dozen years since the 1992 peace agreement.

MORE RECENT CASES OF POWER-SHARING

Starting in 1980, negotiated settlement of civil war became far more commonplace than before. Whereas Licklider found less than a quarter of the civil wars that ended from 1945–93 did so by negotiated agreement, Hoddie and Hartzell say the figure is 65 percent (twenty-four of thirty-seven) for wars that ended from 1980 to 1996.[43] Howard notes a similar trend in all major civil-war databases, which she attributes to a temporary norm of negotiated settlement in the late twentieth century.[44] Only two of the most recent agreements, however, qualify as power-sharing settlements by the five criteria above.

SOUTH AFRICA-1994

The 1948 racial discrimination policy (apartheid) of South Africa's white government spawned an armed black opposition, which eventually spiraled into

---

42. Michel Cahen , "Nationalism and Ethnicities: Lessons from Mozambique," dated 1999, available at http://www.cphrc.org.uk/essays/cahen1.htm (accessed 6 March 2004). See also, Michel Cahen, "Nationalisms and Ethnicities: Lessons from Mozambique," in *Ethnicity Kills? The Politics of War, Peace and Ethnicity in Sub-Saharan Africa*, ed. Einar Braathen, Morten Bøås and Gjermund Sæther (London: Macmillan, 2000), 163–87.

43. Matthew Hoddie and Caroline Hartzell, "Civil War Settlements and the Implementation of Military Power-Sharing Arrangements," *Journal of Peace Research* 40, no. 3 (May 2003): 303–20. The authors do not disaggregate power-sharing and power-dividing agreements.

44. Lise Morje Howard, "The Rise and Decline of the Norm of Negotiated Settlement" (paper presented at the Georgetown Junior Faculty Workshop on Intervention, Georgetown University, 23–24 October 2003), 2. She cites the Major Armed Conflict, Correlates of War, and Intra State War databases, and those compiled by Walter, Doyle and Sambanis, and SIPRI. She believes the norm has faded in the wake of the terrorist attacks of 11 September 2001.

a civil war from the late-1980s to early-1990s that killed thousands. Spurred in part by the white business community, South African president F. W. de Klerk initiated negotiations in the early 1990s, leading to democratic elections in 1994 that established black majority rule.[45] The war clearly was ethnic, involving three main factions: white government security forces, Zulu warriors of the Inkatha Freedom Party, and the mainly Xhosa fighters of the African National Congress.[46] Although a 1993 draft constitution granted limited regional autonomy to nine provinces, it never envisioned autonomous provincial security forces guarding defensible borders; moreover, the final 1996 version further scaled back this autonomy.[47] The peace did not represent a disguised victory, because no side was defeated on the battlefield, and all sides ultimately made significant compromises. Whites surrendered control of the government, the ANC permitted continued white economic dominance, and the Zulu accepted less than full autonomy for KwaZulu-Natal province. No outside peacekeepers were deployed. Though low-level political violence persists between Zulu and ANC supporters, and high crime rates have spurred some white emigration, the ethnic civil war has been successfully resolved by power-sharing for more than a decade.[48]

GUATEMALA-1996

Although Guatemala's civil war began in 1960 as an ideological struggle, by 1980 it had evolved into an ethnic war between the ruling minority elite, of European heritage, and the majority, indigenous Mayan populace who fueled the rebel movement. Peaking in intensity from 1981 to 1983, Army violence killed an estimated 200,000 Mayans overall during the war, but failed

45. Peter Gastrow, "A Joint Effort—The South African Peace Process," European Platform for Conflict Prevention and Transformation, available at http://www.xs4all.nl/~conflic1/pbp/part1/8_joint_.htm (accessed 12 March 2004). A chart of yearly political violence is contained in Phiroshaw Camay and Anne J. Gordon, "The National Peace Accord and its Structures," South Africa Civil Society and Governance Case Study no. 1, Co-operative for Research and Education (CORE), Johannesburg, South Africa, 2000, available at http://www.ids.ac.uk/ids/civsoc/final/southafrica/saf4.doc (accessed 12 March 2004). "Democracy and Deep-Rooted Conflict Case Study: South Africa," Institute for Democracy and Electoral Assistance, available at http://www.idea.int/publications/democracy_and_deep_rooted_conflict/ebook_cs_south_africa.htm (accessed 12 March 2004).
46. "The Zulu of South Africa," Minorities at Risk, available at http://www.cidcm.umd.edu/inscr/mar/data/safzulu.htm (accessed 12 March 2004).
47. David A. Lake and Donald Rothchild, "Territorial Decentralization and Civil War Settlements," in Powersharing and Peacemaking, forthcoming, 8.
48. "Good news for political stability—but South Africans are still insecure," South African Institute of Race Relations, 21 March 2001, available at http://www.sairr.org.za/wsc/pstory.htx?storyID=214 (accessed 12 March 2004). The report concludes that, "Since 1994 political violence has declined consistently."

to defeat the rebels. Accordingly, the two sides turned to negotiations and in late 1996 signed a multifaceted peace deal, agreeing to end the war, disarm the rebels, halt army human rights abuses, ensure equality for the indigenous, and share power over the whole territory in a unitary democracy.[49] The agreement was not a disguised victory because the government was forced to make major concessions before the rebels would agree to peace. The agreement did not grant regional autonomy, nor did it rely on outside military intervention. Although implementation has been slow and bumpy, especially during the domestic political ascension of conservatives from 1999 to 2003, progress is substantial: the rebels have demobilized; the army has downsized and halted some notorious armed patrols; free and fair elections have been held; refugees have returned; and discrimination has been outlawed. Most important, as a 2003 UN report noted, "The armed conflict has definitively ended, as has the state policy of human rights abuses that characterized the conflict."[50] Though work remains, the implementation of power sharing is exemplified by the fact that both candidates in the December 2003 presidential run-off elections ran on platforms of improving the lot of the indigenous.[51] Even more remarkably, although the more conservative candidate won, he appointed to his cabinet the Nobel Prize-winning indigenous activist Rigoberto Menchu to oversee implementation of the agreement.[52] The genocidal violence of Guatemala's ethnic civil war is precisely the type that Kaufmann says should prevent power-sharing agreements of the type that has successfully kept the peace in Guatemala for more than eight years so far.

DISQUALIFIED CASES

Other apparent power-sharing settlements of ethnic war over the past fifteen years cannot be coded as such because of one or more of the tests above. One case, in the Philippines, is disqualified because the peace agreement grants autonomy to a regionally concentrated ethnic group and because violence continues. In 1996, the Catholic-dominated government gave substantial autonomy to the Moro, a group of Muslims concentrated in southern islands,

---

49. Susanne Jonas, "Democratization Through Peace: The Difficult Case of Guatemala," *Journal of Interamerican Studies and World Affairs* 42, no. 4 (winter 2001): 10–14.

50. Hilde Salvesen, "Guatemala: Five Years After the Peace Accords. The Challenges of Implementing Peace," International Peace Research Institute, Oslo (PRIO), March 2002, 9–17. *MINUGUA Report to the Consultative Group Meeting for Guatemala*, Executive Summary, UN Verification Mission in Guatemala, 7 May 2003, 1–2.

51. "Poll Rivals Pledge Boost for Mayans," *Agence France Press*, 27 December 2003.

52. "Menchu Plans to Join New Guatemalan Government," *Milwaukee Journal Sentinel*, 18 January 2004, 8A.

permitting them to maintain a security force of 20,000. The main rebel group has honored the cease fire, but a splinter organization fights on.[53] Three other cases cannot be counted because of the presence of occupation forces, which suggests that peace may result from enforcement rather than power-sharing. In Northern Ireland, 12,000 British forces are still committed to peacekeeping six years after the 1998 Good Friday agreement.[54] In Tajikistan, some 15-25,000 Russian troops have been present since its 1997 peace agreement.[55] In Lebanon, 15,000 Syrian troops remain fifteen years after the power-sharing 1989 Taif agreement ended that country's second civil war.[56] Three more cases are disqualified because they involve both regional autonomy and peacekeeping forces. In Bosnia, 12,000 peacekeeping forces remain nine years after the Dayton accords, which granted significant autonomy (including military) to each of Bosnia's two entities: a Serb Republic, and a Muslim-Croat Federation.[57] Likewise, two civil wars in Georgia's secessionist republics of the early 1990s, South Ossetia and Abkhazia, were halted with grants of autonomy and occupation by Russian troops.[58]

Another recent case of ostensibly negotiated peace is actually a disguised victory. In late 1995, Yugoslav authorities agreed to end hostilities and return to Croatia the region of Eastern Slovenia that they had controlled for four years. They did so, however, only after Croatia forcibly took back other Serb-held regions in Croatia and Bosnia and appeared poised to do the same to Eastern Slavonia. By settling this matter through negotiation rather than war, Belgrade managed to avoid the near total Serb out-migration that occurred in regions re-taken forcibly by Croatia, and thus enabled 80 percent of Serbs

53. After more than two decades of war that killed 50,000, a 2 September 1996, agreement created an autonomous region comprising fourteen provinces. The region was slightly enlarged by an August 2000 referendum. "Moros in the Philippines," Minorities at Risk, www.cidcm.umd.edu/inscr/mar/data/phimoro.htm (accessed 12 April 2004). See also, Rothchild and Hartzell, "Security in Deeply Divided Societies," 260.
54. 12,000 troops are committed to the mission, although only about 4,000 are deployed at any time, while the rest are in various stages of rotation. Peter Almond, "Ulster Vote Hit UK Troop Options," UPI, 28 November 2003.
55. Gregory Gleason, "Power Sharing in Tajikistan: Political Compromise and Regional Instability," Conflict, Security & Development 1, no. 3 (December 2001): 127.
56. Nicholas Blanford, "Syria loosens its grip on Lebanon. Despite the latest troop withdrawal last week, about 15,000 Syrians remain," Christian Science Monitor, 31 July 2003. Kaufmann includes Lebanon-1989 in his database as a case of outside military occupation. Syria has agreed to withdraw its remaining forces, as this article goes to press.
57. http://www.nato.int/sfor/organisation/sfororg.htm (accessed 11 March 2004). See also, Sumantra Bose, Bosnia after Dayton: Nationalist Partition and International Intervention (London: Hurst and Company, 2002).
58. Kaufmann includes Abkhazia-1993 in his database as a case of settlement by regional autonomy.

to remain after the peaceful handover.[59] The result is Croat control, however, not power-sharing.

One additional case, in Bangladesh, cannot be counted even though war has subsided, because the power-sharing agreement has not been implemented. In 1997 the government agreed to settle its two-decade war against rebels of the Chittagong hill tribes, a conflict that killed thousands, by granting limited autonomy and reversing the Bengali land settlement program that had displaced tens of thousands of tribal people. The agreement qualifies as power-sharing because the promised autonomy is extremely limited and makes no provision for autonomous tribal security forces or a defensible internal border. The government has failed to implement most of the agreement, however, especially since the 2001 election of the BNP party that had opposed it. Not only has the government refused to facilitate the return of displaced tribal people, it continues to subsidize Bengali settlers. In 2003, violence erupted anew, displacing 1,500 tribal people.[60] As yet, there has been no resumption of full-blown civil war, but the case cannot be coded as successful resolution of ethnic war through power-sharing until calm is restored and the government substantially implements the agreement.

Yet another intriguing case satisfies all the tests for power-sharing settlement of ethnic civil war—except the death toll was so low that the conflict may not qualify as war. From 1990 to 1995, Mali's army fought a counter-insurgency against northern Tuareg rebels. The fighting clearly was ethnic, as Tuareg spearheaded the rebellion and were singled out for retaliation, though they initially were supported by other northern minorities. The peace agreement did not represent a disguised victory, because both sides realized that victory was impossible and accordingly made significant concessions. The government increased sharply its spending in the north, marginally expanded local political autonomy, and integrated some former rebels into the army and civil service, while the Tuareg rebels abandoned their goal of independence, demobilized, and turned over 3,000 weapons. The grant of autonomy was not tantamount

---

59. "Eastern Slavonia back to Croatia's control: Country returns to its pre-war borders," *CNN*, 15 January 1998, http://edition.cnn.com/WORLD/9801/15/croatia.handover/ (accessed 12 March 2004).

60. "Bangladesh: land disputes perpetuate internal displacement," Global IDP, Norwegian Refugee Council, available at http://www.db.idpproject.org/Sites/IdpprojectDb/idpSurvey. nsf/SearchResults/F8F0406D73E163ADC1256BA2004F010C?OpenDocument (accessed 12 March 2004). "The Chittagong Hill Tracts Peace Accord: Squandering the Peace and Human Rights Dividends," Asian Indigenous & Tribal Peoples Network, New Delhi, India, January 2003, available at http://www.aitpn.org/Briefingpapers/II-03-03-CHTs.PDF (accessed 12 March 2004).

to partition because the Tuareg gave up autonomous security forces. Nor did any third-party occupation enforce peace. Initial grassroots opposition to power-sharing on both sides was mitigated by widespread reconciliation efforts, both by the army and communal groups.[61] Peace was not merely a pause in fighting, because it persists nearly a decade later.[62] The only question is whether the fighting ever escalated sufficiently to qualify as war. Death estimates for the entire five-year conflict run only between 500 and 1,000, which does not qualify as war by most operational definitions.[63]

To Kaufmann's credit, none of the eight cases he codes as settled by regional autonomy is actually an instance of power-sharing resolution of ethnic civil war, although one case comes close. Most of the others never actually were settled at all. For example, the conflict between India and its Naga minority persists at a low level despite the enforcement efforts of 200,000 Indian troops among the 3.5 million populace of Nagaland, because many Nagas reject the 1972 agreement as a surrender.[64] Likewise India's war against its Tripuri insurgency persists after India's perceived failure to implement a 1988 autonomy agreement. [65] Spain's battle against Basque separatists persists at its historic, extremely low level (800 killed in 35 years) despite a 1980

61. Kåre Lode, "Mali's Peace Process: Context, Analysis & Evaluation," ACCORD—Conciliation Resources, http://www.c-r.org/accord/peace/accord13/mapea.shtml (accessed 12 April 2004). Bram Posthumus, "Mali: Successful Mediation Effort Could Lead to Lasting Peace," dated 2000, http://www.conflict-prevention.net/dev/ECCP/ECCPSurveys_v0_10. nsf/0/CB6AEB8CD65E670FC1256B2700317DED?opendocument (accessed 12 April 2004). Lt. Col. Kalifa Keita, *Conflict and Conflict Resolution in the Sahel: The Tuareg Insurgency in Mali* (Carlisle, Penn.: Strategic Studies Institute, 1998), http://www.carlisle.army.mil/ssi/pubs/1998/tuareg/tuareg.htm (accessed 12 April 2004).
62. "Tuareg of Mali," Minorities at Risk, http://www.cidcm.umd.edu/inscr/mar/data/malituar.htm (accessed 12 April 2004). "Background Note: Mali," Bureau of African Affairs, U.S. Department of State, November 2003, http://www.state.gov/r/pa/ei/bgn/2828.htm (accessed 12 April 2004).
63. R. William Ayres, "A World Flying Apart? Violent Nationalist Conflict and the End of the Cold War," *Journal of Peace Research* 37, no. 1 (January 2000): 12, http://darkwing.uoregon. edu/~dgalvan/ps607-w04/ayres-post911.pdf (accessed 12 April 2004). M.G. Marshall, *Measuring the Societal Impact of War* (2002), Appendix A, www.cidcm.umd.edu/inscr/papers/IPAmgmA.pdf (accessed 12 April 2004).
64. "Nagas in India," http://www.cidcm.umd.edu/inscr/mar/data/indnaga.htm (accessed 29 March 2004).
65. R. Radhakrishnan, "Terror strikes in Tripura," Institute of Peace and Conflict Studies, New Delhi, 26 September 2002, http://www.ipcs.org/ipcs/issueIndex2. jsp?action=showView&kValue=84&issue=1014&status=article&mod=b, (accessed March 29, 2004); Paolienlal Haokip, "Election Verdicts in Nagaland, Meghalaya and Tripura: Mandates for Peace?," Institute of Peace and Conflict Studies, New Delhi, 21 March 2003, http://www.ipcs.org/ipcs/issueIndex2.jsp?action=showView&kValue=956&issue=1014&status=article &mod=b (accessed 29 March 2004). "Tripuras/Tripuriin India," Minorities at Risk, http://www.cidcm.umd.edu/inscr/mar/data/indtrip.htm (accessed 29 March 2004).

autonomy agreement.[66] Israel's struggle against the Palestinians continues after collapse of the 1993 Oslo peace accords. Also, as noted above, autonomy agreements have failed to settle the Philippines' struggle against the Moro and Bangladesh's versus the Chittagong tribes, while Georgia's war against secessionist Abkhazia is frozen by the intervention of Russian troops. The case in Kaufmann's database that comes closest to power-sharing is the 1987 peace agreement between Nicaragua's government and its Miskito Indian minority. Though the state nominally granted regional autonomy, in practice local authority has remained so limited that the Miskitos protested in 2000 by boycotting elections. Thus, power is in fact centralized and shared, yet peace has prevailed for more than seventeen years. Like Mali, however, the death toll in the original conflict was so low (a few hundred Miskito deaths) that it probably should not be counted as civil war.[67] Finally, Papua New Guinea's war against Bougainville rebels, which Kaufmann coded as a victory for the state in 1988, actually continued for at least another decade. More recently, the conflict may have been settled by a regional autonomy agreement, but it is too early to tell whether that peace will hold.[68]

SUMMARY AND RECOMMENDATIONS FOR FURTHER RESEARCH

TWO PROMINENT articles on the prospects for negotiated settlement of civil wars reach divergent conclusions for several reasons, including that they (1) rely on different databases; (2) employ different operational definitions of negotiated settlement; (3) overstate the statistical significance of some findings; and (4) make faulty assumptions. The first two reasons, differing databases and definitions, are responsible for most of the divergence. Indeed, in the context of their own databases and definitions, each study generally justifies its own conclusions. One exception is that Kaufmann seems simply to assume, rather

66. http://www.cnn.com/SPECIALS/2001/basque/stories/overview.html (accessed 29 March 2004). "Basques in Spain," Minorities at Risk, http://www.cidcm.umd.edu/inscr/mar/data/spbasque.htm (accessed 29 March 2004).
67. Alma Guillermoprieto, "OAS Study Says Miskito Indians Suffered Abuse From Sandinistas," *Washington Post*, 8 June 1984, A18. George Gedda, "Defector Charges Sandinistas Executed Thousands," *Associated Press*, 18 September 1985. "North Atlantic Coast Miskito Indians," Carnegie Project on Complex Power-Sharing and Self-Determination, http://www.ecmi.de/cps/about_miskito.html (accessed 29 March 2004). "Native Peoples of Nicaragua," Minorities at Risk, http://www.cidcm.umd.edu/inscr/mar/data/indnic.htm (accessed 29 March 2004).
68. "Bougainvilleans in Papua New Guinea," Minorities at Risk, http://www.cidcm.umd.edu/inscr/mar/data/pngboug.htm (accessed 29 March 2004). "Bougainville Case Review," Carnegie Project on Complex Power-Sharing and Self-Determination, http://www.ecmi.de/cps/documents_bougainville_case.html (accessed 29 March 2004).

than demonstrate, that ideological civil wars are more susceptible to negotiated settlement than ethnic civil wars. The evidence provided by Mason and Fett appears to belie this assumption. Kaufmann also overstates the significance of one of his main findings, that all negotiated settlements of ethnic civil wars have involved regionally concentrated ethnic groups. In reality, the vast majority of all ethnic civil wars in his database involve such concentrated ethnic groups, so it is impossible to rule out the possibility that the results observed by Kaufmann occurred solely by chance. In addition, both studies share the problem of excluding from their databases ongoing civil wars, potentially introducing a selection bias.

The difference in case selection in the two studies' databases of resolved ethnic civil wars is remarkable, considering that each study purports to include "all" such cases since the Second World War. Of the twenty-seven and twenty-eight cases in the two databases, respectively, only six overlap. This difference is responsible for some of the discrepant findings between the two studies, as was demonstrated by applying identical tests to the two databases. In particular, when Kaufmann's definition of negotiated power-sharing settlements was applied to his own database, it yielded no such cases, but when applied to the Mason and Fett database, it yielded two such cases, Lebanon-1958 and Zimbabwe-1979. Both these cases of ethnic civil war were resolved by negotiated settlements not based on political autonomy for regionally concentrated ethnic groups—a phenomenon that is impossible according to Kaufmann's theory. Two other cases in Mason and Fett's database, Sudan-1972 and Mozambique-1992, also defy Kaufmann's theory, because ethnic conflicts were settled by power-sharing agreements that entailed neither autonomous regional security forces nor defensible internal borders. Kaufmann's database excludes all four of these cases that contradict his theory. In addition, two ethnic civil wars that were settled too late for inclusion in either study, South Africa-1994 and Guatemala-1996, also defy Kaufmann's theory because peace was based on centralized power-sharing rather than granting political and military autonomy to defensible regions. These few discrepant cases do not disprove the causal mechanism in Kaufmann's theory, but do falsify his hyperbolic claim that power-sharing is an "impossible" solution to ethnic conflict.

In addition, much of the divergence in findings between the two studies results not from their different universes of cases but from differing operational definitions of negotiated settlement, as demonstrated by applying their opposing definitions to each other's database. For example, applying Mason and Fett's definition to Kaufmann's database, we found eight (out of twenty-seven) negotiated settlements, whereas Kaufmann found zero such settlements in this universe using his own definition.

The two databases do yield some common findings when consistent operational definitions are applied. For example, among completed civil wars, there appears to be no significant difference in the likelihood of negotiated settlement (as defined by Mason and Fett) between ethnic and ideological wars. In Kaufmann's database, such settlements were reached in 30 percent of ethnic wars. In their own database, Mason and Fett find such settlements in 26 percent of ethnic wars and 21 percent of ideological wars. These differences are not statistically significant.

In an attempt to reconcile the two studies' findings, this article proposed a two-part hypothesis: (1) Ethnic civil wars involving regionally concentrated ethnic groups are more amenable to negotiated agreement than ideological civil wars; and (2) Ethnic civil wars involving intermingled ethnic groups are less amenable to negotiated agreement than ideological civil wars. If both parts of the hypothesis were correct, ethnic civil wars overall might appear roughly equally as amenable to negotiated agreement as ideological civil wars. This two-part hypothesis was supported by Kaufmann's data on ethnic civil wars, taken in conjunction with Mason and Fett's data on ideological civil wars, although the findings were not statistically significant. Mason and Fett's data on ethnic and ideological wars, however, did not support the hypothesis.

The above analysis sets out a clear agenda for future research. Most importantly, a comprehensive, rigorously defined database of all civil wars, ongoing and completed, ethnic and ideological, should be constructed. Several operational definitions will be important. First, for a war to be categorized as "resolved," the level of killing should have fallen below a specific threshold for a set duration.[69] Second, criteria must be developed for distinguishing a war as ethnic or ideological. While some wars have characteristics of both, Kaufmann's theory would suggest that so long as ethnic groups are pitted against each other in a civil war (even as parts of opposing ideological camps), it should be categorized as ethnic because such identities will harden and then persist after the war. Third, the database should include the number of war-related deaths, either as an absolute figure or as a percentage of population. This will permit low-violence cases to be excluded from tests of Kaufmann's theory, where they are irrelevant, as well as enable more sophisticated statistical assessment of the impact of such violence on prospects for negotiated settlements. Fourth, the

---

69. While this will create a selection bias against recently settled wars, that is unavoidable.

database should exclude cases of one-sided suppression—such as those involving Soviet forces in post-Second World War Ukraine and Lithuania, which are included by Kaufmann—perhaps by requiring a threshold level of deaths on both sides. Fifth, the database should include a sophisticated measure of the regional concentration of ethnic groups, given the potential importance of this variable.[70]

In addition, the outcomes of such civil wars should be broken down into at least four categories: (1) negotiated settlements based on regional political and military autonomy for concentrated ethnic groups with defensible internal borders; (2) negotiated settlements based on regional political autonomy without regional military autonomy and defensible internal borders; (3) negotiated settlements based on centralized power-sharing over a unitary state; and (4) other outcomes, including victory for one side, partition, or third-party occupation. This will permit a test of the main theoretical difference between the two studies: whether or not negotiated settlements of ethnic civil wars must be based on granting autonomy (political or military) to regionally concentrated ethnic groups. Selection effects should be minimized by conducting tests on both ongoing and completed wars where relevant—for example, in testing Kaufmann's corollary that regional concentration of ethnic groups increases the likelihood that ethnic civil wars can be resolved by negotiated agreement. Where inclusion of ongoing wars is not appropriate for a specific test, the potentially distorting impact of excluding ongoing wars should be evaluated by testing for a correlation between included variables and such wars. Finally, it would be useful to construct an additional database of all attempted negotiated settlements of ethnic civil wars. This would enable testing of the two potential versions of the causal mechanism behind Kaufmann's theory, to determine if either is confirmed by the data.

Obtaining and processing data in such a rigorous manner is an essential prerequisite before jumping to any conclusions or prescriptions about the appropriate role of the international community in facilitating resolution of ethnic civil wars via partition.

---

70. Kaufmann argues that the rankings for ethnic-group concentration in the original Gurr database do not capture the phenomenon that has causal power in his theory—the extent to which most members of an ethnic group in a country are concentrated within a single contiguous area. He says this original database incorrectly coded as concentrated many ethnic groups that were dispersed within a large contiguous area, because they were locally concentrated in several small pockets within that larger area. Kaufmann, communication with author, 17 October 1997. This problem has been addressed somewhat by additional codings for regional concentration, based on definitions of Fearon and Laitin, in the Minorities at Risk dataset, Phase IV.

THEORETICAL IMPLICATIONS OF RECENT FINDINGS

Recent research provides some support for both studies examined in this article. In 1995, Licklider found results consistent with Mason and Fett: "Identity and political-economic civil wars are about equally likely to end in negotiated settlements (26 percent and 20 percent)." In addition, he found that identity wars did not last longer and that, "One-third of the negotiated settlements of identity civil wars that last for five years 'stick.' We can not simply say that such settlements do not work." [71]

By contrast, Rothchild, Hartzell, and Hoddie find evidence consistent with Kaufmann. A 1999 study by the first two authors found that peace agreements after ethnic wars were 40 percent less stable than others and that regional autonomy provided more stability than power-sharing such as federalism. [72] More recently, Hartzell and Hoddie have found that among civil wars ended by negotiation, ethnic wars were a remarkable four-to-five times more likely to resume. [73] A study by all three authors also found that partition provided longer peace than other settlements. This last study, however, did not disaggregate ethnic from other wars. Since ethnic wars are more likely to end in partition, this finding indicates that ethnic wars settled by partition last longer than other civil war settlements. Taken in combination with their other studies, this implies that ethnic civil wars settled by power-sharing are the most prone to fail, which strongly supports the causal mechanism of Kaufmann's theory. [74] Although the six cases of ethnic civil war resolved by power-sharing falsify Kaufmann's absolutist claim about the impossibility of this type of settlement, the weight of data confirms that such settlements are difficult to achieve.

The finding that partition reduces the likelihood of renewed civil war between the separated groups is not surprising. Few would dispute that physically separating two groups reduces the security dilemma between them and the opportunities for friction to flare into fighting. Rather, the questions about partition have always been three:

71. Roy Licklider, "The Consequences of Negotiated Settlements in Civil Wars, 1945–1993," *American Political Science Review* 89, no. 3 (September 1995): 686.
72. Donald Rothchild and Caroline A. Hartzell, "Security in Deeply Divided Societies: The Role of Territorial Autonomy," *Nationalism and Ethnic Politics* 5, no. 3&4 (autumn-winter 1999): 267–68.
73. Hartzell and Hoddie, "Institutionalizing Peace," 328.
74. Caroline Hartzell, Matthew Hoddie, and Donald Rothchild, "Stabilizing the Peace After Civil War: An Investigation of Some Key Variables," *International Organization* 55, no. 1 (winter 2001): 183–208.

- Is partition the only feasible negotiated solution to ethnic conflict?
- If not, do the benefits of partition outweigh the human costs of forced population transfers?
- Does partition increase the likelihood of violent conflict within each of the separated groups?

This article answers the first question in the negative, showing that several ethnic civil wars have been settled for long periods without partition. Whether the benefits of partition outweigh the costs depends in part on the alternatives, which are few according to recent research. For example, in a forthcoming study, Lake and Rothchild find that regional autonomy is not a sustainable means to resolving ethnic conflict. Although peace agreements based on regional autonomy may help end civil wars, the authors find that regional autonomy always devolves in one of two opposing directions, toward either hard partition or re-centralization of authority: "We find no evidence of successful institutionalization of [regional autonomy] provisions in a post-war constitutional order."[75] If so, the only long-term alternative to partition may be centralized power-sharing. As noted above, however, power-sharing settlements of ethnic civil wars are the most prone to failure. Still unclear are the long-term prospects for peace achieved by an initial promise of regional autonomy that is subsequently eroded through re-centralization—a pattern that Lake and Rothchild say is common.[76]

The primary theoretical shortcoming in Kaufmann's work is his assumption that each ethnic group is monolithic, at least during and after violent inter-ethnic conflict. In reality, ethnic groups have internal divisions, even during violent conflict against other groups, which has two important implications. First, according to Barak, it is precisely such intra-ethnic divisions, which Kaufmann assumes away, that enable the power-sharing accords Kaufmann says are impossible. As Barak illustrates in the case of Lebanon-1989, inter-ethnic power-sharing comes about when factions of opposing ethnic groups

---

75. David A. Lake and Donald Rothchild, "Territorial Decentralization and Civil War Settlements," in *Powersharing and Peacemaking*, forthcoming. The authors, however, do find nine states that remain "semi-decentralized" following implementation of a negotiated agreement. The authors cite two factors that militate toward partition: governance requires a belief that institutions will last (and fully independent institutions are perceived as longer lasting); and minorities do not accept promises about future benign treatment. They cite one opposing factor: any central institutions inherently promote further centralization. This empirical finding and theoretical argument are in tension with the deductive logic in favor of regional autonomy in Hartzell, Hoddie, and Rothchild, "Stabilizing the Peace," 191–92.

76. Lake and Rothchild, "Territorial Decentralization," argue that the state's promise of regional autonomy, even if not credible, represents a "costly signal" that reassures opposing groups.

realize they have a common interest against factions within their own ethnic groups.[77] Second, according to Licklider and Atlas, the hidden divides within ostensibly monolithic ethnic groups explain why the cause of renewed civil war is "often a breakdown in relations among former allies, not former foes."[78] These dynamics suggest two important caveats about Kaufmann's prescription for the international community to promote partition as a means of resolving ethnic conflict. First, partition may obstruct some paths to peace that rely on alliances between factions within opposing ethnic groups. Second, partition may give rise to violence within one or more of the separated ethnic groups.

Despite these and other shortcomings, partition remains a valid option for managing violent ethnic conflict. Admittedly, partition may require violence, separate people from the land of their ancestors, undermine inter-ethnic moderate alliances, and foster new conflicts within separated groups. These costs, however, may be the lesser evil in cases where partition can end an otherwise insoluble, violent ethnic conflict. Knowing when to apply this draconian prescription thus requires more research into the determinants of success for partition, power-sharing, and hybrid solutions such as regional autonomy, as well as the costs and risks of each. In the absence of such data, it is irresponsible to tout any solution—whether partition or power-sharing—as a silver bullet to resolve ethnic conflict.

77. Oren Barak, "Intra-Communal and Inter-Communal Dimensions of Conflict and Peace in Lebanon," *International Journal of Middle East Studies* 34, no. 4 (November 2002): 619–44.
78. Atlas and Licklider, "Conflict among Former Allies," 36.

ETHNIC UNMIXING AND CIVIL WAR*

DAVID D. LAITIN

CHAIM KAUFMANN'S "Possible and Impossible Solutions to Ethnic Civil Wars"[1] makes the strongest case available that the best cure for ethnic war is viable territorial defense through partition or substantial regional autonomy, and that, in the wake of ethnic civil wars, attempts to bring security to intermingled ethnic groups by means other than partition or regional autonomy are doomed to failure. The key premises of his analysis are, first, that hypernationalist rhetoric and atrocities are part and parcel of civil war and "harden ethnic identities." This makes cross-ethnic appeals as a solution to civil war likely to fail. Second, he takes as theoretically demonstrated that "intermingled population settlement patterns create real security dilemmas that intensify violence, motivate ethnic 'cleansing,' and prevent de-escalation unless the groups are separated." Therefore, he reasons, "stable solutions of ethnic civil wars are possible, but only when the opposing groups are demographically separated into defensible enclaves."[2] As he develops his brief for the separation of populations, Kaufmann systematically addresses several objections to the solution he advocates. All solutions are bad, he concludes, but separation is the least bad, even if least favored by policymakers.

The tight structure, extensive references, and tone of *sang froid* give this article an impressive cogency. Kaufmann's concluding paragraph, urging that "we have a responsibility to be honest with ourselves" not "to offer false hopes to endangered peoples,"[3] leaves the reader with the feeling that cold logic and raw fact rather than dreamy delusions or wishful thinking motivate his recommendations. Nonetheless, there are two fatal flaws in his brief. The first concerns

*This article presents data and arguments from a joint project with James D. Fearon. Support from the National Science Foundation (Grants SES-9876477 and SES-9876530) and from the Carnegie Corporation of New York made the recoding of the group concentration variables for the MAR dataset possible. Ted Gurr and Victor Assal from the University of Maryland participated in the collection of these data, and kindly opened the MAR archives to Fearon and me. Matthew Kocher and Ebru Erdem directed the recoding operation. James Fearon, Peter Katzenstein, Roy Licklider, Jack Snyder, and Barbara Walter helpfully commented on earlier versions of this article.

1. Chaim Kaufmann, "Possible and Impossible Solutions to Ethnic Civil Wars," *International Security* 20, no. 4 (Spring 1966): 136–75.
   2. Ibid., 137.
   3. Ibid., 175.

his inadequate rebuttal to the objection that secessionist warfare can encourage further secession attempts elsewhere. Fearon ("Separatist Wars, Partition, and World Order," in this volume) addresses this flaw. The second flaw concerns the issue of the security dimension of ethnic concentration. In this note, I address this second flaw. My objection does not undermine Kaufmann's conclusion, which compares a variety of bad solutions. Rather, my objection should lead Kaufmann and policymakers considering the separation of populations to add substantially to Kaufmann's assessment of its potential costs.

TERRITORIAL CONCENTRATION AND CIVIL WAR

IN HIS ANALYSIS of "demography and security dilemmas,"[4] relying on Posen's work,[5] Kaufmann points out that the severity of ethnic security dilemmas is greatest when demography is most intermixed, weakest when community settlements are most separate. The more mixed, or so the reasoning goes, the stronger the offense; the more separated, the stronger the defense. "Accordingly [when mixed] each side has a strong incentive . . . to kill or drive out enemy populations before the enemy does the same to it, as well as to create homogeneous enclaves more practical to defend." Ethnic militias in enclaves are less murderous, or so the reasoning goes, as they have defensive value only. Once groups are separated, "any attempt to seize more territory requires a conventional military offensive [and in consequence] normal deterrence dynamics apply. Mutual deterrence does not guarantee that there will be no further violence, but it reduces the probability of outbreaks . . ."[6]

Kaufmann sees unmixing of ethnically different populations, once these populations have been at war with each other, as the key to future interethnic peace. He suggests that this can be achieved through partition (the creation of de jure or de facto international boundaries separating the populations), or by granting regional autonomy and demographic superiority to the minority population in its own region.[7] In this article, I do not address the consequences of partition for peace. Rather, I examine the consequences of enhanced regional concentration of ethnic groups within the boundaries of the state (through the granting of regional autonomy and the movement of peoples) for the likelihood of resurgent ethnic war. I present data, based on analysis of the

4. Ibid., 148.
5. Barry R. Posen, "The Security Dilemma and Ethnic Conflict, *Survival* 35, no. 1 (Spring 1993): 27–47.
6. Kaufmann, "Possible and Impossible Solutions to Ethnic Civil Wars," 150.
7. Ibid., 161.

Minorities at Risk (MAR) dataset,[8] to assess the impact of political strategies to enhance regional ethnic concentration, and to challenge Kaufmann's empirical claim that territorial concentration of ethnic groups results in relatively lower probability of violence even after civil wars.

The core finding from the analysis of MAR is that the concentration of groups within a region of a country, other things being equal, makes these groups better candidates for insurgencies leveled against states.[9] In the MAR dataset, an eight-point scale of rebellion indicates the degree of violence in a civil war. Fearon and I have used the variable MAXREB60 to signify the maximum rebellion score from 1960 through 1998.[10] For group concentration, the MAR dataset includes six different variables (five of them dummies) seeking to delineate the spatial distribution of the group. GROUPCON is a summary index of the five dummy variables. Fearon and I reported in a paper in 1999, referring to table 1 below, that "being either "widely dispersed" or "primarily urban" (GROUPCON = 0 or 1) proves to be *almost a sufficient* condition for a group to have a low MAXREB score in these data." We found that once per-capita GDP is controlled for, GROUPCON is the only robust and significant predictor of group rebellion in the MAR dataset that is plausibly exogenous to the occurrence of group rebellion (at least in so far as the data on concentration reflect population patterns before civil war outbreak).

Fearon and I have already reported several problems with the coding for GROUPCON, and our recoding effort to isolate better what was driving this relationship between group concentration and rebellion.[11] The core concept which we wished to clarify was that of a "regional base," improving upon MAR's conceptualization of group concentration. To determine whether a group had a regional base in a country, we first asked coders whether there were a spatially contiguous region larger than an urban area—that is, part of the country—in which a substantial fraction (25 percent or more) of the minority resided and in which the minority constituted the predominant proportion of the population. If there were such a region, we asked coders to name that

8. The MAR dataset is available at www.bsos.umd.edu/cidcm/mar. For purposes of replication of the models presented herein, request from the author marwork13.dta.

9. James D. Fearon and David D. Laitin, "Weak States, Rough Terrain, and Large-Scale Ethnic Violence since 1945" (paper presented at the annual meetings of the American Political Science Association, Atlanta, GA, September 1999); Monica Toft, The Geography of Ethnic Violence (Princeton: Princeton University Press, 2003); Barbara Walter, "Explaining the Intractability of Territorial Conflict," International Studies Review 5, no. 1 (December 2003): 137–53.

10. Scores are for five-year periods. The last period for which we have data ends in 1998.

11. Fearon and Laitin, "Group Concentration and Civil War" (paper prepared for delivery at the 2002 annual meeting of the American Political Science Association, Boston, 29 August–1 September 2002.

Table 1
REGIONAL CONCENTRATION AND REBELLION IN THE MAR DATASET

GROUPCON	MAXREB45		
	≤3	≥4	Total
Widely dispersed (Reg6)	67	9	76
OR Primarily urban	88.2	11.8	100
(Reg5) OR minority in			
one region (Reg3) %			
Majority in one region	108	84	192
(Reg2 or Reg4) OR	56.3	43.7	100
Concentrated in one			
region (Reg1) %			
Total	175	93	268
%	65.3	34.7	100

$\chi^2_{d.f.=1} = 24.5, Pr = .000$

Note: I assume a threshold of rebellion to be a score of ≥4 on the MAR rebellion variable.

area. We asked them also to assess whether this area was an administrative region of the state (for example, Uzbek Soviet Socialist Republic in the Soviet Union) or a topographical region (for example, the Pyrenees), or a geographical expression (for example, the South).

We sought to capture two separate elements in our specification of a regional base. First, a reasonable percentage of the group (25 percent was our criterion) should live in a well-delineated region of the country. Second, the percentage of the country's minority population living in that region ought to be significantly higher than the percentage of the country's dominant group living in that region. In other words, to have a regional base, a substantial percentage of the minority group must be living in that region, and the probability that a member of this minority group is living in the region ought to be much higher than the probability that a member of the country's dominant group is living in the region. We defined this formally in the expression below:

If:

$m_r \equiv$ minority population in region r
$m_c \equiv$ minority population in country c
$M_r \equiv$ majority population in region r
$M_c \equiv$ majority population in country c

Table 2
DESCRIPTIVE STATISTICS: WORLD REGION, REGIONAL BASE, AND REBELLION

World region	Percentage of groups with regional base	If regional base, percent in rebellion since 1960	If no regional base, percent in rebellion since 1960	Number of groups
Western Democracies and Japan	52	0	0	29
Eastern Europe and former Soviet Union	64	27	0	58
Asia	37	84	23	59
North Africa and Middle East	71	70	38	28
Sub-Saharan Africa	88	42	38	67
Latin America and the Caribbean	59	26	0	32
Total	68.5	45	16	247

The percentage in rebellion is based on a score ≥ 4 on MAXREB60.

Definition: Minority m has a regional base in region r of country c if, and only if, $m_r/m_c \gg M_r/M_c$ and $m_r/m_c > .25$. ("$\gg$" means "is substantially greater than").][12]

As with GROUPCON, the regional concentration of groups—a dummy variable that asks whether a group has a "regional base" (GC2)—is a significant predictor of rebellion (here specified as whether the maximum rebellion score for the eight coding periods since and including 1960—MAXREB60—ever reached the level of 4, our threshold of genuine rebellion).[13] As indicated in table 2, the probability of rebellion in all regions of the world save the Western Democracies and Japan (where no rebellions take place) is much greater if the group has a regional base than if it does not. It is only in sub-Saharan Africa

12. The Fearon/Laitin data for group concentration, that is, for groups having a regional base, differs from MAR's composite variable GROUPCON, but the bivariate correlation is .64. A breakdown of the differences is reported in Fearon and Laitin, "Group Concentration and Civil War." In this article (with one exception), for purposes of replication of Kaufmann's reports, and despite problems of selection bias (addressed in the Fearon/Laitin NSF proposal noted in the acknowledgements), I use only the 273 cases in the official MAR dataset.

13. I use rebellion scores since 1960 for the dependent variable because the data on population dispersion is based on 1960s estimates, and therefore the concentration variables cannot be used to explain earlier rebellion levels (as reported in table 1).

(where only 12 percent of the groups do not have a regional base, thus making the statistical description of likelihood of rebellion without civil war somewhat skewed by the law of low numbers) where the probability of rebellion comes even close for groups without a regional base. It is perhaps a sign of the power of the regional base measure that the numbers are correct in Africa, even though four of the most rebellious groups—the Hutus and Tutsis in Rwanda and Burundi—are widely dispersed.

This relationship between regional base and MAXREB60 holds up even when controlling for GDP and mountainous terrain, two robust predictors of rebellion in the country/year dataset.[14] In the regression reported in table 3, I control as well for ethnic fractionalization, which has come up as significant (or closely so) in several studies of rebellion. Here, it is also entered along with its squared version, which also comes out significantly in some country/year analyses.[15] I also control for whether the group is in a sub-Saharan state which was a colony of France, a variable which has been significant in some of the Fearon/Laitin models using the MAR dataset, and which approaches significance in this specification. Group concentration, even with these controls, comes out strongly. On the eight point scale of rebellion, other things being equal, a concentrated group will have one-and-a-half times higher level in its maximum rebellion score since 1960 than a group which is not concentrated geographically.

Kaufmann, to be sure, agrees about the "decisiveness of territory," but his theory incorrectly leads him to predict that territorial control by one group leads to a higher probability of peace. In fact, territorial control by one group leads to a higher probability of war. He writes that, "population control depends wholly on territorial control. Since each side can recruit only for its own community and only in friendly-controlled territory, incentives to seize areas populated by co-ethnics are strong, as is the pressure to cleanse friendly-controlled territory of enemy ethnics . . . "; and he reasons, therefore, that "military control of the entire territory at issue is tantamount to total victory." Thus, according to Kaufmann's logic, once there are well-defined demographic fronts, "the strongest motive for attack disappears, since there are few or no endangered co-ethnics behind enemy lines."[16] The MAR data,

---

14. I use OLS regressions here because they are easiest to interpret. When Fearon and I incorporate these variables into more complex models, given the distribution on the dependent variable, we will rely on different statistical techniques.

15. In Fearon and Laitin, "Ethnicity, Insurgency and Civil War," *American Political Science Review* 97, no. 1 (February 2003): 75–90, neither ethnic fractionalization nor its square comes out significantly when regressed on civil war onset.

16. "Possible and Impossible Solutions to Ethnic Civil Wars," 149.

Table 3
THE INFLUENCE OF GROUP CONCENTRATION ON REBELLION

Dependent Variable: MAXREB60; OLS
[Specification: reg maxreb60 GC2 frassa ethfrac ethfrac2 lwbpop65 flat lgdp60en
   GC17r GC15all if (GC17r~=6) & [marstat==31 | marstat==41 | marstat==53 |
   marstat==63 | marstat==73 | marstat==83]

Regional base (GC2)	−1.59
	(.37)**
Length of group's residence in country (GC17r)(1)	−.20
	(.15)
Transnational dispersion: kindred groups in power (GC15all) (2)	−.067
	(.11)
GDP/Cap 1960, logged (Lgdp60en)	−1.46
	(.22)**
Flat terrain (flat)	−1.32
	(.66)*
Ethnic heterogeneity (ethfrac)	−1.57
	(2.50)
Ethnic heterogeneity squared (ethfrac2)	.74
	(2.65)
Country population (natural log) (lwbpop65)	.19
	(.109)
French African colony (frassa)	−1.35
	(.81)
Constant	13.45
	(2.34)**
R-squared	.29
Number of observations	254

Notes for table 4: * = significant at p < .05; ** = Significant at p < .01.
(1) GC17r is GC17, but all Roma who were coded as GC17==6 were recoded as GC17==2, that is, they were coded as having arrived in their present country before the nineteenth century. The remaining cases of GC17==6 were deleted from the sample for this specification.
(2) GC15all is GC15, but all cases in which GC14==1 (no close kindred across border) and thus get a missing value for GC15, are recoded as a 0 in GC15all, one step lower than having a kindred group across the border with no access to power.

as our discussion makes clear, do not support this analysis—groups that have some degree of regional concentration appear to have stronger motives for attack compared to groups which are more dispersed.

Kaufmann might offer two distinct rebuttals to the use of MAR data to challenge his plea for partition or autonomy. He might point out that his theory concerns the phenomenon of "unmixing," that is, of ethnic groups that had been interspersed and subsequently, due to civil war, become concentrated. Thus—Kaufmann might offer as a conjecture—the process of fighting a war, agreeing to separation of the populations, and then actively moving into separate territorial zones could have a pacifying affect on the country. In contrast, as would be implied by this conjecture, concentration without previous war is dangerous. This is an intuitively perplexing position, since it would be difficult to explain why group concentration has such a violent effect on groups that have not yet been at war, but a peaceful effect on groups that have ended a war. Nonetheless, it merits scrutiny.

Testing this conjecture, however, would require a clearer specification of the claim. In most cases of ethnic war (as the MAR data make clear) there was already concentration and certain degrees of regional autonomy before the war. Therefore to point out, as Kaufmann does, that successful resolutions to civil wars involve partition or autonomy is not fully informative.[17] Such resolutions do not necessarily involve the movement of peoples or even changes in the administrative structure of the state.[18] Kaufmann therefore needs better to specify the criteria for unmixing—does it, for example, need to be greater than the status quo ante?—before one can test to see if his conjecture is correct. There are many examples of civil war endings in the past half-century—including Abkhazia (Georgia), the IRA (Northern Ireland), the Tuaregs (Mali), Katanga (Congo-Kinshasa), and the Kurds (Turkey)—that have not involved substantial unmixing compared to the prewar situation. If the theory requires *greater* autonomy or *more* unmixing than before the war, it is not clear that Kaufmann's conjecture will withstand empirical scrutiny. Also, there are cases (Chechnya and Southern Sudan) in which wars recurred after substantial grants of autonomy. These cases decrease confidence in Kaufmann's recommendation for autonomy.

A more systematic test of Kaufmann's conjecture, relying on MAR data, is to isolate non-regionally concentrated groups that had been at war with their state, and in which the war ended. We could then ask whether autonomy and the movement of peoples were necessary to avoid a recurrence? In the MAR case list, there are only eleven groups that meet these criteria, and they are listed

---

17. Ibid., 160–61.
18. Kaufmann at times combines partition and unmixing as having the same properties, but at times separates them analytically. This leads to confusion. In "When All Else Fails: Ethnic Population Transfers and Partitions in the Twentieth Century" (*International Security* 23, no. 2 [Autumn 1998]: 120–56), for example, Kaufmann he writes of his four empirical cases "all . . . were accompanied by large-scale population transfers" (121). One of his cases, however, is Ireland, which was a partition but which did not involve large-scale population transfers.

Table 4
IS PARTITION AND THE UNMIXING OF POPULATIONS NECESSARY TO AVOID
RECURRENCE OF CIVIL WARS AMONG NON-CONCENTRATED GROUPS?

Group/country	Rebel history	Unmixing?	Restart?
Santals/India	65–70	No (but quasi-partition)	No
Arabs/Israel	45	No	No
Hmong/Laos	45–75, 85–	No (but attempt by rebels to create an autonomous state)	Yes
Palestinians/Lebanon	65–90	No	No
Sunnis/Lebanon	55, 75–80	No	Yes, No
Berbers/Morocco	55, 70	No	Yes, No
Hutus/Rwanda	60, 98	No	Yes
Tutsis/Rwanda	85–90	No	No
Black Africans/South Africa	75–80	No	No
East Pakistani Hindus/Pakistan & Bangladesh	45, 70	No	Yes, No
Chinese/Malaysia	45–55	No	No

Notes:
(1) Cases include beginning of five-year period where maxreb45 > 3 (that is, there has been at least one substantial rebellion) & GC2==2 (that is, the group was not concentrated regionally) and the rebellion after reaching >3, fell below 4 for at least one five-year period.
(2) Rebel history (five-year periods in the MAR dataset when the rebellion score was >3).
(3) In this table, I use all cases in the Fearon/Laitin dataset (see n. 12) to raise the number of observations for the rare phenomenon of civil wars for unmixed peoples. (The in-progress dataset, owing to an inappropriate coding rule, records the Chams in Cambodia and the Slovenes in Yugoslavia as not regionally concentrated. Although these cases, if included, would bias the results in my favor, I delete them from the analysis. Both groups at the time of their rebellions were geographically concentrated). The MAR dataset counts the East Pakistani (and Bangladeshi) Hindus as two observations—one in Pakistan and one in Bangladesh. I consolidate these into a single observation, as their mobilization in both eras was part of a single history.

on table 4. Resolution in none of these cases involved autonomy along with the compelled unmixing of populations. In six of the cases (55 percent) there was no recurrence of war, despite the lack of unmixing. Whites and Black Africans in South Africa have established a *modus vivendi* after a negotiated settlement that did not involve autonomy or the substantial movement of peoples; Arabs inside the Green Line have not rebelled a second time after their initial rebellion in the wake of Israeli independence, and have lived in remarkable peace with Jewish citizens in spite of regional chaos; the Chinese in Malaysia were at war for over a decade, but today live in peace with the Malays without a regional base. The Santals (along with the Chotanagpurs, a related *adivasi* [tribal] group) live in the forests around the states of Madhya Pradesh, Orissa and Bihar. In response to their insurgency, they were granted a provisional autonomous council and in 2000 a new state of Jharkhand carved out only from Bihar. This might be counted as a legal separation, but it never involved the movement of peoples in or out of the autonomous area. Furthermore, scheduled tribes (of which the Santals and Chotanagpurs are the predominant groups) constitute only 28 percent of the population, which hardly reflects unmixing.[19] This case therefore does not fully meet Kaufmann's criteria for full security. In three of the cases (27 percent) there was recurrence, but there was subsequently a second peace that has not broken, again with no unmixing. In one of these cases, the East Pakistani and Bangladeshi Hindus, the recurrence was in the context of the Bangladeshi war of secession. With the success of the Bengali secession, the Hindu rebellion was crushed. Hindus remain in Bangladesh in peace and mixed with Bengali Muslims. These three cases have experienced a recurrence without unmixing, but they do not support Kaufmann's prediction of hardened identities making it impossible to live next to one another in peace. After all, all three groups ultimately did. Finally, two cases (18 percent), the Hutus in Rwanda and the Hmong in Laos, show a recurrence of rebellion after an initial settlement that did not entail unmixing. These cases go as Kaufmann's theory predicts. Kaufmann has already addressed the Hutu case.[20] The other case is the Hmong in Laos, who in 1966 (with aid from the Vietnamese) declared Meoland as their independent state. Pathet Lao forces crushed this proto-state. It could be argued, in accordance with Kaufmann's theory, that if the self-declared state had remained autonomous, there would not have been a war recurrence in the 1980s.

While there is no comparison set within MAR of post-civil war unmixing and substantial autonomy to compare results, it would be a violation of the historical record to claim that once civil wars begin among interspersed ethnic populations, it is not possible to resume civil peace without unmixing them and

---

19. Data are from the Jharkhand home page (jharkhand.nic.in/about/profile.htm).

20. Kaufmann ("Possible and Impossible Solutions to Ethnic Civil Wars," 168–69) makes a sensible case for partition in Rwanda and Burundi. It is only an oddity of this "test" of his theory that the ongoing war of Hutus in Burundi is not included. Equally odd is the coding of the Tutsis of Rwanda as not having a recurrence, since this is due to the victory of the RPF, an army that they have dominated. In the MAR coding rules, a "minority" can capture the state, but if it does, it cannot have a rebellion against itself. The RPF, however, has shown that it can distinguish Hutus who perpetrated the genocide from those who did not; and there remains a possibility of long term peace without unmixing. Kaufmann's prediction, if Hutus return, of "sooner or later . . . another genocide" is wildly over-confident.

giving each group an autonomous homeland. To the extent that it is possible to specify Kaufmann's theory to allow for a direct test using MAR data, there is little support for it. Only two of the eleven cases lend it support.

Kaufmann's second rebuttal to the use of MAR data to test his theory might be that ethnic concentration as reported in the revised MAR dataset is insufficiently informative about the ethnic demography. There could be macro concentration (by the Fearon/Laitin coding for regional base) along with micro mixing that will enhance the danger of the security dilemma. This too is an extraordinarily difficult issue to address empirically. In Posen's classic article on the subject, he gives insufficiently precise criteria for judging the degree to which a variety of ethnic demographies create a security dilemma.[21] Consider in a rural area a situation in which two ethnic groups have 50 percent of the population but each lives in well-bounded villages that are themselves homogeneous. Now consider a comparable case where each village has 50 percent of each group. It should be obvious that the security issues in these two different regions are quite different, but they are lumped together in Posen's article. Furthermore, cross-sectional data on this level of ethnic mixing are not available. It is therefore not possible with current data to decide conclusively whether this objection—that truth is in micro concentration—stands up to empirical scrutiny.

There is evidence, however, which should give pause to Kaufmann's conclusion that ethnic mixing in the context of hostility is inherently unstable. Take, for example, Kaufmann's data presented on his table 1.[22] Here Kaufmann relies on Ted Gurr's dataset on civil war endings in the past fifty years. From this table, he concludes "the data supports (sic.) the argument that separation of groups is the key to ending ethnic civil wars." This is an unfortunate misreading of at least two of the cases—and perhaps more of them. Kaufmann codes Ukraine's war against the USSR that began in 1945 as ending in *de facto* or de jure partition. He codes the Basque war vs. Spain beginning in 1959 as ending in autonomy. In neither of these cases, however, did the war settlement involve the separation of groups. Russians continued to live peacefully in eastern and southern Ukraine after Ukraine became a federal republic. By 1989, 22 percent of the residents in the Ukrainian SSR were Russian.[23] Extramadurans and other non-Basques from Spain continued to live peacefully in Basque country after autonomy was granted, and today make up about half the population of *País Vasco*.[24] Both civil wars ended without any significant separation of groups, in

---

21. "The security Dilemma and Ethnic Conflict."
22. "Possible and Impossible Solutions to Ethnic Civil Wars," 160.
23. 1989 USSR Population Census, East View Publications, available on the web at www. statistischedaten.de/products/ciscen.htm

direct contradiction to Kaufmann's assertion to the contrary. The "unmixing" of peoples, Kaufmann's condition *sine qua non*, was unnecessary to preserve the peace at least in these two civil wars.

Other cases of ethnic wars in this list of ethnic civil wars resolved are not cogent examples of hardened identities making future mixing impossible. The Somali clans have been at war for a decade and there is de facto partition; however, it would be a wild exaggeration to claim that the Isaaqs of the now rump Somaliland Republic could never be secure in the south should a political solution be reached. Similarly in Ethiopia; while the Tigreans were victorious in their war in Ethiopia, Amharas and Tigreans live peacefully in Addis Ababa. Evidence does not support Kaufmann's argument that the separation of groups is the key to peace.

To be sure, ethnic war can have a powerful *short-term* effect of ethnic unmixing. Kaufmann provides illustrations of Ibos leaving the north in Nigeria in the wake of the massacres in Kano in 1966 and the subsequent civil war (1967–70) in which the federal government defeated the Biafran secession. Kaufmann, however, omits from his example the fact that after the war, Ibos returned in large numbers to Kano, the site of the massacres. Indeed it would be hard to account for the killings and intimidation of Ibos in Kano and other northern cities connected with the Sharia court crisis of 1990 had there been a full separation of groups in the wake of the Biafran civil war.[25] Similarly in Sri Lanka. Kaufmann points to the rapid unmixing in Colombo after the massacres in 1983. He omits mentioning, however, that shortly thereafter the population of Tamils in Colombo continued to increase. In 1953, 9.5 percent of the population in Colombo was Tamil. In 1981, the figure rose to 11.2 percent. Suppose there was a vast exodus in 1983. By the time of the 2001 census, the percentage of Tamils in Colombo had increased to 12.4 percent.[26] If civil wars and massacres make ethnic mixing unbearable, it is difficult to explain why members of formerly massacred groups would return to the scene of the crimes. Kaufmann's evidence of fleeing ethnics with "hardened . . . identities," unable

24. BBC news, 30 September 2002, news.bbc.co.uk/1/hi/world/europe/2289036.stm
25. The Nigerian census of 1991 did not include questions of ethnicity and religion, and it therefore is not possible to get precise figures on Ibo populations in Kano. See Rotimi T. Suberu, *Federalism and Ethnic Conflict in Nigeria* (Washington, D.C.: U.S. Institute for Peace, 2001), 157. On the flight of Ibos in 2000 from northern cities, consult www.usafricaonline.com/shariashowdown_chido.html, a report from 29 February 2000. Kaufmann ("When All Else Fails," 156) addresses the security implications of Ibo return for non-Ibos, but doesn't address the question of why, if antipathies are so hardened after civil wars, Ibos returned to the sites of the 1966 massacre directed against them.
26. See *Census of Ceylon 1953* (Columbo: Department of Census and Statistics, 1957), sec. 4, table 16. For 1981 and 2001, see www.statistics.gov.lk/abstract/population/ch02tab10.htm and www.statistics.gov.lk/abstract/population/ch02tab09.htm. Thanks to Kanchan Chandra for these data and to Val Daniels for help in the analysis of them.

Table 5
ETHNIC MIXING IN REGIONAL BASE AND REBELLION

Population of group/total population living in regional base (GC7a)	Mean of maximum rebellion scores since 1960 (maxreb60)
25–50%	2.70
51–75%	4.32
76–100%	3.31

Note: Only groups with regional base are included. Of the 187 groups with a regional base, 102 were missing values (coders not able to make a reasonable estimate).

to live in security mixed with the ethnic other, is undermined by the demographic facts of voluntary return. Most likely, middle class Tamils considered Colombo (where they would not face armed confrontations) safer than Jaffna. In Colombo, through the creation of micro security zones with fellow Tamils and links to officialdom in the army and police, Tamils secure a modicum of protection. However secured, their return demonstrates that political autonomy *and* mass population exchange is not the only hope for peace in Sri Lanka.

Two final pieces of evidence put to question the argument purporting to link ethnic mixing, security dilemmas and ethnic war. These concern the proportion of the minority group in the region and in the country. First, consider table 5, in which I present the mean maximum rebellion score for groups that constitute different percentages of the total percentage in their regional base. Confirming Kaufmann's point, the highest maximum rebellion scores are for groups that are most mixed in regional bases (50–75 percent).[27] The greatest security, however, comes from having the regional group more insecure in its region (25–50 percent of the population) than more secure (75–100 percent). From these ambiguous data, it would be foolhardy to take as strong a position as Kaufmann has done in regard to the relationship of ethnic mixing and the probability of renewed ethnic war.

Second, the MAR dataset has information on the proportion of the group in the country population. If I add that to the regression presented on table 3,

27. The difference between the average maximum rebellion scores for the 50–75 percent and 75–100 percent groups, however, is not statistically significant in a two-tailed t-test ($p = .11$). I am using a measure of "group percent of regional base" that is measured for 1960 and is missing many observations (a total of 100 groups). When I use the same variable measured for 1990, which has 133 observations, the average rebellion scores, in order of increasing group percentage in region, are 2.1, 4.1, 3.6

the result is a near significant positive relationship with rebellion.[28] In one sense, this confirms Kaufmann's security dilemma argument inasmuch as there should not be a security dilemma if the group is too small for any hope for success in fighting. In fact, smaller groups are less likely to rebel. In another sense, the data do not work well with Kaufmann's overall argument, as they imply that giving large groups their own region will make them even more dangerous than if they were dispersed.

This accumulating but insufficiently decisive evidence debunking the argument about ethnic mixing leads to further reflections on another observable implication of Kaufmann's security dilemma argument. If the argument is correct, we should see the effects of regional concentration to be strongly positive on rebellion when states are weak than when they are strong. If states are strong, they can protect minorities, and therefore mixing should be no less secure than separation. If states are weak, however, minorities are less likely to be protected. Under these conditions, regional concentration should serve as a substitute for state protection.

The data give little support to this observable implication. To test it, I divided the groups up into two halves—each group had a GDP value for its country. I computed the median group/country/GDP value to separate the groups as to whether they were living in rich or poor countries. The assumption here is that country wealth is a proxy for state capacity to provide order. In both rich and poor states, the mean rebellion score goes substantially down under conditions of the group not having a regional base. (For groups in states with greater than or equal to median GDP, maximum rebellion score goes from .78 for groups with no regional base to 2.18 for groups with a regional base. For groups in states with less than the median GDP, the maximum rebellion score goes from 1.61 for groups with no regional base to 3.96 for groups with a regional base.) Rebellion is less likely with ethnic mixing in both strong and weak states. This finding suggests that regional concentration is not a substitute for state protection for ethnic minorities, again challenging the security dilemma framework. This test is not perfect. Rich countries may have the capacity but not the desire to offer protection to regionally concentrated minorities. Even so, it reduces confidence in a theory of civil war resting on a security dilemma foundation.

28. I added the variable "gpro98," which is the proportion of the group in the country in 1998. It would be inappropriate to present this in the regression on table 3 because data from 1998 cannot be used to explain rebellion from 1960. If, however, there were available group proportion data from 1960, I doubt the result would be much different. In the run with gpro98, the coefficient is 2.17 and the standard error is 1.15. No significant changes occur for the other variables in the model.

Why, then, is the situation of unmixed populations which do not face a security dilemma so dangerous for rebellion in the past half century, when Kaufmann's theory predicts the opposite? For one, Kaufmann adds additional criteria for the peacefulness of regional bases, and does not base his entire theory on settlement patterns. While the separation of populations need not provide sovereignty to afford security, he judges, it ought to have a "regional self-defense capability that abrogating the autonomy of any region would be more costly than any possible motive for doing so" (p. 162). Also, he argues, peace cannot be maintained if there are militarily significant minorities in any region. It could well be the case that the regional bases in the MAR dataset consistently lack these criteria, and that is why they have been so dangerous.

There are, however, other avenues to explore which may account for the MAR data that contradict Kaufmann's theory. Consider Kaufmann's assumption that groups having their own territory lose their strongest motive for attack.[29] This needs to be reassessed for two reasons. First, ideologues in groups that live in a regional base sometimes have visions of a homeland far larger than their current base, and have ambitions for fulfilling an historic mission of reaching those boundaries. In our coding of concentration patterns, ideologues in 96 out of the 171 MAR groups (56 percent) have articulated a vision of their homeland that far exceeds their current regional base.

An example of this phenomenon may be culled from Kaufmann's case studies of partition, in which he presents evidence that in the wake of violence, partition has an ameliorating affect.[30] Post-partition ideas of a wider homeland (wider than was granted in the partition) by Israelis drove the government to encourage pioneers to settle in secure Arab zones, undermining both communities' security. The reality of territorial control—whether through partition or regional autonomy—along with a dream to incorporate a wider homeland, give groups an incentive to disrupt the peace. Kaufmann argues that much of the violence in places such as Punjab and Ireland come from the "incompleteness of separation,"[31] but the incommensurate boundaries of regional base and imagined homeland make incompleteness—at least in cases of contested imaginary homelands—a virtual certainty.[32]

29. "Possible and Impossible Solutions to Ethnic Civil Wars," 162.
30. "When All Else Fails."
31. Ibid., 121.
32. Thus, given sharp and conflicting views between Muslims and Hindus about the boundaries of their homeland, I am less certain than Kaufmann ("When All Else Fails," 141–42) that Kashmir could have been cleanly partitioned.

Second, without sovereignty, groups in militarily secure regions can still be taxed, and from their point of view, unfairly so. Ibos, for example, were not afraid of extermination if they remained in the eastern region of Nigeria in 1966, but they fought to retain rights to eastern region oil revenues.[33] So any granting of autonomy can lead to further demands for sovereignty, re-igniting violent conflict, especially if the state faces lost mineral reserves if sovereignty were granted.

On a larger scale, Fearon and I have suggested an alternative theory to Kaufmann's. The importance of group concentration as the only group level variable that clearly and consistently comes out significantly in predicting rebellion—while variables such as economic inequality, religious discrimination, and denial of recognition of a group's ancestral language, are either not significant or not robust across a range of model specifications—provides strong support for the interpretation provided in Fearon's and my country/year analysis.[34] The conditions allowing for successful insurgency, we argue, are a better guide to the occurrence of civil violence than are the social, economic, political and cultural conditions that might motivate a group to organize a rebellion. Consistent with this interpretation, the concentration of a group in a country can be seen as allowing for low-cost communication among the population in whose name the insurgency is being fought. In our reckoning, concentration gives insurgents a strategic advantage in knowing who amongst them is collaborating with the state, and the concomitant ability to restrain and sanction such collaboration. Thus a regionally concentrated group raises the costs for the government to weed out insurgents from a densely planted minority population. Insurgents are activated, we argue as an alternative to Kaufmann, with the strategic advantages for warfare that group concentration allows.

I have not made here a cost assessment of alternate solutions to civil war as compared to partition or autonomy. Indeed Kaufmann ("When All Else Fails") provides several examples where partition has lowered violence, and so his brief cannot be ruled out entirely. I have shown, however, that autonomy along with the ethnic unmixing of peoples, the least bad outcome in Kaufmann's ordering, has a dire implication ignored in his analysis. I have also shown that there have been successful solutions to civil wars fought by non concentrated groups that did not involve concentrating them. Kaufmann pleads that all

---

33. Micahel Ross, "How Does Natural Resource Wealth Influence Civil War? Evidence from 13 Case Studies," *International Organization* 58 (Winter 2004): 35–67.

34. "Ethnicity, Insurgency and Civil War."

solutions other than separation of populations provide only "false hopes." As it currently stands, his plea overestimates the risk of post-civil war ethnic mixing and underestimates the risks of partition or autonomy coupled with unmixing. The hope he offers is no more true, as the evidence now stands, than the ones he calls false.

VENGEANCE AND INTERVENTION: CAN THIRD PARTIES BRING PEACE WITHOUT SEPARATION?

DAVID CARMENT AND DANE ROWLANDS

F ROM a legal and practical point of view, separation is never easy. On the one hand, there is the perceived need to support struggling minorities who demand self determination as an inalienable right. This impulse is demonstrated by the fundamental role of the 1947 UN Human Rights Sub-commission on the Prevention of Discrimination and Protection of Minorities, associated with the post–Second World War decolonization process. Occasionally, this and other UN declarations of self-determination are cited as support for a minority's claims about historical injustice or threats to identity.[1] On the other hand, there are the legal, theoretical, and practical imperatives of maintaining a functioning state-based international system, which require reasonably coherent and stable nations.

During the cold war, the international community was willing to recognize the self-determination of peoples as a bulwark against "imperialism" but not at the cost of disrupting the integrity of the state-system. Parts of UN Resolution 1514 reveal the inherent dilemma in granting self-determination:

(2) All peoples have the right to self determination . . .

(4) All armed action of repressive measures of all kinds directed against dependent peoples shall cease in order to enable them to exercise peacefully and fully their right to complete independence . . .

(6) Any attempt at the partial or total disruption of the national unity and the territorial integrity of a country is incompatible with the purposes and principles of the Charter of the United Nations.[2]

David Carment is associate professor of international affairs at Carleton University; Dane Rowlands is associate professor and associate director at the Norman Paterson School of International Affairs at Carleton University.

1. Another example would be Article 1 of both the International Covenant of Civil and Political Rights and the International Covenant of Social, Economic and Cultural Rights, drawn directly from UN General Assembly Resolution 1514 (Declaration of Decolonization, 1960): "By virtue of that right they [self-designated minorities] freely determine their political status and freely pursue their economic, social and cultural development" (Daniel Patrick Moynihan, *Pandaemonium: Ethnicity in International Politics* [Toronto: Oxford University Press, 1993: 150]).

2. Ibid., 151.

Studies of attempts at ethnic conflict management by third parties underscore the complex problem in finding a balance between rights to self-determination and maintaining the integrity of states. For example, in their examination of five failed domestic "Peace Accords" (Canada, Cyprus, India, Sri Lanka, and Sudan) Samarasinghe and de Silva suggest that without the presence of a third party, the potential for transforming existing state structures is minimal.[3] Third party involvement has the potential to do two things. External involvement can partially reduce levels of conflict between separatist groups and the state-centre when there is support for the state-centre. If one side of the international community supports self-determination, however, while the other supports the state-centre, then the possibility of conflict diffusion is greatly increased. The latter situation describes the cold war situation as well as the Yugoslavian case and other post-cold war scenarios because of the potential for involvement by external actors on both sides of the ethnic issue.

Principles of conflict management and responses to ethnic separatism served a specific purpose during the cold war, a period which was perceived in the West as a Manichean struggle of right versus wrong. Within this struggle, international instruments were developed to hold in check the expansionist aims of some states and to prevent separatist conflicts from spreading. Maintaining international stability, at least for the West, was a system-wide concern.[4] In contrast, today's struggles often consist of impossibly competing ethnic identities and mutually incompatible dreams of national self-determination. Within this matrix of competing claims, the conventional wisdom persists in the belief that the sovereignty, territorial integrity and independence of states within the established international system, and the principle of self-determination for peoples, are compatible.

Chaim Kaufmann offers a potential way out of this international law vs realpolitik debate. Kaufmann's argument relies on simple indicators or thresholds to determine when separation of ethnic groups should be the preferred option. Kaufmann argues that in cases of massive and ongoing ethnic tensions, partition should be undertaken resolutely and swiftly. He goes further by suggesting that after a substantial amount of civilian killing has occurred, the least-worst solution above all else is full separation. This should be done by outside forces since otherwise it will be done by the two sides at a much higher cost.

3. K. M. de Silva, and S. W. R. de A. Samarasinghe, eds., *Peace Accords and Ethnic Conflict* (New York: Pinter, 1993).
4. Astri Suhrke and Lela Garner Noble, eds., *Ethnic Conflict and International Relations* (New York: Praeger, 1977); Michael Brecher, *Crises in World Politics* (Oxford: Pergamon, 1993); Moynihan, *Pandaemonium*.

At face value, Kaufmann's argument makes eminent sense, but it runs contrary to both the bulk of traditional ethnic conflict management practice and UN Charter law. In some other important ways, however, his argument is consistent with current practice on intervention which places far greater emphasis on individual and group protection from the state.[5] For example Kaufmann argues that when ethnic conflicts turn violent they generate spontaneous refugee movements, and thus "the question ... is not whether the groups will be separated, but how. With protection, transport, subsistence, and resettlement organised by outside institutions, or at the mercy of their ethnic enemies."[6] Looking further back in time, Kaufmann suggests that it was the failure to partition completely India and Pakistan in 1948 that led to the protracted conflicts there and the immediate deaths of over one million people.[7]

Cases like the Indian partition are suggestive of what can happen when competing groups separate themselves, but the fact that it was messy there doesn't mean it will be less messy if it gets done by outsiders. Kaufmann concludes by arguing that the international community needs to devise ways to identify those cases where partition is the only option because there is no hope of attaining civil peace. Partitioning must be "complete" and it must "unmix" the populations or it will lead to renewed hostilities.

This article has two purposes. First, we examine whether the empirical record provides any a priori support for Kaufmann's claim that extended conflicts involving extensive bloodshed require partition as a solution. Second, on the basis of the case evidence we use to examine Kaufmann's theory, we try to identify any implications that arise regarding the role of third parties in ending these types of disputes. We begin by considering some of the difficulties that arise both from testing Kaufmann's argument, and from teasing out its implications for third party interveners.

5. See the *Independent International Commission on Kosovo*, and *The International Commission on Intervention and State Sovereignty* which both elaborate on basic criteria justifying intervention, for example, the suffering of civilians owing to human rights violations or the breakdown of government, the commitment to protect the civilian population and the calculation that the intervention has a reasonable chance of ending the conflict.

6. Chaim D. Kaufmann, "When All Else Fails: Ethnic Population Transfers and Partitions in the Twentieth Century," *International Security* 23, no. 2 (Fall 1998): 120–56.

7. Partition is not the only answer. Cloughley, for example, argues that with respect to Kashmir, combining an agreement to move mortars out of range of the Line of Control with a withdrawal of Indian and Pakistani troops from the Siachen Glacier to pre-1971 positions and holding Pakistan to the Simla Accord vis-à-vis insurgents, should help prepare the ground for de-escalation of hostilities. While all of these actions are confidence building measures (CBMs), because of the deep suspicion between India and Pakistan the CBMs themselves would require third-party verification. Cloughley explicitly believes that no aspect of the Kashmir conflict can be dealt with purely on a bilateral basis, despite India's desire to keep relations that way. Brian Cloughley, "Violence in Kashmir," *Security Dialogue* 30, no. 2 (June 1999): 225–38.

INTERPRETING KAUFMANN

IT IS perhaps fitting to start with Kaufmann's conclusions regarding partition. He draws three lessons from his analysis.[8] First, we must "identify the threshold of intergroup violence and mutual security threats beyond which we must resort to separation and partition."[9] Second, partition should be pursued only when the pre-existing separation of the warring ethnic groups is extensive. Third, refugee flows must be facilitated instead of prevented due to the greater risk of continued and escalating violence compared to the risks of flight. Implicitly all three lessons are to be learned by the international community, and they are deemed to thus have a central role to play in the management of these conflicts.

Kaufmann's lessons are not without their practical problems, many of which he acknowledges. There are nuances in all three of these recommendations that require the exercise of considerable judgement on the part of intervenors. Taking the recommendation in order, the first difficulty is indeed to identify the threshold of intergroup violence beyond which attempting to maintain a state's integrity is both futile and bloody. Through case studies Kaufmann can identify some important factors that may influence how such a threshold is to be determined, but there is no testable model or formula that can be applied in general. The feasibility of this first central requirement, then, is debatable.

Second, by the time a conflict has reached clearly identifiable thresholds it may be too late for third parties to act effectively, no matter how unanimous they may be on the need for separation. A delay in response is problematic since many players, both state and non-state, internal and external, will have at this stage become involved in the conflict on an ongoing basis—making separatist conflicts inherently less manageable but also making the tasks of separation even more difficult. An increase in the number of stakeholders, and the hardening of positions in any conflict means, by definition, that resolution and the negotiated solution upon which a lasting separation depends, will be more difficult to obtain and enforce over the long run. Further, waiting for a clear signal of having crossed the threshold also means waiting for additional deaths, the presumed best signal.

A similar problem of judgement lies in Kaufmann's second conclusion, that separation should be used only when the "national communities are already largely separate or will be separated at the same time."[10] There is

8. Kaufmann, "When All Else Fails."
9. Ibid., 155.
10. Ibid. 155.

the obvious problem of how separate should "largely separate" be. There is also the related problem in implementation of the extent to which warring parties need to be physically isolated from one another. Obviously, the idea of complete partition is difficult to attain even under the best of conditions; in practice it is extremely difficult to unmix populations. Ghosh, for example, traces the complex ways that population flows resulting from ethnic hostilities, environmental disasters, and wars in South Asia, continue to cause ethnic hostilities in their host states even after unmixing has occurred.[11] Partitions are no barrier to the movements of people. Ghosh argues that instead of considering separation as an alternative, the community of states need to sign, ratify and more stringently adhere to international refugee treaties to ensure fair treatment for displaced persons.

It also needs to be noted that in his normative policy proposals Kaufmann seems to have assumed two reasonable but opposing elements of the intervener's preference structure, and then sought to balance them. First, there is the assumption that third-parties value a peaceful settlement, presumably to reduce casualties and promote stability. As a consequence he concludes that since separation of the warring sides is the only (or at least the most effective) way of achieving a peaceful settlement, this ought to be the goal of intervention. Against this preferred option, however, Kaufmann appears to weigh the costs of the intervention by suggesting that the policy be pursued only when the two sides are already largely separate. Therefore Kaufmann's approach to handling these severe conflicts seems to require a delicate balance between the necessity of separation and the presence of circumstances that facilitate such a separation. What is not clear is whether the balance is contingent on intervener effort, or whether there is yet again a fundamental threshold of required pre-separation of the hostile groups beyond which any level of resource expenditure is futile.

In some sense Ghosh's suggestion is diametrically opposed to Kaufmann's last conclusion, that the movement of people should be facilitated rather than suppressed. Ghosh takes what Kaufmann identifies as the UNHCR policy approach of improving the safety of people where they are, instead of moving them. Once again the problem lies in the detail: how much effort to move people how far? To be even more pointed, when does facilitating the separation of populations become collaboration in ethnic cleansing? Implicitly it seems that Kaufmann is taking the quite legitimate position that saving lives in the

---

11. Ghosh, Partha, "Regional Security and Cross-Border Population Movements in South Asia," in *Regional Security, Ethnicity and Governance*, ed. Justus Richter and Christian Wagner (New Delhi: Manohar Publishers, 1998), 66.

immediate conflict outweighs the associated problems of moral hazard in terms of potentially encouraging those who maliciously use ethnicity as a political tool.

Notwithstanding these practical difficulties, Kaufmann has presented a coherent and compelling argument with crucial policy implications. In this article we take up the challenge of testing aspects of Kaufmann's argument to see whether his theoretical and policy inferences stand up to the stylized facts of identity-based conflicts. Specifically, we consider two interrelated components: is there a threshold which divides conflicts between those in which separation is essential and those in which it is not, and are third parties necessary for the process of separation.

The remainder of this article unfolds as follows. First we derive the propositions for testing by reviewing Kaufmann's argument. We then test these against a database of conflicts. We focus on two related types of conflict. We initially consider as a more direct test of Kaufmann's arguments those conflicts in which separation has been identified as an important causal factor. These are the cases for which Kaufmann's argument is arguably the most appropriate, as there is at least a clearly identified party willing to be separated from the current state. We then examine how the outcomes of these conflicts are related both to the level of violence and the activities of third party interveners. One observation worth noting at the outset is that there are few cases where there is outright international support for separatists and there are far more cases of international support for state integrity, so much of our investigation is necessarily of the conjectural what-if variety. We then widen the analysis to consider conflicts with an important ethnic dimension, but not an explicitly separatist conflict. In these cases separation is also theoretically possible though perhaps less tenable. Inclusion of these latter cases, then, constitutes the weaker test of the hypotheses we derive from Kaufmann. We consider ethnic conflict cases where separation is a stated goal of the rebels as well as where it is not.

In evaluating the empirical content of the hypotheses we do not engage in a formal statistical analysis. Instead, we use the data to test whether the empirical record conforms to the a priori expectations derived from the hypotheses. We believe this approach is justified because Kaufmann has presented a valuable yet very general theory that, as we have argued, is insufficiently developed to deduce formal propositions due to the critical role of judgment. Thus we wish to supplement our analysis with inductive insights from the data that may help to guide further refinements of Kaufmann's theory. This approach can be justified as a tool to evaluate the logical consistency of a model, to clarify the propositions, and examine critical questions of inference.[12] This method allows us to evaluate the underlying assumptions that are embedded in the ad hoc elements of Kaufmann's argument. Further, it stimulates the production of additional propositions for later testing. Finally, we recognize that irregularities between our findings and Kaufmann's claims are not insufficient to refute or prove the hypotheses we have identified, or Kaufmann's theory as a whole. This approach, however, may lead us to question or reject some interpretations of his theory, while pointing to alternatives that are more clearly consistent with the empirical record.

HYPOTHESES

KAUFMANN'S ANALYSIS lends itself to the identification of several hypotheses. Some are quite explicit, others need to be teased out from the underlying logic. Further, some of these hypotheses deal with very general elements of conflict and conflict resolution, while others can be made specific to the context of third party intervention. We frame the hypotheses so as to make the null the contrary to our interpretation of Kaufmann's argument.

The central hypothesis that emerges from Kaufmann's builds on his argument that after a certain level of violence has been reached, and after the different sides in a dispute suffer a sufficiently high number of casualties, groups will find it impossible to live peacefully with one another. The level of hostility and the generation of group-based myths will ensure that the two sides continue their conflict, with vengeance for past misdeeds driving a cycle of violence. Consequently, the only viable solution would be to separate the combatants territorially. The strongest form of this argument would be to say that peaceful coexistence cannot be brought about after an intergroup conflict has resulted in high number of casualties. It is possible, however, that some intermediating factors could dilute the proposition to one which stipulates that a conflict with a high number of casualties would significantly reduce the probability of post-conflict coexistence. By investigating cases of conflict with high numbers of casualties we may thus examine the degree of empirical

12. Bruce Bueno de Mesquita, "An Expected Utility Theory of International Conflict," *American Political Science Review* 74 ask (December 1980): 917–31, Bruce Bueno de Mesquita, "Toward a Scientific Understanding of International Conflict: A Personal View," in "Symposium: Methodological Foundations of the Study of International Conflict," *International Studies Quarterly* 29, no. 2. (June 1985): 121–36, Bruce Russett, *Power and Community in World Politics* (New York: W. H. Freeman, 1974); Gary King, Robert O. Keohane, and Sidney Verba, *Designing Social Inquiry: Scientific Inference in Qualitative Research* (Princeton: Princeton University Press, 1994).

support for Kaufmann's hypothesis, as well as identify what the associated threshold of violence might be. We can write the first hypothesis as:

HYPOTHESIS 1: If a Conflict Generates a High Number of Casualties, then any Peaceful Settlements should be Based on Territorial Separation

Although some general insights may be derived from an examination of Kaufman's central hypothesis, our other interest here is to translate Kaufmann's ideas into propositions regarding the role of third party interveners and the outcomes of their efforts. Intervention, therefore, might be one of those important intermediating factors which dilute the purer forms of Kaufmann's hypotheses. For example, the strength of the intervention, as well as the strength of the other protagonists, will clearly influence how hypothesis 1 might be modified.

First, if the intervener is sufficiently strong it may be possible to suppress the violence and potentially promote a settlement regardless of its orientation or bias. The capacity of the intervener to impose a settlement, in turn, depends on the absolute and relative strength of the combatants. An intervention on behalf of a weaker side may prolong a conflict by encouraging it to prosecute the war rather than surrender its desire for a separate state, on the one hand, or a unified state, on the other. These modifications to the hypothesis are of practical importance as well, since interveners seem loath to support separatist movements for a variety of reasons.[13] Therefore, there are unlikely to be many observations of interventions in support of separation. Therefore a related hypothesis can be identified.

HYPOTHESIS 2: If a Conflict Generates a High Number of Casualties, then Peaceful Settlements that do not Involve Separation will Require Either Very Strong and Extended Interventions, Very Weak Separatist Groups, or a Very Strong Central Government

Finally, we can consider the nature of the intervention. For our purposes we can think of three pure forms of intervention: those that support the integrity of the state, those that support partition, and those that are effectively neutral. In addition there may be multiple interveners with different goals. These interventions may also come in various forms of robustness, and will interact with combatants of various strengths. What hypotheses might emerge from the consequences of intervention?

---

13. Heraclides, "The Ending of Unending Conflicts: Separatist Wars," *Millennium: Journal of International Studies* 26, no. 3 (summer, 1997): 679–703."

Kaufmann's argument is that separation is essential for the resolution of ethnic conflicts with high-numbers of casualties, because the bitterness engendered by the amount of killing will make the peaceful integration of the fighting communities impossible. Interventions that support the separatists in such a conflict should thus be more successful in bringing about a rapid end to the violence and inducing a settlement than those that are either neutral or support the integrity of the pre-existing state. Interventions of the latter kind, therefore, should be expected to be longer and more protracted, without necessarily arriving at a permanent solution. We might thus consider the following hypothesis as a consequence of Kaufmann's theory:

HYPOTHESIS 3: If a Conflict Generates a High Number of Casualties, then Faster and More Stable Settlements will Result if Third Party Interventions Support Separation

Before proceeding to the data, we want to stress that we do not want to formulate a normative test of what third parties ought to do to try and mitigate the violence of a conflict, as that would not necessarily have any relevance for testing the content of Kaufmann's argument. Kaufmann has argued that third parties ought to try and separate warring factions when it is clear they can no longer reside within the same state. This does not mean that we will necessarily observe any such cases, as other policy options may well have been pursued, correctly or otherwise. For these reasons we focus on the positive side of how conflict outcomes are linked to casualties and third part activity.

CASE SELECTION

IN EVALUATING Kaufmann's argument we consider two sets of cases. The first set comprises cases where separation is deemed to be more tenable, and are pre-identified by the presence of an agenda that includes separation. In other words, where there is a the potential for territorial demarcation, an informal or formal declaration of intent, a concentration of ethnic groups and divided political leadership on the desirability for separation. Therefore, tenable cases of separation are situations where at least one party to the conflict wants separation.

If neither party has ever identified separation as an option, or there is little potential for territorial demarcation (because groups are scattered), then the third party is likely to find separation to be extremely difficult. Therefore, the first component of our test will focus on cases identified specifically as having a core separatist component, as identified by Heraclides.[14]

In tenable cases, when a separatist group makes a formal declaration of independence, that certifies the separatist group as "secessionist *stricto sensu.*"[15] Secessions stricto sensu usually follow on from "incremental secessions" that involve ongoing and gradually increasing political and military activity aimed at independence or some form of autonomy. Incremental secessions are usually and more accurately referred to as separatist movements because, initially at least, there is no formal declaration of independence.

It is important to note that both secessions stricto sensu and incremental separatist movements possess a territorial base for a collectivity and a sizeable and distinct minority, both key ingredients in determining whether separation is viable.[16] There are also claims that there is an unequal relationship between the minority group and the state-centre, another important factor for third parties to consider since much of their judgement on the viability of separation and who to support should depend on how the parties to a conflict treat one another.[17]

We have selected Heraclides' 1997 study of separatist wars to evaluate third party involvement in tenable cases. According to the Heraclides study, six outcomes are possible:

1) Nineteen cases involve victory by the state-centre (as in the Thai Malay of Thailand);
2) Twenty-two conflicts involve some form of autonomy or accommodation through a peace accord (as in the Gorkhas in India or the Serbs in Bosnia-Herzegovina);
3) Eight conflicts remain unresolved with the separatist group either in disarray or temporarily quiescent;
4) Eight cases have tenuous or ambiguous cease-fires as in the Shan, Mon and Karen separatist movements in Burma;
5) Thirteen conflicts remain deadlocked with sporadic and ongoing violence (as in Kashmir or the Kurds of Iraq), and

---

14. Alexis Heraclides, "The Ending of Unending Conflicts: Separatist Wars."
15. Alexis Heraclides, *The Self-determination of Minorities in International Politics* (London and Portland, OR: Frank Cass, 1991), 344.
16. Alexis Heraclides, "Secessionist Minorities and External Involvement," *International Organization* 44, no. 3 (summer 1990): 341–78.
17. Heraclides, *The Self-determination of Minorities in International Politics.*

6) Only five conflicts have resulted in outright victories by the separatist group: Tigray, Bangladesh, Eritrea, Croatia, and Slovenia.[18]

Of the seventy-five cases where the state-centre opted for a military solution against a minority, the result has been either de-facto autonomous administrations or lost territory for the state-centre. Only in eleven of the seventy-five major separatist conflicts of the last half century has successful military conquest led to the settlement of the conflict between a minority and the state-centre (either victory by the state-center or by the separating group).

Heraclides' evaluation highlights several characteristics of violent separatist conflict. First, at one of the end of the spectrum it is important to note that all separatist wars have occurred in settings where power is highly centralised and democracy is weak or non-existent.[19] Second, there are outside partisan actors in those instances where separation is pursued through violence.[20] Finally, all seventy-five of Heraclides' separatist wars involve minorities at risk of political and economic discrimination or military repression, though data problems eliminated some of these observations.

A fair assessment of Kaufmann's arguments requires, however, that we also consider other cases where separation was never at the core of the conflict but where levels of violence are so high that separation is viable compared against either continued fighting or brokering a negotiated power sharing agreement. In these cases ethnicity is specified as a motivating dimension of the conflict, suggesting that there are grounds for distinguishing between combatants on some reasonably transparent basis. Kaufmann's logic still seems applicable to these cases, despite the potentially extreme difficulty of executing a reasonable policy of territorial separation. Even if different factions in a country did not originally contemplate separation, the emergence of ethnic or other affiliations on different sides of a conflict and the potential ill will generated by casualties may make reconciliation extremely difficult. Indeed a subsidiary test of hypothesis 1 is to examine the case evidence to see whether a high number of casualties in conflicts with some form of identity component eventually produce a separatist element.

18. Heraclides' 1997 assessment excludes low-intensity, low fatality separatist conflicts such as the Basque separatist movement in Spain ("The Ending of Unending Conflicts").

19. George Tsebelis, *Nested Games: Rational Choice in Comparative Politics* (Berkeley and Los Angeles: University of California Press, 1990); Timothy Sisk, *Power Sharing and International Mediation in Ethnic Conflicts* (Washington, D.C.: United States Institute for Peace Press, 1996).

20. David A. Lake and Donald Rothchild, "Containing Fear: The Origins and Management of Ethnic Conflict," *International Security* 21, no. 2 (fall 1996): 41–75.

To examine this wider set of conflicts, Heraclides' set of separatist wars was augmented by data from Regan, Licklider, HIIK, and the Europa World Yearbook.[21] The conflicts identified as ethnic, religious, or identity-based by these authors, but not identified as separatist, constituted an additional sample of cases.

In the context of balancing minority claims of unfair treatment against maintaining state integrity, third parties have been important but extremely uneven players.[22] This variability results from the fact that, during the post-cold war era, most ethnic conflicts have not been directly connected to broader patterns of competitive international relations, as was the case during the cold war. Even though there has been a considerable shift away from supporting proxy wars—a major source of conflict escalation in many cases in the past—toward mutual reconciliation, few international efforts have been directed towards specific problems in reconciling ethnic tensions or even in considering the possibilities and viability of separation.

EVALUATION OF THE HYPOTHESES

FOR A very basic examination of hypothesis 1 we need only look at the set of conflict situations and compare the outcomes of high casualty and low-casualty conflicts. Four problems with this approach arise very quickly. First, how do we define "high" in a conflict with a high number of casualties? Casualty levels may be determined in absolute terms as the number of deaths, or in relative terms, by the rate of casualties relative to the size of the population. Should we define a conflict with ten thousand fatalities out of a population of one million people as a conflict with a higher casualty level than one with one thousand fatalities out of ten thousand people? The former is ten times worse in absolute terms, but only one tenth as bad as a proportion of population. We have chosen the absolute casualty numbers as the better indicator, though we

---

21. Patrick Regan, "Conditions for Successful Third Party Intervention in Intrastate Conflicts," *Journal of Conflict Resolution* 40, no. 2 (1996): 336–59; Roy Licklider, "The Consequences of Negotiated Settlement, 1945–1993," *American Political Science Review* 89, no. 3 (September 1995): 681–90; Heidelberger Institut für Internationale Konfliktforschung (HIIK) e.V., 2001, www.hiik.de/de/index_d.htm; *Europa World Yearbook* (London: Europa Publishing, 2002).

22. Third parties are important under those very rare instances when separation is agreed to by both sides. Though only a handful of cases can be characterized as such, peaceful separation has occurred in the last fifty years in at least five cases and this has been due largely to the presence of three factors: a) a constitutional basis for managing the dispute peacefully; b) a formal declaration of the intent to separate; and c) the presence of outside powers. Young, "How do Peaceful Separations Happen?" 45–60; and Heraclides, "The Ending of Unending Conflicts."

acknowledge that this is far from perfect and may perturb the comparisons. The justification is that it is difficult to know exactly which is the relevant population base to choose. A highly regionalized dispute between two ethnic groups within a very large country (such as India, for example) may appear to have a low rate of casualties based on total national population. For the local groups involved in the violence, however, these casualties might be quite significant and contribute to hardening of community feelings. Conflicts with 5,000 deaths or fewer are classified as low-casualty, while conflicts with 45,000 deaths or more are classified as high casualty.

Second, Kaufmann's conceptual framework is not formal enough to identify specific thresholds that might be relevant to the analysis. Is the relationship between casualties (in either absolute or relative terms) and the diminished likelihood of peace without separation, linear, or even monotonic? Or does the level of casualties cross some sort of (possibly context-specific) threshold below which reconciliation may be possible? If Kaufmann's idea is theoretically correct, it might not be reflected in the data if current conflict levels have not crossed this threshold, or have not done so with sufficient frequency to permit for solid statistical tests of significance. Thus we will pay particular attention to those conflicts with casualty levels similar to those discussed in Kaufmann.[23]

A similar problem arises in identifying cases of territorial separation. Partition into two (or more) states is the most extreme case of potential separation, though even this dramatic step may not be sufficient to separate warring ethnic groups without further population transfers. What is less clear is whether less formal arrangements are sufficient. Will the creation of autonomous regions suffice? Will decentralization or even federalism suffice?

Third, the question of causality, and the possibility of tautology, must be taken into account. High-casualty conflicts are often associated with conflicts of long duration. Why is there such a high number of casualties in the conflict? Because both sides have resisted peace. The causal factors relating these two clearly linked events may, or may not, have anything to do with the forces identified and analyzed by Kaufmann.[24]

---

23. "When All Else Fails."

24. The causality issue is also closely tied to the timing and data problems that emerge. At the beginning of a conflict, casualties may be quite low, but these will eventually accumulate. When we examine a case, therefore, timing matters in terms of how the conflict is characterized. Further, the data on conflict casualties are problematic. Estimates are often very poor, and may or may not include civilian deaths that are more indirectly linked to the actual fighting. For example, famine killed many in Biafra, but some estimates of casualties for that conflict put it below the high casualty cut-off we are using. The actual conflict data, therefore, may only give us some rough notions about the plausibility of Kaufmann's argument, rather than a definitive test of their legitimacy.

Finally, the presence of complicating factors mean that a simple examination of the data can only be suggestive, not definitive. Unfortunately, it is difficult to determine the degree to which high casualties as a causal factor determining conflict outcomes interacts with other determinants. A perusal of the actual cases may, however, help to identify explanatory variables for more formal testing. Of specific interest is the role of third party interveners, on whom we focus our later analysis.

We first examined the sixty cases of separatist-driven conflict, of which twenty-three are classified as low casualty and twenty-one were classified as high casualty. The remaining sixteen cases are between the limits discussed above. The high casualty cases are identified in table 1. We have used the 2002 *Europa World Yearbook* to update the status of each conflict as a supplement to the coding provided by others.

There are two primary tests for hypothesis 1. As a general examination we compare first the outcomes of the low and high casualty separatist conflicts. The evidence is weakly supportive of the hypothesis. Of twenty-one cases of high-casualty conflict, nine have some degree of settlement and six are clearly still active. Of the remaining six cases four involved separation and two are primarily suppressed. In contrast, of the twenty-two lower-casualty conflicts, thirteen have some degree of settlement and only three are clearly active. Of the remaining six cases there is one separation and five primarily suppressed.

The second test of hypothesis one involves a focus on the high casualty conflicts. In discussing these we can also identify the degree to which hypothesis 2 is supported or not. There are six cases that conform to hypothesis 1 in so far as high-casualty civil conflicts have endured. Some of these are fairly recent in their modern form, having emerged (or re-emerged) after the dissolution of the Soviet Union (Chechnya-Russia and Abkhazia-Georgia). Three cases are of particular interest due to their longevity and the display of a common cycle of violence, partial settlement, and renewed violence. The conflicts involving the Karen in Myanmar, the Tamils in Sri Lanka, and the Southern areas in Sudan, have all moved through ebbs and flows of violence.

The case of Sudan is illustrative. In the earliest phase of the civil war in Sudan, lasting from the early 1960s until the early 1970s, the government and the opposition attempted a peaceful reconciliation after the two sides had fought to a military stalemate. After a decade of relative calm the arrangement collapsed, however, and civil war returned. Although there have been sporadic ceasefires and agreements between the two sides, at the time of writing no solution has yet emerged on anything approaching a permanent basis. This case would appear to conform with Kaufmann's argument, while also being a ripe candidate for his recommendation of formal separation. Although by

Table 1a
SEPARATIST CONFLICTS: LOW CASUALTY[1]

Case	Number of deaths	Outcome	Third party (current)	Third party (past)
India/Nagas	0	Partial settlement/ dormant	Absent	None
India/Bodoland	34	Partial settlement/active	Absent	None
India/Mizoram	63	Mostly settled	Absent	None
Slovenia/Yugoslavia	100	Separation/settlement	Absent	None
China/Xingjiang	200	Suppressed	Absent	None
Niger/Tuareg	200	Mostly settled	Absent	None
Mali/Tuareg	1000	Mostly settled	Absent	None
Moldova/Transdniestra	1000	Mostly settled/dormant	Absent	Rebel
Spain/Basques	1000	Partial settlement/active	Absent	None
Senegal/Casamance	1250	Active/partial settlement	Absent	State
India/Assam	2000	Mostly settled	Absent	None
Yemen/South Yemen	2000	Suppressed	Absent	None
Burma/Rohingyas	2500	Suppressed	Absent	None
Burma/Karenni	2800	Active	Absent	None
Burma/Mon	2800	Suppressed	Absent	None
Iran/Kurds	3000	Suppressed	Absent	Rebel
Northern Ireland	3000	Mostly settled	Absent	None
Papua New Guinea/ Bougainville	3000	Mostly settled	Absent	State
India/Tripura	3500	Partially settled	Absent	None
Cyprus	5000	Suppressed/separated	Neutral	Divided/ neutral
Indonesia/Aceh	5000	Active	Absent	None
Indonesia/Irian Jaya	5000	Active	Absent	None

[1]The tables were based on the data present in Heraclides ("The Ending of Unending Conflicts: Separatist Wars"); Regan ("Conditions for Successful Third Party Intervention in Intrastate Conflicts"); Licklider ("The Consequences of Negotiated Settlement, 1945–1993"); and the Heidelberg Institut für Internationale Konfliktforschung data. The level of casualties were generally taken from Regan or an average of the HIIK data. The outcome column refers to coding presented in the data sets supplemented by updated information from the *Europa World Yearbook 2002*. In the outcome column there are several adjectives. "Active" refers to conflicts in which substantial violence is ongoing. "Partial settlement" implies that there has been some degree of political settlement though important issues remain unresolved. "Mostly settled" refers to cases in which the large majority of the aggrieved group or groups appear to have accepted a political settlement, though some tension remains. Dormant conflicts are those for which no apparent political solution was reached but violence appears to have largely ceased. Suppressed refers to conflicts where a dominant party has overwhelmed an

no means perfectly separated, the main combatants can be roughly (though not completely accurately) divided into two ethnically divergent groups that are also geographically more clearly separated than in several other cases of conflict. In the absence of formal political separation or the interposition of third party forces to separate the two sides, Kaufmann's logic suggests that this conflict will remain unsettled and violent.

Hypothesis 1 is also supported to a degree by the presence of peaceful agreements accompanied by territorial separation. In the most successful case of peace, Bangladesh's independence from Pakistan, settlement emerged as a consequence of territorial separation.[25] The fact that the two do not share a border undoubtedly limited the opportunities for subsequent violent interaction.

There are three other cases of formal separation in this group that offer mixed support for hypothesis 1. The India-Pakistan partition and the Eritrean-Ethiopian split both conform to Kaufmann's requirement of setting up separate states for combatants. Neither relationship, however, has been subsequently free of violence. Both borders have been the scene of renewed tension and fighting since the acceptance of independence. What the level of violence would have been in the counter-factual case of no separation, however, is unknown. Though it is tempting to say that violence would likely have been much worse, the potential for a nuclear exchange in the Indian sub-continent is arguably greater now given the presence of two independent states. The fourth case of successful separation, East Timor, was accompanied by considerable protracted violence, though there were many years of relative calm due to the successful suppression of the relatively weak separatists by a powerful central government. It is too early to determine the long-term prospects for bringing peace to the island, though outside support for the new nation will likely ensure its survival.

Two cases have been classified primarily as suppressed, with little or no evidence of an attempt to engage the separatists in a settlement. One case is the Tibet-China conflict. There is little information to allow us to judge

---

opponent and is able to end most violence without addressing the root causes of the conflict. The presence and activity of third parties are described in the last two columns. Present activity refers to the presence or absence of third parties in providing significant presence in enforcing the current outcome of a conflict, and identifies which combatant is being supported. Past activity refers to the presence, absence, and the combatant supported by third parties in the past with significant effort at crucial periods of the conflict.

25. There are additional cases of territorial separation not considered here. These are the cases emerging from the dissolutions of the Soviet Union and Yugoslavia. In the latter case there were few casualties directly relating to independence struggles, while in the latter the casualties were either conflated with other ethnic violence (Croatia, Bosnia-Herzegovina) or limited in scope (Slovenia, Macedonia).

Table 1b
Separatist Conflicts: High Casualty

Case	Number of Deaths	Outcome	Third party (current)	Third party (past)
Ethiopia/Eritrea	45 000	Separation	Absent	Divided
Burma/Karen	50 000	Active	Absent	None
Indonesia/W. Sumatra	50 000	Active	Absent	State
Burma/Kachin	54 000	Partial settlement/suppressed	Absent	None
Philippines/Moros	60 000	Partial settlement/active	State	State
China/Tibet	65 000	Suppressed	Absent	None
Croatia/Serbs	65 000	Settled	Absent	Divided/state
Sri Lanka/Tamil	65 000	Active	Absent	Neutral/state
Russia/Chechnya	72 000	Active	Absent	None
Georgia/Abkhazia	100 000	Active	Absent	Rebels
Laos/Meos	100 000	Partial settlement/suppressed	Absent	Divided
Iraq/Kurds	186 000	Suppressed	Rebel	Divided/rebels
Indonesia/East Timor	200 000	Separation	Rebel/neutral	Rebels
Bangladesh/Chakmas	200 000	Mostly settled	Absent	None
Bosnia/Croats	200 000	Mostly settled/suppressed	State	State
Bosnia/Serbs	200 000	Mostly settled/suppressed	State	State
Congo/Katanga	300 000	Partial settlement/suppressed/dormant	Absent	State/divided
India/Pakistan Partition	500 000	Separation/active	Absent	Rebels/neutral
Bangladesh	1 259 000	Separation/not contiguous	Absent	Rebels
Nigeria/Biafra	1 500 000	Mostly settled/suppressed/dormant	Absent	None
Sudan	1 500 000	Active	Absent	Divided

whether and to what extent the Tibetans have come to accept the authority of the Chinese government. In the second case of the Kurdish people in Iraq, overt conflict has been suppressed by the central authority in some years, or by third parties since the first Gulf War. In Iraq the northern protectorate and no-fly zone effectively kept the Iraqi army from pursuing the conflict against the Kurds between 1990 and 2003. It should be noted, however, that the Kurds and the Iraqi regime have a complex relationship, and that the Kurds themselves are split into competing factions. Periodic evidence of reduced tension and cooperation, however, seem to be just that: periodic. A permanent appraisal of Iraqi-Kurdish relations is currently impossible due to the recent war and American-led coalition occupation. In some sense this case does conform to hypothesis 2, where powerful third-party forces have been able to overcome the violent tendencies identified by Kaufmann by enforcing a de facto separation of forces without acknowledging political independence.

Nine cases that have involved some degree of settlement present the clearest challenge to hypothesis 1, though some conform to hypothesis 2. Thus, the Myanmar-Kachin and Laos-Meos settlements seem largely to have come about through successful suppression. A third case, that of the Moros in the Philippines, is difficult to assess since it involves a mix of successful government counter-insurgency, partial settlement, and remaining activity.

Three cases are of special interest due to the recentness of their settlement and the role of third parties. The Croatian and Serbian separatist groups in Bosnia, and, to a degree, the Serb rebellion within Croatia, were all pacified to a degree by the imposition of de facto solutions. Furthermore, though Croatia's settlement with its Serb population seems to be remarkably robust, inter-ethnic contact has been reduced by previous population transfers and expulsions.

In Bosnia, the Croats and Serbs were wrestled into political accommodation that maintained the territorial integrity of Bosnia while recognizing the de-facto separation of Serbs from the Federation. Peaceful political ties between the different component parts, however, seem to be maturing. Furthermore, the withdrawal of active support from neighbouring ethnic brethren in Serbia proper and their apparent abandonment of irredentist sympathies has undoubtedly diminished the capacity of separatists in Bosnia to pursue their struggle. Four factors are of particular interest appear in this case. First, the sides are, to a degree, separated both administratively and ethnically. Ethnic cleansing during the civil war left large areas of Bosnia more homogeneous than before, and the three distinct groups based on ethnicity and religion have been given considerable local autonomy in a quasi-federalist arrangement. Thus, one of Kaufmann's main requirements has been fulfilled, at least in part.

Kaufmann says little about two other potentially interesting elements of these types of conflict. Thus, a second feature of the Bosnian case is the relatively advanced economic state of the country prior to the civil war, at least in comparison to many other cases. With more to lose materially, and with greater prospects for wealth through trade and investment ties with Europe, the combatants in Bosnia may be more open to considering political accommodation. Slovenia's rapid political and economic stabilization and ties to the European Union provide a powerful example to those contemplating their future in Bosnia. Therefore, it seems reasonable to ask whether economic circumstances can blunt or cancel the kinds of forces that drive Kaufmann's analysis.

History, and possibly ideology—a third factor—provide similar potential challenges to Kaufmann. Thousands of Yugoslavians died during the Second World War at the hands of either partisans or Nazi sympathizers. These divisions were themselves exacerbated by interethnic hostilities of even longer pedigree. Yet, after 1945, Yugoslavia was held together in relative peace and prosperity, if only by the presence of powerful internal forces based partly on ideology. Nonetheless, these forces were sufficient to repress ethnic violence and maintain territorial cohesion. This period of more than forty years can hardly be treated by a theory as a temporary aberration. Having succeeded in dealing with ethnic divisions once, Bosnians may be encouraged to try ethnic accommodation yet again.

Fourth, the question of how permanent and peaceful the settlement actually is remains open. The current structure can hardly be considered stable, self-sustaining, and cordial. The presence or threat of force applied by NATO's SFOR, and the significant involvement of the EU, UN, and OSCE in the current administration of the country, highlights the potentially crucial role outside intervention may play in these cases. We return to this fourth factor later on.

In all three of these cases, therefore, the currently observed reduction in violence has been accompanied by the engagement of third parties that have made the pursuit of conflict either extremely difficult or unnecessary. Once these third parties leave, it is not clear that system stability will be maintained. Indeed, what emerges after their eventual departure will serve as a good test for hypotheses 1 and 2. Yet, it appears that third parties can indeed overwhelm the violent tendencies identified by Kaufmann, at least temporarily and if the intervention is sufficiently forceful.

The most direct challenge to Kaufmann's ideas emerge from the remaining three cases. Of these the Bangladesh-Chakma settlement is fairly recent and it is unclear the degree to which further suppression of the insurgency is required to maintain the peace. Nonetheless, it is a situation where a largely peaceful settlement has emerged without territorial separation, and without complete victory by the government forces.

The final two cases, of Biafran-Nigeria and Katanga-Congo, seem clearly to contradict Kaufmann's arguments. Although these conflicts were settled initially by outright government victory (in one instance with third party assistance), they have remained peaceful, or at least dormant, for an extended period of time. There are occasional acts of violence or calls for independence, but these areas have managed to exist within their nations for long periods of time without substantial enmity being exhibited, without the need for extraordinary government suppression targeting the dissenting group, and with an apparent genuine acceptance of their participation in national affairs. What may explain these cases?

It took UN intervention on the side of the government in the 1960–63 period eventually to bring a settlement in the Congo-Katanga war. The departure of the intervening troops, however, did not lead to a significant re-ignition of the conflict. Despite an estimated 300,000 casualties (Regan puts this number lower at 60,000), and the presence of sporadic fighting that emerged afterwards (particularly 1977–78), this conflict may hold some lessons for how the two sides in a bloody conflict might be sufficiently reconciled to live in the same country. One potential interpretation is that the Congo was a largely dysfunctional kleptocracy which was hardly capable of exerting significant control over its more distant regions, making Katanga effectively separate. The absence of a full-fledged war of independence, though, or even of particularly violent relations between Katanga and the central government, makes this qualification a weak defense. In fact, given the virtual collapse of the Democratic Republic of the Congo during its recent civil war, it is remarkable that regions such as Katanga did not more forcefully assert their independence.

The Biafran civil war in Nigeria offers another case of a violent conflict which has failed to erupt into renewed civil war. Ethnic tensions remain in Nigeria, and occasionally give rise to violence, but the focus does not seem to be exclusively or predominantly along the ethnic fault lines that characterized the Biafran war. Much of the current violence focuses on religious and North-South differences, albeit with strong ethnic and religious undertones, as groups in the north agitate to establish Islamic law. The presence of authoritarian governments has undoubtedly helped to suppress any attempts to unravel the Nigerian federal system, but there has been a remarkable absence of any effort to rekindle the arguments and animosities that animated the previous war. Indeed, the failure of recent episodes of ethnic violence to spark a wider rebellion by appealing to the ethnic hatreds that underpin Kaufmann's analysis calls into question the general applicability of the hypotheses.

In these two cases third parties have not played a significant role in maintaining the peace after the initial conflict. It is possible to suggest that there is a force acting in opposition to Kaufmann's argument regarding the accumulation of enmity: fear. In the face of a bloody quelling of their uprising, could it be the case that an ethnic group will abandon its separatist cause for fear of provoking another round of violent suppression? Such a response would certainly be consistent with rationalist models of conflict. It is then necessary to determine how desirable, stable and permanent the emerging peace should be considered.

It should be noted that these conclusions cannot be ascribed to an inappropriate identification of the high-casualty threshold. First, one of Kaufmann's own cases (Cyprus) is, in fact, in the low-casualty list, suggesting that all of the high-casualty cases are well above the threshold Kaufmann implicitly used. Second, the two most challenging cases have casualty levels that are extremely high (in the top five) and with an order of magnitude similar to Kaufmann's case of the India-Pakistan partition.

For purposes of comparison, the low-casualty cases of attempted or successful separation were also examined. A slightly higher proportion of these seemed to have been at least partially settled without the need for extensive or continuing third party involvement, an observation consistent with hypothesis 1. The relative absence of third-party interveners, both as short-term mediators and long-term participants, contrasts sharply with the situation in high-casualty conflicts. Some of the settlements that do arise, however, are the consequence of the outright victory of the state centre and the effective political and military suppression of the opposition. In fact, many of the cases seem to involve fairly small independence movements against a very large state center, making suppression fairly easy and the likelihood of a high number of casualties fairly low.

As a third test of the first two hypotheses, the preceding analysis was repeated with the set of cases in which ethnicity, religion or other identity-based conflicts were present. Of the twenty-five cases we examined, eleven were identified as having casualty levels above 45,000, eight are low casualty, and six are ranked in between.

Of the high casualty cases two (Tajikistan and Guatemala) seem to be largely settled. Both, however, are of questionable relevance to Kaufmann's hypothesis. The Tajikistan conflict was largely a battle over who would govern after the collapse of the Soviet Union, and ideology and personality seemed to be as prominent as the ethnic dimensions exhibited by the participants? Similarly, Guatemala is probably better classified as an economic conflict, though the fact that indigenous groups were overwhelmingly on one side due to their poverty gave the conflict an identity dimension.

Three conflicts that are somewhat harder to interpret in the context of hypothesis 1 occurred in Uganda, Somalia, and Angola. In Uganda, there are many facets to the conflicts that have erupted, and some seem to pass away for extended periods of time while others erupt. There are some connections between different bouts of conflict, but the composition of the various factions shift, making it difficult to determine the extent to which accumulated ethnic rivalry and hatred contribute to each manifestation of violence. Thus, while Milton Obote's overthrow of Idi Amin, the coup against Obote and subsequent victory of Yoweri Museveni, and Museveni's own problems with various rebel groups, all provide vehicles for the expression of ethnic competition, their weight relative to other factors is not definitive.

Somalia provides yet another challenge.[26] The overall number of casualties is estimated to be high, but these figures would be divided between many factions. With the high level of bloodshed, however, it is reasonable to expect that Kaufmann's process of unquenchable ethnic hatred should arise. Separation has indeed occurred with various bits (Somaliland and Puntland) declaring their own unrecognized independence. These areas, however, saw relatively little fighting compared to the South. Yet an accord of sorts has been reached between the various fairly evenly balanced warring factions, without strong and current third party intervention. This would appear to violate both hypothesis 1 and 2, although no stable government has emerged and the peace remains fragile.

The third case, Angola, shares with Somalia the difficulty in projecting forward from the current fragile agreements for peace. At different junctures of the Angolan civil war, military stalemate and external pressure brought the UNITA guerrillas and the MPLA government to the negotiation table, though the cease-fire and political accommodations were generally stillborn or short-lived. Only the military defeat of UNITA and the death of Savimbi provide grounds for optimism regarding the current peace settlement. Furthermore, it is difficult to say categorically that the Angolan civil war was primarily founded

---

26. Somalia represents a challenge for those using the empirical record to investigate Kaufmann, rather than challenge to his theory. The case of Somaliland's de facto (though unrecognized) separation from the rest of the country occurred at the same time as the violent power struggles in the south of the country. The casualty figures for the general conflict were not separated from those associated with the secession. Therefore the general breakdown of order in Somalia and the data problems make this observation largely inadmissible, though anecdotal evidence suggest that casualties in the north were probably quite low.

on separatist intentions, territorial ambitions, or even ethnicity. While ethnic divisions played a major role in the conflict, ideological differences derived in part from external sponsorship were prominent in the early stages of the conflict. As casualties mounted, ethnic divisions hardened.

Lebanon, Syria, and the Iraq-Shi'ite conflicts all seem to be largely suppressed. Of these, the Syrian conflict seems to be settled, though it is obviously impossible to say definitively that similar tensions will not arise in the future. The Iraq-Shi'ite conflict is at least in stasis until a wider settlement in Iraq is reached.

Of these cases, Lebanon casts the greatest doubt on the need for territorial separation as a precursor to restoring reasonably peaceful relations. Despite the bitterness of the Lebanon conflict, a war that claimed more than 100,000 lives according to Regan's data, the country has managed to remain both intact and relatively calm. The likelihood that civil war will re-emerge is difficult to determine. Political accommodation among the various groups is probable. The role of a third party (Syria) in freezing the current situation, the degree to which accommodation rested on the military defeat of one of the key combatants, and the presence of more than two combatants, all play some role in modifying Kaufmann's central argument. At the least, the Lebanon case reinforces questions about when political accommodation is voluntary rather than coerced, the meaning of territorial separation, and to what degree must violence be eliminated before peace is considered to have been restored

The remaining three conflicts in table 2 that need to be mentioned all support hypothesis 1. The conflicts in Rwanda, Burundi, and Liberia have all been coded as still active. While partial accommodations have been reached in all three of these cases at the time of writing, it is too early to identify these efforts as successful.

Finally, the low-casualty identity based conflicts can also be examined to see whether they provide support for Kaufmann's argument. While the test is far less conclusive, it is none-the-less true that for low casualty conflicts there are several instances of conflict settlement. These settlements, however, are more frequently based on victory and suppression by states rather than voluntary political accommodation.

Therefore hypothesis 1 seems to have some support in a probabilistic sense (from the first test) but does not hold universally. Aspects of Kaufmann's argument appear as highly accurate in certain cases, while in others it applies only when modified to reflect other conflict characteristics. Finally, there are some cases that simply seem to contradict hypothesis 1.

Insights into hypothesis 2 also emerge from the high casualty cases. Settlements without separation that arise are often linked to the presence of

Table 2
NON-SEPARATIST CONFLICTS

Case	Number of Deaths	Outcome	Third party (current)	Third party (past)
Mauritania/Polisario	1,000	Settled/state withdrawal	Absent	Divided
Nigeria/Muslims	1 000	Mostly settled	Absent	Absent
China/Taiwan	1 400	Separated/dormant	Absent	Absent/rebels
Uganda/Obote	1 500	Mostly settled/suppressed	Absent	Rebels
Oman/Dhofar	2 000	Suppressed/dormant	Absent	Divided
Paraguay	2 500	Suppressed/mostly settled	Absent	State
Indonesia/ Islam	5 000	Suppressed	Absent	Absent
Iraq/Shammar	5 000	Suppressed/dormant	Absent	Divided
Angola/Unita	50 000	Suppressed/partly settled	Absent	Divided
Burundi	100 000	Partly settled/active	Absent	State/divided
Guatemala	100 000	Mostly settled	Absent	Absent/state
Tajikistan	100 000	Mostly settled	Absent	Divided/state
Lebanon	125 000	Mostly settled/suppressed	State	Divided/state
Liberia	150 000	Active	Absent	State/divided
Syria	200 000	Suppressed/dormant	Absent	Absent
Somalia	410 000	Partial settlement/partial separation	Absent	Neutral/none
Uganda	500 000	Partly settled/active	Absent	Rebels
Iraq/Shi'ites	500 000	Unclear/partial settlement/suppressed	Rebels	Rebels
Rwanda	520 000	Partly settled/active/suppressed	Absent	Divided/neutral

either a strong government suppressing a relatively weak separatist group, or a strong third party intervener forcing or maintaining a peaceful arrangement. For example, there is no doubt that strong central governments or supporting interveners played a role in initially suppressing the rebellions in Biafra and Katanga. The absence of subsequent third party involvement or extensive, enduring and regionally specific repression suggests, however, that other factors seem to be at play in explaining the relative calm that emerged after the extensive violence.

Examining hypothesis 3 and the nature of third party intervention more generally is difficult. Not only are there few cases of support for separatists, but situations of intervention include even more room for interpretation. Among the complicating factors is the potential for both neighbouring states and global powers to intervene in a conflict. These interveners may have divergent interests in terms of who they are supporting, and different motives ranging from territorial to humanitarian. It is also difficult to gauge the extent of the support interveners may offer their clients, especially if it is provided secretly or through other third party channels. Related to this problem is the question of formal versus informal support or intervention. In some cases ethnic groups may offer support to their brethren in a neighbouring country without the explicit support of their own government, or governments may themselves offer support through clandestine means.

Further, third-party behavior is far from constant over the life of a conflict. Beside ebbing and flowing in terms of the amount of support, sides can be switched and motivations changed with great fluidity. Variance in third party behaviour may well be endogenous to a conflict, or related to their own civil wars. For example, a meddlesome third party might be quite happy to support a rebel group in a neighbouring country if it keeps that country unstable, and possibly unable to support rebel groups on its side of the border. The conflicts in Sudan and Uganda may be illustrative of this situation. Third parties may also be induced into intervention as a consequence of a high number of casualties, particularly if concerns over regional stability are raised or affective humanitarian emotions aroused.

Finally, for a strict test of hypotheses 3 we would need more data. The timing of third party intervention in terms of the increasing number of casualties is necessary for a solid test of whether certain forms of intervention appear successful in terms of reducing subsequent violence. Even more data are required to try and establish statistically robust counterfactual benchmarks for comparison. What follows, then, is a preliminary and informal test. Additional insights into hypothesis 2, or reinforcement of those observed above, are also found by focusing on the question of intervention.

From table 1, four cases of separation occurred in high casualty conflicts with separatist dimensions. In two of these cases the participation of third parties in support of the separating group were crucial. Bangladesh's independence was won partly as a consequence of India's intervention on its behalf. Similarly, in East Timor, a UN intervention was instrumental in securing independence from a politically weakened Indonesia. In the other two cases, third parties played minimal roles, due to the two sides reaching an agreement regarding partition, amicable or otherwise. Eritrea's independence from Ethiopia was the consequence of its central role in the rebellion that led to the overthrow of the Dergue regime (1974–91) that ruled Ethiopia after the toppling of Emperor Haile Selassie. Independence, in a sense, had been prearranged with the other rebel groups, and was the reward for victory. Third party intervention was unnecessary since the new government was willing to grant independence, though there were external supporters of both sides during the initial civil war. Similarly, the partition between India and Pakistan, was jointly agreed to by both sides and supported by the departing colonial power, Britain, though the agreement was far from harmonious.

From these four cases it is tempting to make the preliminary observation that in the first two cases where third parties supported separatists, postpartition violence has been limited. In the other two cases, subsequent wars have emerged between the separated sides. The evidence needs to be viewed with caution, however. On the one hand, Bangladesh, and Pakistan do not border each other and so the role of India in suppressing post-separatist violence is rather moot. The case of East Timor is probably too recent to compare with the other separations in terms of opportunity for violence to be renewed, although undoubtedly the continued presence of UN forces have prevented anti-independence militias from escalating further violent conflict. On the other hand, the latter two cases suggest that third party participation may be useful in preventing subsequent conflict. Care must be taken even with this restricted conclusion, however, as Somaliland's self-declared independence has received no recognition or third party support, and yet has not provoked a violent challenge. This case, however, is one of a low number of casualties.

There are few general lessons that emerge from reviewing the pattern of outcomes and the pattern of past and current third party intervention into high casualty disputes. Coding is extremely difficult, however. In the cases selected, separation did not emerge when there was strong support by a third party for the state center, though separation did occur either with support for the rebels, or weak or divided support. Intervention was not necessary for peaceful settlement to be brought about either, as the Kachin, Chakma, and Biafran rebellions illustrate. There were no instances of settlement (partial or complete) when rebel groups received substantial assistance. These conflicts are either settled through separation (East Timor and Bangladesh), suppression (Iraqi-Shi'ites) or coded as on-going (Uganda, Abkhazia).

To give a sense of the complexity of the potential relationships, however, consider the case of Angola. American support for UNITA in Angola ebbed and flowed for a variety of mainly political reasons (including the actions of other states, such as South Africa and Cuba). Support faded away to a more neutral stance born of humanitarian concerns, before shifting in favour of the MPLA government derived in part from economic motivations. South Africa's support for UNITA similarly faded. Thus, by the end of the conflict most third parties to the Angolan conflict either supported the government to various degrees, or were neutral.

Great power or strong multilateral support is not a guarantee of victory for either side in a separatist conflict, nor is the direction of support always the same. In some cases strong third parties have supported the rebel movements (Russia in Georgia, the UN in East Timor) with very different outcomes. The degree of support and goals of the intervener are important, however. Russia is unlikely to desire Georgia's partition, merely its acquiescence to Russia's other security goals. When deployed on behalf of the state, strong power support has generally been associated with a settlement that supports the integrity of the state (Congo and Bosnia). One interesting possible exception in a low-casualty case is Cyprus, although, again, the competing visions for a permanent settlement have been successfully subordinated to the more immediate intervener requirement of a cessation of hostilities. Therefore a guarded but intuitively appealing conclusion seems to be that committed intervention by a strong third party is generally successful in achieving the intervener's primary goals, regardless of whether it supports the separatist side or the state centre.

Such a conclusion begs some questions, however, and these are highlighted by a consideration of the non-separatist cases. Table 2 contains two of the more dramatic failures of third party intervention, in Lebanon and Somalia. In both cases local groups challenged the commitment of some interveners and successfully drove them out. So the intuitive appeal of a proposition that committed strong interveners always win is at least partly, or potentially, tautological.

Intervention by other regional powers or neighbouring countries are even harder to summarize. Again, commitment and strength of all the parties to the conflict, including the interveners, can potentially play a role in determining the outcome; no simple rules emerge. In some cases (Iraq's Kurds, for example) rebel groups are defeated despite their receipt of external support. In other cases (Somali opposition victory against a Libyan-supported government) rebels can win despite the state being supported. In other cases, such as India's intervention in Sri Lanka, no permanent change in the conflict is perceptible.

There is, therefore, qualified evidence in support of hypotheses 2 and 3. In cases of a high number of casualties, separation seems less likely to occur when third parties support the state center, and are less likely to remain peaceful in the absence of third party support for the secessionists. Overall, however, the evidence from the cases suggest that simple relationships do not exist. Not surprisingly, there appear to be several potential explanatory variables that need to be taken into consideration when trying to determine the likelihood of peaceful settlements in secessionist or ethnically based conflicts. So while the number of casualties may play an important intervening role in determining the prospects for peaceful settlement, at best it interacts with, rather than subordinates, these other explanatory factors.

Assessing Kaufmann's Claims: Summary

OUR PRELIMINARY findings indicate that, to some extent, third parties have been usually unwilling to support the separation of states even when the number of casualties is high. Our data and the evaluation of it against the hypotheses derived from Kaufmann's argument, however, should not be taken as a definitive test of the legitimacy of separation or of the ability of third parties to achieve a definitive outcome.

We began by suggesting that there has been a bias against the disruption of the integrity of the state-system especially during the cold war era. In order to meet the challenge of violent separation, third parties must be in a position to at least partially reduce levels of conflict between separatist groups and the state-centre. Several cases, however, present problems for Kaufmann's hypothesis by challenging, in varying degrees, the notion that a high number of casualties prevents political accommodation and, further, that third parties can reduce violence. Some of these challenges arise because many of the cases evaluated for this study are either on-going, stalemated without settlement, or have ended with military victory by one side. In other cases of severe conflict, however, the levels of violence have subsided substantially without separation having occurred. In sum, some important cases cast doubt on the need for territorial separation as a precursor to restoring reasonably peaceful relations between ethnic groups that have engaged in extensive bloody conflict with one another.

Separatist Wars, Partition, and World Order

James D. Fearon

HOULD ETHNONATIONALIST wars be resolved by formally partitioning states? The answer cannot be decided on a case by case basis, because two incentive problems cause ad hoc partitions to have effects that extend beyond the specific case for which the ad hoc partition was tailored. First, if some level of violence is the implicit criterion for major-power intervention in support of partition, then this encourages the use of violence by movements seeking to mobilize cultural difference to claim statehood. The Wilsonian diagnosis is wrong. Perpetual civil peace cannot be achieved by properly sorting "true" nations into states. Nations are not born but made, partly in response to international incentives and major power policies.

Second, an international order in which major powers carve up lesser powers on an ad hoc basis would make all states less secure. Ad hoc use of partition to solve civil wars would undermine an implicit and relatively stable bargain among the major powers, in place since the 1950s. The bargain rests on the expectation that if any one major power seeks to change interstate borders by force, others may follow, to the detriment of the first.

I argue that this norm has been valuable, functioning in some respects like an arms control agreement. It would be irresponsible to undermine it without a thought given to what might replace it, but this is what the advocates of ad hoc partition are doing: They urge us to use partition more liberally as a solution to ethnic conflict, with little regard to the ramifications of such a policy.

If the major powers want to start redesigning states, they need a political and legal framework that mitigates these two incentive effects. The best feasible solutions may be: (1) strengthening and making more precise international legal standards on human (and perhaps group) rights; (2) threatening to impose sanctions on states that do not observe these standards in regard

James D. Fearon is professor of political science at Stanford University.

An earlier version of this paper was presented at the conference, "EthnoNational Conflicts: Solutions and Dissolutions," held 13–14 June 2000, at the Hebrew University of Jerusalem. That version appeared as no. 88 of the Leonard Davis Institute series of Occasional Papers. I thank the conference organizers and participants for their valuable comments.

to minorities, possibly including support for agents of the oppressed group; and (3) supporting the norm of partition only when it is accepted by mutual consent, but providing carrots and sticks when the state in question refuses to abide by minimal standards of nondiscrimination.

A HISTORY OF AD HOC RESPONSES

CIVIL WARS OF separatist nationalism raged around the globe in the 1990s, in the Balkans, India, Russia, Azerbaijan, Sudan, Indonesia, Great Britain (Northern Ireland), Turkey, Georgia, the Philippines, and Burma, to name only some of the more prominent examples. These wars caused considerable loss of life, massive refugee crises, economic devastation, considerable strains on great power relations and important international institutions such as NATO and the United Nations, and a significant risk of nuclear war in South Asia.

What should be done? Thus far, the Western powers' approach has been ad hoc, with little public discussion of the broader implications of particular cases and the problems for the international system posed by separatist nationalism.[1]

At least five sorts of ad hoc responses can be identified:

1. The imposition of weak international protectorates by stronger states through international organizations, as in Bosnia, Kosovo, Northern Iraq, and, earlier, in Cyprus.
2. Disapproval but little or no direct action, either due to lack of interest (Kurds in Turkey, Tamils in Sri Lanka, Tuaregs in Mali, and many other such cases) or due to the power of the states involved (Russia/Chechnya, China/Tibet, India/Kashmir).
3. Weak international attempts to facilitate partition when this is by mutual consent of some sort (East Timor, Eritrea, the Czech Republic and Slovakia, and, in a halting way, the West Bank).

---

1. Exceptions include Amitai Etzioni. "The Evils of Self Determination." *Foreign Policy* 89 (winter 1992/93): 21–35; David D. Laitin, *Identity in Formation* (Ithaca, NY: Cornell University Press, 1998), ch. 12; and Gideon Gottlieb, "Nations without States," *Foreign Affairs* 73, no. 3 (May/June 1994):100–12. Alan Kuperman and Timothy Crawford have written on how the prospect of international intervention might encourage civil war. See Alan J. Kuperman, "Transnational Causes of Genocide, or How the West Exacerbates Ethnic Conflict," in *Yugoslavia Unravelled: Sovereignty, Self-Determination, Intervention*, ed. Raju G. C. Thomas, (Lanham: Lexington Books, 2003), 55–85; "Reducing the Moral Hazard of Humanitarian Intervention: Lessons from Economics" (paper presented at the 2004 annual meetings of the American Political Science Association, Chicago; and Timothy Crawford, "Pivotal Deterrence and the Kosovo War: Why the Holbrooke Agreement Failed," *Political Science Quarterly* 116, no. 4 (winter 2001–02); 499–523.

4. Stable ceasefires and de facto partitions, as in Nagorno-Karabagh and Somaliland.
5. Some efforts to help negotiate powersharing agreements, as in Northern Ireland and Angola (the latter with a largely ethnic but not separatist war).

That international responses to wars of separatist nationalism have been ad hoc is not surprising. International relations is the realm of the ad hoc, and even if it were possible, it would be hard to imagine a general, one-size-fits-all approach which would make sense. The lack of discussion about the broader implications of different possible policies in particular cases is surprising, however. Here is a possible explanation.

For the Western powers, separatist nationalism is so perplexing and fundamental a problem that it has to be ignored as a general phenomenon. The problem is that the overwhelmingly accepted diagnosis of the cause of separatist nationalism implies a policy remedy no major power can stomach.

In brief, the standard diagnosis is Wilsonianism, the theory that separatist nationalism stems from bad borders and incompatible cultures. Wilsonianism holds that violent separatism arises when state borders are not properly aligned with national groups, which are fixed, preexisting entities. Separatism is due to the injustice of depriving proper nations of proper states. If one accepts this, then the remedy for nationalist wars is obvious. Just redraw the borders. Impose partitions.

Indeed, with each nationalist war foreign policy analysts in the—United States and elsewhere have called for partition as the obvious and proper solution.[2] In the wake of the intense killing and brutality of conflicts like those of Bosnia and Kosovo, partition has often seemed inevitable. Even if these people lived together once, analysts say, how can they live together now? If one accepts the general diagnosis, the argument for partition seems inescapably strong.

Why not do it, then? Why are the major powers not leaping on partition as the obvious solution, rather than setting up costly and ineffectual protectorates? Are there good reasons to oppose partition, or are the Western powers just

---

2. A few examples are: John J. Mearsheimer, "The Only Exit From Bosnia," *New York Times*, 7 October 1997, A27; Mearsheimer, "A Peace Agreement That's Bound to Fail," New York Times, 19 October 1998, A17 [regarding partition of Kosovo and Serbia]; Mearsheimer and Stephen Van Evera, "Redraw the Map, Stop the Killing," *New York Times*, 19 April 1999, A23 [Bosnia, Serbia, and Macedonia]; Makau Mutua, "The Tutsi and Hutu Need a Partition," *New York Times*, 30 August 2000, A23 [Rwanda]; Thomas L. Friedman, "Not Happening," *New York Times*, 23 January 2001, A21 [Bosnia]; Peter Schweizer, "Partition Provides Best Afghan Solution," *USA Today*, 29 October 29, 15A; Leslie H. Gelb, "The Three-State Solution," *The New York Times*, 25 November 2003, A27 [Iraq].

misguided, cowardly, or transfixed by a naive and dangerous commitment to multiculturalism?[3] I argue below that there are indeed good reasons to be skeptical of partition as a general solution to nationalist wars. The most important of these are two types of incentive effects.

First, ad hoc partition applied to one trouble spot may help produce more violent separatist nationalist movements elsewhere, in addition to making existing nationalist wars more difficult to resolve. The world is not composed of a fixed number of true nations, so that peace can be had by properly sorting them into states. Rather, there is literally no end of cultural difference in the world suitable for politicization in the form of nationalist insurgencies. As long as controlling a recognized state apparatus is a desirable thing and nationhood is understood to ground claims to a state, ambitious individuals will try to put together nationalist movements to claim statehood. A de facto policy of partition that says, in effect, that a state can be gotten by mounting a bloody enough insurgency provides the wrong incentives. The more general point is that whether partition is good idea depends in part on one's theory of what causes separatist nationalism. I will argue that the dominant theory of Wilsonianism is misleading, and implies ad hoc responses that states are right to shy away from.

Second, the incentive effects of imposing partitions on weak states apply not just to relations between insurgents and governments, but also to relations among states. An international order in which coalitions of major powers go around carving up lesser powers on an ad hoc basis would make all states, including the major powers themselves, less secure. Such an order would publicly proclaim that a state's territory is secure only if it is militarily strong enough to be coded as a major power, and even then it must be lucky enough to find itself in the right major power coalitions. Incentives for arms build-ups, nuclear weapons proliferation, and other Realpolitik strategies would increase. In effect, ad hoc use of partition and recognition to solve civil wars would undermine a tacit bargain among the major powers in place since the early 1950s: If you don't seek to change interstate borders by force, then neither will we. I argue that this norm has been valuable, functioning in some respects like an arms control agreement. It would be irresponsible to undermine it without any thought to what might replace it.

If the major powers want to start redesigning sovereign states, they should have a political and legal framework that mitigates the two incentive effects just described.

---

3. John J. Mearsheimer and Stephen Van Evera, "When Peace Means War," *New Republic* 18 December 1995, 221–42; Mearsheimer and Robert A. Pape, "The Answer: A Three Way Partition Plan for Bosnia and How the U.S. Can Enforce it," *New Republic*, 14 June 1993, 22–28.

NATURE AND CAUSES OF SEPARATIST NATIONALISM

W HAT OUGHT TO be done about separatist nationalist wars depends in part on how one thinks about the nature and causes of separatist nationalism. In this section I quickly summarize the most prominent views and then sketch an alternative. First, however, a brief discussion of the meanings of nationalism.

TWO CLUSTERS OF MEANINGS

The word nationalism, as it is used in both academic and everyday discourse, has two clusters of meanings. These are rarely distinguished in academic writing on the subject. Instead, authors typically force the word into a single definition, with unfortunate consequences. Failure to distinguish the two meanings is an unrecognized source of dispute in the main academic debates on nationalism.

In the first cluster of meanings, nationalism refers to a feeling of affection or loyalty to one's nation, especially with a negative connotation of chauvinism regarding other nations. In this sense, nationalism is something like the dark side of patriotism, and it is not far from the capacious idea of group loyalty. An explanation for nationalism in this sense need have nothing to do with questions about separatism.

In the second cluster, nationalism refers to the political doctrine holding that the boundaries of states and nations should coincide.[4] Nationalism in this sense refers to the doctrine of national self-determination, which in the hands of American foreign policymakers is called Wilsonianism. One can do no better than quote Elie Kedourie's formulation:

> Nationalism is a doctrine [that] pretends to supply a criterion for the determination of the unit of population proper to enjoy a government exclusively its own, for the legitimate exercise of power in the state, and for the right organization of a society of states. Briefly, the doctrine holds that humanity is naturally divided into nations, that nations are known by certain characteristics which can be ascertained, and that the only legitimate type of government is national self-government.[5]

Failure to distinguish these meanings causes trouble. For instance, one of the central debates in the literature on nationalism has concerned the question of when nationalism began, with some saying it has deep premodern roots and others (the modernists) arguing that nationalism is a product of modernity, even the nineteenth century. Plausibly, nationalism as feelings of affection and

---

4. Ernest Gellner, *Nations and Nationalism* (Ithaca: Cornell University Press, 1983), 1.
5. Elie Kedourie, *Nationalism* (New York: Praeger), 1.

chauvinism on behalf of cultural groups is old, even eternal, and no doubt one can find examples of premodern cultural groups whose leaders argued for political privileges on the basis of cultural difference. It is equally plausible, as the modernists assert, that we do not encounter the formulation, and certainly not the success, of nationalism as a generalized doctrine of political legitimacy until the modern period.

This distinction is also important for understanding the causes of nationalism. Asking about the causes of nationalism-as-group-loyalty-and-chauvinism is not the same as asking about the causes of nationalist separatist movements.

PRIMORDIALIST AND MODERNIST EXPLANATIONS

Our concern here is with nationalism in the second sense, in particular with the causes of separatist movements that claim unjust violations of the doctrine that state and national borders should coincide. Two types of arguments are given.

First, there is what may be called the primordialist variant of nationalist doctrine itself. This holds that not only is humanity naturally divided into nations, but proper nations find the violation of self-determination intolerable and so naturally strive for independence. The cause of separatist nationalism is simply the violation of the principle of self-determination for some proper nation. Thus, the obvious and morally appropriate remedy is to redraw borders. It may be that this cannot be done without making some nation unhappy about the new borders, so that population transfers may be necessary. These are necessary compromises that will bring about peace and justice in the end, however.

This view implies that the project of redrawing borders can be completed. After enough redrawing, separatist nationalism will disappear as a problem because all proper nations will have received their own states. By this argument, there is no need to worry about the incentive effects of a policy of ad hoc partition. Proper nations are going to rebel when their self-determination is violated regardless of what is going on with other cases. In this Wilsonian form, nationalist doctrine is a theory of perpetual peace, with partition the means of getting there.

As a positive explanation for separatist movements and strife, the primordialist view is either implausible or tautological. Either we admit that the world is filled with proper nations that are not seeking self-determination, or the proposition is true by definition (that is, proper nations are those that actively seek their own state).

The second main view of the causes of separatist nationalism is associated primarily with the work of Ernest Gellner, Karl Deutsch, Benedict Anderson, and Eric Hobsbawm.[6] These modernists reject as unhistorical the idea that nations have always existed. Instead, they see nations and nationalism as the local political and psychological consequences of macrohistorical forces, economic modernization most of all. The core argument goes as follows: Nationalist movements arise in the modern period as economic modernization makes upward social and economic mobility possible for individuals, but contingent on the individual's culture (and especially, first language). When the son of the Czech-speaking peasant moves to town and finds his upward progress in local industry or the Habsburg bureaucracy blocked because his manners and language are insufficiently German, he becomes resentful and ready to be mobilized for a Czech nationalist movement. Separatist nationalist movements are argued to arise out of ascriptive barriers to upward mobility imposed by the state or the majority cultural group.[7]

For most modernist writers, the central determinant of whether a country will get a separatist nationalist movement is the extent of premodern cultural differences between populations. Deutsch argues that when these are large—as for example, between Germans and Magyars in Austria-Hungary—the rate of assimilation will be too slow relative to the rate of social mobilization. Gellner argues that psychological bias will lead the dominant group to attribute the effects of different educations to inherent cultural or genetic properties of the minority, giving rise to discrimination and oppression. When preexisting cultural differences are smaller, successful assimilation and national homogenization is more likely. For the modernists, the paradigmatic case of such assimilation is "peasants into Frenchman."[8]

If the modernist account is valid, then two natural remedies for violence arising from separatist nationalist movements present themselves. First, states or majority cultures can somehow be brought not to discriminate along cultural

6. Gellner, *Nations and Nationalism*; Karl W. Deutsch, *Nationalism and Social Communication* (Cambridge, MA: MIT Press, 1953); Benedict Anderson, *Imagined Communities* (London: Verson, 1983); and Eric J. Hobsbawm, *Nations and Nationalism since 1780: Programme, Myth, and Reality* (Cambridge: Cambridge University Press, 1992).

7. In *Imagined Communities*, Anderson relies on the idea of barriers to upward mobility in his "blocked pilgrimages" argument explaining new world nationalist movements (chap. 4, "Creole Pioneers"). In pointing to these new world movements, Anderson is also suggesting that the barriers need not be cultural—the creoles of Latin America shared the culture of Spain. Rather, the key is that upward bureaucratic "pilgrimages" be blocked by an ascriptive trait, in this case, birth in the new world. Still, in the old world that Gellner and Deutsch had in mind, the barriers to upward mobility typically fell along cultural lines (see Anderson, *Imagined Communities*, chap. 3, on the "linguistic nationalisms" of Europe).

8. Eugen J Weber, *Peasants into Frenchmen* (Stanford, CA: Stanford University Press, 1976).

lines of difference, the basis of popular support for separatist nationalism should be less. As a result, states with problems of separatism should, for their own good, be urged not to discriminate and oppress cultural minorities. Of course, this is something they shouldn't do in any event, from a moral perspective. Second, the modernist argument has nothing in it that makes redrawing borders a bad thing, subject to practical constraints. As in the primordialist view, redrawing boundaries is a project that can come to an end, when the lines around states correspond to the set of preexisting cultural zones 'activated' by the secular tidal wave of economic modernization or "print capitalism".[9]

As a positive explanation for separatist nationalism, the modernist version is vastly more plausible than nationalist doctrine itself. Surely discrimination and oppression along cultural lines can breed resentment, anger, group solidarity, and movements on behalf of the group. It also remains largely untested, however. That is, we have almost no systematic efforts to measure and code the extent of preexisting cultural differences between minority and majority groups, and show that where these have been greater, ethnonational movements are more likely.

There are reasons to doubt that such a project could be wholly successful, for at least two reasons.[10] First, by any measure of what preexisting cultural differences might consist of, there will be cases where similar levels of difference produced quite different levels of nationalist mobilization. Compare, for example, the case of Prussia/Germany with Serbia/Yugoslavia. Both had significant Catholic religious minorities that spoke varied dialects of similar languages. It would be difficult to argue that the degree of cultural difference between a Prussian and a Bavarian peasant was smaller in 1800 than was the difference between a Catholic peasant from Croatia and an Orthodox peasant from Serbia. It is not even clear that levels of political and economic discrimination

9. On print capitalism, see Anderson, *Imagined Communities*, ch. 2.

10. See, however, James D. Fearon and Pieter Van Houten, "A Return to the Theory of Regional Autonomy Movements," (presented at the annual meetings of the American Political Science Association, San Francisco, 25 September 1998), who show that language distance helps predict regionalist parties in Western Europe. Using the Minorities at Risk data set (Ted Robert Gurr, "Minorities at Risk III Dataset: User's Manual." CIDCM, University of Maryland, 1996,. http://www.cidcm.umd.edu/inscr/mar/home.htm), James D. Fearon and David D. Laitin, in "Weak States, Rough Terrain, and Large-Scale Ethnic Violence since 1945" (presented at the annual meetings of the American Political Science Association, Atlanta, GA, 25 September 1999); and Ted R. Gurr, *Minorities at Risk: A Global View of Ethnopolitical Conflicts* (Washington, D.C.: United States Institute of Peace, 1993), find no clear relationship between measures of cultural distance from the dominant group and a minority's probability of being involved in rebellion against the state. Using a much larger list of ethnic groups, Philip G. Roeder, "Clash of Civilizations and Escalation of Domestic Ethnopolitical Conflicts," *Comparative Political Studies* 36, no. 5 (June 2003): 509–40, does, however.

were appreciably different.[11] Croatian elites resisted incorporation in the Serb-dominated interwar Kingdom and some developed an enduring separatist or autonomist ideology. By contrast, Bavaria was successfully incorporated into Germany after 1871 despite bitter anti-Prussian popular and elite sentiment as late as 1866.[12]

Second, it seems implausible to take "the degree of cultural difference" as a wholly exogenous factor, rather than something itself produced by politics. The perception of cultural difference is made as much as it is born. This point is relevant to the Germany/Yugoslavia comparison. What mattered for getting separatism in one case and not the other probably had less to do with degrees of cultural difference and discrimination "on the ground" as it did with the different ways that politics among the elites played out in the two cases, along with more international factors such as the advantage and prestige conferred by Germany's great-power status.

SEPARATIST MOVEMENTS AS A CONSEQUENCE OF THE STATES' SYSTEM

Despite some sharp differences, the primordialist and modernist explanations have something important in common. Both are bottom up in the sense that they locate the motivation for separatist nationalism in popular sentiments taken as inherent or as the result of economic and political discrimination along cultural lines. Separatist movements are indeed often animated by a powerful, popular sense of cultural nationalism. It is a mistake, however, to treat such sentiments as exogenous variables, as in primordialism, or things produced out of a fixed set of preexisting cultural difference by the slow, secular process of economic and political modernization. Rather, the sentiments of separatist nationalism can be and are shaped by elite politics. Here is a complementary account that focuses more on such factors.

Instead of lying in particular groups' cultures or in relations between particular groups, the deeper sources of separatist nationalism are to be found in the logic of a system of nation-states. Think of a formally recognized state as a kind of candy that is hard to get. States are very good things for those who run them, and in short supply relative to demand. They are the object of great ambition and contestation.

11. Perhaps they were even greater in nineteenth century Germany than in the first Yugoslav state. Recall the Kulturkampf in Germany.

12. Many in late nineteenth-century Europe, including in the Balkans, saw Serbia as naturally playing the role of Piedmont or Prussia for the South Slavs.

How do you get a state? Either by winning control of an already established state or by establishing a new one. In the latter case, it helps enormously to have a claim to statehood that other states recognize as potentially valid. All manner of concrete benefits can flow from recognition of a valid claim, including military support in an independence struggle and, after independence, development aid, balance-of-payments finance, more military support, and a battery of rights, protections and privileges in international law on which other states condition some actions. Formal admission to the club of states is tremendously valuable.[13]

Interstate borders are pure conventions, a matter of tacit agreement among the states that respect them. States have powerful incentives to naturalize the boundaries, however, to provide a justification for why they are as they are so as to fend off internal and external challenges. Since the French Revolution, the nationalist doctrine has gradually become the dominant justification. Existing states justify their boundaries as delimiting the property of the nations they represent. Thus, those who would seek to establish a new state have an incentive to appeal for recognition and external support in precisely these terms, to say that they merit a state because they are a true nation, just like all the rest.

Ambitious state seekers therefore have an incentive to render their claim more plausible by actively cultivating the sense and appearance of distinct nationality in the population they wish to govern. One of the best ways to do this is to get a nationalist insurgency going with the current state, since the violence tends to divide populations according to putatively primordialist lines.[14]

If there were only a limited amount of cultural difference out there in the world suitable for politicization in nationalist terms, then this might not be so bad. A Wilsonian project of ad hoc partitions could conceivably come to an end, because eventually political entrepreneurs would run out of cultural differences they could develop into nationalist claims for autonomy or independence. If the primordialist and modernist views are wrong, however—if

---

13. For example, the Taliban regime in Afghanistan several times offered the U.S. and the U.N. to end poppy cultivation, a major source of their tax revenues, in exchange for international recognition (Ahmed Rashid, *Taliban: Militant Islam, Oil, and Fundamentalism in Central Asia* [New Haven: Yale University Press, 2000]).

14. For example, John Mueller, "The Banality of 'Ethnic War'," *International Security* 25, no. 1 (summer 2000); Chaim Kaufmann, "Possible and Impossible Solutions to Ethnic Civil Wars," *International Security* 20, no. 4 (spring 1996): 136–75; David Laitin, "National Revivals and Violence," *European Journal of Sociology* 36, no. 1 (1995); 3–43; and James D. Fearon and David D. Laitin, "Violence and the Social Construction of Ethnic Identity," *International Organization* 54, no. 4 (autumn 2000): 845–77.

the world is filled with cultural differences that can be politicized, sharpened and interpreted in the direction of nationality claims—then a Wilsonian project of partition is inherently selfundermining.

To use an idea from economic theory, the nation-state system is not incentive compatible, meaning that the system itself creates incentives that work to undermine the system. Separatist movements will be a problem for as long as the "club" of states defines membership in terms of nationhood. Not only will dividing up states not make separatist nationalist movements go away, it may even increase their number.

PROBLEMS WITH AD HOC PARTITION

THERE ARE at least three sets of problems with using partitions imposed by strong states to settle ethnic nationalist civil wars. First, there are questions of practicality, efficacy, and justice in particular cases, such as Bosnia. Almost all of the public debate on partition has focused on these matters. I will quickly rehearse the main objections and discuss some points of contention, but my focus is on the incentive problems that have been little addressed. These come in two forms. There is the issue raised above in connection with theories of the causes of separatist nationalism: Would a policy of ad hoc partition increase incentives for more separatist wars and render current conflicts more intractable? Next, how would a policy of ad hoc partition affect states' incentives in their dealings with each other? I will argue that such a policy would undermine some desirable features of the post-1945 international system.

EFFICACY AND JUSTICE

The question of partition arises in the first place when competing nationalisms seek to mobilize within a common international boundary, and especially when violence ensues. Drawing a new line to separate populations is problematic if any line will leave an unhappy and fearful minority on one or both sides. Unfortunately, this is by far the most common case.[15] What to do when the area claimed by the disgruntled national minority contains a distinct group that prefers to remain in the undivided state? Examples include English-speakers and Native Canadians in Quebec; Serbs in Bosnia, Kosovo and Croatia (formerly); Hindus in Kashmir; Sinhalese and Muslims in the Sri Lankan Northern

---

15. Czechoslovakia, Slovenia, and Singapore are exceptions.

and Northeast provinces; Azerbaijanis in Nagorno-Karabagh; Georgians in Abkhazia; and so on.

Advocates of ad hoc partition tend for this reason to favor population transfers, arguing that this is likely to happen anyway: Why not have international actors intervene so that it is done properly and with a minimum of violence?[16] I find the idea of internationally sponsored and legitimized ethnic cleansing loathsome, all the more so since it will often be at the behest of opportunistic thugs. Advocates of partition often seem to make the sole moral standard the number killed due to ethnic fighting, at the expense of considerations of justice on other dimensions. Is it right that people should be uprooted from homes of longstanding and made permanent refugees? If the answer is no, then at a minimum we need to consider tradeoffs rather than making the number not killed the only value. It is not sufficient to argue that if partition is the policy that maximizes this, it is necessarily best.

Relatedly, critics have observed that partitions are often accompanied by significant violence, and may simply replace civil conflict with interstate conflict in the form of revanchism. Ireland, India, Palestine, and Cyprus are leading examples, with the world-threatening nuclear confrontation between India and Pakistan the most dramatic.[17] Kaufmann maintains that the problem with these partitions was simply that they were incomplete and did not take the Wilsonian logic far enough.[18] For instance, the problem with the Indian partition was the failure to divide Jammu and Kashmir and sort out populations there. A "clean" partition with population transfers need not eliminate revanchist tendencies, however. The relatively clean de facto partition of Azerbaijan has created camps filled with displaced, bitter Azeris who are actively developing a political ideology of revenge and return, for instance. In any event, the argument for partition needs to address politically feasible rather than hypothetical pure cases.

None of these objections are in principle insuperable for any particular case. Indeed, if there were no implications of ad hoc partition that extended from one case to another, then there really would be no argument against considering

---

16. Kaufmann, "Possible and Impossible Solutions to Ethnic Civil Wars."

17. See for example Radha Kumar, "The Troubled History of Partition," *Foreign Affairs* 76, no. 1 (1997): 22–34; Nicholas Sambanis, "Partition as a Solution to Ethnic War: An Empirical Critique of the Theoretical Literature," *World Politics* 52 (July 2000): 437–83; and Robert Schaeffer, *Warpaths: The Politics of Partition* (New York: Hill and Wang, 1990).

18. Kaufmann, "When All Else Fails: Evaluating Population Transfers and Partition as Solutions to Ethnic Conflict," in *Civil Wars, Insecurity, and Intervention* ed. Barbara F. Walter and Jack Snyder, (New York: Columbia University Press, 1999).

the merits and demerits of partition case by case.[19] If, however, partition in one case of separatist nationalism can influence incentives elsewhere, then arguments for partition that refer only to the pluses and minuses of particular cases can't be decisive by themselves.

INCENTIVES FOR INSURGENCY AND COUNTERINSURGENCY

Any policy of ad hoc partition sets an implicit threshold or criterion for applying the policy. When major powers impose or push for the division of war-torn country X, they are saying, essentially, that if things get bad, they may step in to push the players toward a partition and recognition of a new state. To see that this is problematic, consider a hypothetical case of a very low threshold. The example is intentionally unrealistic.

Suppose that a small, violent separatist movement develops in the New York borough of Staten Island (which did see a 60 percent positive vote for independence from New York overturned in the courts in 1993). The active rebels begin threatening and assassinating individuals associated with the city, state, and federal governments, along with prominent Staten Islanders who do not agree with their program. Facilitating partition—sorting out those who identified with New York and those who identified with Staten Island—and giving the new state of Staten Island a UN seat would clearly be a huge mistake. No advocate of partition could deny that setting the implicit threshold this low would be an absolute disaster for international peace, order, and justice. No advocate of partition could deny that a threshold this low would encourage opportunistic thugs all around the world to try similar gambits.[20]

Exactly the same issues arise at higher, more realistic thresholds, however. Making the implicit criterion for international intervention in favor of partition some level of violence and chaos gives the leaders of nationalist insurgencies an incentive to reach for this level of violence. For example, prior to the Dayton agreement, there had been an ongoing debate among Kosovan Albanians about whether a violent insurgency or peaceful civil disobedience in the form

19. Kaufmann, "Possible and Impossible Solutions," makes a much stronger claim, that the only appropriate and effective solution for a country beset by ethnic war is to partition it. Presumably, Kaufmann believes there is some threshold of ethnic violence such that below this, it is not necessary to partition the state; otherwise, many countries would fall under his knife. The criteria for deciding where this threshold is, however, are neither clear nor sharp (see Kaufmann's brief mention of the issue on p. 159 of "Possible and Impossible Solutions"), making the strong claim quite difficult to evaluate or apply.

20. If this example is too fanciful, imagine that the radical wing of the movement for an independent Hawaii becomes more radical.

of a shadow government was the best course for attracting international support and redressing wrongs in Kosovo. After Dayton, which the Kosovars reasonably interpreted as rewarding the violent Bosnian Serb leadership with virtual independence, the KLA broke ranks and initiated a guerrilla campaign. Deliberately provoking Serbian attacks, they succeeded beyond what must have been their wildest dreams, with NATO intervening on their behalf in 1999.[21]

Chaim Kaufmann, the only partition advocate I know of who has addressed this first incentive problem at all, dismisses the issue in one sentence: "because government use of force to suppress them makes almost all secession attempts extremely costly . . . only groups that see no viable alternative try."[22]

There are two mistakes here. First, the argument implicitly treats ethnic groups as if they were unitary actors, making a collective decision about whether to fight for secession. This is rarely a plausible assumption, especially at the onset of violence. Instead, nationalist insurgencies are frequently initiated by small minorities within an ethnic group who take it as one of their central projects to cultivate and enforce support for their project. Violence directed at insufficiently supportive co-ethnics is one important means; provoking indiscriminate counterinsurgency by the state is another.[23] With respect to Kaufmann's claim above, the implication is that the costs of government suppression will mainly be born by publics with little say in the decision about how to oppose the government. For the active rebels, possible costs are offset by their relative extremism and the prospect of heading a new state or autonomy.

Second, even if we could treat the minority ethnic group as a unitary actor choosing rebellion, it is still true that lowering the expected costs of separatist war by increasing the likelihood of international intervention increases the incentive for new nationalist insurgencies, while making intransigence a more attractive option in ongoing conflicts. This might be partially offset by an increased incentive for governments to be nice to cultural minorities in the first place. As I will discuss, however, there are better ways to provide such an incentive.

---

21. Another important factor enabling the KLA insurgency (such as it was) was the procurement of weapons out of the Albanian anarchy in 1996; see Kuperman, "Transnational Causes of Genocide," 81n36, on this and other factors behind the KLA escalation. On NATO's moral hazard problem with respect to encouraging violence by the KLA in Kosovo, see also Crawford, "Pivotal Deterrence and the Kosovo War."
22. Kaufmann, "Possible and Impossible Solutions," 170.
23. Kaufmann, "Possible and Impossible Solutions," 140–45, is aware that violence "hardens" ethnic identities, but sees violence purely as a product of mutual fears produced by a weakened central government, rather than by individuals and factions with their own ambitions and agendas. Cf. John Mueller, "The Banality of "Ethnic War" on the war in Bosnia.

In arguing that secession attempts are very costly and "only groups that see no viable alternative try," Kaufmann suggests that the "elasticity" of supply of separatist movements is negligible with respect to changes in international support for partition. Evidently, he thinks would-be leaders of nationalist movements do not condition their behavior much on anticipated international support or censure. I suspect this is incorrect. Even if it is not, however—even if the elasticity is very small—the potential effects would still need to be considered to make a serious case for partition as a solution to particular ethnic conflicts.

For one thing, there is a tremendous amount of "raw material" for violent separatist movements in the world, so even if the elasticity is small the implications may be significant. In other work, I provide a list of 822 ethnic groups in 161 countries that formed at least 1 percent of country population in the 1990s.[24] Of the 708 of these groups that are minorities, at least 100 (14.1 percent) had members engaged in significant rebellion against the state on behalf of the group between 1945 and 1998.[25] In the 1990s alone, almost one in ten of these ethnic minorities engaged in significant violent conflict with the state. Not all of these groups had avowedly separatist or autonomist aims, but some three quarters did.[26] In addition, many of the minorities that did not openly rebel were coded by the Minorities at Risk Project as displaying "latent," "historical" or "active" separatism (69 of the 198 quiescent groups coded by MAR, or 35 percent).

These data suggest, first, that violent conflict between states and ethnic groups or their would-be leaders has been quite common since 1945, with most of it occurring in the form of separatist struggles.[27] Second, though common, there is ample potential for more, both from the groups with members who have already demonstrated the possibility, and those that have not but that have

24. James D. Fearon, "Ethnic and Cultural Diversity By Country," *Journal of Economic Growth* 8 (2003): 195–222.

25. I matched the groups in Fearon, "Ethnic and Cultural Diversity by Country," with the Minorities at Risk (MAR) groups (Gurr, "Minorities at Risk III Dataset"), and then counted the number of matched groups that scored 4 or higher on the MAR rebellion scale (that is, "small," "intermediate," or "large-scale" guerrilla activity, or "protracted civil war") for at least one five-year period since 1945). This underestimates the number of ethnic groups in violent conflict, since the non-MAR groups are not considered. Because MAR tends to select, in effect, on violence, however, the underestimate is probably not very far off.

26. Judging by the scores of the MAR groups in my list that were coded as showing separatism on the MAR variable SEPX.

27. Compare, for instance, the one-in-seven minority-state dyads experiencing violent conflict to the 3.2-in-1000 share of the contiguous country dyads that fought an interstate war in the years from 1946–1992. This figure was calculated using data generated by EUGene (D. Scott Bennett and Allan Stam, "EUGene: A Conceptual Manual," *International Interactions* 26, (2000): 179–204).

latent or active but nonviolent separatist movements. Finally, these statistics do not account for the possibility discussed earlier, that political entrepreneurs may cultivate new "ethnic groups" and movements in response to domestic and international political incentives. In other words, we should not take my list of 822 groups listed as primordially fixed in stone (or DNA).[28]

To recap, a policy of ad hoc partition would implicitly set criteria for international intervention in support of redrawing borders or otherwise reconstituting states. If the implicit criterion is some level of violence and chaos, this creates perverse incentives. There are ample grounds for thinking that a responsible consideration of partition as a means to resolve ethnic wars should to take this into account.

Would some other criterion be workable? If nationalist doctrine were literally true, then we could objectively ascertain which of the world's cultural groups are proper nations, and propose to intervene only on their behalf and at their behest, irrespective of levels of violence. The nationalist doctrine is false, however. What is a proper nation is political question, a matter of dispute. No one agrees on just which the proper nations are, and no one agrees on objective, non-manipulable criteria defining nationhood. This is one reason that violence has become the implicit criterion. Scholars, journalists and government officials often infer proper nationhood from the costs that "groups" are willing to bear in struggles for independence.

An extreme alternative would be self-selection. Why not have the international community support the claim of any self-defining national group, or a majority of the putative group in a plebesite, that demands self-determination and its own state? Showing a clear understanding of the incentive problem, international lawyers recognized early on that self-determination could not be construed as a right to be exercised voluntarily. In a report on the 1920 dispute in which a League of Nation's Commission of Jurists heard demands by Aaland Island residents that they be allowed to secede from Finland to join Sweden, the Jurists wrote:

> To concede to minorities, either of language or religion, or to any fractions
> of a population the right of withdrawing from the community to which

---

28. A reviewer wondered if these observations were inconsistent with the argument I made in James D. Fearon, "Commitment Problems and the Spread of Ethnic Conflict", in *The International Spread of Ethnic Conflict*, ed. David A. Lake and Donald Rothchild (Princeton: Princeton University Press, 1998), 107–26, against the likelihood of significant transnational "demonstration effects" of ethnic conflict. There I was arguing against the proposition that the mere presence of an ethnic conflict in one country would raise the likelihood in other countries. Here my concern is with a change in great power policies that would affect cost-benefit calculations for many different ethnic disputes.

they belong, because it is their good wish or pleasure, would be to destroy order and stability within States and to inaugurate anarchy in international life; it would be to uphold a theory incompatible with the very idea of the State as a territorial and political unity.[29]

A more promising alternative would be to condition international support for cultural minorities on the state's treatment of the minority. Suppose that international intervention and pressure in favor of partition were linked to measures of systematic political and economic discrimination and a plausible case that these were unlikely to change. Then governments with cultural minorities would have an increased incentive to treat their members as equals in the polity. If authorized international observers saw a nationalist insurgency but no systematic discrimination, no support would be offered, thus undercutting the incentive problem.

In fact, such moves represent a long-standing tendency in international legal attempts to deal with the "destabilizing and anti-statist tendencies" of the norm of self-determination.[30] For example, many international lawyers agree that a group has a case for secession and independence if it is subject to genocide in the state it inhabits. Even in the reports on the Aaland Islands dispute, both commissions allowed that "secession might be justifiable as a remedy of last resort in states that failed to respect minority rights."[31] In addition, efforts to articulate a human rights regime since the Second World War, whether focused on individual or, more recently, group rights, in effect seek to develop internationally certifiable criteria of good behavior by states regarding their citizens.

While much better than using violence as the criterion for support for partition, conditioning the international response on aspects of government behavior is still problematic. In the first place, who adjudicates the application of the criteria in particular cases? While one can imagine states authorizing international courts to rule on whether a state is respecting some aspect of

---

29. Cited in David Wippman, ed., *International Law and Ethnic Conflict* (Ithaca: Cornell University Press, 1998), 9–10. It is ironic that the generally neorealist-influenced advocates of partition in the United States should not see the threat to the states system that the lawyers have long understood.

30. See Wippman, *International Law and Ethnic Conflict*, 10. Also, Stephen D. Krasner. *Sovereignty: Organized Hypocrisy*, (Princeton: Princeton University Press, 1999), who sees international agreements and interventions in favor of minority rights as evidence that the norm of sovereignty is continually violated. I would argue that minority rights regimes are better understood as attempts at agreements among sovereigns to preserve or make sovereignty viable despite incentive incompatibility.

31. Wippman, *International Law and Ethnic Conflict*, 10.

human rights in its domestic practices,[32] it remains hard to imagine them allowing courts to authorize international intervention to break up a state if its domestic practices are sufficiently bad. Second, moral hazard problems do not disappear. The state can write laws that are technically neutral, but enforce them selectively or not at all. The authorized international authorities, whoever they might be, would require an intrusive apparatus and method for making determinations about state and majority group behavior, which it is again difficult to imagine the great powers authorizing. On the separatists' side, many examples show rebel leaders deliberately seeking to bring down counterinsurgency on the heads of their own people. Clearly, if violations of human rights in the course of counterinsurgency were enough to justify international support for partition, then the incentive problem remains. Separatist insurgents would have strong incentives to provoke the state into counterinsurgency that violates human rights. Finally, prior to these questions there is the problem of deciding and getting agreement on what would constitute discrimination that justifies partition if it were not remedied. The U.S. government refused to sign the 1948 Convention on the Prevention of Genocide until 1989 in part out of fear that the definition of genocide was insufficiently tight. Definitions of actionable discrimination and oppression would seem impossibly more difficult.

INCENTIVES FOR INTERSTATE COMPETITION

The bad incentive effects of imposing partitions to resolve ethnic wars concern not only relations between insurgents and governments within states, but also relations among states. If the major powers recognize and support as a new state a government of rebels trying to secede from an already recognized state, they are setting a precedent that is potentially dangerous for themselves. What is to stop other states from recognizing a breakaway movement in one's own territory? If some majority of powerful states can agree to carve up a recognized state, what keeps one's own state safe from this end?

Realist international relations theory would probably say that the answer is only self-help, one's own armed strength. And because this is already the case, there is nothing lost if the major powers start carving up minor powers without their consent.

Actually, much would be lost. Members of the club of sovereign states have an agreement that says, in effect, "I will not support the de jure division of your

---

32. To an extent this has been happening, as in the ruling of the European Court of Justice against Britain's counterinsurgency practices in Northern Ireland in the 1970s.

state if you will not support the division of mine." This agreement is rendered more or less formally in the UN Charter and in much prior international law. Realist theory has long argued the irrelevance of international law, but at least in this case the argument is weak.

The agreement on mutual respect of territorial integrity among recognized, sovereign states is functionally similar to an arms control agreement. Such an agreement says, in effect, that one party will not increase its arms if the other party agrees to the same. This does not replace or render "self-help" irrelevant. States still keep arms as insurance against other states' use of arms and against potential internal challengers. An arms control agreement can add to states' security and welfare by spelling out the terms of a mutually advantageous form of coordination, however. If you armed more, I would want to race to keep up, yielding the risks and costs of a pointless arms build-up. Even though arms agreements are nothing more than words and beliefs, they can have the real effect of helping to avert this bad outcome.[33]

The same is true of an agreement on mutual respect of the territorial integrity of sovereign states. States of course do not rely wholly on this convention to protect their control of territory from internal and external challenges. They maintain armies and police forces. The scale of these costly efforts depends on the scale of other states' efforts, however. All can be better off if they can make a tit-for-tat deal that limits the extent and nature of challenges to territorial integrity, and thus the scale of self-help necessary to protect it.

To be sure, states have often violated the norm against supporting separatists in another country with shelter or military aid, probably as much since 1945 as before.[34] In this period, however, the major powers have refrained from interventions to carve up a previously recognized state to make new states without the consent of the state. In marked contrast to prior great power politics, the major powers since the 1950s have stuck to the norm of "no border changes imposed by force" with very few exceptions.[35]

---

33. Cf. Alexander Wendt, *Social Theory of International Politics*, (New York: Cambridge University Press, 1999) on Hobbesian versus Lockean world orders. Also, Charles Glaser, "Realists as Optimists: Cooperation as Self-Help." *International Security* 19, no. 3: 50–90; and George W. Downs and David M. Rocke. *Tacit Bargaining, Arms Races, and Arms Control*, (Ann Arbor: University of Michigan Press, 1990).

34. See, for examples, Steve Saideman, *The Ties that Divide: Ethnic Politics, Foreign Policy, and International Conflict* (New York: Columbia University Press, 2001). Still, there might be much more support for separatists in a world without the convention of mutual recognition of sovereignty. In Alexis Heraclides, *The Self-Determination of Minorities in International Politics*, (London: Frank Cass, 1990), Heraclides claims, for instance, that since 1945 insurgents in separatist wars have been less likely to receive international support in the form of military aid than have insurgents in non-separatist civil wars.

35. Germany's recognition of Croatia on 23 December 1991 is a plausible exception, although it might be argued that the federal government of Yugoslavia had ceased to exist by December

In a large part, the leaders of the major powers recoil from a policy of ad hoc, imposed partitions to settle ethnic wars for just this reason, out of concern for what seems to them a valuable standard. They realize that the formal equality of sovereign states is worth respecting, even if it is patently obvious that states are wildly unequal in substantive terms. The more the de jure fiction is abandoned, the more states have incentives to protect themselves de facto by arming, acquiring nuclear weapons, forming alliances, and so on. For instance, if Bosnia is forcibly partitioned but Chechnya left to Russia and Tibet to China because they are militarily stronger, how does this affect the incentives of minor and middle powers with potential separatist troubles, or Russia and China for that matter?

This is one important reason why Germany's unilateral recognition of Croatia in December 1991 and the subsequent recognition of Bosnia were so ill-advised. Prior to these acts, there would have been no legal obstacle to discussing the redrawing of Yugoslavia's internal borders to make successor states in a just and sensible way. Once Croatia and Bosnia were recognized, however, the internal administrative borders designed by Tito's regime became external frontiers enclosing new members of the states' "club" with all the formal rights and privileges this implies. Any partition plan now faces the obstacle of either discarding or implausibly finessing the norm of "no border changes of recognized states by force."[36]

Of course, the strong states could simply cast these issues aside if they wish to dismember UN member state Bosnia-Hercegovina. They could do the same with Yugoslavia, by stripping off an independent Kosovo. They could declare each a one-time or otherwise special exception and employ international lawyers to find arguments to justify this. Doing so would take a toll on the overall implicit bargain, however. Ignored by advocates of partition, this issue ought to be considered in a responsible assessment of whether partition and recognition are good ways to resolve an ethnic war. How many one-time exceptions or special circumstances can be declared? Does doing this increase the demand for exceptions? At what cost to a possibly valuable interstate norm concerning sovereign equality? With what effect on the prevailing legal structure through which the major powers sometimes coordinate to resolve collective concerns and problems?

1991 and so there was no question of "consent." (This does not mean that recognition was a good idea in this case; see below.)

36. See Steven R. Ratner, "Ethnic Conflict and Territorial Claims: Where Do We Draw the Line?" in Wippman, *"International Law and Ethnic Conflict,"* 112–27, on the doctrine of uti possidetis and whether it was a good idea to apply it to Yugoslavia's internal frontiers.

The incentive effects described in this section would apply only, or at least mainly, to cases of forcibly imposed partition. If partition has the formal consent of the state losing territory, then the norm of no border changes by force is formally respected, even if the consent is in part the product of a long fight (East Timor or Eritrea, for example). One way to mitigate the interstate incentive problem posed by partition might be to say that there is consent, and there is "consent." The Yugoslav government does not want to allow the secession of Kosovo, but perhaps sufficient carrots and sticks might persuade them to "sign off."[37] The Bosnian government after Dayton is a federation, so it might be "legally" divided just by arguing that the state no longer exists when a component part votes "out" in a referendum; to hell with what the Muslim leaders say.

If partitions are going to happen, this is the most likely route. The major powers' strong desire to formally respect the norm of no forcible border changes will make sure of this. It is equally clear that consent produced by big international sticks and carrots is not the same as consent. Rather, it is a form of coercion, or forcibly imposed partition. The more bald the coercion, the more the arguments and questions above apply.

Nonetheless, if some level of carrots and sticks will work to get a consensual partition of an country mired in an intractable ethnic war, this may be much better than imposing partition by military intervention and/or outright recognition of the separatists. It would still be problematic to condition the carrots and sticks on levels of violence reached in the civil war, for the reasons already described. Consider, however, conditioning the carrots and sticks— perhaps economic sanctions, quiet military support for the separatists' efforts, public statements that a mutually acceptable partition should be considered by international negotiators—on the state's unwillingness to do X, Y, Z with respect to policies of nondiscrimination. Such an approach might get around both kinds of incentive problems.

Against Ad Hoc Partition

M Y INTENTION has not been to argue against partition as a solution for problems posed by ethnic war in any and all circumstances, forever

---

37. John Mearsheimer and Stephen Van Evera, in "Redraw the Map, Stop the Killing" (*New York Times*, 19 April 1999, A23) suggest offering the Republika Srpska to Yugoslavia in exchange for agreement to let Kosovo go. They do not say if anything would be offered to the Bosnian Muslims in the Bosnian government to gain their assent, or if the partition would simply be imposed on them. In general, partition advocates have been unclear about how they would manage or direct the imposition of partitions on unwilling parties.

more. Rather, I have argued against a policy of ad hoc partition that would treat each case in isolation. Partition cannot be justified on an ad hoc, case-by-case basis, because the effects of a policy of major-power-imposed partitions extend across cases in diverse ways.

Before partition can be contemplated as a plausible and responsible policy option, two incentive problems posed by partition must be seriously addressed. First, if violence is the implicit criterion for major power intervention in support of partition, this will encourage violent separatist movements seeking to mobilize cultural differences to claim statehood. Second, for the major powers to forcibly intervene to carve up sovereign states would be to abandon a valuable agreement that has helped structure international relations since 1945—the standard of no border changes by force. Wholesale abandonment of this convention would move international affairs a step further in the direction of *sauve qui peut*.

What, if anything, can be done to get around these incentive problems? It would seem incredibly unjust to declare that the current interstate borders are the only possible borders, regardless of what is going on inside them or how murderous a state is to some fraction of its population. There is no obvious or clean answer, however, because the problem is foundational. It arises from the internal logic of a nation-state system, which justifies its organization by treating already recognized nations as given even as it creates incentives for new or unsatisfied nations to challenge the existing organization. To have a court that could authoritatively rule on and enforce who gets a state would be to end the states system!

At least at present, the best solutions are second-best and the first-best unclear. The best I can do here is this: Condition international support and pressure for a consensual partition on a state's unwillingness to observe some set of internationally agreed standards regarding human and minority rights.

The first incentive problem would be mitigated because separatist violence and ethnic civil war would not necessarily gain international support for partition; it would depend on the policies of the state in which the separatists lived. The second incentive problem would be mitigated because wholesale carving up of recognized states would be rejected in favor of inducements, and these in turn would be, in a weak sense, a matter of law. That is, there would be some notion of justifiable and general conditions under which the threats and inducements should be applied. Serious thinking is required to work out how to define and state such conditions, and it is not even clear that this can be done in a way that would be both practicable and acceptable to the major powers. The alternatives of the status quo or blundering from one ad hoc partition to another, though, are not attractive either.

Living Together After Ethnic Killing: In Theory, in History, and in Iraq Today

Chaim Kaufmann

I have argued that in some intense communal conflicts a stable end to the killing can only be attained by separating the warring populations into defensible territories; that in such cases efforts to keep warring ethnic communities together in mixed settlements, or to put them back together after they have become separated in the course of the war, are misguided and actually dangerous; and that in such circumstances demands for very loose regional autonomy or even for partition of sovereignty should not be resisted.[1]

This is nearly the opposite of what was for many decades a virtually unexamined consensus—that separation of populations and partition of sovereignty should never be encouraged, accepted, or even tolerated. The United Nations Charter favors states over non-state groups or individuals in almost all circumstances.[2]

What Roy Licklider and Mia Bloom have called the "Chaim Kaufmann argument" has certainly not replaced the old consensus, but the consensus has broken down far enough that at least some scholars among them the eleven contributors to the present volume and the editors of *Security Studies* who sponsored the special journal issue of which this volume is an expansion[3] have concluded that the question now requires serious investigation. Further, all eleven contributors—Licklider, Bloom, R. William Ayres, David Carment, Dane Rowlands, Alexander B. Downes, James D. Fearon, Alan J. Kuperman,

This chapter (and I) owe debts to Alex Downes, James Fearon, Carter Johnson, Roy Licklider, Dan Lindley, Charles Lipson, Bruce Moon, Robert Pape, and John Mearsheimer.

1. Chaim Kaufmann, "Possible and Impossible Solutions to Ethnic Civil Wars," *International Security* vol. 20 no. 4 (Spring 1996), pp 136–75; and Kaufmann, "When All Else Fails: Ethnic Population Transfers and Partitions in the Twentieth Century," *International Security* vol. 23 no. 2 (Fall 1998), pp. 120–56. See also John J. Mearsheimer and Stephen W. Van Evera, "When Peace Means War," *New Republic*, December 18, 1995, pp. 16–21; and Mearsheimer and Van Evera, "Redraw the Map, Stop the Killing," *New York Times*, April 19, 1999.

2. Since the mid-1990s, however, we have seen increased willingness of U.N. Security Council members and other important powers to seek creative interpretations in order to assist people at risk in failed states such as Somalia, Bosnia, Cambodia, Haiti, Albania, Kosovo, Indonesia (East Timor), Sierra Leone, and Sudan.

3. Bloom and Licklider, eds., *Living Together After Ethnic Killing: Exploring the Chaim Kaufmann Argument, Security Studies* vol. 13 no. 4 (Summer 2004).

David D. Laitin, Raul Roe, and Nicholas Sambanis—express support for separation and partition as the appropriate policy prescription in at least some circumstances, although some would resort to partition less often than they estimate that I would.[4] This result would have been unthinkable ten years ago.

The logic of what I call the security dilemma theory of ethnic conflict has four components. First, ethnic wars create security dilemmas that escalate violence and act as a bar to de-escalation. Once inter-communal violence escalates beyond a certain threshold,[5] all involved individuals and groups face security dilemmas—they have realistic reasons to fear rival groups, and few ways to improve their own security except by offensive action against those groups.[6] Such security dilemmas are intensified in places where the groups live intermixed, creating strong strategic pressures for all sides to create safe, defensible communal enclaves, often by ethnic cleansing of mixed settlements.

Second, ethnic wars separate communities. This follows directly from the impact of population geography on the intensity of security dilemmas.

Third, communal killing hardens group identities. Atrocity tales continue to circulate within all the rival groups for many years after the end of the most intense violence, providing unanswerable arguments to hard-liners on all sides and undermining individual trust that might allow refugees to return to homes in what has become 'enemy' territory—as well as the likelihood that the 'enemy' will allow such returns.[7]

As a result, options for ending ethnic wars are path-dependent. Regardless of the mix of opportunity, fear, or other motives that led to the initial outbreak

---

4. Bloom; Licklider; Downes, "The Problem with Negotiated Settlements," pp. 230–79 at 234; Roe, "Which Security Dilemma? Mitigating Ethnic Conflict: The Case of Croatia," pp. 280–313 at 313; Kuperman, "Is Partition the Only Hope? Reconciling Contradictory Findings About Ethnic Civil Wars," pp. 314–49 at 349; Laitin, "Ethnic Unmixing and Civil War," pp. 350–66 at 351; Carment and Rowlands, "Vengeance and Intervention: Can Third Parties Bring Peace Without Separation," pp. 366–93 at 371–72; Fearon, "Separatist Partitions and World Order," pp. 394–415 at 405 (with very strong caveats), all in *Security Studies* vol. 13 no. 4 (Summer 2004): Sambanis, "Partition as a Solution to Ethnic War. An Empirical Critique of the Theoretical Literature. *World Politics* vol. 52 no. 4 (July 2000), pp. 437–483 at 482; Ayres 15th page (unnumbered).

5. Stephen Walt once suggested that the threshold should be considered to be passed when, for most members of at least one group, the most likely cause of death has become murder by a member of a rival group. This logic is difficult to operationalize exactly, but often not hard to measure within a shortish time span. Bosnia almost certainly had not passed the threshold before the elections of December 1991, but almost certainly had by the time that ethnic Serb policemen began defecting, and Serb death squads began operating, both in March 1992.

6. Barry R. Posen, "The Security Dilemma and Ethnic Conflict," *Survival* vol. 35 no. 1 (Spring 1983), pp. 27–47.

7. Croatian atrocities 1941–1991; Israel, Jordan and Egypt after 1948. Bosnia population 2000.

of violence, dynamics created by the war itself—including security dilemmas, atrocities, and hardening of identities—influence possibilities for de-escalation or resolution.

What this means for policy is that outside powers seeking to help resolve ongoing communal wars should rarely attempt to resurrect the failed multi-ethnic state or, worse, pressure refugees to return to places where they may simply be victimized again; instead they should protect and resettle refugees behind defensible borders.[8] These elements make up the core logic of the security dilemma theory of ethnic conflict resolution.

There is another possible, indeed common, solution to ethnic wars that need not separate the populations—namely, complete victory by one side and forcible suppression of the losers—but outsiders motivated by humanitarian concerns never aim at this.[9] Such outcomes are also stable only so long as the military balance remains the same.

THE SECURITY DILEMMA IN THE MARKETPLACE OF IDEAS

One point in the security dilemma argument is sometimes misconstrued—that its logic "undercuts the rationale for all multi-ethnic states."[10] Far from it. Ethnic conflict, even far short of war, tends to separate populations, while peace tends to integrate them as individuals move to places where it seems that they can improve their lot despite ethnic diversity.[11] It is not clear whether there is a global trend toward either integration or separation.

Three further important points are not always fully recognized. First, the security dilemma is a theory of *escalation* and *de-escalation*, not of the initial sources of conflict. At least one side must have a prior suspicion that the other intends to resort to violence before security dilemma dynamics can operate;[12] whatever may be the source of such suspicions, they are exogenous

8. Kaufmann, "When All Else Fails," p. 156. Attempts to forestall refugee movements often increase ethnic cleansers' incentives to resort to mass killing. Benjamin A. Valentino, *Final Solutions: Mass Killing and Genocide in the Twentieth Century* (Ithaca, N.Y.: Cornell University Press, 2004), pp. 74, 76, 80, 82, 87, 90.

9. Unmixing may be dampened when one side's control of the disputed territory is so complete that escape options of defeated minorities are constrained.

10. Bloom and Licklider, "What's All the Shouting About?" *Security Studies* vol. 13 no. 4 (Summer 2004), pp. 219–29 at 223.

11. Multi-ethnic societies with highly integrated settlement patterns are likely to suffer terrible human disasters if they do have communal wars, but in any given society integration itself is evidence that that society may have few serious communal disputes.

12. Andrew Kydd, "Game Theory and the Spiral Model," *World Politics* vol. 49 no. 3 (April 1997), pp. 371–400; Charles L. Glaser, "The Security Dilemma Revisited," *World Politics* vol. 50 no. 1 (October 1997), pp. 171–201.

to the theory.[13] We should expect the theory to perform better at explaining escalation to extreme violence, the dynamics of communal violence, and the ends and aftermaths of communal wars than at explaining how large-scale communal violence comes to be a thinkable choice.

Second, security dilemmas explain behavior only under conditions of *mutual* threat; when power imbalances are so great that one side is completely secure and the other completely insecure, security concerns cannot influence the behavior of either.[14] It is almost never necessary that warring communities be entirely separated, only that the rump minorities left on the "wrong" sides of the lines be small enough, militarily and politically weak enough, and so located that they pose no threat to the dominant communities.[15]

Finally, while the intensity of inter-communal security dilemmas is a function of people living in places where they appear simultaneously both vulnerable as well as threatening, this is not determined by population geography alone. Other factors can sometimes be as or more important, including technology (what is the offense-defense balance?), physical geography (can the sides get at each other?), infrastructure networks (who would have to fight for which road junctions?), and mass constraints on elite behavior (has moderation become politically untenable?). Designing defensible borders requires taking into account all these factors.[16]

I appreciate the careful attention paid to my work by the eleven leading scholars of ethnic conflict and civil wars named above. Ten of the eleven engage directly with the logic of the security dilemma theory and offer extensions, critiques, or qualifications based on logical, methodological, or empirical

13. Instances of elite manipulation of discourse to create such suspicions are well attested. Some of the more famous include Francis M. Deng, *War of Visions: Conflict of Identities in the Sudan* (Washington, D.C.: Brookings Institution, 1995); V. P. Gagnon, Jr., "Ethnic Nationalism and International Conflict: The Case of Serbia," *International Security*, vol. 19 no. 3 (Winter 1994/95), pp. 130–66; Stuart J. Kaufman, "Spiraling to Ethnic War: Elites, Masses, and Moscow in Moldova's Civil War," *International Security*, vol. 21 no. 2 (Fall 1996), pp. 108–38; Gerard Prunier, *The Rwanda Crisis: History of a Genocide* (New York: Columbia University Press, 1997). See also Paul Roe's contribution to this volume.

14. Genocides of militarily helpless groups occur, but usually only when leaders of the dominant group have persuaded themselves that the victim group is actually much more powerful and dangerous than it appears. Valentino, *Final Solutions*, pp. 67, 75–77.

15. After the 1921 partition of Ireland, Protestants made up 9% of the population of the Republic and were politically unorganized; Catholics made up 34% of the population of Northern Ireland, a proportion that almost immediately began to increase. They were also largely mobilized along communal lines, and were supported by coreligionists across the border.

16. Intensity of security dilemmas can vary sharply from place to place within a country, which may allow us to predict where ethnic cleansing will be fiercest and most difficult to prevent.

investigation of aspects of the theory.[17] The first main section of this chapter offers comments on these contributions. Some of the contributions seek to evaluate aspects of theory based on large-N datasets, but are hampered by the fact that none of the datasets capture certain essential features of communal security dilemmas, such as the locations of particular settlements or infrastructure in relation to each other. A second problem is that reliability across different datasets is poor, even on matters so basic as cases included.[18]

The second section engages with David Laitin's contribution, which is the most ambitious. Laitin rejects the logic of security dilemma theory entirely; he favors an alternative model under which security concerns play a much less important role than do opportunities to indulge greed for wealth or power, and in which differences in the logics and determinants of communal wars and civil wars are minor at best. He presents empirical tests which he argues undermine the credibility of the security dilemma theory as an explanation of either onset of outcomes of communal wars.

As we will see, Laitin's proposed tests of security dilemma theory are not valid because they incorporate a number of serious theoretical and empirical errors. Full engagement with Laitin's analysis is nevertheless worthwhile because of both his standing in the field and that of his own rational choice, opportunity-based, theory of civil wars. Another even more important reason for engagement is the question is that Imre Lakatos would ask of us: what happens when our theories are confronted with new data? Accordingly, the second main section of this chapter evaluates the usefulness of both theories for understanding and coping with current communal conflict in Iraq. Many

---

17. The most important criticism not represented in this volume is that of David A. Lake and Donald Rothchild, who argue that inter-communal security dilemmas are primarily information failures rather than structural facts. "Containing Fear: The Origins and Management of Ethnic Conflict," *International Security* vol. 21, no. 1 (Fall 1996), pp. 41–75. This, however, is not so much a fundamental objection as an attempt to fill in an important intermediate step in the causal logic—many security dilemma theorists, such as Robert Jervis and Charles Glaser, explain security dilemmas as operating through information. Jervis, "Cooperation Under the Security Dilemma, *World Politics*, vol. 30 no. 2 (January 1978), pp. 176–218; Glaser, "Realists as Optimists: Cooperation as Self-help," *International Security*, vol. 19 no. 3 (Winter 1994/95), pp. 50–90. Lake and Rothchild's more important challenge is an empirical one—if we could show that perceived intensities of security dilemmas in ethnic conflicts were little related to objective histories of the harm that the sides had inflicted on each other or to their capabilities to inflict yet more, my argument would be damaged.

18. Sambanis, "What is Civil War? Conceptual and Empirical Complexities of an Operational Definition," *Journal of Conflict Resolution*, vol. 48 no. 6 (December 2004), pp. 814–858; Licklider, comment on war termination listserv (war-term@columbia.edu. June 6, 2005); Kuperman, "Is Partition Really the Only Hope?" p. 315.

were surprised at the escalation of communal conflicts in Iraq after April 2003, as well as by the timing, actors involved, scale, and trajectory of these conflicts.

The third section offers policy advice for Iraq based on the findings of the first two sections.

LIVING TOGETHER AFTER ETHNIC KILLING

ALL but one of the contributions discussed in this section address how well security dilemma theories of ethnic conflict resolution fit the empirical record, and offer possible limitations, modifications, or extensions to the theory based on their findings. The last (by James Fearon) addresses policy.

At one time I believed that separation of warring populations into defensible regions was a nearly sufficient condition for reducing inter-communal security dilemmas and suggested that so long as this was done, minor differences in governing arrangements between loose autonomy, *de facto* partition, and *de jure* partition would not matter much. Alexander Downes convinced me long ago that I was wrong: after communal wars, solutions short of partition—power-sharing, federalism, or regional autonomy—are usually politically unworkable within the damaged state because they do not satisfy the nationalist ambitions and security demands induced or intensified by the war, and are likely to relapse into more war.[19]

R. William Ayres tests nine hypotheses concerning ethnic conflict resolution against the records of 48 ethnic wars that ended between 1945 to 1996. Two of these are intended to address parts of the logic of the security dilemma theory. First, Ayres finds that "level of violent behavior" is associated with higher likelihood of separation outcomes.[20] Second, he finds that ethnic "stereotyping," presumably meant to capture the impact of hypernationalist mobilization rhetoric, is not related to the likelihood of separation outcomes.[21] Whether these findings should be construed as weak support for the theory, weak disconfirmation, or neither is not clear.

---

19. Downes, pp. 248, 265–67, 276–79, Cf. Kaufmann, "Possible and Impossible Solutions," pp. 161–62, versus "When All Else Fails," p. 123 fn. 7. Sovereign states also receive advantages in international law and practice that make them less vulnerable to future *revanchism*, further reducing future inter-communal security dilemmas.

20. Ayres, 6th, 7th, 10th unnumbered pages. Violent behavior is coding using Minorities at Risk (MAR)'s 0 to 7 scale for intensity of civil wars. Casualties, either absolute numbers or in relation to population, are only weakly associated.

21. Ayres, 8th, 9th, 13th unnumbered pages. N = 23 because of missing data. We are not told much about the coding rules for "stereotyping."

Paul Roe points out that the initial sources of ethnic conflict may often have less to do with structural security dilemmas than with hegemonic ambitions—in the Croatian-Serb conflict that began in 1991, these were the ambitions of Franjo Tudjman.[22] Roe points out, rightly, that my argument does not really cut in until the next two stages: escalation to full-scale communal war or ethnic cleansing, and barriers to de-escalation of such conflicts.[23]

David Carment and Dane Rowlands extract from my work three hypotheses for use in testing security dilemma theory against the record of 14 high-casualty communal conflicts that had been settled by 1995. They find that nine of the fourteen count against the security dilemma argument because they were settled without separation of the warring communities.[24] Five of these cases, however, are misinterpreted: they ended in the total or near-total victory of one side and suppression of the other, and so cannot be counted either for or against the security dilemma argument.[25] The other four are miscoded: the Croatian-Serb conflict was "settled" by wholesale ethnic cleansing. Croatian military offensives in Summer and Fall 1995 recaptured virtually all of the territory that Croatia had lost in 1991, driving out Serb inhabitants in the process. The "settlement" consisted of Serbian surrender of the tiny slice of Croatia (part of Eastern Slavonia) that it still held; most of the Serb inhabitants left. The Serb-Bosnian war ended after ethnic cleansing of most people on the 'wrong' sides of what became the Dayton lines. The conflicts between Bosnians and Croats and between the Chakma hill peoples and Bangladesh are both coded as "mostly settled." What is not noted is that in both cases the rival groups were largely separated at the start and became more so, conditions under which the security dilemma approach would expect resolution to be (relatively) easy.

Nicholas Sambanis attempts to evaluate the security dilemma argument against a set of 125 communal and other civil wars from 1945 to 1999. He finds support for the security dilemma argument on some points: ethnic wars are more likely than others to end in partition or secession, as are wars with

22. Roe converts this analysis into a sliding scale for the severity of security dilemmas and resultant escalatory pressures. "Which Security Dilemma?" pp. 280–313.
23. Roe, p. 313.
24. Carment and Rowlands, "Vengeance and Intervention," pp. 373–74, 379–83.
25. Tibetans vs. China, Kachins vs. Burma, Meos (Hmong) vs. Laos, Katangans vs. Congo, Biafrans vs. Nigeria.

higher death tolls (contra Ayres, above),[26] and partition (along with other factors) improves prospects for postwar democratization.[27]

Sambanis' most important claim, however, is that ethnic partition or secession has a positive effect on the recurrence of war within two years, instead of the negative effect that he thinks that security dilemma theory should expect.[28] His test design is wrong, however, because security dilemma theory predicts that partitions should reduce violence *only* when they separate populations in a manner that improves the physical security of both (or when the populations are already separated in a way that provides reasonable security from each other). Partitions without ethnic separation often intensify security dilemmas and increase violence.[29] Testing effects of partition without respect to separation is pointless.[30]

Sambanis also reports that "ethnic heterogeneity" (EHET) has a negative effect on war recurrence when it should, under security dilemma theory, have a positive one.[31] This may sound closer in flavor to the theory, but actually repeats the same error. The size of a rump minority matters only if it is so small that everyone understands that it cannot possibly compete for political power, whether by ballot, bullet, or any other means. Then there can be no

26. Sambanis, p. 456. Both variables are significant at the .01 level in three of three probit models.

27. Sambanis, pp. 459–64. The effect is significant at the .01 level in five of five OLS and 2SLS models. Sambanis suggests (p. 463) that performance may be worse in unrecognized *de facto* partitions. If true—and anecdotal evidence seems to support the suggestion—this would support Downes' claim about the value of sovereignty.

28. The coefficients are not significant in any of the eight models tested. Sambanis, pp. 466, 470.

29. Kaufmann, "Possible and Impossible Solutions," pp. 161–62.

30. Sambanis makes at least three coding errors that he counts against the security dilemma argument. The Kashmir insurgency that started in 1989 is counted as a partition case even though the partition occurred 41 years before; the Serbo-Croatian war is counted as two separate wars, dated "1991" and "1995" even though the 1991 war is coded as having restarted within two years; and the *de facto* partition of Iraq in 1991 is omitted. The overall impact is unclear since I did not search for miscodings that might have had the opposite impact.

31. Sambanis, pp. 467, 470. The effect is significant at the .05 level or better in three of six models. Sambanis says (p. 471 fn. 75) that the partition and heterogeneity variables do better at predicting war recurrence within 10 years, but does not report those models because of the large number of missing observations. The definition of EHET is Tatu Vanhanen's: the sum of the inverses of the population shares of the largest 1) racially defined, 2) linguistically or tribally defined, and 3) religiously-defined communities. Vanhanen, "Domestic Ethnic Conflict and Ethnic Nepotism: A Comparative Analysis," *Journal of Peace Research* vol. 36 no. 1 (January 1999), pp. 55–73 at 59. Vanhanen's measure has a weakness in that countries where rival communities are divided on only one or two of these dimensions will show only moderate EHET scores, but division on one or two dimensions can easily lead to hostility just as intense as division on all three. Vanhanen (p. 65) lists nine underpredicted outliers, seven of which have this property—Rwanda, Burundi, Croatia, Bosnia, Afghanistan, Somalia, and Guatemala (the others are Israel and Sudan).

security dilemma. But once over the threshold where both sides believe that the weaker side could threaten the stronger—even if the balance of power remains quite uneven—the logic of the security dilemma operates with full force, which means that population geography, physical geography, etc., may matter as much or more than further increases in the strength of the weaker group or in ethnic heterogeneity.[32]

Bosnia in 1992 ranked very high for ethnic heterogeneity, but in fact there was little fighting between Croatians and Muslims at any time between 1992 and 1995 except in the city of Mostar because elsewhere there were few places where they lived intermixed with each other. The heaviest fighting and most extensive ethnic cleansing took place in the (initially) mixed city of Sarajevo; in the Drina Valley, where Muslim towns sat astride the roads that the Serbs believed that they needed to organize their own defense; and, worst of all, in the North-Central "Posavina Corridor" that was roughly half Muslim at the start of the war—but also the only possible connection between the largest mostly Serb area in Bosnia, in the Northwest, and the main centers of Serb power in Eastern Bosnia and in Serbia itself. In contrast, the Muslim "Bihac Pocket" was left alone because it threatened no communication lines, was too far from the main centers of Muslim strength, and was the largest and most defensible of the isolated Muslim enclaves.

Carter Johnson study of the same partitions studied by Sambanis[33] shows that the findings reverse when communal partitions are stratified on the sizes of remaining minorities on the "wrong" sides of the new lines:[34]

---

32. If the strength of the potential warring sides approaches parity and relatively few of either community are vulnerable, mutual fears should decline if all sides can perceive that the likely outcome of any war would be stalemate. Equal strength with mutual vulnerability, however, may not prevent war because one or both sides may be unable to control ethnic cleansing by some of their own members who are focused on their local situations rather than on the overall balance. Comparable potential strength may not help either if one side perceives a window of opportunity, as in Bosnia.

33. Johnson, "Sovereignty or Demography? Reconsidering the Evidence on Partition in Ethnic Civil Wars" (2005). One of Sambanis' cases, Tajikistan, was excluded because the war was not over in 2004. One, Kosovo, was added because the de facto partition occurred in 1999, the year that Sambanis' dataset closed.

34. Johnson, pp. 25–32. PPEHI (Post Partition Ethnic Heterogeneity Index) $= \frac{(O - \max_{[N_1, N_2]})}{O} * 100$

Where: O = Original minority percentage. N_1, N_2 = minority percentages in new states. Despite its virtues, PPEHI is not an optimal indicator of what security dilemma theory might predict because it is a measure of *reduction* in sizes of rump minorities, not of the sizes of rump minorities in proportion to population. As it happens this makes a difference in only one case—Chechnya—which has a negative PPEHI score even though the Russian share of the population after 1996 was only 2.5%. Although the factors at work in this case are more complex than this one statistic, we could consider this reason to call Chechnya a "high separation"

Table 1
COMMUNAL SEPARATION AND RECURRENCE OF WAR

Category	Partition, populations highly separated (PPEHI > 95)	Partition, populations not fully separated (PPEHI < 65)	No partition
N	6[35]	12[36]	63
Recurrent war within 5 years	0	5	21
No recurrent war within 5 years	6	7	42
% recurrent war	0%	42%	33%

This result is not an artifact of careful placement of category thresholds. If we move the threshold down from "high" separation (the larger of the minorities in the two rump states averaging about 1% or less) to "moderate" separation (larger minority about 10% or less),[37] the findings become stronger:

These findings are as predicted by the security dilemma theory. It is true that this research design does not take account of population geography within rump states, but for this test it does not matter because none of the ten

---

case. Since there was recurrent war. Chechnya would then count against the security dilemma theory.

35. The *de facto* partition of Iraq in 1991 could be included, as could Yugoslavia-Slovenia 1991 and Indonesia-East Timor 2000. An argument could he made for excluding Algeria as a colonial case; Johnson's justification for including are presumably its legal incorporation into France or its unusually large settler population. Finally. Johnson includes the 1965 and 1989 Kashmir wars separately from the partition of India itself. This is justifiable, because, the terriory in dispute, underlying grievances, and proximate causes of the wars were all differences and the communal identities not identical to those in the main Indo-Pakistani dispute of 1947. On the same ground, he could also include the 1948 partition of Kashmir as a separate case from the 1947 partition of India.

36. The *de facto* partitions of Iraq in 1961 and in 1970 could be included, as could the *de* facto partition of Congo since 1997. If we made all eleven of the coding changes suggested in this and the two previous footnotes, we would add six right predictions for the theory while removing one (Algeria), add one wrong prediction (Kashmir 1948), shift one from right to wrong (Chechnya), while two (Kashmir 1965 and 1989—one right, one wrong) would be unaffected. The impact on Table 1a below would likely be identical, although I have not investigated all the relevant censuses.

37. The choice of this alternate threshold is not arbitrary; it happens that there are four cases clustered around this level with large gaps between these and the next cases either above or below.

Table 1a
COMMUNAL SEPARATION AND RECURRENCE OF WAR[38]

Category	Partition, populations mostly separated (PPEHI > 57)	Partition, populations not separated (PPEHI < 37)	No partition
N	10	8	63
Recurrent war within 5 years	0	5	21
No recurrent war within 5 years	10	3	42
% recurrent war	0%	63%	33%

"moderate" or "high" separation cases contained minorities strong enough to be perceived as even potentially threatening.[39]

James Fearon grants that partition and separation might reduce loss of life in certain conflicts, but argues that recognizing even a few partitions could generate many more secessionist movements worldwide; he says that "wholesale abandonment of this convention [no border changes by force] would move international affairs a step further in the direction of *sauve qui peut*."[40] Here Fearon raises a spectre that most would judge imaginary: a re-writing of international law and practice to read, more or less, "all secession-ists will receive approval and aid," something advocated by no one to my knowledge.[41]

Fearon's position are also mutually contradictory. Elsewhere he speculates oppositely "against the likelihood of significant transnational demonstration

38. For "good" partitions vs. "bad" partitions, Kendall's tau-b = −0.694, ASE = 0.137; 1-sided Fisher's exact test p = .007. For "good" partitions vs. non-partitions: tau-b = −0.253, ASE = 0.047; Fisher's exact test p = .025.

39. The four largest rump minorities were Israeli Arabs after 1948 (14%); Indian Muslims after 1948 (10%); Serbs in Kosovo after 1999 (6%); and Serbs in Croatia after 1995 (4.5%). Johnson, pp. 31–32. The first two of these communities were, and were understood to be, much weaker than their numbers might suggest because they were unorganized (both had lost most of their political elites to emigration) and lacking in economic, political, and military skills and resources.

40. Fearon, "Separatist Wars, Partition, and World Order," pp. 405,414.

41. Even if security dilemma-based logic comes to dominate international responses to communal conflict disasters secessionists will rarely receive active international aid or encour-agement in part because it will remain difficult to persuade first-world publics that the potential recipients deserve help—especially those that are easily demonized as the sorts of bandits or thugs that Fearon thinks dominate most secessionist movements. Kaufmann, "Intervention in Ethnic and Ideological Civil Wars," *Security Studies* vol. 6 no. 1 (Autumn 1996), pp 62–103 at 92–93.

effects of ethnic conflict."[42] In the present volume Fearon attempts to reconcile this contradiction by speculating further that "the prospect of international acceptance of ethnic partitions would have a fundamentally different effect than do the outcomes of actual rebellions."[43] This is illogical; both effects should point in the same direction for the same reasons, and Fearon offers no basis for estimating relative magnitudes.

There is no systematic data on contagion of ethnic secession movements.[44] Historical accounts of particular separatist rebellions since 1945, however, are remarkable for the rarity with which separatist elites refer to (or seem aware of) separatist movements by different communities against different states.[45] Further, the costs of secession attempts are usually very high and the odds of attracting international aid low, facts of which potential separatist elites and masses are usually aware.[46]

ESCALATION OF SCIENTIFIC DISPUTES (AND OF CIVIL WARS IN IRAQ)

David Laitin's organizes his contribution mainly as a competitive test of security dilemma theory against his own theory of civil wars. His theory, based on an individualist, materialist logic, is that opportunity, not fear, is the main driver of internal violence.[47] The main reason for the increase in civil

42. Fearon, "Commitment Problems and the Spread of Ethnic Conflict," in David Lake and Donald Rothchild, eds., *The International Spread of Ethnic Conflict* (Princeton: Princeton University Press, 1998), pp. 107–26.
43. "Separatist Wars," p. 408 fn. 28.
44. The most obvious evidence for demonstration effects might seem to be the large wave of state creation in the 1950s and 1960s, but what contagion there was occurred among European governments, not between potential rebel movements: there were many more decolonizations than colonies that experienced rebellions.
45. One instance where a community did pay close attention to a nearby ethnic war counts in the opposite direction. The lesson that Ibrahim Rugova, the dominant figure among Kosovar Albanians after an unofficial election in 1992, drew from Bosnia was that if Kosovars remained quiescent under Serb provocation and repression, they could expect that the international community would eventually come to their aid as it had the Bosniaks. Over several years these hopes were not realized, leading eventually to decline of Rugova's credibility and to the rise of the violently secessionist Kosovo Liberation Army by 1998. Richard Caplan, "International Diplomacy and the Crisis in Kosovo," International Affairs vol. 74 no. 4 (October 1998), pp. 745–61 at 751–54. See also Downes, p. 278, on how little international efforts to hold Bosnia together purchased in for estalling other conflicts.
46. Fearon argues (p. 407) that many secession movements are composed of gangsters who expect to profit even if the likelihood of gaining independence or autonomy is low. In fact the death rates of insurgent leaders are so high that it seems unlikely that this could be a frequent motive.
47. Laitin, "Ethnic Unmixing," p. 365; Fearon and Laitin, "Ethnicity, Insurgency, and Civil War," *American Political Science Review* vol. 97 no. 1 (February 2003), 75–90. For broad-ranging discussion of opportunity-driven or "economic" theories of political violence, see Sambanis,

wars since the 1950s is the rise of a particular technology and practice of "rural guerrilla warfare"[48] that "can be harnessed to various political agendas" from communism to Islamic fundamentalism to right-wing reaction to ethnic nationalism. There is little or nothing special about ethnic conflicts.

The main thing that Laitin says about the logic of security dilemma theory for deescalating or resolving conflicts is that he cannot understand it: "Kaufmann might offer as a conjecture [that] the process of fighting a war [and] separat[ing] the populations . . . . could have a pacifying effect on the country" but he finds it "intuitively perplexing" that population geography could have different effects during and after severe ethnic violence than it does in states that have not known civil war.[49]

What is so "perplexing" to Laitin? Laitin assumes causal invariance across the whole domain of civil wars. Security dilemma logic, however, poses three challenges to this assumption: the escalation dynamics of communal wars may be different from others; they may be fought differently than others; and, most important, their dynamics of de-escalation and resolution may be different from others.

OPPORTUNITY VERSUS SECURITY

More is at stake than ontologies of civil wars. Opportunity-based and security-based interpretations of internal conflicts imply different understandings of much of state and interstate politics over the last half-century. For Laitin, "the prevalence of internal war in the 1990s is the result of an accumulation of protracted conflicts since the 1950s" because decolonization "gave birth to a large number of financially, bureaucratically, and militarily weak states." It has little to do with either the Cold War or its end. Security dilemma theorists argue that two distinct waves of sudden imperial collapses—first European decolonization and then the collapses of the Soviet and Yugoslav empires—removed the prior guarantors of inter-communal order without provision for replacement. Ethnic and religious communities suddenly responsible for their own protection felt compelled to move either to capture the state or to defend themselves against it.

"Do Ethnic and Non-Ethnic Civil Wars Have the Same Causes? A Theoretical and Empirical Inquiry (Part 1)," *Journal of Conflict Resolution* vol. 45 no. 3 (June 2001), pp. 259–282; and Paul Collier and Anke Hoeffler, "Greed and Grievance in Civil War," World Bank Working Paper no. 2355 (2000).

48. The fall in price of automatic rifles and of land mines since the 1940s has certainly lowered the financial ante at least for the smallest rebellions. The overall impact of technological and social change on contests between governments and armed opponents is less clear.

49. Laitin, "Ethnic Unmixing and Civil War," p. 357.

The two theories also imply different futures. Laitin should expect continued high prevalence of internal conflict until and unless many Third World states make considerable advances in economic development and state capacity. Border changes or population movements, however, should be nearly irrelevant. A security dilemma model would expect peaks and valleys in communal conflict following (and sometimes precipitating) the ends of some of the world's remaining multi-national empires.[50]

COMMUNAL CONFLICT OUTCOMES

Laitin proposes two tests of security dilemma theory. The first concerns outcomes, and not the theory's main logic but its included contention that communal wars cause unmixing of populations. Laitin grants that war can cause substantial unmixing in the short term, but argues that the refugees often return later: "If civil wars and massacres make ethnic mixing unbearable, it is difficult to explain why members of formerly massacred groups would return to the scenes of the crimes.[51] Based on his readings of the outcomes of sixteen rebellions by eleven "non-concentrated" ethnic minority groups, he finds that ethnic unmixing (or not) played a role in only two of the outcomes.[52]

This is both theoretically and empirically misguided: first, *all* communal wars, even between relatively concentrated groups, cause ethnic unmixing. Recent examples include Bosnia, Croatia, Kosovo, Abkhazia, South Ossetia, Chechnya, Karabakh, Afghanistan, and Iraq.[53] Second, eleven of the

50. Candidates, though not of equal likelihood, include Iraq, Afghanistan, Russia, Georgia, Azerbaijan, all of the Central Asian states, Lebanon, Turkey, Iran, Pakistan, India, Myanmar, China, Indonesia, and many African states.
51. Laitin focuses (pp. 361–62) on the city of Colombo where, despite devastating anti-Tamil riots in 1983, by 2001 the Tamil proportion of the population had risen higher than before. This case is one where escape options were constrained (see fn. 9). The government had military control of nearly the whole country. Over time hundreds of thousands of Tamils were displaced from formerly mixed rural areas, most of whom could not escape either to Tamil-controlled regions or out of the country. Many moved to or near Colombo, into segregated neighborhoods that often amounted to semi-permanent refugee camps, where they were often subject to harassment or worse. Suzanne Goldenberg, "Tamils Fear Mob Violence At Funeral Of Sri Lanka's Slain Populist President," *Guardian*, May 6, 1993; Feizal Samath, "Refugees-Sri Lanka: Left to Fend for Themselves," *Inter-Press Service*, December 8, 1998.
52. Laitin, p. 358–59. Laitin wonders (p. 357) whether my argument implies that resolution of wars between already well-separated communities requires yet further unmixing. The answer is: not if the sides are already relatively secure from each other, as Finland and the Soviet Union in 1918, Serbia and Slovenia in 1991, Georgia and Abkhazia in 1992–93, the Bangladesh hill peoples in 1997, or Somaliland and the rest of Somalia today.
53. As does nearly all communal conflict, even at levels short of war. Between 1891 and 1931 the proportion of Cypriot villages that were ethnically mixed declined from 43% to 36%; then, after the 1931 riots, to 18% by independence in 1960 and to 8% by 1970, by which time most of the remaining "mixed" villages were sharply segregated into ethnically homogeneous

fourteen "non-concentrated" cases that Laitin proposes to count against security dilemma theory are miscoded. Six—the civil war in Palestine in 1947–48, the rioting in Bengal in 1946–47 (there was no war), the Lebanese civil war from 1975 onward (counted twice),[54] the Hutu capture of Rwanda in 1959, and the Tutsi re-capture in 1994—did cause large refugee movements out of those countries (of Arabs, Hindus, Christians, Tutsis, and Hutus respectively). Five cases—the "Malayan Emergency" of 1948–1960, the first Hmong rebellion in Laos, black Africans against South Africa in the 1970s, the Hindu rebellion against Pakistan/Bangladesh in 1970–71,[55] and the Hutu insurgency against Rwanda in 1998 all ended in decisive government victories.[56]

Johnson's study on recurrence of communal war by size of remaining minorities is a better way to address these issues.

ONSETS OF COMMUNAL WARS

Since Laitin's theory is concerned with onset and says nothing about resolution, while security dilemma theory is concerned principally with resolution, the two are not fully comparable. As discussed above, the transformative effects of large-scale violence mean that there can be no necessary connection between explanations of the beginnings of communal wars and explanations of their ends.[57] Nevertheless, there is something at stake here because we want not only to resolve ongoing communal conflicts but also to predict and, perhaps, prevent some wars. The security dilemma, as theory of escalation, should be of use in understanding onset given certain minimum conditions—substantial prior levels of inter-group suspicion as well as of communal mobilization, and

---

parts. Richard Patrick, *Political Geography and the Cyprus conflict.* Waterloo, Ontario: University of Waterloo, (1976), pp. 8, **XX?**.

54. Once each for Palestinians and for (native) Lebanese Sunnis. Considerable communal unmixing occurred despite the re-imposition of order by Syrian occupation from 1976 onward. Absent the intervention there would have been more.

55. More or less simultaneous with the much larger Bengali rebellion against Pakistan.

56. A twelfth case—the second Hmong rebellion—is listed as ongoing, which, as Laitin explains his design, should be reason for not including it.

57. Regardless of what motives initially instigated violence, the dynamics of war produce security dilemmas and hardening of identities that constrain possible routes of de-escalation or resolution; solutions to ethnic wars do not depend on their causes. Thus, even if we found that security dilemma theory performed indifferently at predicting onsets, this would not necessarily undermine its usefulness as a theory of ethnic conflict resolution—providing that the findings did not somehow destroy the core logic of the security dilemma entirely, e.g. by showing that inter-communal security dilemmas do not exist at all, or do not vary. It should be noted, however, that Posen's original formulation of the impact of security dilemmas on ethnic conflict was concerned with explain the reason for large-scale communal violence in certain countries but not others.

both sides' possession of capacity (or perceived capacity) to threaten the other. Unfortunately Laitin's proposed tests ignore these domain limitations, rendering his findings invalid.

Laitin asks whether "dispersed" or "concentrated" communities are more likely to become involved in ethnic violence. Above the thresholds where security dilemma logic is activated, the intensity of security dilemmas should predict something about likelihood of further and intermixed population geography should produce more intense security dilemmas than would separation. Opportunity-based logics, however, favor groups with secure regional bases.[58]

Laitin surveys 268 cases from the Minorities at Risk III (MAR) dataset and finds that 44% of regionally concentrated minorities (MAR GROUPCON values of 2 or 3)[59] became involved in at least a moderate level of violence between 1945 and 1998,[60] compared to only 12% of minorities that were thinly dispersed, primarily urban, communities, or a minority in one region (MAR GROUPCON 0 or 1).[61]

This test, however, is not valid, because of three theoretical errors. The first is that to neglect that the security dilemma is a theory of *escalation* (and de-escalation), not of the initial sources of disputes. The minimum criterion for its operation is a level of inter-group suspicion high enough that individuals can plausibly imagine being attacked by members of the other group—e.g., because of previous conflict history, or rhetoric within the other community that calls for violence either explicitly or implicitly, or because of some actual violence.[62]

MAR's coding rules for groups "at risk," however, are much broader than this, including groups that were (1) discriminated against: or (2) disadvantaged because of past discrimination; or (3) an "advantaged minority" being challenged by others: or (4) if there existed an identifiable organization pressing for greater rights or autonomy for the group.[63], pp. 3–4, 7. It is probable that

58. Fearon and Laitin, "A Cross-Sectional Study of Large-Scale Ethnic Violence in the Postwar Period" (1997), p. 33.

59. Ted Robert Gurr, dir., *Minorities at Risk Phase III User's Manual* (College Park: University of Maryland, 1996), pp. 9–11, 88, C8–C9.

60. A maximum rebellion score of 4 or more ("small-scale guerrilla activity"). Laitin, p. 353. MAR III covers 1945–1995, but Laitin adds conflict data through 1998.

61. Similar findings based on essentially the same test design were reported in Monica Toft, *The Geography of Ethnic Violence: Identity, Interests, and the Indivisibility of Territory* (Princeton: Princeton University Press, 2003).

62. For the same reason, it is not clear what relationship we should expect between intermixed settlement patterns and war initiation. Given inter-communal hostility, intermixed settlement produces severe security dilemmas—but there may be few well-integrated societies that experience dangerous inter-communal tension at all, since integration itself is very often a result of people's confidence that communal conflict is unlikely.

63. Gurr, *MAR III* User's Manual

MAR III includes many cases in which expressions of inter-communal conflict over the whole 50-year period were so mild that they cannot be construed as sufficiently threatening to activate the logic of the security dilemma. We could attempt to capture this by excluding cases that did not experience any deadly violence at any time between 1945 and 1998,[64] 68 in all.[65]

Laitin's second error is to forget that security dilemmas require mutual threat. If one group is so small or so weak that no matter what its members' grievances it could not improve its situation by war, there is no security dilemma, escalation driven by fear cannot occur, and population settlement patterns do not matter.

This matters most in two categories of cases: urban and nomadic groups. A community settled mainly in cities, without rural presence over any significant land area, normally has virtually no potential for military mobilization, and so is usually absolutely insecure while the surrounding majority is absolutely secure from the city dwellers.[66] Laitin, however, misreads security dilemma theory to predict that communities such as the Turks in Germany and Indians in Malaysia, and indians in South Africa should be among those most frightening to dominant groups in their countries. This reverses his predictions in 28 cases.

In addition, some "dispersed" groups are incapable of posing a threat to the nations among whom they live. The most obvious are the Roma in thirteen different European countries. The Roma are few (ranging from less than 1% to a maximum of 9% in Slovakia), very poor, partly nomadic, and lack cohesive organizations that could serve as bases for military mobilization. Laitin, however, includes the Roma among those whom he says security dilemma theory should most expect to rebel, reversing his predictions in 13 more cases.

Urban and nomadic communities are not the only ones in MAR III that are so weak as to be both absolutely insecure and offensively incapable,[67] but trying to count all incapable communities would require case-by-case judgments that

64. A REBEL level of 0 and a COMCON (communal conflict) level of 2 or less for all years. Gurr, MAR III *User's Manual*, p. 87. At first glance this may appear circular, since one of indicators used for the dependent variable would also be used as a control variable, but it is not. Because the security dilemma is a theory of escalation, not of the initial sources of conflict, it seeks to predict changes in levels of conflict *within a certain range*. Levels below that range are outside the domain of the theory.

65. A better operationalization of the minimum at which suspicions of possible attack might become plausible would be attempts by any side to organize communally-based armed forces. But MAR III does not contain this information.

66. Laitin, p. 352, observes, rightly, that a rural base area is nearly a necessary condition for any insurgency, ethnic or otherwise. The base need not be inside the disputed region, however: e.g., RPF operations from Uganda in 1990–1994.

67. Among communities coded "dispersed," some that would seem to fall below the lowest possible threshold for activation of a security dilemma include the Hui in China; Germans in Kazakhstan; Blacks in Costa Rica, Colombia, and the United States; Hawaiians and Native

would not be reliable across a judges. The 68 non-violent cases and the 41 in the urban and nomadic categories have the advantage that we can easily locate their boundaries as well as explain clearly why they fall outside the domain of the security dilemma. There is, however, some overlap between the 68 non-violent cases and the (at least) 41 incapable ones.

Laitin's third error is that a simple dichotomy between "dispersed" (GROUPCON 0 or 1) and "concentrated" (2 or 3) settlement patterns is too coarse to capture the logic of the security dilemma. Geography, including population geography, generates security dilemmas when and to the extent that particular people live in places where they appear both vulnerable and threatening. At the extreme where two communities live in every alternate house, if for some reason they come to fear one another everyone in the country will face an intense security dilemma;[68] at the other extreme where all groups live in purely homogenous cantons with mountains separating them, even intense disputes cannot generate much of a security dilemma for anyone.[69]

In almost all real countries, however, settlement patterns much more complex than a simple scale from most integrated to most regionalized. If most or nearly all of one community live in a well-defined region, but members of a rival group also live within that region, then the intensity of the security dilemma will depend on the number of the second group within the region, the vulnerability of their settlements as well as their locations in relation to sites with mobilization potential, transportation infrastructure, and strategic terrain, and the amount of military strength that the second group could potentially generate outside this region. As Kosovo demonstrated, even a 10 percent minority can threaten a 90 percent majority if it has powerful support from outside the province—and, if its settlements are scattered across much of the province, can also remain fearful of the majority group even with such support. In Iraq in 2003, Kurds, Sunni Arabs, and Shia each constituted nearly all the population of certain regions, but the presence of mixed belts between them generated strong security dilemmas in the mixed areas.

If one community lives mainly in a number of enclaves some of which are separated by regions dominated by a rival community, the security dilemma is likely to be severe. It will vary, however, based on how valuable the isolated enclaves are and how vulnerable they are, as well as on how vulnerable are settlements of the rival group that stand in the way of linking the isolated

---

Americans in the United States; and the indigenous peoples/aborigines in Taiwan, Australia, Canada, and Argentina. More could surely be found among groups coded "concentrated."

68. The situations of the main communities in Rwanda at the start of 1994 approached this extreme.

69. The situations of the main communities in Switzerland approach this extreme.

enclaves. Almost all of Israeli strategy in the civil war of 1947–48 was aimed at capturing those Arab towns that stood on or commanded the roads that could link the main Jewish enclave around Tel Aviv and Haifa with the two main isolated enclaves—West Jerusalem and the Huleh Valley in Eastern Galilee.[70] This was also the main problem facing all sides in Punjab in 1947, in Nagorno-Karabakh in 1991–1994, dates? and in Bosnia in 1992. All of the communities mentioned in these examples could be considered "concentrated" or "largely concentrated" in MAR's coding scale.

Thus Laitin's simple division on GROUPCON values does not capture very much about the predictions of security dilemma theory. Part of the problem, as the Palestine example illustrates, is that neither MAR III nor any existing large-N dataset captures the complexities of population geography, other elements of geography, or any of the other variables (technology, prior conflict history. etc.) that affect the intensity of inter-communal security dilemmas.[71] Laitin recognizes this problem, and makes a start at addressing it by recoding GROUPCON into six categories rather than four, but then discards the information gained. For purposes of testing he still divides at the original boundary between GROUPCON values of 0 or 1 versus values of 2 or 3.[72]

Laitin's effort thus leaves us with two conclusions: first, for now our only appropriate method for testing security dilemma theory may be comparative case studies that can capture variables that existing large-N datasets do not.[73]

---

70. To the extent that there were coherent Arab strategies, they were driven by the same logic. The Arab Liberation Army sought to capture settlements that would separate the Hulch from other Jewish areas while the Jordanian Arab Legion sought to reduce Jewish Jerusalem and nearby smaller settlements as well as bar Israeli advances from the direction of Tel Aviv. Success would have protected many Arab and mixed settlements that the Israelis ultimately overran, as well as potentially contributing to the chances of capturing all of Palestine.

71. MAR III is also missing at least 80 cases of potential interest. First, 47 groups that were included in MAR I (1993) were dropped from MAR III on the grounds that by 1995 they were no longer "at risk," although some of these had been involved in communal civil wars between 1945 and 1985. Second, a number of communities that certainly met one or more of the four "at risk" criteria in 1995 are nevertheless missing. A back-of-the-envelope count identifies at least 33: Okinawans in Japan; Kazakhs, Mongols, Dai, Lolo, Miao, and Zhuang in China; Dayaks in Indonesia; Tajiks and Karakalpaks in Uzbekistan; Uzbeks in Kyrgyzistan; Uzbeks and Badakshanis in Tajikistan; Adyge, Cherkassians, Kabardins, North Ossetians, Dargins, Kalmyks, Bashkirs, and Chinese in Russia; Armenians in Georgia; Romanians in Ukraine; Sunnis (advantaged minority) and Shi'ites in Bahrain; Turkmen in Iraq; Kurds in Syria; Alawites in Turkey; Orthodox Christians in Lebanon; Druze in Israel; Turks in Cyprus; Flemings in Belgium; Welsh in Britain; and blacks in Cuba. As with the 268 cases that are included, many of these 80 do not meet the minimum suspicion or minimum capability thresholds to be possible candidates for involvement in inter-communal conflict—although some have been involved in large scale communal wars. The overall impact on an attempt to replicate Laitin's claims would be hard to guess.

72. Laitin, pp. 352–55 and table p. 353.

73. Construction of usable large-N datasets is probably possible, but will require greatly simplified yet still reasonably faithful specificatins of certain complex variables. Neither I nor

Second, to the extent that MAR III data might be able to shed light on the validity of security dilemma theory. Laitin's test design is not based on valid use of that data.[74]

EXPLAINING IRAQ

Another at least equally important question to ask of competing theories is to ask how well they fit new facts that had not yet occurred when the theories were formulated. This points us to current communal conflicts, of which the ones of most interest today are in Iraq.

The first question that we can ask of both theories is what would have been their *ex ante* predictions about the odds that regime change in April 2003 would spark communal civil wars. Although Laitin's main concern is civil war onset, his and James Fearon's model, explained in their 2003 "Ethnicity, Insurgency, and Civil War," would have expected little chance that Hussein's overthrow would lead to communal war.

The logic of the theory is based mainly on opportunity: conditions that favor insurgents' ability to survive and prosper, such as mountains or other difficult terrain, an unstable or resource-poor state, and easily cashable resources in insurgent-controlled territory.[75] External economic or military aid also plays an important role: outside aid can enable insurgents, while aid to the state should "increase the relative advantage of government forces against potential insurgents and thus associate with lower rates of civil war onset."[76] Popular grievances and communal identities play little role.[77]

---

other proponents of security dilemma theory nor opponents have yet done this. It will also, of course, require more resources.

74. Laitin makes a fourth theoretical error of uncertain impact given the others. His dependent variable, which he does not justify, is whether the maximum REBELxx value in each case ever reached 4 ("small scale guerrilla activity") or higher. One strength of security dilemma theory is that it can predict which conflicts are most likely to escalate all the way to the most extreme violence—in MAR terms, REBELxx = 7 ("protracted civil war") or COMCONxx = 6 ("protracted communal conflict"). Gurr, MAR III *User's Manual*, pp. C14–C16. Cases in which the rival populations are well-protected from each other by physical separation and perhaps other factors should be, even given some violence, relatively unlikely to escalate to the most intense possible violence. Thus, if Laitin had used a more appropriate dependent variable he might have been forced to reverse his predictions in yet another category of cases. But investigating this would require another substantial paper.

75. poverty is said to favor insurgencies in three ways—by limiting other options for young men, and by reducing the state's revenues and internal discipline. Larger total populations make it harder for the center to monitor potential rebels, and oil exporters are likely to have relatively weak state institutions because they have little need to tax. "Ethnicity, Insurgency, and Civil War," pp. 80–81.

76. "Ethnicity, Insurgency, and Civil War," pp. 80, 81, 86.

77. Variables tested and found not significant include language and religious discrimination, ethnic and religious fractionalization, income inequality, economic growth rate, Islam, the

Laitin and Fearon present three logit models of civil war onset worldwide from 1945 to 1999, two predicting "civil war" and one "ethnic war." The independent variables in all three include "percent mountainous," "noncontiguous state," "oil exporter," "ethnic fractionalization," "religious fractionalization," "prior war," "population," "new state," "instability," "per capita income," and "democracy;" the last five of these are lagged one year.[78] One model seeks to capture the logic of Jack Snyder and Karen Ballentine's idea that states in transition from autocracy to democracy might be especially vulnerable;[79] this model includes a variable called "anocracy" (an intermediate degree of political freedom), and codes "democracy" differently.[80] The same variables are significant in all three models (see Table 3 below), meaning that the determinants of civil wars generally and of the subclass of ethnic civil wars are the same.[81]

With the exceptions of democracy and anocracy, coding the variables for Iraq for 2002–2005 presents few problems.[82] Democracy is harder because the Polity project codes Iraq as "missing" for 2003–2004 due to the presence of foreign troops.[83] Presumably Fearon and Laitin could argue that

Middle East as a region, the number of males aged 15 to 24, or the proportion of males in secondary school. Fearon and Laitin, "Additional Tables for 'Ethnicity, Insurgency, and Civil War'," (February 2003).

78. "Prior war" means whether the state was already engaged in a civil war. "New state" covers a state's first two years. "Instability" is coded as a change of 3 or more in Polity IV score in any year of the previous three; and "democracy" is the state's Polity IV score, ranging from −10 (most autocratic) to +10 (most democratic). GDP per capita is in PPP, mainly from Penn World Tables 5.6, with some country years, including Iraq 1988–1991, imputed from other sources. Fearon says that on reconsideration the 1988–1991 figures appear high; I agree. "Ethnicity Insurgency and Civil War," pp. 81, 84, 85; "Additional Tables," pp. 1–3; "APSR 2003 replication data," apsr03redata.zip, http://www.stanford.edu/~ifearon/Fearon 2003; Fearon personal communications, January 4, 6, 2006.

79. Snyder and Ballentine, Nationalism and the Marketplace of Ideas," *International Security* vol. 21 no. 2 (Fall 1996), pp. 5–40.

80. "Anocracy" is coded as a Polity score of −5 to +5, while "democracy" is dichotomous: a positive Polity score. "Ethnicity, Insurgency, and Civil War," pp. 81, 84.

81. Sambanis found oppositely that ethnic heterogeneity is a significant predictor of onset of ethnic wars but not of other civil wars, and that per capita income—which plays a large role in Fearon and Laitin's theory—is a significant predictor of non-ethnic civil wars but not of ethnic ones. Sambanis, "Do Ethnic and Non-Ethnic Civil Wars Have the Same Causes?" pp. 273–74, 278. Vanhanen, "Domestic Ethnic Conflict," pp. 65–66. found that ethnic heterogeneity accounted for 54% of variance in ethnic violence, while democratization, the inverse of GDP, and Human Development Index scores accounted for 8%, 9%, and 17% respectively.

82. Income estimates for 1999–2004 are from the CIA World Factbook at www.cia.gov/cia/publications/factbook and www.indexmundi.com, and population estimates are from Unstats.org, unstats.un/unsd/snaama. The U.S. CPI deflator series was obtained from the International Monetary Fund, http://imfstatistics.org/imf/. The remaining eight variables are coded from Fearon and Laitin's replication data. I assumed that ethnic fractionalization, religious fractionalization, which are coded as unchanged from 1945 to 1999, remained so through 2005.

83. http://bsos.umd.edu/cidcm/polity.

Table 1a
FREEDOM HOUSE RATINGS AND ESTIMATED POLITY SCORES FOR IRAQ,
2002–2005[86]

	FH "political rights"	FH "civil liberties"	Polity (estimated)
2002	7	7	−9.5
2003	7	7	−9.5
2004	7	5	−6
2005	7	5	−6

given this missing data their model should not be expected to predict any-thing about Iraq after 2002, but there is limited value to a theory that can say nothing about a case that scholars and policy makers care about very much.[84]

Fortunately, Freedom House, the other highly respected source of rat-ings of political freedom worldwide, does code Iraq for 2003–2005—and it turns out that that Freedom House ratings and Polity scores are so closely correlated that the latter can be estimated from the former.[85]

The following table replicates all three of Fearon and Laitin's civil war models for Iraq in 2003.[87] Lagged variables The "ethnic war" model vields a predicted probably of ethnic war onset that year of about $2\frac{1}{2}\%$. The two "civil war" models yield probabilities of about $2\frac{1}{2}\%$ and 4%.[88]

---

84. Fearon and Laitin say that they treat "foreign occupation years" as missing, but inter-polate values for "transition period years" from Freedom House (pp. 79 n. 11, 81 n. 18). This standard would make Iraq missing for 2003 but not for 2004 or 2005. Actually the data is coded so unevenly that it is difficult to tell whether any standard was used: None of the Eastern European countries occupied by the Soviet Union are counted as occupied, nor is Austria, nor Afghanistan from 1978 to 1989, nor Panama in 1989, nor Congo from 1997 to 1999. On the other hand Fearon and Laitin count South Vietnam (in 1954 only), Hungary in 1956, Uganda in 1979, Cambodia from 1979 to 1987, and Kuwait in 1990. APSR 2003 replication data.

85. Polity $= 13.60 - 2.73$ FHpol $- .50$ FHciv which accounts for 83% of the variance over the 4.640 cases for which data exists on both. Bruce E. Moon, Can Iraq Democratize? How Long Will it Take?" (manuscript, 2006), appendix 3.

86. http://www.freedomhouse.org/.

87. For logit coefficients and significance levels see Fearon and Laitin. "Ethnicity, Insurgency, and Civil War," p. 84; APSR 2003 replication data.

88. Chaim Kaufmann, "Fearon and Laitin Civil War Models Iraq Replication Worksheet," http://www.lehigh.edu~ininr/faculty/ kaufmann.htm

Table 1a
PREDICTED LIKELIHOOD OF CIVIL WAR ONSET IN IRAQ IN 2003

Model→ Independent Variables *(lagged variables)*	#1: "Civil War"		#2: "Ethnic War"		#3: "Anocracy" → "Civil War"	
	Coefficient	Iraq 2003	Coefficient	Iraq 2003	Coefficient	Iraq 2003
Prior war	−0.954**	0	−0.849**	0	−0.916**	0
Per capita income $000s	−0.344**	−0.826	−0.379**	−0.909	−0.318**	−0.763
Log (1,000s population)	0.263**	2.678	0.389**	3.963	0.272**	2.771
Log(% mountainous)	0.219**	0.426	0.120	0.234	0.199*	0.387
Non-contiguous state	0.443	0	0.481	0	0.426	0
Oil exporter	0.858**	0.858	0.809*	0.809	0.751**	0.751
New state (L)[89]	1.709**	0	1.777**	0	1.658**	0
Instability (L)	0.618**	0	0.385	0	0.513*	0
Democracy (Polity IV)	0.021	−0.200	0.013	−0.124		
Ethnic fractionalization	0.166	0.060	0.146	0.053	0.164	0.059
Religious fractionalization	0.285	0.140	1.533*	0.754	0.326	0.160
Anocracy (Polity −5 to +5)					0.521*	0
Democracny (dichotomous)					0.127	0
Constant	−6.371**	−6.371	−8.450**	−8.450	−7.019**	−7.019
LOGIT		−3.23	−3.67			−3.65
Approximate likelihood		3.8%		2.5%		2.5%

The logit models omit a factor that Fearon and Laitin describe as one of the most important in their theory—external aid to one or both sides.[90] If the model were to take into account the vast disproportion between Coalition aid available to the Iraqi government in 2003 and the relatively tiny *jihadist* contribution that Sunni rebels could expect, the predicted probabilities of rebellion would be lower.[91]

---

89. Iraq does not qualify as a new state, which Fearon and Laitin define as "a newly independent state that loses the coereive backing from a former imperial power (p. 85)." The opposite happened: the Iraqi government gained the military backing of a strong outside power. Of the U.S.-enforced regime changes in Panama in 1989 and in Haiti in 1994, and the conquests of Uganda by Tanzania in 1979. Afghanistan by the Taliban in 1995–96, and Zaire/Congo by a Rwandan-led coalition in 1997, none are counted by Fearon and Laitin as new states.

90. "Ethnicity, Insurngency, and Civil War," pp. 80–81, 86.

91. Fearon and Laitin argue (2003, p. 86; 2005, p. 10) that they could not find adequate *ex ante* measures of the availability of aid, but such an argument cannot hold water for Iraq: even in April 2003, all observers could already see how wildly disproportionate would be the external help available to the sides.

Recently Fearon and Laitin published on the web a retrospective look at the performance of their model in predicting Iraqi civil wars.[92] This survey covers only 1945 to 1992, but nevertheless includes several observations of interest:

1) Fearon and Laitin grant that their model in "Ethnicity, Insurgency, and Civil War" greatly underpredicts ethnic wars in Iraq. The model predicts .60 civil wars over 47 years, compared to an actual six (five ethnic). They also grant that nearly every war onset is miscoded.[93] In addition, five of the six onsets occurred in years when the predicted probability of civil war was lower than a year or two earlier.[94]

2) Mountainous terrain seems to play a larger role than estimated in the model. Although most of Iraq is flat, four of the six rebellions began in the mountainous north. This is a result that would be expected by both rational choice theory (greater opportunity) and by security dilemma theory (a minimal level of opportunity plus a wide band of mixed settlement on the plains between the mountains and Baghdad).[95]

3) As originally theorized, availability of external aid seems to make a large difference, although Fearon and Laitin still see no way to test for the impact of this factor.[96]

Fearon and Laitin could defend their theory's record by pointing out that it did at least recognize 2003 as a relatively dangerous year, with a predicted probability of rebellion of 3.8% (for Model 1) compared to an average of about 1.3% per year for 1946 to 1992. This would be misleading, however, since about three-fourths of this difference is accounted for by the decline in Iraqi GDP per capita under economic sanctions, from an average of $4,256 during 1945–1991 to $2,400 in 2003.[97] Controlling for the sanctions would lower the logit by 0.64 and the predicted likelihood of war onset in 2003 from 3.8% to 2.0%. Income fluctuations so dominate the model that the predicted

92. Fearon and Laitin, "Iraq: Random Narrative" (undated; 2005?). http://www.stanford.edu/group/ethnic/Random%20Narratives/ IraqRN1.2.pdf.
93. Originally they counted two: the 1959 Shammar incident and a 1961–1974 Kurdish rebellion. Their revised count totals five: they drop Shammar, but count the 1963 overthrow of the Qasim regime (non-ethnic), the 1945–46, 1961–70, and 1974–75 Kurdish rebellions, and the 1991 Shia rebellion. "Iraq," pp. 1, 3–8. Unaccountably, they do not include the 1980–88 Kurdish rebellion, which is conventionally estimated to have cost 150,000 lives in its last year alone. David McDowell, *A Modern History of the Kurds* (New York: St Martin's Press, 1996), p.'359. This makes six. CHECK > 100 Iraqi government losses.
94. One war started in 1945, the first year studied. "Iraq," pp. 1, 8, 18.
95. *Ibid.*, pp. 8–9.
96. *Ibid.*, pp. 10–11.
97. **GET COMPLETE CIA DATA AND RE-ESTIMATE.**

likelihoods of civil war onset are virtually identical for 2000, 2001, 2002 and 2003 under all three models.[98]

Opportunity-based theory, at least in Fearon and Laitin's formulation, seems unable to cope with the possibility that the likelihood of communal civil war can go from near-zero to near-certain in a very short time. Security dilemma theory, however, predicts exactly this when authority in a multiethnic state either collapses or becomes captured by one community. Each community must mobilize for its own defense; depending on population geography, other geography, and past conflict history, the only feasible defense may be attack, including ethnic cleansing.[99]

Iraq was a multinational empire ruled by its third largest community, who suddenly lost control of all state organs. The Sunni-controlled regime had employed extreme repression against both Kurds and Shia, and had fought wars with both as recently as 1991. Both Kurds and Shia nursed atrocity grievances, including massacres and forced relocations. Although all three groups had regional bases, they were also settled intermixed with each other in two wide belts in the north and in the center. Both belts contained mixed cities of high economic and strategic value—Kirkuk and Baghdad. The physical geography of both mixed regions favored offense—mainly flat terrain with good infrastructure. All three communities had ample access to

---

98. "Fearon and Laitin Civil War Models Replication Worksheet." Estimates for 1993–1999, when the economic pain was worse, would be higher. The predicted likelihoods for 2004 and 2005 (if we assume that war had not broken out already) are slightly higher; see below.

99. Posen, "Security Dilemma and Ethnic Conflict." Many observers of Iraq did predict that regime change would lead to communal war based on this logic: "Outside experts say the nightmare chain of events will be that the Ba'ath Party will collapse quickly and completely and Iraq will tumble into civil war, with its deep divisions between the Kurds, Arabs, Sunni Muslims and Shi'ite Muslims." Ian Fisher, "Experts See High Risk of Strife In Iraq if Hussein Is Deposed," *New York Times*, March 1 2003. Peter Galbraith, an expert on Iraqi Kurdistan, argued in December 2002 that the idea of a "democratic and unified Iraq" was a dangerous contradiction. "The breakup of a country is a terrible thing, but it can be even worse to try to hold them together." Quoted in Hugh Pope and David S. Cloud. "After Hussein: Ethnic, Religious, Political Rifts Test U.S. Hopes for a Stable Iraq," *Wall Street Journal*, December 11, 2002. Iraqi exiles, international aid experts, and CENTCOM, the U.S. military command responsible for planning the invasion, all warned that regime change would be followed by widespread violence, while the Saudi government warned that deposing Hussein could break up Iraq. Joel Brinkley and Eric Schmitt, "Iraqi Leaders Say U.S. Was Warned of Disorder after Hussein, but Little was Done," *New York Times*, November 30, 2003; Anthony Shadid, "War's Aftermath Now Arabs' Focus; Most See Conflict as Inevitable," *Washington Post*, February 21, 2003. As far back as 1991 Dick Cheney foresaw that "Once you've got Baghdad, it's not clear what you do with it. Is it going to be a Shi'ite regime, a Sunni regime, or a Kurdish regime? How much credibility is that government going to have if it's set up by the U.S. military when it's there? How long does the military have to stay, and what happens once we leave?" Doug Saunders, "Iraq and a Hard Case," *Globe and Mail* (Toronto), February 15, 2003.

weapons.[100] Of the two communities that were the main instigators of communal violence, the Kurds did not have to take on United States forces, and Sunni rebels were not deterred.

The second main question about Iraq that we can ask of the two theories is who should have been expected to rebel and why. An opportunity based-theory would have expected almost the opposite of what happened; the Kurdish and Shia communities should have been the most likely to generate rebels.

The Kurds had mountains, high confidence in external aid from the United States, and a chance to gain control of about 20% of Iraq's oil.[101] Further, opportunity based-logic should expect that disputes over valuable prizes would produce at least some fighting between factions drawn from the same community. The two main Kurdish factions, Massoud Barzani's Kurdish Democratic Party (KDP) and Jalal Talabani's Patriotic Union of Kurdistan, who have a long history of rivalry, and occasional combat, should have been good bets to fight over the oil riches around Kirkuk. This has not happened. Although the KDP and PUK remain rivals in Kurdistan, they have been careful always to present a solid front to the Sunnis and Shia.[102] Arguably this case could be counted as a partly right call for Fearon and Laitin: although the Kurds have stuck together, they could be considered *de facto* rebels in that the Shia eventually found (by early 2005) that they had to make immense constitutional concessions to keep the Kurdish parties in the government and in Iraq.

Shia factions wishing to rebel would have the advantages of difficult terrain (marshes), high confidence in external aid from Iran (for certain factions), and hope of capturing—or at least holding hostage—roughly 80% of the country's oil, the most lucrative and easily cashable resource available to any side.[103] Since communal grievances should matter little, and the Shia were already divided among themselves,[104] rebel entrepreneurs would have every incentive and excellent opportunities to split the community further. Such oil-based rebellions should have been likely even if other Shia controlled the

---

100. And would have even if the U.S. had not disbanded the Iraqi Army. The Kurds and Sunnis were already very well armed, and Shia not only made up much of the army but certain factions also had large militias already trained and equipped in Iran.

101. Although exporting it in the face of the hostility of other communities would be (and has proved) difficult.

102. "Kurds' Disconnect Bigger than Phones," *Al-Mendhar* (November 11, 2005). The KDP and PUK, both secular-oriented, did use violence against much smaller religious parties competing in the December 2005 elections. Jonathan Finer, "For Kurds, a Surge of Violence in Campaign," *Washington Post*, December 14, 2005.

103. A faction that controlled the extreme south of Iraq would not face the same export difficulties that the Kurds do.

104. The major factions, leaders, and their histories and interactions are profiled in Sammy Salerno, Kathleen Thompson, and Jennifer Chalmers, "In Post-War Iraq, Placating the Shi'a is Paramount" (Center for Non-proliferation Studies, January 30, 2004).

central government. It would, of course, make a big difference which Shia or other faction(s) the United States was expected to support—if any in such a confused situation. Even if a strong U.S. presence deterred such adventures initially, they should have come sooner or later.

The one community that should not have been likely to generate rebels were the Sunni Arabs, who did not control either good defensive terrain nor cashable resources,[105] and could expect only the smallest trickle of foreign support. Foreign fighters assisting the insurgency as of November 2005 were estimated at between 700 and 2,000, between 3% and 10% of active rebels.[106] Any Sunni rebellion would also have to face the power that the United States could deploy both directly and indirectly.[107] Between April 2003 and November 2005 the U.S. and allied foreign powers built up Iraqi government forces from 8,000 to 214,000 toward a target of 270,000, have supported the government with 160,000 to 180,000 foreign troops armed on a scale vastly superior to the insurgents, and have provided several tens of billions of dollars in budgetary, reconstruction, and other aid.[108]

Security dilemma theory should have expected the collapse of Hussein's imperial regime—whether or not caused by outside intervention—to promptly generate two wars: between Kurds and (mainly Sunni) Arabs and between Sunnis and Shia. Kurds and Shia harbored deep grievances based on atrocity memories; Sunnis were angry at the U.S. and the Shia for the loss of their former privileged status, on simple nationalist grounds, and—almost immediately—for both real and exaggerated abuse. None of the communities trusted their safety under the power of any other. Both the Kurdish/Arab and Sunni/Shia settlement frontiers were fuzzy, not sharp, with deep belts

---

105. Al-Anbar Province contains large tracts of desert, but these cannot support significant numbers of guerrillas or anyone else; the fighting has been mainly confined to the cities and towns, the roads, and along the Syrian frontier.

106. Expert estimates vary, up to a maximum of about 10%. Between 6% and 7% of insurgents killed between March and August 2005 were non-Iraqis. Michael O'Hanlon and Nina Kamp, *Iraq Index: Tracking Variables of Reconstruction and Security in Post-Saddam Iraq* (Washington, D.C.: Brookings Institution, December 27, 2005), pp. 16, 17.

107. Or, if the U.S. stayed out, Iranian aid to certain Shia factions, especially the Supreme Council for Islamic Revolution in Iraq (SCIRI). Mary Jacoby, "The Rule of the Turban," Salon.com, June 16, 2004.

108. 62,000 Army, 37,000 border police, 142,000 other police, and 29,000 others. O'Hanlon and Kamp, *Iraq Index*, pp. 19, 24. Admittedly improvement in the readiness of government forces has been painfully slow. James Fallows, "Why Iraq Has No Army," *Atlantic* vol. 296 no. 5 (December 2005), pp. 60–77 at 60–63. Nevertheless potential Sunni rebels would have to expect that with U.S. aid Iraqi government strength could only grow over time. Foreign troop totals have varied slightly month to month. Confusing accounting, including incomplete enumeration of programs, makes it impossible to guess the total of other aid. The single most visible program, the Iraq Relief and Reconstruction Fund, had disbursed $12.1 billion by November 2005. "Iraq Weekly U.S. Status Reports" (Washington, D.C.: Department of Defense), various dates, cited in O'Hanlon and Kamp, *Iraq Index*, p. 30.

of intermixed population in which no one could be confident of their safety, until or unless their own community could establish secure control.[109] Identities did not fragment in order to take advantage of opportunities to profit by rebellion; instead they hardened to cope with security needs. Shia leaders not only papered over most of their own community's internal divisions but also reached a consensus on a painful decision to give up on the integrity of Iraq, at least for the foreseeable future. In mid-2004 most Shia leaders opposed the Kurds' rather extreme autonomy demands, but by late spring 2005 the Sunni threat seemed so dire that denying the Kurds became an unaffordable luxury.[110]

A third question concerns the make-up of rebel and non-rebel forces. Opportunity-based theory should also expect that not all army, police, militia, or bandit forces (if these types could be distinguished) would be organized solely on communal lines. After two and a half years of energetic U.S. effort to recruit Sunnis for government forces, and some effort by Sunni moderates, the most that U.S. spokesmen would claim in November 2005 was 5,000 out of 214,000 government security forces.[111] Instead, as security dilemma theory would predict, all non-official forces and most Iraqi government units are mono-ethnic.[112]

---

109. The Sunni/Shia mixed belt is at least 100 miles deep, with Baghdad roughly in the center. Had there been more than a few Shia settled in Kurdish-claimed areas there might have been three wars with potentially shifting alliances.

110. Since making the deal, many religious Shia have discovered the virtues of regional autonomy for themselves as well, although Moqtada al-Sadr among others have dissented. The Kurds made concessions on Islamic law on the understanding that regions could nullify such legislation. Minor concessions to Sunni interests, not touching the main deal, were made later. "Iraq's Kurds, Shiites Quarrel on Eve of UN Security Council Resolution," *Agence France Presse*, June 8, 2004; Edward Cody, "In Iraq, Showdown Looms over Self-Rule for Kurds," *Washington Post*, July 11, 2004. "Leaders among the Shi'ites and Kurds have already begun cutting deals over contentious issues like the powers of a federal Kurdistan and the status of oil-rich Kirkuk," Noah Feldman, "A Backroom Constitution?" *Wall Street Journal*, April 8, 2005. "The Shi'ites and the Kurds might have been able to do a deal, but the addition of Sunni Arabs to the mix [for drafting the constitution] appears to have thrown the timetable off. The Sunni Arabs don't like the first sentence of the draft, which proclaims Iraq a federal state." Juan Cole, *Informed Comment*, July 10, 2005, www.juancole.com. See also Jonathan Finer and Omar Fekeiki, "Iraqis Finish Draft Charter that Sunnis Vow to Defeat", *Washington Post*, 29 August 2005; International Crisis Group, "Unmaking Iraq: A Constitutional Process Gone Awry" (Amman/Brussels: September 26, 2005); and "A Chance for Iraq's Charter," *Washington Post*, October 25, 2005.

111. Robert F. Worth, "Sunni Clerics Urge Followers to Join Iraq Army and Police," *New York Times*, April 2, 2005; *National Strategy for Victory in Iraq* (Washington, D.C.: National Security Council, November 2005), p. 21. This number may be slightly low, as an estimated 7% of votes cast in December 2005 by Iraqi security forces, hospital patients, and prisoners (combined) went to Sunni parties. Richard A. Oppel, "Iraq Vote Shows Sunnis are Few in New Military," *New York Times*, December 27, 2005.

112. Tom Lasseter, "Iraqi Army Magnifies Ethnic Divisions," *Knight Ridder Newspapers*, January 1, 2006; Eric Schmitt, "Iraq Facing Hurdles, U.S. General Warns," *New York Times*, January 6, 2006.

Fifth, how do we account for the high rate of suicide attacks in Iraq totaling 107 by June 2005?[113] Opportunity-based logic cannot explain why these people should be willing; they could only be coerced, duped, or enticed by promised rewards to their families. Coercion or brainwashing, however, hardly ever play roles in suicide attacks; most suicide attackers since 1980 have been patriotically motivated to defend what they see as their own national territory from foreign military occupation.[114] Although not all of the attackers in Iraq have been Iraqis, most of the others appear to have been Saudis, Syrians, or Kuwaitis—all countries vulnerable to U.S. occupation as long as we retain so many men in Iraq.[115]

Opportunity also cannot explain why we have seen 107 attacks by Sunnis but not one retaliation in kind by Shia or Kurds—both communities that have used suicide attack in other conflicts.[116] This behavior does make sense under a security-driven logic: in Iraq the Sunni Arabs are by far the weakest side, and—like the Kamikazes in World War II—they are resorting to extreme measures.

Finally, what do the theories have to say about expected trajectories of Iraq's civil wars? Fearon and Laitin's model in principle covers onset only, but it is reasonable to take the series of predictions over several years as at least vaguely indicative of whether conditions for insurgencies are becoming more favorable or less so. Since most of the variables are static, the main factors would be rising GDP per capita, which exerts downward pressure on the estimate, and democratization, which exerts upward pressure. The overall trend over several years would depend on performance on both economic and political fronts.[117]

Security dilemma theory should predict that Sunni/Shia violence would, once the cycle was well started, go on escalating until a process of ethnic

113. 20 in 2003, 49 in 2004, and 56 in the first six months of 2005. Robert Rape, *Dying To Win: The Strategic Logic Of Suicide Terrorism*, paperback ed. (New York: Random House, May 2006).

114. Pape, "The Strategic Logic of Suicide Terrorism," APSR vol. 97 no. 3 (August 2003), pp. 1–19. Thus far there is no evidence of payments to those who commit suicide attacks in Iraq or to their families. Pape, *Dying to Win* (2006 edition).

115. Pape, *Dying to Win*. We know little for certain; the most detailed count is by Reuven Paz, who identified 33 foreign suicide bombers, 23 of them Saudis. Paz, "Arab Volunteers Kill in Iraq," Project for the Research of Islamist Movements occasional papers vol. 3, no. 1 (March, 5, 2005). Gregory Gause has pointed out, however, that Paz relied on internet chat rooms and that several of the supposedly identified dead terrorists have been located alive. Comment on Robert Art's listserv, October 2005.

116. Against the United States, France, and Israel and against Turkey, respectively. Pape, *Dying to Win*, p. 15.

117. "Ethnicity, Insurgency, and Civil War," pp. 81, 85. In addition, a single year Polity score improvement of +3 or better makes a state "unstable" in Fearon and Laitin's terms; conversely not only reversal but also stagnation of political development would reduce estimates because Iraq would no longer qualify as "unstable."

cleansing—whether more or less mutual or predominantly one-sided—
effectively partitions the country into a Shia canton and a Sunni canton.[118]

Sufficiently heavy foreign occupation might dampen or interrupt the process as long as the occupation lasted, but not indefinitely.[120] The option in the
constitution for a Shia autonomous region can be read as anticipating partition.[121] Minorities would likely remain, but too few to affect each community's
secure control of its canton.[122]

Since the main Kurdish territorial aims—beyond the three provinces are
(Dohuk, Erbil, and Suleimaniyah) that they already dominate—are limited to
Kirkuk Province[123] and they have had the upper hand militarily from the start,

118. "The complex webs of tribal affiliations and social status that rule everyday life in Iraq
do not always line up as simply as Shi'ite against Sunni. But increasingly, despite the urging
of some Shi'ite religious leaders and Sunni politicians, the attacks have been. A mostly Sunni
Arab fringe is carrying out vicious attacks against civilians, often Shi'ites, while Shi'ite death
squads are openly stalking Sunnis for revenge, and the Shi'ite-dominated government makes
regular arrests in Sunni Arab neighborhoods. Expressions of prejudice have been making their
way onto walls and into leaflets, too." Sabrina Tavernise, "Sectarian Hatred Pulls Apart Iraq's
Mixed Towns," *New York Times*, November 20, 2005. According to the International Institute
for Strategic Studies, "The last six months have also seen an upsurge in murders being carried
out with a distinctly sectarian motive. Although radical Sunni jihadists originally drove these
trends, militias and death squads on both sides of the sectarian divide—those aligned with the
insurgency and [with] the government—now carry them out." "Iraq After the Referendum,"
IISS Strategic Comments, vol. 11 no. 8 (October 2005). Many of the killings of Sunnis have been
carried out by Iraqi police who are also members of the Badr Brigade, one the three main Shia
militias. Tom Lasseter, "Iran Gaining Influence, Power in Iraq through Militia," *Knight Ridder
Newspapers*, December 21, 2005. See also Nancy Youssef and Mohammed al-Dulaimy, "Shi'ites
Fleeing Sunni Neighborhoods of Baghdad," *Knight Ridder Newspapers*, September 21, 2005;
Juan Cole, "Sunni-Shi'ite Warfare Breaks Out in Southeast Baghdad," "Informed Comment,"
October 28, 2005, juancole.com; Edward Wong and John F. Burns, "Iraqi Rift Grows after
Discovery of Prison," *New York Times*, November 17, 2005; Edward Wong, "Shi'ite Cleric
Increases His Power in Iraq," *New York Times*, November 27, 2005.

119. Tavernise, "Sectarian Hatred."

120. Army Chief Of Staff General Eric Shinseki estimated that "Something on the order
of several hundred thousand soldiers are probably a figure that would be required" to impose
order in a conquered Iraq. Testimony before the Senate Armed Service Committee, February 25,
2003, quoted in Rowan Scarborough, "Wolfowitz Criticizes 'Suspect' Estimate of Occupation
Force," *Washington Times*, February 28, 2003.

121. Shia leaders have ambitions to control the central government as well, and could potentially extend the Shia autonomous region to include Baghdad Province, making a total of
10 provinces.

122. Even then, the fact that the border will run mostly through flat land would predict
a higher than usual likelihood of additional rounds of fighting. Alternatively, the Shia might
become so strong that they could utterly defeat, occupy, and repress the whole Sunni population.
Barry Posen has argued persuasively that the costs of this are likely to be higher than any Shia
faction or government would pay. Comments on Robert Art's listserv, June–August 2005.

123. Kurds claim that Kirkuk was predominantly Kurdish before forced expulsions of Kurds
and colonization by (mainly Sunni) Arabs in the 1980s. A referendum on the status of Kirkuk
Province is planned for 2007. Potentially also in dispute is a small part of Ninewa Province east
of the Tigris. See "Heremi Kurdistan," http://www.globalsecurity.org/military/world/war/
kurdistan-maps.htm.

Figure 1
SUNNI AND SHIA REFUGEE MOVEMENTS, LATE 2005[119]

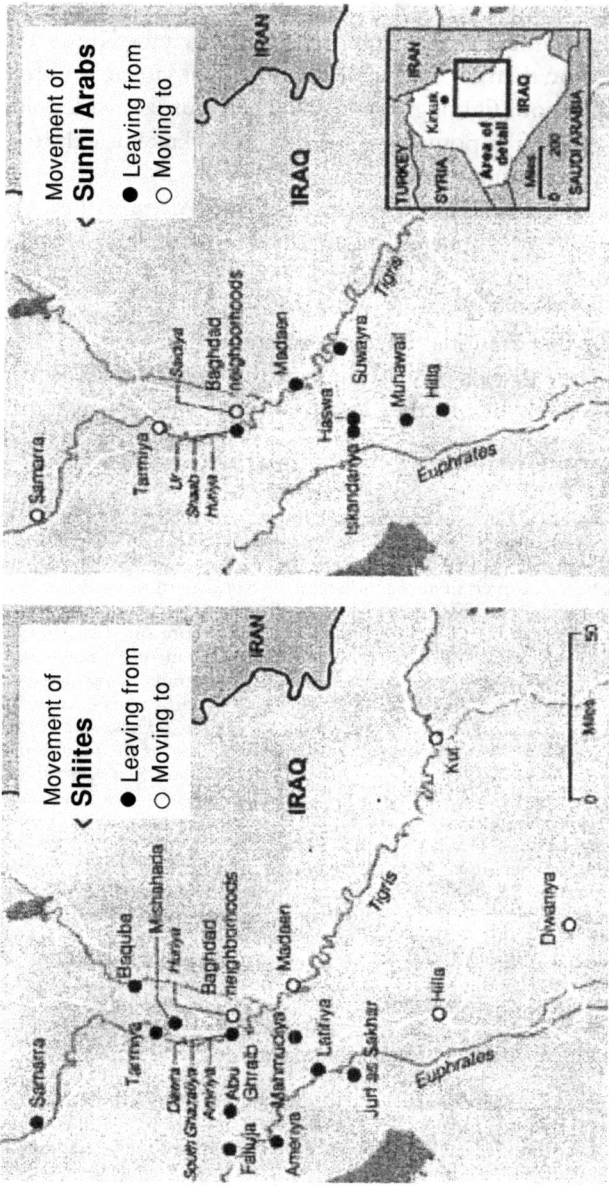

Sources: Local shiites; nongovernmental organizations; Iraqi military officials

The New York Times

the prediction for the northern front should be that violence would be of lesser intensity than in the south and should show less tendency to escalate. After a surge in expulsions of Arabs and Turcomen right after the collapse of the Hussein regime, anecdotal reports suggest that the Kurds have relied more on colonization than on intimidation or outright violence, although these still continue.[124] Serious fighting should end when Kurdish leaders are satisfied that they have altered the population balance in Kirkuk enough to secure control of it and the surrounding oilfields.[125]

Security-based motives explain most of the dynamics of the conflicts in Iraq so far, including the antagonists, the locations of most of the violence, why initially low rates of ethnic cleansing between Sunnis and Shia have snowballed steadily upward while the same has not occurred on the Sunni/Kurdish front, why pre-existing factional divides among both Kurds and Shia have shown more tendency to close to common fronts than faction leaders have taken opportunities to split further apart, and the most important single policy

124. Estimates of killings range around 100 for April 2003; Arab and Turcoman sources claim hundreds more since, as well as kidnappings, but it is difficult to get neutral confirmation. Estimates of expulsions are in the thousands for April 2003 and perhaps 100,000 by mid-2004. Some Arabs have accepted financial inducements to leave. In Kurdish returnees are estimated anywhere from 85,000 to 350,000 by November 2005, compared to a city population of 800,000 (1,100,000 for the province) before the war. Relying more on colonization than on ethnic cleansing may have helped the Kurds 'fly underneath the radar' of many observers who have been focused on the more violent conflict further south, minimizing damage to relations with the U.S. and with the Shia. The Kurdish proportion of the province population was estimated at 38% in the 1977 census, no more than 20% before March 2003, around 35%–40% at the time of the October 2005 constitutional referendum. In December the main Kurdish list got 52% and the Islamic Union of Kurdistan another 1% (according to a Kurdish source; consistent with seats ultimately awarded). Nouri Talabani, *Mantikat Kirkuk Wa Muhawalat Taghyeer Wakiiha Al-Kuwmy [The Kirkuk District and Attempts at Changing Its National Reality]* (London: 1999), p. 81; Mary Beth Sheridan, Returning Kurds Force Arabs from Northern Cities," *Washington Post*, April 22, 2003; Kim Sengupta, "Americans Accused of Turning Blind Eye to Killings by Kurds," *The Independent*, April 23, 2003; Dexter Filkins, "Kurds Advancing to Reclaim Land in Northern Iraq," *New York Times*, June 20, 2004; Jim Krane, "Kurdish Exiles Pouring Back into Northern Iraq City They Once Fled," *New York Times*, September 15, 2004; Steve Fainaru and Anthony Shadid, "Kurdish Officials Sanction Abductions in Kirkuk," *Washington Post*, June 15, 2005; Fainaru, "Kurds Reclaiming Prized Territory In Northern Iraq: Repatriation by Political Parties Alters Demographics and Sparks Violence," *Washington Post*, October 30, 2005; Edward Wong, "Kurds Are Flocking to Kirkuk, Laying Claim to Land and Oil," *New York Times*, December 29, 2005; "Iraqi Parliament After Elections," December 22, 2005. http:/northerniraq.info/blog/?p=31.

125. Since the Kurdish population share was only about 20% in April 2003, the opportunity to reverse perceived historical injustices could be considered at least as persuasive as security motives for the beginning of this campaign, even though Kurds argued that Kirkuk was needed to secure the whole of Kurdistan against future Arab threats. Since then, the rise in the Kurdish population share has certainly given them a security motive to continue the project even if we judge that this was not primary at first.

reversal by any side so far—the Shia consensus from about April 2005 that they had to let Kurdistan go.

What Now for Iraq?

Examination of the various comments on and criticisms in this volume of the security dilemma theory of ethnic conflict resolution suggest that the core logic of the theory is valid. But does it have policy usefulness? What should the United States do in Iraq now?

Any policy choice require not only understanding of the situation and of causal process that can be expected to operate, but of preferences. The United States has at least five important interests in Iraq now:

1) Minimize the number of Iraqis who will be killed in future communal or other internal conflict. This is in part a normative interest, which others may not rank as high as I do, and in part a strategic one. All sides in Iraq, the region, and in much of the rest of the world, will blame us for all damage to Iraq and Iraqis since 2003, including whatever happens after our departure.
2) Minimize future instability in the Persian Gulf region arising from spread of Sunni/Shia conflict or from any other source.
3) Avoid unnecessary conflict with the Iraqi state, Iran, and Turkey.
4) Minimize damage to relations with Sunni Arab countries although considerable damage has already been done and more is inevitable. Arabs already blame us for making war on Iraqi Sunnis and for empowering the Shia, and will also blame us for all future perceived injuries.
5) Avoid, as far as possible, generating new opportunities for anti-American terrorist movements.

Initially, this discussion will ignore domestic constraints on U.S. policy; we cannot know what internal political interests or actors may have to accommodated—or persuaded—unless we can first decide what policies we believe would be in the national interest.

THE KURDS

There is every reason to expect that the Kurdish campaign to establish demographic and military control of al-Tamim Province will continue, and that it will be successful. The four provinces will become an autonomous region as provided for under the Iraqi constitution. Beyond this the Kurds' only interests in Iraq are to preserve and extend their autonomy and to achieve full independence if they can. They have no interest in power-sharing at the center except as a tool to protect their own autonomy.[126]

The most important threat is Turkish fear of demonstration effects of a successful Kurdish state on Kurds in Southeastern Turkey. Declaration of a formally independent Kurdistan would likely spark Turkish (and perhaps Iraqi and Iranian) military intervention, and even without this Turkey might intervene anyway once U.S. forces are gone.[127]

Both threats can be avoided by making continued client assistance to the Kurds contingent on remaining at least formally in Iraq, and by a U.S. or Coalition guarantee of the security of the Kurdish autonomous region. This might require long-term deployment of some U.S. forces (though an international force would be better), and could offend Turkey mightily, but the alternative is to risk a holocaust nearly as bad as what could happen between the Sunni and Shia.[128]

THE SUNNIS, THE SHIA, AND THE IRAQI GOVERNMENT

We have three options: "cut and run," "stay the course," and managed partition. The dominant view as of February 2006 appears to be "cut and run"—that is, full withdrawal by a scheduled date regardless of the situation in Iraq or subsequent consequences.[129] There is good reason to expect, however, that if U.S.

126. Bashdar Ishmaeel, "For Kurds, Sovereignty Easily Beats of the Constitution, *Daily Star* (Beirut), September 16, 2005; Edward Wong, "A Celebration of Kurds' Hopes for Their Region, Not the Country," *New York Times*, December 16, 2005.

127. In early April 2003, General Hilmi Ozkok, chief of the Turkish armed forces, faced pressure from some of his own generals to intervene to prevent the Kurds from seizing Kirkuk. At the time Turkey had 70,000 mechanized forces massed on the border, while the U.S. had only a few special forces in northern Iraq. Philip P. Pan, "Turk General Faces Tough Choice in Iraq; Military Could Step In To Block Kurd Gains," *Washington Post*, April 9, 2003. See also Kathleen Ridolfo, "Turkey Proposes Cross-Border Action to Rein In Kurdish Fighters," *Agence France Presse*, July 20, 2005; and Karl Vick, "Wary Eyes Cast on Iraqi Kurds: Neighboring Nations Fear Consequences if Charter Passes," *Washington Post*, October 15, 2005. Nir Rosen points out that Turkey has no desire to annex more Kurds, but the point of intervention would be to smash Kurdish military power and to destabilize Iraqi Kurdistan. Rosen, "Once the Americans Leave, Sunnis Will Have No Common Cause with Foreign Mujahideen," *Boston Review* (January/February 2006).

128. As well as yet another lesson to possible clients anywhere of the risks of trusting the United States; Iraqi Shia have not forgotten that we abandoned them in 1991, and we have paid heavily for that.

129. On June 16, 2005, Representative Neil Abercrombie introduced into the House of Representative a resolution calling for complete U.S. military withdrawal by October 1, 2006; the bill attracted 64 co-sponsors. . . . not counting a few who later withdrew. On November 17, Representative John Murtha, a decorated Marine and known as a hawk on most issues, introduced

and Coalition forces leave before a powerful Shia[130] army is ready, Sunni/Shia fighting would immediately escalate to full-scale war. As Barry Posen points out, thus far U.S. intervention has served to inspire overconfidence on both sides: many Sunni rebels have believed up till now that they could beat the Shia if foreign forces left, and at the same time withdrawal will concentrate the minds of many Shia who have thus far seen little urgency about genuinely effective military mobilization.[131]

The war would convert into a fairly conventional battle for settlements and other strategic points, with the main battle zone in the communally mixed belt—Baghdad and parts of five surrounding provinces.[132] The pace of ethnic cleansing would escalate radically.[133] The war would continue until a military line of control and demographic frontier are established; this is the only way that either side can stop ethnic cleansing by the other. The Shia especially will be concerned to establish a border that no suicide bomber could cross and that harbored no potential recruits within it. This partition could generate more than a million refugees, the majority of them Sunni since the Shia are the stronger side. How many might be massacred is anyone's guess, as would be the ability of a small, poor, disorganized Sunni statelet to absorb so many.[134]

---

another resolution saying that deployment of U.S. forces in Iraq "is hereby terminated" and calling for complete withdrawal "at the earliest practical date." **CITE**. James Fallows quotes a Marine lieutenant colonel that either "we can lose in Iraq and destroy [the morale of] our army, or we can just lose. Similar views are now common among U.S. officers in Iraq. Fallows, "Why Iraq has No Army," p. 63. William Odom argues that everything that opponents of a pullout say would happen if the U.S. left Iraq—including escalated civil war and ethnic cleansing is happening already and cannot be prevented by staying longer. "What's wrong with cutting and running?," *Niemann Watchdog*, August 3, 2005; http://www.niemanwatchdog.org. See also Martin Van Creveld, "Costly Withdrawal Is the Price To Be Paid for a Foolish War," *Forward*, November 25, 2005; Robert Dreyfuss, "Iraq: Game Over," *TomPaine.com*, December 22, 2005; http://www.tompaine.com/articles/20051222/iraq game over.php. Barry Posen argues for a modified cut and run: 18 months to train government forces sufficient to defend the main Shia regions, with U.S. withdrawal during the last 6 months. Posen, "Exit Strategy: How to Disengage from Iraq in 18 Months," *Boston Review* (January/February 2006).

130. Shia, not total government forces, are what are relevant here. Units that are actually composed of Kurdish *peshmerga* whose loyalties are first to their faction leaders and second to Kurdistan would have little interest in dying for Baghdad or for Shia. Tom Lasseter, "Kurds in Iraqi Army Proclaim Loyalty to Militia," *Knight Ridder Newspapers*, December 27, 2005.

131. Posen, "Exit Strategy."

132. Diyala north of the capital, a small part of Al-Anbar just to the west, and Karbala, Babil, and Wasit to the south. The small Sunni minorities in the far south will be in (somewhat) less danger since they present no threat, although revenge pogroms have already occurred.

133. Posen, "Exit Strategy," predicts that the Sunni/Shia war will become a stalemate, but as he has pointed this will not initially be obvious because of both sides' overconfidence. Even if both sides do eventually scale back territorial ambitions this would not stop large-scale ethnic cleansing, not only for revenge but because the success of ethnic cleansing could itself decide control of key pieces of territory.

134. Significant help from other Arab countries seems unlikely because the refugees would be too useful as justifications for international grievances, as were Palestinian refugees after 1948.

Another cost to U.S. interests would be that Iraq would have to accept military aid from Iran, making Iraq an Iranian client ruled by the most pro-Iranian factions.[135]

Some argue that "cut and run" could actually reduce conflict because U.S. withdrawal would improve the legitimacy of the Iraqi government, further expose divisions within the insurgency, force the Sunni and Shia to face the full costs of failure to co-operate, and allow the full complexity of communal relations in Iraq, including clans with both Sunni and Shia branches, to assert itself in ways that would bridge the now communalized political divides.[136] Divisions among Sunnis exist as do mixed clans, but the remaining power of cross-communal appeals was tested on December 15 by Iyad Allawi's Iraqi National List; it got 8% of the vote.[137] se matter less than they might have before nearly three years of war; the one.

By now there remain few advocates of the position that that the U.S. should "stay the course" as long as it takes to establish a peaceful, democratic, communally inclusive Iraq that can and will suppress the terrorist organizations that have grown up in the country since 2003, the most important of whom is President George W. Bush.[138] This policy is failing for several reasons, of which the most important is that the powerful players in Iraq—the Shia religious parties combined in the United Iraqi Alliance (UIA) and the Kurds do not want a united or inclusive Iraq. They have long since decided to work together to exercise their autonomy options in a way that will leave the Sunnis with no political power nor access to more

---

IGO and NGO help would presumably depend on what local political and security conditions permit.

135. Especially SCIRI. Mary Jacoby, "The Rule of the Turban," Salon.com, June 16, 2004.

136. Nir Rosen, "Once the Americans Leave, Sunnis Will Have No Common Cause with Foreign Mujahideen;" and Barbara Bodine, 'Establishing a Credible, National, Legitimate Government is a Critical Predicate to Withdrawal," both in *Boston Review* (January/February 2006); and John J. Zakarian, "Presumptuous to Plan Iraqis' Future." *Times Union* (Albany), January 16, 2006.

137. And 9% of Council of Representative seats. *Certification of Council of Representatives Elections Final Results* (Baghdad: February 10, 2006), p. 2; actual certification took place January 20, 2006.

138. President George W. Bush, "President Outlines Strategy for Victory in Iraq," November 30, 2005, http://www.whitehouse.gov/news/releases/2005/11/20051130-2.html. Others have proposed stay the course strategies involving various reforms of current U.S. policy, but not ones with realistic hopes. Kenneth M. Pollack, "Five Ways to Win Back Iraq," *New York Times*, July 1, 2005, proposes buying off Sunni sheikhs. We have tried this; those who can be bought do not have influence with the insurgents. Thomas Friedman says that "My own visits to Iraq have left me convinced that beneath all the tribalism, there is a sense of Iraqi citizenship and national identity eager to come out. But it will take more security, and many more Iraqi leaders animated by national reconciliation, for it to emerge in a sustained way." He does not say what would motivate these leaders' changes of heart. Friedman, "The Measure of Success," *New York Times*, December 21, 2005. David Brooks, "Taking a Long View of the Iraq Conflict," *New York Times*, December 18, 2005, proposes that the U.S. act as an honest broker between communities, which is what we tried during the constitutional negotiations and failed.

than a tiny share of oil revenues.[139] Long-term U.S. occupation might undermine some Sunnis' confidence in their military chances,[140] but would also
maximize opportunities to infuriate more Iraqi Sunnis and more Arabs and
Muslims worldwide, as actual and perceived U.S. and Shia atrocities continue
to do every day. This policy would also provide terrorist recruiters with the
best arguments and the longest time in which to use them.[141] The Sunnis are
also too divided to enforce on themselves acceptance of any deal, good or
bad.[142]

U.S. officials have tried to push the Shia and the Kurds toward inclusion,
but to no avail. We pressured the constitutional commission to pay more
heed to Sunni interests and the government to include more Sunni Arab and
secular Shia officials, to accept oversight of police acting as death squads
and, since December 2005, to push sectarian figures and parties out of the
Premiership and Defense, and Interior Ministries that they now control and
to wrest control of the Iraqi Army and police away from sectarian militias in
favor of arrangements more responsive to the government.[143] None of this

139. The October 2005 constitution allows the autonomous regions to retain revenues from
"new" wells, which in practice will be classified so as to include virtually all wells. O'Hanlon,
"The Iraqi Constitution: Potentially Fatal Flaw," *Washington Times*, September 2, 2005. Abdul
Aziz al-Hakim, head of SCIRI, the largest UIA party, has suggested that the Kurdish and Shia
regions be joined as a confederacy with special privileges under the Iraqi government. Moqtada
al-Sadr, head of one of the other two factions, dissented. *Agence France Press* [Arabic], cited in
Cole, "Informed Comment," December 31, 2005, Juancole.com
140. Even this may be optimistic. Official U.S. figures estimate that the insurgency has four
times the strength it had in January 2004—despite claims that we have killed or captured more
than 10 times the numbers that we said it had then. O'Hanlon and Kamp, "Iraq Index," p. 17.
141. For additional critiques of options to stay the course, or even escalate, see Daniel Byman,
"Five Bad Options for Iraq," *Survival* vol. 47 no. 1 (Spring 2005), pp. 7–32; and Posen, "Exit
Strategy."
142. A number of Sunni candidates seeking to take part in the December 2005 elections were
assassinated, both by Sunni rebels and by Shia death squads. Edward Wong, "Sunni Candidates
in Iraq Find Enemies on All Sides," *New York Times*, December 5, 2005. As of January 6, 2006, the
MIPT Terrorism Knowledge Base listed 40 active terrorist groups in Iraq; this includes some of
minor importance as well as a handful of Shia or Kurdish groups, but omits rebel organizations
that have not sought public recognition. http://www.tkb.org/Category.isp?catID=192. U.S.
and Iraqi officials estimate that there may be as many as 100 independent rebel groups. Dexter
Filkins, "Profusion of Rebel Groups Helps Them Survive in Iraq," *New York Times*, December
2, 2005.
143. Paul Richter, "U.S. Goals Adapt to New Iraq: Disappointed with Vote Results, Washington is now Focused on Keeping Security Forces Out of the Hands of Religious or Nationalist
Parties," *Los Angeles Times*, January 21, 2006. In January 2006, a person in the U.S. intelligence
community told me that the U.S. is trying to transform the Iraqi 7th Division, stationed into
Fallujah, into a predominantly Sunni force. The most recent record I could find described this
unit as overwhelmingly Shia. Jonathan Finer, "Iraqi Official's Visit to Sunni Province Under-
scores Depth of Distrust," *Washington Post*, December 13, 2005. Whether such an attempt would
be wise would depend on whether we have reason for confidence that such a unit would not
ultimately fight on the other side of a civil war.

has accomplished anything beyond infuriating some of the most powerful Shia politicians.[144]

"Stay the course" might slow the continued escalation of ethnic cleansing but would not affect its ultimate scale. It would also inspire rising Shia resentment as we continue to stand in the way of full Iraqi independence, of sufficient mobilization to allow the Shia to handle their communal security problems in their own way, and of certain factional interests. Eventually the Shia would demand that we go. Like cut and run, this course too would likely end with Iraq being forced or seduced into clientship with Iran.

There are signs that the administration is now laying the political groundwork to cut and run. In a January 25, 2006 interview with David Ignatius, U.S. Ambassador Zalmay Khalilzad demanded of the dominant Shia United Iraqi Alliance that "The security ministries have to be run by people who are not associated with militias and who are not regarded as sectarian" and that "if you choose the: If you choose the wrong candidates, that will affect U.S. aid."[145] On February 1. Secretary of Defense Donald Rumseld told reports that he did not expect that Iraq would be a long war; unannounced but generally credited U.S. plans call for reducing troop levels to 100,000 by the end of 2006.[146]

There are a few intermediate proposals, but they operate within the same bounds as the two main ones. Michael O'Hanlon proposes that the U.S. should withdraw 75% of its forces at a rate matched to improvements in the capacities of Iraqi forces, government institutions of all types, and economic infrastructure. 30,000 to 40,000 U.S. or NATO forces would remain indefinitely

144. **HAKIM CITE**. See also Borzou Daragahi and Alissa J. Rubin, "Shiite-Kurd Goals Stymie U.S.: The alliance America helped build appears set to create a religious, federal state, opposite of the secular, united Iraq that Washington seeks," *Los Angeles Times*, January 22, 2006; and, on control of the Army and police, Eric Schmitt, "Iraq Facing Hurdles, U.S. General Warns," *New York Times*, January 6, 2006.
145. Ignatius summarized Khalilzad's message as: "America's money and patience aren't unlimited. . . . If [Iraqis] can't pull together, they will eventually have to face the nightmare of a shattered Iraq on their own. Ironically, that's America's hidden leverage in Iraq—the power to walk." Ignatius, "America's Message to Iraq," *Washington Post*, January 25, 2006. See also Khalilzad, "The Challenge Before Us," *Wall Street Journal*, January 9, 2006: "There has to be a government of national unity, which includes all major players—including Sunni Arabs. A repeat of the current Shiite-Kurdish alliance government will not solve Iraq's problems. . . . "the constitution will likely need to be amended in the coming year to broaden support [including] compromises on . . . federalization in Arab regions of Iraq [i.e., reduction of Shia autonomy privileges]." . . . "Iraq's leaders [must] reform security institutions and eliminate a number of militias and other armed groups [i.e., the Shia and Kurdish militias that control much of the Army and police]."
146. Rowan Scarborough, "Rumsfeld Doubts 'Long War' in Iraq; Secretary Mum on Cuts in Troops," *Washington Times*, February 2, 2006.

to continue training missions and to guarantee the government's security.[147] In essence this is a more optimistic and more drawn-out version of "cut and run."

James Fallows argues that the U.S. cannot leave Iraq honorably until it has "a national army strong enough to deter militias and loyal enough to the new Iraq to resist becoming the tool of any faction," as well as comparable improvements in the police,[148] which will require revamping policies on many dimensions[149] as well as making "very long-term commitments to stay." Then the U.S. "can leave with a clear conscience—no matter what might happen a year or two later." The alternative is to "face the stark fact that [the U.S.] has no orderly way out of Iraq."[150] In sum, a policy for those ashamed to "cut and run" but pessimistic about the chances that "staying the course" can succeed.[151]

The third and least destructive option—actively managing the partition of Iraq to minimize its human costs—is not represented in current policy debates.

This option should not be undertaken lightly; not all analysts accept that a Sunni/Shia partition is inevitable. The question is whether the civil war has already passed the tipping point beyond which real inter-communal security dilemmas will force separation of the communities. Qualitative indicators such as escalating communal massacres and escalating hate discourse suggest that

147. Time scale hopes are given as 18 or 24 months. O'Hanlon, "Plan a Moderate Iraq Exit Strategy," *Christian Science Monitor*, November 22, 2005; and "The State of Iraq: An Update," *New York Times*, December 14, 2005. O'Hanlon also recommends involving European powers and international institutions in Iraqi reconstruction and regional security, and amending the Iraqi constitution to give more oil money to the Sunnis. The latter will not happen because the Shia and Kurds don't want to, and would see little point—Sunni rebels outside the political system will not care whether or not Sunni politicians inside succeed in begging a little money for themselves. Byman, "Five Bad Options," offers a basically similar prescription, and makes the additional point that a slower drawdown would allow maintaining counter-terrorist intelligence assets longer than would cut and run.

148. It is hard to see what could induce most officials or rank and file who are now loyal to particular Shia factions to transfer their loyalties to the state—to say nothing of the Kurds.

149. Including supplying Iraqis with heavy weapons, basic equipment such as armored personnel carriers and body armor, forming and training functional command organizations above battalion level, communications, logistic, and medical services, and supplying more and better (by altering career incentives) U.S. officers for training and advising missions. Fallows, "Why Iraq has No Army," pp. 74–76; Michael Moss, "Lack of Armor Proves Deadly for Iraqi Army," *New York Times*, October 30, 2005.

150. Fallows, "Why Iraq has No Army," pp. 76–77.

151. Andrew Krepinevich recommends shifting from "sweep" or "search and destroy" operations, pursuing insurgents, to "clear and hold" aiming at protecting the population by strongly garrisoning every town captured. To some extent U.S. command in Iraq is already moving in this direction, which is recognized by academic counterinsurgency experts as best practice. Krepinevich also recommends training "competent and incorruptible" police but admits that this would be "incredibly difficult" in Iraq. Interviewed for "What Should Be the U.S. Exit Strategy from Iraq?" (Council on Foreign Relations, November 28, 2005); http://www.cfr.org/publication/9288/what_should_be_the_us_exit_strategy_from_iraq.html.

it may have, but these are not decisive in part because security dilemma theory itself does not provide quantitative thresholds for recognizing the tipping point in real time. How many calls for ethnic cleansing, from leaders with how much following, are too many to reverse?

We are likely, however, to learn the answer from the process of coalition-making in the new parliament that will already have occurred by the time this sees print. The most obvious sign will be the make-up of the coalition. Of the 184 seats needed to form a government, the Shia religious parties together with the main Kurdish bloc have exactly 184.[152] The Shia religious parties have already demonstrated that they are not interested in power-sharing or even in regional autonomy on terms that offer anything to Sunnis, nor are the Kurds.[153] If we see a narrow Shia Kurdish coalition, or "fig leaf" power-sharing in which the Shia parties accept into the government a few small Sunni parties who are allowed no influence, that will augur badly.[154]

Additional important signs will include the fates of any Sunni Arab politicians who do join the government: that is, whether they lose their legitimacy with most or nearly all Sunnis, and whether announcement of the coalition is followed by further significant increases in ethnic cleansing and or by public pessimism in both communities about prospects of re-integrating Iraq.[155] The worst possible sign would be defection of many of the Sunni Arab police and soldiers that U.S. officials continue to try to force on a mainly unwilling government. It is difficult to pinpoint, even in retrospect, the exact moment after which Bosnia's disaster was unavoidable, but that moment had surely passed

152. United Iraqi Alliance 128, Progressives 2, al-Ezediah Movement for Progress and Reform 1 (both considered loyal to al-Sadr) [CHECK al-Ezediah], Kurdistan Alliance 53. Electoral Commission, *Certification of Council of Representatives Elections Final Results*, p. 2. It is not clear whether the (Sunni) Islamic Union of Kurdistan, with 5 seats, is a likely coalition partner. On February 12 the UIA voted to retain Ibrahim Ja'afari of the al-Da'awa Party as Premier, a compromise among the coalition's three components: SCIRI, al-Da'awa, and the Sadrists. Ja'afari is widely perceived by Sunnis as too close to sectarian militias and as responsible for purging of Sunni officials; Dr. Adel Abdul Mehdi of SCIRI is expected to retain the Interior Ministry. Borzou Daragahi, "Shiite Bloc Votes to Retain Iraq Premier," *Los Angeles Times*, February 13, 2006; See also Cole, "Informed Comment," February 12, 2006.

153. After meeting with Khalilzad, Jalal Talabani, one of the two key leaders of the Kurdistan Alliance, said that he would not support a government that did not give Allawi's (secular) Iraqi National List at least one ministry. Cole, however, argues that the UIA cannot afford to unravel its own internal deal and that the Kurds owe the UIA more than the other way around. "Informed Comment, February 12, 2006, www.juancole.com.

154. According to Ra'ad Alkadiri, a former advisor to the British government in Baghdad, "We've reached a point of no return now. Are Iraqis willing to put aside their narrow interests? Is there a real Iraqi state? You can't fudge this. This is the edge of the precipice." Quoted in Ignatius, "America's Message to Iraq."

155. There was a Sunni insurgent attempt to assassinate Abdul-Aziz al-Hakim, head of SCIRI, the day that the election results were certified. "Iraq Foils Plot Against Shi'ite Leader—Source," *Reuters*, January 20, 2006.

when in March 1992 essentially the whole ethnic Serb component of Bosnia's police force deserted.

If we must manage Iraq's partition and population exchanges, we must first choose a side (the dominant Shia religious parties are the only choice), and arm and train government forces on a far more massive scale than we have planned—hundreds of thousands of soldiers with plentiful heavy weapons and all the other equipment, organizations, and skills of a respectable second-rank power.[156] Forces this strong are need both to ensure the outcome and because the more uneven balance of forces, the more may be accomplished by intimidation and the less by combat. Readying this force, even if we transform our policies today, will take at least two years; in the meantime Coalition forces cannot be drawn down significantly. During the same period, the Coalition and the Shia must agree on a *de facto* border to be established that will be satisfactory to the latter; the fact that the line will be dictated to the Sunnis will not matter.

What we must extract in return for such generous aid is Shia concession that when Iraqi government forces eventually advance to establish the new border is carried out, the flight of Sunni refugees in front them will be managed by the Coalition and by whichever international relief IGOs and NGOs can be persuaded to help. This is one reason why the U.S. and Coalition forces cannot be drawn down before this point; they will be needed to stand between Shia forces and Sunni settlements scheduled for Shia control long enough for secure transit and resettlement to be provided.[157] If possible, arrangements should be made for compensating refugees using property abandoned by other refugees who had moved in the opposite direction—and there will not be enough to go around on the Sunni side of the line.[158]

There are several advantages to fixing the border in advance. First, both sides' knowledge of the final lines will limit their concerns about security of particular places with mixed populations and thus reduce felt needs for ethnic

156. Any Iraq that can master its own internal security will also be able to threaten its Arab neighbors; that cannot be helped. Veterans Alliance for Security and Democracy, "Iraq: What Must Be Done Now," advocates training an Iraqi forces of about 600,000, about the same as before 2003, but does not explain goals or strategy. http://www.vetpac.org/iraq2.htm.

157. For advice on a number of related problems, see Posen, "Military Responses to Refugee Disasters," *International Security*, vol. 21 no. 1 (Summer 1996), pp. 72–111.

158. Spontaneous refugee movements among Greece, Turkey, and Bulgaria during 1923–1925 caused terrible suffering, but after 1925 more serious relief capabilities were deployed by the League of Nations and more than 1,000,000 more people moved with virtually no losses. Michael R. Marrus, *The Unwanted* (New York: Oxford University Press, 1985). Some Iraqis are already exchanging houses by private arrangement Tavernise, "Sectarian Hatred Pulls Apart Iraq's Mixed Towns."

cleansing—especially, the Shia may not feel the need to eject the more than a million Sunni residents of Baghdad if they are assured of control of the whole city anyway. Second, the border could be used as a coercive tool to restrain atrocities by either side. Similar arrangements should be made for refugees fleeing from Sunni areas, although of course U.S. troops will not be usable as guarantors of order on that side of the border. The Coalition—or better, an international commission—could punish incidents by promptly moving the planned final border one village or one town against the offending side.[159] Third, international sanction, if it can be obtained, could help reduce Sunni resistance, moderate Shia demands, and, most important, improve the chances that the new border will remain peaceful afterwards. If important world powers can be persuaded of these points, hope of obtaining such sanction may not be as absurd as it may appear at first glance.

This option would be risky: some of those that we would be supporting have already shown themselves eager to commit murder, which means that the policy would only save lives if the complex dance of relief together with alternating military permissiveness and prohibition—something never before attempted on this scale—can be executed with few missteps.

There is also little stomach among American and other Western publics for accepting a continuing burden in Iraq, let alone re-thinking why. The policy would also be nearly impossible to explain because its rationale is complex and because it flies in the face of certain accepted legal and moral norms: the U.S. and any other states or agencies participating would be accused of abetting ethnic cleansing and worse. But we have already seen ethnic cleansing in Iraq and have reason to think that we may soon see much more. In that case responsible elites should at least try to explain why managed partition is necessary.

AFTERMATH

U.S. forces would depart promptly, as they would be no longer needed nor welcome. The governing arrangement would probably have to be loose federalism amounting to *de facto* partition, which is essentially what the current constitution already envisions.[160] An internationally recognized partition between the Sunnis and Shia would be safer for both, but if Kurdish sovereignty were

159. This may be especially important for the safety of refugees fleeing southward, since Coalition forces will not be usable as guarantors of order on the Sunni side of the border.

160. This puts me on the wrong side of Downes' point about the near-hopelessness of successful functioning of federal states after communal civil wars; little should be expected of such a government beyond continuation of the wartime Shia-Kurd alliance, if that.

permitted Turkey might be unrestrainable, and a rump Sunni Arab/Kurdish state would be a non-starter for both sides. Still, U.S. and—if it can be had—international sanction for the zonal boundaries would have some calming influence. Perhaps even more important, the stronger side would be the satisfied side.

The proposed policy also holds out the possibility of retaining Iraq as a client or at least as a friendly state and might improve chances for rapprochement with Iran, putting us on the right side of Persian Gulf politics for the coming decades. Iran has traditionally been the strongest power in the region, and will be again if it is not already.[161] The second strongest has traditionally been Iraq. The United States's best hope for stabilizing the Persian Gulf is to triangulate between the two. The first step toward that is to decide decisively in favor of the Iraqi Shia; we want Iraq's valuation on its relationship with us as high as possible.

One major cost is that U.S. relations with the rest of the Arab world would be badly damaged, and the long-awaited destabilization of Saudi Arabia could be accelerated. It is not clear, however, that our losses in the Sunni world would be smaller under any other option.[162]

Finally, the implications for terrorism are ambiguous. None of the options can really secure Sunni Iraq nor avoid further infuriating Sunni militants everywhere,[163] although some observers argue that transnational terrorist organizations will no longer be welcome in Iraq after the end of the civil war. At least the United States will no longer be an occupation threat anywhere in the region except in a small way in Kurdistan.

We can cut and run or we can try to fight it out to the end, but neither promises much hope of avoiding the effective partition of Iraq. We have a human responsibility to do what we can to reduce the harm done in the ethnic cleansing that is coming, and a national interest in retaining the best relations we can with the new Iraq.

161. The United States and the EU-3 would have to relax about the prospect of Iranian nuclear weapons, but responsible experts increasingly rate this as inevitable anyway. **CITES**.

162. If future U.S. relations with Iraq and Iran went well, U.S. forces would be neither welcome nor needed in the rest of the Persian Gulf. If these relationships went badly, we would have to revert to the offshore balancing strategy that we used before 1990. See Pape, *Dying to Win*, pp. 247–50.

163. Douglas Jehl, "Iraq-Based Jihad Appears to Seek Broader Horizons," *New York Times*, November 11, 2005.

INDEX

For Product Safety Concerns and Information please contact our EU
representative GPSR@taylorandfrancis.com
Taylor & Francis Verlag GmbH, Kaufingerstraße 24, 80331 München, Germany

www.ingramcontent.com/pod-product-compliance
Lightning Source LLC
Chambersburg PA
CBHW060142280326
41932CB00012B/1608

9 781138 010543